MW00396267

An American Genealogy: The Finney Family History and Genealogy

Long live the Finneys!
Love Cousette Copeland
Nov 2011

by

Cousette Copeland

with

Rosamary High Finney

The Library of Congress has cataloged this book as follows:

Copeland, Cousette

An American Genealogy: The Copeland Family of Montgomery County Kansas – First Edition

1. REFERENCE / Genealogy / Finney Genealogy / Finney Pictorial Genealogy / Finney Family History / United States / Kansas / Montgomery County

Library of Congress Number: 2011915153

ISBN: 978-1466235779

Printed in the United States of America

1466235772

Dedication

To Rosamary High Finney – a genealogist and family historian of the old school. Without computers, Rosamary worked tirelessly researching the genealogy and family history of the Finneys.

Rosamary corresponded with Finneys across the U.S., ordered research materials, sat in libraries, read books/letters, peered at rolls of microfiche and bare legible documents. She used a typewriter to type endless outlines of Finneys based on published material, microfiche records, word-of-mouth, public records, and what she knew about Tommie's family.

In 1992, Rosamary published her findings in *"History of Finney Family 1692-1990"* and distributed it among her family. Unfortunately, Rosamary passed in 1997 at the age of 73.

Rosamary's husband Tommie Finney gave me permission to use Rosamary's book as the core of this *American Genealogy* book. I hope I honor her hard work with this updated genealogy.

Acknowledgements

I would like to thank each of the Finney and Copeland descendants who provided me with an abundance of photographs and stories.

I'd like to give a special "thank you" to Bonnie and Harold Finney, who invited me to the Finney reunion in Kansas. There I met and began enjoying the heart and warmth of the many Finneys that I came in contact since then. A special thanks to Harold Finney, who contributed his DNA to the Finney DNA Project, **with results that will reject previously published Finney genealogies**.

I would like to thank Lynn Finney Stuter and Gerald Finney for engaging in a debate about Finney genealogy, and then a special thanks to Gerald Finney for running the Finney DNA Project – resulting in astonishing discovery and changes that must be made to all Finney genealogies.

I would like to thank Pastor Grady Miller of the Bolton Friends (Quaker) Church in Bolton, Kansas. He responded to my request and rescued precious family photos and memorabilia from the home and estate of Ralph Copeland, who passed in August 2011, and Arlene Copeland, who passed in June 2010.

A belated thank you to Ralph and Arlene Copeland, who treasured and stored family photos and memorabilia their entire lives, ensuring that countless relations would benefit from these treasures.

A special thank you to George and Maxine Copeland, and Virginia Copeland Noble, who traveled to Bolton to retrieve many photos and memorabilia, and then forwarded those items to me.

A special thank you to Melvin Koons, who will store the majority of the Copeland memorabilia in his later mother Pearl (Copeland) Koons' trunk, along with other Copeland and Koons photos and memorabilia.

All the genealogists, past and present, are an inspiration for the countless hours preserving family histories so that we can all understand the people whose life and times made us the people that we are today.

As always, the love and support of my family and friends keeps me going!

Introduction

Finney genealogists must correct their ancestry charts and copies of previously published Finney genealogies! My book *An American Genealogy: The Finney Family History and Genealogy* contains Controversy, Science, and Revelation provides DNA evidence that cannot be disputed!

Modern genealogists, including myself, rely on "facts" drawn from ancestral research, using published genealogies, family trees and facts on Ancestry.com, records from the Church of the Latter Day Saints, Google, research with microfiche and other photographed records, as well as the research of historians and other amateur genealogists. Genealogists battle over details. It was such an online battle that led to one Finney genealogist – Gerald Finney – to monitor a Finney DNA database that provided evidence to support another Finney genealogist's – Lynn Finney Stuter – contention that there was a major error in all previously published Finney genealogies, including family trees on Ancestry.com and other online genealogy databases. Harold Finney's DNA provided the scientific proof and a new direction for this family's Finney ancestry.

An American Genealogy: The Finney Family History and Genealogy continues my tradition of the pictorial genealogy – where images of the Finney descendants come alive next to names, dates, and places. I began with the late Rosamary High Finney's 1992 family publication of *"History of Finney Family 1692-1990."*

Rosamary began with the traditional Finney genealogy, which has Robert Finney as the "father" of American Finneys. She covered descendants, narrowing her focus to Joseph and Rachel Finney, and then to their son Joseph and Mary Polly Long Finney. The book then focuses on Wesley and Mary Matilda Finney, and the family who settled in Montgomery County Kansas. While there is an emphasis on the Kansas descendants, Rosamary also included the hundreds of other Finneys who descended from Robert Finney. As of 1990, she accumulated the most amount of available information available at that time.

Twenty years later, using the power of the internet, as well as the abundance of information and contacts on Ancestry.com, I began building my Finney family tree. The Finneys were prolific and soon I had a posse of new "cuzzins." Living Finney descendants shared knowledge, information, and photographs – helping me to build a picture of our large and wonderful family.

I hope I have brought the Finney family history alive using a pictorial genealogy. Photographs document our ancestors and their descendants. I hope the reader enjoys discovering their ancient and close Finney relations, as well as learning about Finney lives and their history.

IMPORTANT REVELATION THAT CONTRADICTS PREVIOUSLY PUBLISHED FINNEY GENEALOGIES!

While working on this book, I was in contact with two Finney genealogists – Lynn Finney Stuter and Gerald Finney. I observed their debates on genealogy message boards. Lynn disputed published and accepted genealogies that stated that my gr gr gr grandfather Joseph Finney (husband of Mary Polly Long) descended from the Finney patriarch – Robert Finney of Thunderhill. Gerald disputed her findings.

Gerald is the administrator of the Finney DNA Genealogy Project. He asked if I knew of a male descendant of Joseph and Mary Polly (Long) Finney. I did – Harold Finney. Harold participated in the DNA project.

The results will astonish readers and genealogists because it turns established and accepted "FACTS" on their ear! Read about it in the chapter "Controversy, Science, and Revelation."

I have no greater joy than to hear that my children walk in truth.

3 John 4

Behold, children are a heritage from the Lord, the fruit of the womb a reward. Like arrows in the hand of a warrior are the children of one's youth. Blessed is the man who fills his quiver with them! He shall not be put to shame when he speaks with his enemies in the gate.

Psalm 127:3-5

TABLE OF CONTENTS

About the Author

Cousette Copeland is the author of three books available on Amazon.com. *"Silicon Valley: Fact and Fiction"* is a memoir with observations about the changes in Silicon Valley from 1961 to Present. *"Wild Rider and Other Paintings"* presents her paintings and drawings.

The third book is *"An American Genealogy: The Copelands of Montgomery County Kansas,"* which was the first in a series of her family history and genealogy books.

One final *An American Genealogy* book will cover the McKays and McKinlays of Montgomery County Kansas and their descendants. Readers are encouraged to contribute McKay and McKinlay stories and photographs to: codyhaha@comcast.net.

Cousette is a professional writer, living and working in Silicon Valley. She has worked for over two dozen high-tech companies since 1986. In addition, she has had articles published in journals, including SPUR Equestrian News, Lapidary Journal, Diabetes Forecast, and numerous newspaper editorials.

Phinney
Origin:
Irish
Coat of Arms:
A red shield
with three
black mullets
on a gold
chevron,
between three
gold martlets.

Motto: Spes mea Deus
Translated: God is my hope

Part One

The History of the Finney Family: 1692 – 1992

By Rosamary High Finney, with updates by Cousette Copeland

HOW TO READ THIS BOOK

Part One contains the original text by Rosamary High Finney. She typed her manuscript using different typewriters and included materials typed by others, printed out pages of microfiche records, as well as photocopied materials – so the fonts, images, and so on may appear inconsistent, but honest in their presentation.

Updates had page numbering that related to the original text pages. For example, if updates were added to page 100, that page was followed by pages 100-a, 100-b, and so on.

In some cases, the entire original page has been deleted because of comprehensive updates. In other cases, minor updates were added, so the original page was left in the book. Sometimes, underlines were used to indicate minor changes.

In traditional genealogies, birth information for living people was included. Wherever possible, I have eliminated or not included such information due to the concern for privacy.

Parts Two through Five are new material from Cousette Copeland.

Part Six is the original index by Rosamary High Finney.

History of

FINNEY FAMILY

1692 - 1990

by Rosamary (High) Finney

Cousette Copeland

Family: FINNEY

No. 1 on this chart is the same person as No. ___ on chart No. ___

1. Tommie Milton Finney
Born 2 Oct 1927
Where Montgomery Co., Ks.
When Married July 1946
Where Wichita, Sedgwick Co., Ks
Died
Where
Cemetery
Where
Occupation Sales Representative
Military

Loris J. Griswold
Name of husband or wife of No. 1
Born 30 Sep 1927
Where Wichita, Ks.
Died 4 Jan 1962
Where Wichita, Ks.
Cemetery White Chapel Cem.
Where Wichita, Ks.
Occupation

Date 1989
Compiler Rosamary Finney
Address 1506 Deep Creek Lane, Manhattan, Ks. 66502

PARENTS

2. Carl Chester Finney
Born 13 May 1905
Where Montgomery Co., Ks.
When married 20 Oct 1926
Where Caney, Ks.
Died 15 Nov 1987 - California
Cemetery Mt. Hope Cemetery
Where Independence, Ks
Occupation Machinist
Military

3. Vivia Jay McClure
Born 3 Mar 1910
Where Caney, Montg. Co., Ks
Died
Cemetery
Where
Occupation
Military

4. Daniel Webster Finney
Born 7 Nov 1868
Where Parke Co., Ind.
When married 13 Dec 1896
Where Montg. Co., Ks.
Died 10 Dec 1927
Cemetery Mt. Hope
Where Montg. Co., Ks.
Occupation Farmer-banker
Military

5. Mary Ann Farlow
Born 12 Mar 1872
Where Orange Co., Ind.
Died 2 Jan. 1952
Where Independence, Ks.
Cemetery Mt. Hope
Where Independence, Ks.
Occupation

6. James Harvey McClure
Born 9 Sept 1892
Where Ceney, Ks
When married 20 Mar 1909
Where Caney, Ks
Died Feb. 1981
Cemetery
Where
Occupation
Military

7. Almeda Jay Sharp
Born 24 Mar 1894
Where Chautaqua Co., Ks
Died 27 Dec 1943
Where
Cemetery
Where
Occupation
Military

Lineage Chart

Family: FINNEY

No. 1 on this chart is the same person as No. ____ on chart No. ____

1. Tommie Milton Finney
Born 2 Oct 1927
Where Montgomery Co., Ks.
When Married July 1946
Where Wichita, Sedgwick Co., Ks
Died
Where
Cemetery
Where
Occupation Sales Representative
Military

Loris J. Griswold
Name of husband or wife of No. 1
Born 30 Sep 1927
Where Wichita, Ks.
Died 4 Jan 1962
Where Wichita, Ks.
Cemetery White Chapel Cem.
Where Wichita, Ks.
Occupation

Date 1989
Compiler Rosamary Finney
Address 1506 Deep Creek Lane, Manhattan, Ks. 66502

PARENTS

2. Carl Chester Finney
Born 13 May 1905
Where Montgomery Co., Ks.
When married 20 Oct 1926
Where Caney, Ks.
Died 15 Nov 1987 - California
Cemetery Mt. Hope Cemetery
Where Independence, Ks
Occupation Machinist
Military

3. Vivia Jay McClure
Born 3 Mar 1910
Where Caney, Montg. Co., Ks
Died
Cemetery
Where
Occupation
Military

4. Daniel Webster Finney
Born 7 Nov 1868
Where Parke Co., Ind.
When married 13 Dec 1896
Where Montg. Co., Ks.
Died 10 Dec 1927
Cemetery Mt. Hope
Where Montg. Co., Ks.
Occupation Farmer-banker
Military

5. Mary Ann Farlow
Born 12 Mar 1872
Where Orange Co., Ind.
Died 2 Jan. 1952
Where Independence, Ks.
Cemetery Mt. Hope
Where Independence, Ks.
Occupation

6. James Harvey McClure
Born 9 Sept 1892
Where Ceney, Ks
When married 20 Mar 1909
Where Caney, Ks
Died Feb. 1981
Cemetery
Where
Occupation
Military

7. Almeda Jay Sharp
Born 24 Mar 1894
Where Chautaqua Co., Ks
Died 27 Dec 1943
Where
Cemetery
Where
Occupation
Military

Cousette Copeland

GREAT GRANDPARENTS

8. Wesley Finney
   - Born 10 May 1823
   - Where Lawrence Co., Ind.
   - When married 29 Aug 1850
   - Where Indiana
   - Died 3 Oct 1904
   - Where Montgomery Co., Ks.
   - Cemetery Fawn Creek Cemetery
   - Where Montgomery Co., Ks.

9. Mary Matilda Hinshaw
   - Born 29 Oct 1829
   - Where Indiana
   - Died 5 Feb 1900
   - Where Montgomery Co., Ks.

10. Nathan Maris Farlow
   - Born 5 Jan 1842
   - Where Orange Co., Ind.
   - When married 4 Feb 1869
   - Where Orange Co., Ind.
   - Died 26 Mar 1920
   - Where Bolton, Ks.
   - Cemetery Harrisonville Cemetery
   - Where Montgomery Co., Ks.

11. Martha Cloud
   - Born 21 Feb 1849
   - Where Orange Co., Ind.
   - Died 14 Jan 1921
   - Where Montgomery Co., Ks

12. James Martin McClure
   - Born 2 Apr 1861
   - Where Henry Co., Tenn.
   - When married 9 Oct 1881
   - Where Chautaqua Co., Ks.
   - Died 5 Apr 1940
   - Where Montgomery Co., Ks.
   - Cemetery
   - Where

13. Mary Jane Hopper
   - Born 31 Aug 1866
   - Where Putnam Co., Mo.
   - Died 14 Dec 1949
   - Where Ceney, Montg. Co., Ks.

14. William Humbolt Sharp
   - Born 19 Nov 1859
   - Where Shawnee Co., Ks.
   - When married 8 Mar 1888
   - Where Fall River, Ks.
   - Died 21 Nov 1933
   - Where Harlingen, Texas
   - Cemetery
   - Where

15. Myrtle Jay Smith
   - Born 16 Feb 1872
   - Where Huntsville, Ark.
   - Died 18 July 1900
   - Where Monett, Ks.

GREAT GREAT GRANDPARENTS

16. Joseph Finney
   - Born 18 Sep 1784
   - Where Orange Co., NC
   - When married 10 Sep 1805
   - Died 8 Mar 1867
   - Where Parke Co., Ind.

17. Mary Polly Long
   - 2 Apr 1786 - 27 Sep 1872

18. Jesse Hinshaw
   - Born 1 July 1797
   - Where
   - When married 24 Sep 1817
   - Died
   - Where

19. Hannah Moon
   - 14 Mar 1798

20. Jonathan Farlow
   - Born 17 July 1807
   - Where Orange Co., NC
   - When married 15 Nov 1832
   - Died 14 Sep 1873
   - Where Orange Co., Ind.

21. Ruth Maris 1814 - 1843

22. Daniel Cloud
   - Born 1 Jan 1815
   - Where
   - When married 20 Oct 1841
   - Died 14 Sep 1874
   - Where Orange Co., Ind

23. Mary A. Milliken 1827 - 1868

24. Wiley A. J. McClure
   - Born Dec. 1838
   - Where Tennessee
   - When married
   - Died
   - Where

25. Mary Jane Owen - 1843 Tenn

26. James L. Hopper
   - Born 9 May 1836
   - Where McCoupin Co., Ill.
   - When married
   - Died 17 Feb 1912
   - Where Montgomery Co., Ks.

27. Mary Elizabeth Thompson
   - 26 June 1841 - 26 Sep 1935

28. John Gilbert Sharp
   - Born 30 Oct 1830
   - Where Claiborne Co., Tenn.
   - When married 8 Aug 1854
   - Died 29 Dec 1912
   - Where Chautaqua Co., Ks.

29. Elizabeth Hasting Johnson
   - 21 Apr 1830 Mo - 11 Mar 1924

30. Wright J. Smith
   - Born 1848
   - Where Tennessee
   - When married Nov 1868
   - Died 6 Nov 1900
   - Where

31. Martha Almeda Jay
   - 1 Nov 1847 - 1 June 1879

GR GR GR GRANDPARENTS

32 Joseph Finney

33 Rachel Barkley

34

35

36 Jesse Hinshaw

37 Mary Marshall

38 Jacob Moon 1756 - 1822

39 Ruth Hinshaw 1763-1803

40. Joseph Farlow

41 Ruth Lindley

42 Thomas Maris

43 Jane

44 Daniel Cloud ?

45 Martha

46

47

48

49

50

51

52

53

54

55

56 William Sharp 1805-1891

57 Sarah Parker 1810 -1890

58 William Johnson b. 1808

59 Sarah Ellen Clements

60

61

62 James A. Jay b. 1809

63 Mary Suttle - b. 1820

Chart No. ___

Family: FINNEY

SEE "CONTROVERSY, SCIENCE, AND REVELATION FOR STARTLING NEW DETAILS!

No. 1 on this chart is the same person as No. 32 on chart No. 1

1. Joseph Finney
Born 2 Apr 1765
Where New Castle Co., Del.
When Married 13 Dec 1783
Where Orange Co., NC
Died 22 Mar 1837
Where Parke Co., Ind.
Cemetery Rawlins Cemetery
Where Annapolis, Ind.
Occupation
Military

Rachel Barkley
Name of husband or wife of No. 1
Born @ 1770
Where
Died 1795
Where Surry Co., NC
Cemetery
Where
Occupation

PARENTS

2. John Finney
Born 1732
Where Chester Co., Pa.
When married 9 Jan 1758
Where Wilmington, Del.
Died 5 July 1783
Cemetery Old Swedes Church
Where Wilmington, Del.
Occupation
Military

3. Ruth Lloyd
Born @ 1730
Where
Died
Cemetery
Where
Occupation
Military

4. Lazarus Finney
Born
Where Northern Ire.
When m[illegible]
Where
Died 17[illegible]
Cemetery Thun[illegible]ll
Where Chester Co., Pa.
Occupation
Military

5. Cather[illegible]
Born
Where
Died
Where
Cemetery
Where
Occupation

6. Joseph Lloyd
Born @ 1700
Where
When married
Where
Died
Cemetery
Where
Occupation
Military

SOURCES

Allegheny Co., Pa. Deeds
Belmont Co., Oh. Marriage Records
Buster, Nancy (Finney) James
Chester Co., Pa. Wills
Clinton Co., Ind. Death Records
Daughin Co., Pa. Register of Wills
Daughin Co., Pa. Orphans Court Docket
Douglas Co., Ill. Death Records
Farlow Family Bible
Finney Family Bible
Finney Family History 1732 - 1946
Finney, Charles Wesley Research
Finney, Vivia (McClure)
Fountain Co., Ind. Death Records
Greene Co., Tenn. Marriage Records
Greene Co., Oh. Land Purchases
Greene Co., Oh. Court of Common Pleas
Harrison Co., Oh. Death Records
Hartford Co., Md. Death Records
History of Emporia, Ks. by French
Holmes Co., Oh. Land Grants
Holmes Co., Oh. Death Records
Holmes Co., Oh. Federal Census 1850, 1860, 1870
Jacobson, Arabelle (Finney)
Jefferson Co., Oh. Death Records
Lancaster Co., Pa. Land Records
Lancaster Co., Pa. Registers Office
LaSalle Co., Ill. Death Records
Lyon Co., Ks. Probate Court Records
Marion Co., Ind. Marriage Records
Miami Co., Oh. Federal Census 1850, 1860, 1870, 1880
Miami Co., Oh. Court of Common Pleas
Mitchell Co., Ks. Death Records
Montgomery Co., Ks. Marriage Records
Montgomery Co., Ks. Federal Census 1850, 1860, 1870, 1880, 1900, 1910
Northumberland Co., Pa. Death Records
Notebooks of Howard Finney, Sr.
Old Swedes Holy Trinity Church Records - Wilmington, Del.
Orange Co., NC Federal Census 1850
Orange Co., Ind. Federal Census 1850, 1860, 1870, 1880, 1900, 1910
Orange Co., Ind. Cemetery Records
Parke Co., Ind. Cemetery Records
Parke Co., Ind. Federal Census 1850, 1860, 1870, 1880, 1900, 1910
Parke Co., Ind. Marriages and Deaths
Parke Co., Ind. Tax Lists
Quaker Church Records
Richland Co., Oh. Births and Deaths
Riley Co., Ks. Birth Records
Sedgwick Co., Ks. Marriages and Deaths
Union Co., Pa. Court of Common Pleas
U. S. National Archives - Pension Records, Military Service Records
Vermillion Co., Ind. Death Records
Wabaunsee Co., Ks. Birth Records
Ward, Evelyn Towell
Washington Co., Pa. Tax Roll
Washington Co., Pa. Death Records
Will Co., Ill. Death Records
Woodson Co., Ks. Federal Census
Woodson Co., Ks. Death Records

A special recognition and thank you to the friends and families who contributed to this book — with information and family records — and who loaned their treasured photographs and personal documents for everyone to share — now and in the future.
Rf

I. ROBERT FINNEY - b. Scot or England - d. Aug 1692 Londonderry, Ire. His will on record Londonderry dated Aug 1692, witnessed by Hugh Thomson and John Patersone, indicates him to be a man of extensive land interest.

1. Henry Finney - b. 30 Nov 1657 Ireland
2. James Finney - b. 4 July 1659 Ire - d. 10 Aug 1659
3. William Finney - b. 4 May 1664
4. Mary Finney - b. 29 Aug 1666
5. Robert Finney - b. 1667/8 Ulster Co., Ire. - d. Mar 1755 Chester Co., New London Twp., Pa. - buried Thunder Hill Estate - m. Ireland Dorothea FRENCH - b. 1670 Ire - d. May 1752 Chester Co., Pa.

    i. Dr. John French Finney - b. @ 1690 Londonderry, Ire - d. Mar 1774 New Castle, Del. - m. Elizabeth FRENCH - b. 1693 New Castle Co., Del - d. Apr 1740 - m [2] Sarah RICHARDSON

    ii. Robert Finney - died @ 1782, physician, unmarried

    iii. William Finney - b. 1700 Ire - d. 1750 New London, Pa., a carpenter, will dated 12 Jan 1749, probated Apr 1751 - m. Jane STEPHENSON - they had 11 children

    iv. Thomas Finney - died @ 1767 - m. Mary CHESTER

    v. Ann Finney - died after 1778, buried Thunder Hill - m. John McCLENAHAN - d. after 1778

        a. Elijah McClenahan - b. 3 Nov 1728 - d. 23 Feb 1810 New London, Pa - m. Mary - b. 1737 - d. 30 Apr 1780

            1. Samuel Blair McClenahan - b. 1 May 1775 - 11 Sep 1851 - m [1] Amay CHARLTON, m [2] Sarah JOHNSON

    vi. James Finney - died @ 1774 - m. Jean

    vii. Letitia Finney - died @ 1742 - m. William McKEAN

    viii. Lazarus Finney - b. Ire - d. 1740 Chester Co., Pa., bur. Thunder Hill - m. Catharine SIMONTON [Symonton]

THUNDER HILL

Early Finneys, including Robert Finney, were Presbyterians

"Presbyterianism refers to a number of Christian churches adhering to the Calvinist theological tradition within Protestantism that are organized according to a characteristic Presbyterian polity. Presbyterian theology typically emphasizes the sovereignty of God, the authority of the Scriptures, and the necessity of grace through faith in Christ. [1]

PRESBYTERIANISM IN AMERICA

"Just at this time when Presbyterianism was coming into prominence in England, the settlement of the English colonies in the New World began and Puritans and Presbyterians took a leading part in the colonization program. Everyone knows of the Puritan settlements in New England.

Although these Puritans were spiritual brothers of the Presbyterians back home, the connection was more informal as they came to the New World before the Westminster Assembly sat. John Cotton, leader of the New Englanders, was invited to attend the Assembly but did not go.

By 1707 the Presbyterians of the Middle Colonies were numerous enough to form the first presbytery in America. Within a few years and under the efforts of Francis Makamie and other Presbyterians, the movement spread from New York and Pennsylvania into Virginia and the Carolinas. As a result, in 1789, the first General Assembly was held.

The original growth of Presbyterianism in the Middle Colonies was largely due to the huge emigration of Scots and Scottish-Irish (Scots who had fled to Ireland in times of persecution). For instance, over 30,000 Presbyterians arrived from Ireland alone in the two years 1771-1773. And at the time of the Revolutionary War it was reliably estimated that two million of the three million persons in the colonies were Calvinists (Reformed) of some sort. [2]

[1] http://en.wikipedia.org/wiki/Presbyterianism#United_States

[2] http://www.fpcjackson.org/resources/apologetics/story.htm

Addendum to Page 1

I. Robert Finney

5. Robert Finney + Dorothea French

From James G. Finney

I believe I've seen the old picture you mentioned (Thunder Hill) but haven't seen a good one. My wife and I visited Thunder Hill in 2007. There was a farm house that somebody told us was built on the site of the original and we stopped to inquire of the residents who, unfortunately, were kind of standoffish and seemed anxious to get rid of us.

We stopped at the dairy farm across the road from the cemetery (the current owners of the cemetery plot) and got permission to go up to the cemetery. They were very friendly and even gave us a ride across a pasture full of dairy cows and mud to get there. They knew nothing of the history of the cemetery other than that a branch of Finneys from the east coast had taken care of it in years past, but were no long doing so, which was apparent by the overgrowth of weeds and trees obscuring nearly all of the headstones.

My wife found Robert's and Dorothea's headstones and we cleared away a lot of plant matter before shooting the photos. If we had had garden tools we would have cleared a lot more.

Robert Finney and Dorothea Finney headstones, photos by James G. Finney

Two things in the family history I believe may be errors are the attribution of the surname “French” to Dorothea. I've never seen evidence supporting this. Also, John Finney, whose line I am descended from (son of Robert and Dorothea) is often referred to as John French Finney. There was a John French Finney in his descendants, but I don't believe that was his middle name.

It's all very interesting, indeed. I would love to exhume the body of Robert and get a full DNA profile for comparison. Through DNA testing I've “met” two cousins online who descended from Robert. Gerald Finney of Fresno is one of them. He is a treasure trove of family information, knows more than anybody else about our descendancy. You might consider contacting him; I'll append his email address. The other is Fred Finney, Ph.D., an archaeologist from Illinois, very interesting guy with archaeology publications and books all over the internet.

1 **Robert FINNEY**

2 **Robert FINNEY** b: 1668 d: MAR 1755

+ **Dorothea FRENCH** b: 1670 d: MAY 1752

3 **John FINNEY** b: 1690 d: BET MAR 1774 AND APR 1774

+ **Elizabeth FRENCH**

6 **John French FINNEY** b: 09 FEB 1798 d: 25 MAR 1865

+ **Rebecca BUTLER** b:08 OCT 1807 d: 11 MAY 1870

7 **David FINNEY** b: 26 FEB 1827 d: 18 MAY 1879

+ **Rachel WILLIAMS** b: 2 21 AUG 1828

6 **David Thompson FINNEY Jr.**b:27 NOV 1799 d:13 SEP 1881

+ **Hannah BUTLER** b: 04 FEB 1801 d: 30 JUL 1884

6 **Washington FINNEY** b: 04 MAY 1804 d: 06 JAN 1875

+ **Martha BELL** b: 04 JUL 1809 d: 24 MAR 1883

7 **Johnson FINNEY** b: 25 OCT 1836

+ **Elizabeth CRAWFORD**

8 **Roy Lovell FINNEY** d: 12 OCT 1934 b: 22 AUG 1878

+ **Alice REED**

9 **Robert Crawford FINNEY** b: 25 MAR 1911 d: 03 DEC 1975

+ **Juanita OLSEN**

10 **James** G. Finney

James G. Finney descendancy from Robert Finney

As far as the DNA testing, I first got the 67 marker test and recently upgraded to the 111 marker and am awaiting results. Gerald, Fred and I are comparing markers as we go along. The three of us are pretty close genetically. Gerald has as yet been unable to find his paper connection into the family before his ancestor Isaac Finney of Ohio in the 1800s, but his DNA pretty much proves that he is a descendant of Robert.

As you said, there is so much repetition of names it all gets very confusing. The family spread all over, too. My line went from Pennsylvania to Delaware to Ohio to Iowa, where my father was born, then to Colorado which is where my father went to college and medical school. I've found gravestone pictures for some, but not all. John, David, and Washington are missing. I'm just glad that Robert's is still in such good condition as to still be readable.

By the way, we all thought we were Irish originally, but have concluded that we are actually originally from Scotland, coming to Ireland during the Transplantation of King James I in the 1600s. Our ancestors were all Presbyterians, intermarried with McKeans, McClenachans and the like and pretty much "acted" like Ulster Scots, or Scots-Irish if you prefer.

In the Name of God Amen the first
Day of June, one thousand seven hundred & seventy
Eight, I Robt. Finney of Thunder Hill in ye County of Chester
And Province of Pensylvania practitioner of Physick, being
of Sound & disposing mind & memory, doe make & ordain
this my last will & testament in manner following. First
I Commit my soul to Almighty God who give it, and my
Body to be decently intered at ye discretion of my Executors herein after Named, & as to such Estate, real and
personal as I shall dye possessed of, I devise & bequeath
ye Same in manner following, first I order all my just
debts to be paid. Item I will & order, one Acre in the
Corner of my land, where my Fathers are Buried, for a burying place to my relations for ever. Item I will & order
ye Sum of fifty pounds to be put out on interest, which
interest I allow yearly for ever for ye repairing or
[illegible]
[illegible]
be over plus from ye use, to be given to ye poor of said
Township. I Expect that ye Elders of said Meeting will
be careful in this, that so it may be handed down until
time be no more. Item I bequeath to my Sister Ann Mc Clenachan ye Sum of one hundred pounds if alive, I will to
Cousn Robt. Finney Saddler & to Cousn Elijah Mc Clenachan
ye Sum of Twenty to Each of them, I say Twenty pounds.
Item I will to Cousn John Mc Clenachan ye Sum of ten pounds
I will to my Sister in law Mary Finney & to her Daughter
Ann Finney ye Sum of ten pounds to Each of them if
alive. Item I Devise & Bequeath to young Robt.
Finney Son to Agnes Finney Eighty Six Acres & half
of land by Patten for Ever adjoining ye Noreast Side
of Thunder Hill, also one hundred & fifty pounds money
& to his brother William Finney I will ye Sum of one
hundred & fifty pounds, and [illegible] two Sisters now
born as followeth to Dorothea Finney I will ye Sum of
fifty pounds, & to Ann [illegible] ye Sum of thirty pounds

Robert Finney's handwritten will

Bottom of page 1

From James G. Finney

Thanks for clearing up a couple of misconceptions and mysteries for me about names. I was aware of Lazarus (the tavern keeper?), well pretty much the whole bunch, having read a lot of historical documents about the family several years ago.

vii. Lazarus Finney

To his Majesties Justices At their Court of Quarter Sessions held At Chester for ye sd County ye 26 day of August Anno Domo 1729

The Petition of Lazarus Finney

Sheweth

That your Petitioner living on ye Great road leading from Susquehanna River to Philadelphia & ye road from [illegible] to Newcastle in the Township of New London, where there is a great resort of Travellers who Frequently Travel Along ye said Road And Are often [illegible] to your Petitioner & Several of ye Neighbours For Entertainment for want of A house of Entertainment on ye Aforesd Roads to entertain Travellers At. Your Petitioner humbly prays this Court to grant him A recomendation to ye Governour for A Lycence to Keep A publick house of Entertainment on ye Aforesd Road And your petitioner will pray

Lazarus Finney

Know all men by these Presents that We Lazarus [illegible] Both of ye County of Chester are held & firmly Bound unto Patrick Gordon Esqr Governr of ye province of Pennsylvania in ye Sum of Sixty pounds Currt money of America to be paid unto him ye sd Patrick Gordon or to his Legal Successors to them or Either of them to ye which paymt well & truly to be made we hereby Bind our selves our heirs Exrs & Admrs firmly by these presents Sealed with our Seals dated ye 27 Day of August Anno Domo 1729

The Condition of this obligation is Such that if above Bounden Lazarus Finney on Obtaining his Lycence to Keep A publick house of Entertainment for Seling of Wine Beer Syder Ale Brandy Rum & other Strong Liquors &c if therefore ye [illegible] Shal not During ye Continuance of ye sd Lycence Suffer Any unlawful game to be used in his house Nor Shal make use of Any Molasses or other Meterials in Brewing of Beer or Ale but Shal During ye said time use & Mentain good order & Rule therein & observe all ye Laws & Ordinances which Are or Shall be made relating to Inn-keepers or Taverns within this Province then this Obligation to be void & of no Effect or Else to Stand in full force And vertue

Sealed & Delivered in the presence of

[illegible] Parker

Laz: Finney

[illegible] Clenachan

A document signed by Lazarus Finney in 1729. It is a petition for him to open an Inn for travelers to visit. (From Gerald Finney)

i. Dr. John French Finney, s/o Robert & Dorothea - b. 1690 Ire - d. Mar 1774 Del, a physician and surgeon - m [1] Elizabeth FRENCH b. 1693 Del - d. Apr 1740. She had brother David FRENCH [children of Robert & Mary [Sandeland] French] - m [2] Sarah RICHARDSON, d/o John Richardson of Christiana Hundred, New Castle Co., Del.

a. David French Finney - b. 1726 Pa - d.May 1806 New London, Pa - m. Mary Ann THOMPSON - b. 1741 - 1805, d/o John Thompson

David F. went to Ireland for his education where he studied law, practicing in New Castle and was judge of the Supreme Court of Delaware. He inherited considerable property from both his father and mother and at one time was reported to be the wealthiest citizen in Delaware. His estate, however, was reduced during the Revolutionary War by depreciation of Continental money, almost exclusive currency of that day.

1. John French Finney - died 1794, unmarried, lvd. New Castle Co., Del.
2. Elizabeth Finney - m. 1793 James MILLER - no children
3. Ann Dorothea Finney - b. 1775 - d. May 1792 - m. William MILLER, brother of James MILLER above - they had two children
4. David Thompson Finney - b. 20 Jan 1773 New Castle, Del. - d. 22 Nov 1863 Holmes Co., Oh at daughter Rachel's home - m. 9 Mar 1797 Mary JAMES - b. 10 Sep 1775 Del - d. 13 July 1859, d/o Major John JAMES & Elizabeth

David T. was a judge and early settler in Holmes Co., Oh - listed in 1850 census - moved to Washington Co., Pa. 1811 and was then awarded land grants in Holmes Co.

A. John French Finney, s/o David T. - b. 9 Feb 1798 Del - d. 25 Mar 1865 Oh - m. 14 Feb 1826 Rebecca BUTLER - b. 8 Oct 1807 Oh - 11 May 1879. Rebecca was said to be a very haughty, beautiful and proud woman, the d/o Jonathan and Sarah Butler. They and Rebecca lived in Richardland Co., Oh. just west of Mansfield, then in Holmes Co. John F. shown 1850 Holmes Co. census as farmer with $5,000 real estate.

[1] David Finney - b. 16 Feb 1827 Oh - d. 18 May 1879 - m. 12 Apr 1852 Rachel D. WILLIAMS - b. 2 Aug 1829 NY

[a] Tillotson Finney - b. 8 June 1853 Holmes Co - m. 12 Nov 1885 Emma Celia CHURCH

i. Corinna Finney - b. 12 Apr 1887

[b] Albert E. Finney - b. 9 Nov 1854 Oh - m. 27 Feb 1882 Laura ALLISON

[c] Geneva Finney - b. 5 Nov 1858 - 26 June 1881 - m. 26 Apr 1879 Albert O. McCLELLAND

[d] Clyde Finney - b. 8 Feb 1863

[2] Jonathan Finney - b. 30 Dec 1830 Oh - d. 1905 - m. 1854 Agnes S. BIVENS - b. 21 Apr 1836, d/o Ira

[a] Mary Louise Finney - b. 10 June 1855 Oh - m. 7 Oct 1885 Harold WARD STONE
[b] Walter Finney - b. 1856 - d. 1858
[c] John Finney - b. 9 Apr 1858
[d] Horace Finney - b. 13 Dec 1860
[e] Albert Carlyle Finney - b. 12 May 1863 Brown Co., Oh.
[f] Helen May Finney - b. 15 Jan 1865 - m. 27 June 1888 William Clarence BICKWELL
[g] Olive W. Finney - b. 14 Aug 1870
[h] Clara R. Finney - b. 7 Aug 1874

[3] John Albert Finney - b. 9 Dec 1834 Oh - 22 May 1882 - m. Kezia NUMBERS
[4] Mary H. Finney - b. 4 July 1838 Oh - m. Newton DICKINSON
[5] Thomas Corwin Finney - b. 27 Oct 1840 Holmes Co - d. 9 Mar 1895 - m. 11 Apr 1864 Emma Jane WHITMAN - b. 9 Apr 1843 Alexander, Pa - d. 16 July 1876 Paxico, KS where they moved in 1870 - m [2] 9 Sep 1877 Martha HOLLAND - b. 24 July 1860

Addendum to Page 2

i. John French Finney

NOTE: John Finney built the current house (Amstel House), after purchasing the property in 1738. Finney is reputed to have owned half a dozen town houses and vast properties in the county, and is uncle to Declaration of Independence signer, Thomas McKean.[1]

Amstel House, by James G. Finney

From James G. Finney

Thanks for clearing up a couple of misconceptions and mysteries for me about names. I was aware of Lazarus (the tavern keeper?), well pretty much the whole bunch, having read a lot of historical documents about the family several years ago. I did know John was a doctor and visited his house, the Amstel House in Newcastle, Delaware in 2007. It's a beautiful old brick house kept up by the local historical society.

A. John French Finney

[2] After Jonathan Finney, a sister was not included. Her name is Anna Dorothea French

This is how Anna Dorothea Finney's ancestry should be recorded.

4 **Ann Dorothea FINNEY** b: 1735 d: 1817 [2]

+ **John FINNEY** b: 1745 d: 1814

NOTE: Family lore informs us that Anna had been so distraught at the loss of her fiance, a British officer under Colonel Braddock in the French and Indian War, that her father quickly married her to her cousin, John Finney of Pennsylvania.

5 **John FINNEY Jr.** b: 1777 d: 08 JUN 1862

[1] http://www.newcastlehistory.org/houses/amstelhistory.html

[2] http://awtc.ancestry.com/cgi-bin/igm.cgi?op=DESC&db=breamefford&id=I2689

+ **Jane BOOTHE** b: 1789 d: 16 APR 1846

6 **Ann A. FINNEY** b: 29 OCT 1809 d: FEB 1881

+ **James K. LOGAN**

6 **Walter FINNEY** b: 1810 d: 1852

+ **Rebecca E. SLAWSON** b: 1813 d: 10 NOV 1895

7 **John FINNEY** b: died young

7 **William FINNEY** b: 1841 d: 1850

7 **Kate A. FINNEY** b: 15 NOV 1844 d: 30 MAY 1874

+ **Clemens CLACIUS** b: 06 NOV 1829 d: 06 FEB 1886

7 **Walter FINNEY** b: 1849 d: 01 MAR 1867

7 **Carrie D. FINNEY** b: 03 FEB 1851

+ **George BUTLER**

6 **William FINNEY** b: 1812

6 **Catherine FINNEY** b: 1814 d: 20 OCT 1891

6 **Mary FINNEY** b: 1816 d: 1826

6 **John FINNEY Jr.** b: 1819 d: 1850

6 **William FINNEY** b: 1822

6 **Robert FINNEY** b: 1823

+ **Annie E. EMERSON** b: 1826

7 **Frank FINNEY** d: 1851

7 **Lillie FINNEY** b: 11 SEP 1846 d: 21 MAR 1868

7 **Blanche FINNEY** b: 23 NOV 1849

+ **Thomas M. KING**

7 **Henry or Harry FINNEY** b: 08 AUG 1852

+ **Kate MCELROY**

8 **Anna C. FINNEY** b: 25 NOV 1878

8 **Jane E. FINNEY** b: 08 MAR 1880

8 **Josephine FINNEY** b: 08 OCT 1882

7 **Florence FINNEY** b: 1854

7 **Brady W. FINNEY** b: 11 FEB 1855 d: 22 SEP 1890

+ **Lillian WARWICK**

7 **May FINNEY** b: 08 AUG 1857

+ **John C. TEMPLE**

7 **Jennie FINNEY** b: 27 AUG 1859 d: 25 NOV 1884

+ **Henry M. BISSELL**

7 **Maud FINNEY** b: 15 JUL 1861

+ **William R. HERSCHBURGH OR HERSBERBER**

7 **Robert FINNEY** b: 10 AUG 1863

7 **Ann Dorothea FINNEY** b: 20 AUG 1866

+ **William Holden CHACE**

From James G. Finney

I received a new book *Genealogy of One Branch of the Descendents of Robert Finney of Londonderry, Ireland.* The book contains a portrait of Anna Dorothea Finney, daughter of Dr. John French Finney.

Anna Dorothea Finney – "A High and haughty dame, exercising centurion-like authority, prone to issuing of orders, and very vigilant and determined in seeing that they were promptly and vigorously executed."

PORTRAIT — Oil painting of Anna Dorothea Finney, daughter of Dr. John Finney, by Benjamin West, *(from the September 1962 issue of National Geographic Magazine, page 367).*
"BENJAMIN WEST, known as the father of American painting. He started his career as a self taught limner and face painter. He was the son of a Quaker innkeeper outside Philadelphia and according to legend learned to mix paints from the Indians. Later a group of Pennsylvania businessmen raised funds to send him to Europe for study. In London he became the favorite painter of King George III and president of the Royal Academy. He turned his studio into a home-away-from-home for young American painters studying in England. Without his help some of America's best talent might not have weathered the trials of student days. He died in 1820 and was buried among England's great in St. Paul Cathedral."
(Included in the article is a colored portrait of Sarah Ursula Rose who posed for the portrait in 1756. This was approximately the same time that Anna Dorothea Finney posed for the above portrait.) Anna, who inherited wealth from her parents, was described as "A high and haughty dame, exercising centurion-like authority, prone to issuing of orders, and very vigilant and determined in seeing that they were promptly and vigorously executed." Anna Dorothea was a sister of David Finney and daughter of Dr. John Finney.

The Ancient Arms of
Finney

[a] Mary Finney - b. 11 July 1865 Millersburg, Oh - m. Newton DICKINSON - b. 3 May 1865 Ill
[b] Christiana Finney - b. 6 May 1867 Holmes Co., Oh - m. John C. MADDEN - b. 20 July 1867
[c] Hallie Finney - b. 25 May 1870 Tecumseh, KS - m. Robert B. FERGUSON - b. 9 Apr 1859
[d] John Edgar Finney - b. 14 Feb 1872 Paxico, Ks - 1951 - m. Olive DICKINSON - 28 July 1872 Ill - 20 June 1958

i. Whitham D. Finney - b. 17 Sep 1898 Wabaunsee Co, Ks - m. Irma WRAY

a. Whitham Wray Finney

ii. William F. Finney - b. 19 Feb 1901 - m. Dorothy CLIBORNE

a. William C. Finney b. 1929 Okla
b. James H. Finney - b. 9 Jan 1935

[e] William Albert Finney - b. 5 Mar 1874 Wabaunsee Co, Ks - drowned 25 June 1884
[f] Thomas Arthur Finney - b. 30 Dec 1878
[g] James Garfield Finney - b. 30 Dec 1879
[h] Susan Albertine Finney - b. 17 Nov 1881
[i] Jessie Elizabeth Finney - b. 11 Aug 1884
[j] Louise Rebecca Finney - b. 18 Jan 1887
[k] Horace David Finney - 10 Aug 1890 - d. 31 July 1892

[6] Rebecca Finney, d/o John French - b. 9 July 1842 Oh - d. 25 Dec 1874
[7] George Gordon Finney - b. 25 Apr 1845 Oh - m. Mary Jane ARMSTRONG

[a] Walter Scott Finney - m. Anna McGILLWOOD

i. Cecil Gordon Finney - b. 25 Nov 1907 Okla City - m. Gladys BOSWELL

a. Della Lee Finney - b. 5 Mar 1928 Okla City
b. Sylvia M. Finney - b. 22 Sep 1933

ii. Alice V. Finney - b. 3 Feb 1910

[b] Carrydon Finney
[c] Alice Finney
[d] Ollie Olive Finney
[e] Lillian Finney
[f] Lulu Finney

[8] William Finney - b. 3 Apr 1832 - d. 1 Sep 1836

B. David Thompson Finney, s/o David Thompson - 1 27 Nov 1799 Del - 13 Sep 1881 m. 10 Jan 1827 Hannah BUTLER b. 1 Feb 1804 Oh - 30 July 1884 - lvd. Holmes Co., Oh. 1850

[1] Sarah Finney - b. 17 Dec 1828 Oh - m. 22 Dec 1851 REv. Milton W. BROWN
[2] John Finney - b. 10 Aug 1830 - d. 11 Sep 1839
[3] Mary Finney - b. 19 Sep 1832 - d. 8 Dec 1836
[4] James McKenna Finney - b. 20 Jan 1834 Oh - m. Mary E. PHILLIPS b. 1848

[a] Louis C. Finney - b. 20 Aug 1871
[b] Bessie Finney - b. 29 Aug 1875
[c] Bertie Finney - b. 12 June 1882

[5] Rebecca Finney - b. 2 Apr 1837 - 12 Sep 1839
[6] Ann Dora Finney - b. 13 Feb 1840 Oh - m [1] 24 Feb 1864 Ephraim CRIST - died 24 Oct 1873, m [2] William HAGUE
[7] Jane Finney - b. 4 July 1842 Oh - m. 11 Mar 1864 Milton F. LAW
[8] Lucretia Finney - 1 Jan 1844 Holmes Co., Oh - m. 13 Oct 1870 William McCAUGHEY

[9] Jonathan B. Finney - m. 10 Feb 1876 Callie CHATLAIN

[a] DeAlvin Finney
[b] Laura Eva Finney
[c] Lena C. Finney
[d] Ward Finney
[e] Lulu May Finney - b. 7 Jan 1890

[10] Laura Finney - b. 5 July 1850 - m. Rev. Alexander EAGLESTON

C. Elizabeth Finney, d/o David T. - 16 Aug 1801 - 15 Feb 1807
D. Washington Finney - b. 4 May 1804 Del - 6 Jan 1875 - m. 1827 Holmes Co., Oh. Martha BELL b. 4 July 1809 Pa - 24 Mar 1883, d/o John Bell

[1] David Philander Finney - 15 June 1832 - 23 Nov 1887 - m [1] Isabella BIRD, m [2] Mary, m [3] Nellie OSBORN

[2] Samuel Bell Finney - 22 Aug 1834 - d. Delta, Oh. during Civil War - m. Rachel Ellen LEE

[a] Jane Finney - m. Thomas KIRKHAM
[b] Elmer Grant Finney - m. Martha ZIMMERMAN

i. Percy Finney
ii. Fern Finney

[3] Johnston Finney - b. 25 Oct 1836 - m. Elizabeth CRAWFORD

[a] Alma M. Finney - 6 Nov 1856 Holmes Co - m.28 Nov 1882 Jonathan AVERY
[b] Walter Finney
[c] Nettie Finney
[d] Fred Finney - b. 1868 Montour, Iowa
[e] Guy W. Finney - b. 1872 - m. Alice FOGELMAN

i. Clyde E. Finney - b & d 1894
ii. Merrill Finney b. 1896 Iowa - d. 1935 Calif. - m. Lucille JENKINS b. 1896 - d. 1935

a. Lyman Finney - b. 1921 Calif.
b. Eva May Finney - b. 1924
c. W. Louise Finney - b. 1925

iii. Max R. Finney - b. 1900 Iowa - m. Sue CORK b. 1900

a. Robert A. Finney - b. 1926 Calif.
b. Donald L. Finney - b. 1927

iv. Glenn E. Finney - b. 1904 - m. Rosemary McCOMB b. 1913
v. Rex O. Finney - b. 1909

[f] Rodney E. Finney
[g] Roy L. Finney- died 1934 Delta Co., Colo - m. Alice REED

i. Robert Finney
ii. Rodney Finney
iii. Freda Finney

[4] Mary Elizabeth Finney, d/o Washington - b. 7 Dec 1838 - m. Andrew J. BORTZ
[5] Rachel Helen Finney - 17 Aug 1840 - m. John WEATHERBEE
[6] Mary Ruhanah Finney - 10 May 1843 - m. John BOLING
[7] Clarissa Jane Finney - 28 May 1845 - m [1] 21 Nov 1867 James SHANK - b. 9 Dec 1842 - June 1880 - m [2] Sylvanus AYLESWORTH
[8] Clemza L. Finney - 19 July 1847 Holmes Co., Oh - m. Frank HOYER
[9] Thomas Thompson Finney b. 2 Aug 1830 - 1907/1910 - m. 1849 Mary J. RICHARDSON b.21 Feb 1831 Pa - 11 Sep 1883 Oh - m [2] Nancy or Mary SCHALL

[a] Covington Finney - b. 3 June 1850 - d. young
[b] George W. Finney - b. 13 Nov 1851 Oh - m. 6 Mar 1873 Laura TAYLOR

i. Walter W. Finney - 14 Dec 1873 - m. Maud BROWN

a. Orville Finney - 23 Sep 1901 m. Leona DEMPSTER-4 May 1904

b. Mildred Finney - m. H. HARPER
c. Beatrice Finney - m. R. CHAMBERS
d. G. Eugene Finney - lvd. Dennison, Ohio
e. Agnes Finney
f. Lois Finney - b. 23 Feb 1918

ii. Orvel O. Finney - b. 18 Jan 1876 - 18 Dec 1883
iii. Myrtle Finney - b. 3 Oct 1877

[c] Joseph Alexander Finney - 18 May 1853 - d. 1910
[d] Bernard Sylvester Finney - 5 July 1855 - 29 Apr 1893 - m. Mary F. ADAIR
[e] Thomas Grant Finney - b. 1855 - d. 1861
[f] Carrie Finney - b. 18 May 1859 m. Oreo Holmes PRICE
[g] Ella Laura Finney b. 6 May 1861 m. Alonzo E. ADAIR
[h] Luella [Lula] b. 1 Dec 1861 m. 10 Sep 1885 William Mack DEVOR
[i] Maude Finney - 13 Jan 1874 - d. Mar 1924

[10] Sarah Maria Finney - 13 Oct 1828 - m. 1856 Amos BRITON
[11] Josephine Eugenie Finney - m. Cornelius SHANK of Nashville, Oh

E. Mary Jane Finney, d/o David Thompson - b. 4 July 1806 - d. 6 May 1888 - m [1] 7 Jan 1831 Thomas BELL, m [2] 25 Mar 1840 William L. BINGHAM who d. 10 Apr 1873

F. Ann Evans Finney - 10 Dec 1808 - 2 June 1896 - m. 2 May 1837 Rev. George GORDON b. 8 Jan 1806 - 11 Dec 1867

G. William James Finney b. 6 Dec 1811 Pa - 7 Nov 1883 m. 1847 Louisa GRIST - b. 1 Apr 1827 - 15 May 1909

[1] Thomas D. Finney - 30 Sep 1849 Oh - m. 1868 Louisa NUMBERS b. 1850

[a] D. W. Finney

[b] J. E. - m. 26 Sep 1895 J. A. GRAVES

[2] Ann Finney - b. 25 Oct 1854 - 29 Aug 1870
[3] William Finney - b. 3 June 1856 - unmarried
[4] Arthur Finney - 16 Aug 1860 Oh - d. 25 May 1884

H. Rachel James Finney - 1 Dec 1813 - 1 Oct 1876 - m. 2 Oct 1844 David MARSHMAN b. 1811 Pa, w/her parents David & Mary in 1850 Holmes Co., Oh.

[1] Mary E. Marshman - b. 1846 Holmes Co., Oh.
[2] Joanna Marshman - b. 1848

I. Thomas McKean Finney - b. & d. 10 May 1815

J. Thomas McKean Finney - 12 Nov 1817 - July 1859 - m. 28 Oct 1841 Jane Reed ORR - b. 15 June 1817 - d. 18 Sep 1865

[1] James Edwin Finney - 17 Aug 1852 - 3 Sep 1933 - McAlester, Okla - m. 10 May 1877 Alice HOPKINS - b. 1856

[a] Ora Kate Finney - b. 19 Feb 1878 - m. W. F. MIDDLECOFF
[b] Robert Floran Finney - b. 5 Aug 1880

[2] Susan Mary Finney - b. 3 July 1843 - m [1] 7 Aug 1862 Ebenezer Bigham BELL, m [2] 1866 Joseph BURKHOLDER b. 1819 - d. 1904

[3] Laura Finney - 12 Aug 1844 - 12 May 1875 m. 21 Mar 1865 John K. RANKIN
[4] Gertrude Finney - 26 June 1846 - m. 3 May 1877 Joseph Lindsay STUBBS
[5] Anna Finney - b. 5 Aug 1848 - 14 Mar 1904 Okla. - m. 27 July 1869 John Newton FLORER
[6] David Thompson Finney - b. 24 Sep 1850 Knox Co., Oh - 24 Nov 1925 San Jose, Calif - m [1] 10 June 1875 Lida WINAN, m [2] Mrs. Maggie NELSON

[a] Della G. Finney - b. 30 Apr 1876
[b] Ethel M. Finney - b. 3 Apr 1878
[c] Maud Ann Finney - b. 27 Apr 1882

[7] Thomas McKean Finney - b. 13 May 1856 - m. 20 July 1879 Abbie York STILLVERT b. 2 Aug 1850

[a] Frank Florer Finney - 15 June 1884 m. Ila Gray BERRY b. 30 Nov 1886

i. Thomas McKean Finney, s/o Frank Florer - b. 4 Mar 1913 Bartlesville, Okla.
ii. Frank Florer Finney - 26 Nov 1917
iii. Robert Berry Finney - b. 11 Dec 1921

[8] Frank M. Finney, s/o Thomas McKean - b. 13 May 1858 Oh - 23 Mar 1919 LaJunta, Colo. - m. 11 Oct 1882 Grace HOUGHTELING

[a] Royal H. Finney - b. 29 Dec 1883
[b] Carrie G. Finney - b. 4 Aug 1889

5. Washington Lee Finney, s/o David French - b. 20 Jan 1773 - 1804 m. 19 Dec 1797 Christiana BICKHAM, d/o George - she died 1857

6. Sarah Maris Finney - m. 1805 [cousin] French McMULLEN

b. Robert Finney, s/o John French -, died 1771, unmarried

c. Elizabeth Finney - died 30 May 1788, unmarried

d. Ann Dorothea Finney -

e. John Finney, Jr. - b. Nov 1749 - 19 Jan 1753 [Sarah's son]buried within brick enclosure Quaker Burying Ground - New Castle, Del.

NOTES FROM DR. JOHN FINNEY'S WILL: Will dated 5 Sep 1770, New Castle, Delaware -0 Codicil 21 Mar 1774 - 8 Apr 1774, K 129 - Wife Sarah Finney - daughters Elizabeth and Ann Dorothea; sons David and Robert and brother Robert Finney. Codicil - Grandson John French Finney - grand-daughters Elizabeth and Ann - Executors - wife Sarah and son David Finney

<u>HOME OF DR. JOHN FINNEY</u> [Writers' Project, 909 West Street, Wilmington, Del. - Clyde W. Young, 7 May 1940

AMSTEL HOUSE, N. corner 4th and Delaware Streets, New Castle. Open weekdays, 10 to 5, admittance 25 cents. Repositary maintained by the New Castle Historical Society, founded 6 June 1934, for the preservation of antiquities in New Castle. The building once served as the home of Dr. JOHN FINNEY, who practised medicine in New Castle in the middle of the eighteenth century, and was the dwelling place of Nicholas Van Dyke, Governor of Delaware in the latter part of the eighteenth century. It was during the occupancy by Dr. Finney after 1738 that the main building was added to the older one. Governor Van Dyke, while living in the house, was not the owner. He surrendered the lease to his son-in-law Kensey JOHNS, Sr. on 25 Mar 1785. [Johns was afterward Chancellor of Delaware.]

The names of the builder and original owner of the house are unknown, and its exact age has never been definitely determined. Architects have dated the construction of the main house at 1730, but some have thought the service wing to be considerably older. There is a record of a public sale of the house about 1738, immediately prior to which William GODDARD was the owner. It is two stories high, with dimensions of forty by sixty feet.

The principal facade is southeastward upon Fourth Street. One side, including the service wing, looks southwestward on Delaware Street; onthe north side is a modern formal garden, with a suggestion of Southern influence in its protection from the street by a brick wall.

The exterior walls are of locally made brick, laid usually in Flemish bond; the entrance, window frames, and frieze are of wood, painted white. The front of the residence is generously broad. A friendly though comparatively small doorway, only two steps directly above the brick sidewalk, occupies the middle of this front. Four good-sized windows, guarded by solid, paneled wooden shutters, look on the street - two from each side of the central entrance - where the shadows of old trees creep across cobblestone and brick paving. A central window above the doorway gives the second story five front windows. A broad gable, its peak high above the doorway, spans the house-front; it affords room for a fairly spacious attic story, with three somewhat smaller windows. The facade is further enhanced by broad shutters and the wide-angled hatch of the roof. A double cornice creates an impression of heaviness. No two windows in the house are exactly alike.

The Delaware Street side of the main building is narrower than the front, and has but two windows on the ground floor and only one, directly over the rear member of this pair, in the second story. A single dormer window is thrust boldly out from the gentle slope of the roof directly above the blank of the absent second-story window.

The service wing, containing kitchen and pantry, is a continuation of the Delaware Street side of the main house. The floor levels of this older section are somewhat lower. The ends of the manion's low-pitched roof extend a bit over the portico. This extension is trimmed with a simple wooden cornice, of which the main element is a broad, smooth, and deeply concave strip. A lower cornice of the same pattern extends straight across the house-front, just above the top of the second-story windows, from tip to tip of the eaves. The entrance, though not wide, is flanked by substantial woodwork, crowned by a deeper pediment, and treated with heavier ornament than are the entrances of later designed mansions. Its fanlight contains exceptionally broad wooden strips separating the rather narrow panes. The chimney that rises from the rear of the main residence is tall and solid; the chimney on the garden side, springs up from the eaves, matches its services ability. The brick-work on the garden side shows signs of having been relaid in relatively recent times.

The doorway, somewhat narrow for the size of the building, opens directly into a central hall of moderate size. The ceiling is high for an early dwelling dependent on fireplace heating. At the left of the hall, as one enters, a door opens into the dining room; at the right a corresponding door opens into the music room, the main apartment of the house. Its walls and ceiling have been painted a light, water green - approximately the color workmen foundunder layers of wallpaper given at a later date. The paneling, finished in a deep cream color, covers the entire side wall opposite the door from the hall, an integral part of the system of cupboards and mantel of the fireplace. A broad stone slab extending out from the hearth and flush with the broad pine floor boards, bears a modern incised inscription stating that George Washington here attended the wedding of Ann VAN DYKE, on 30 April 1784, to Kensey JOHNS, Sr. Washington did not arrive in time for the nuptial rites, but did attend the reception and banquet that followed the ceremony. It is one of the few places in the country where Washington made a visit for the specific purpose of attending the wedding of a friend. Portraits of Ann Van Dyke and of Kensey Johns, Sr. hang in the room. It is furnished with reproductions of pieces of the period of the wedding, given by Mrs. Coleman DU PONT, a descendent of Governor Van Dyke.

A spirit of complete informality was displayed by Washington at the bridal party, for, according to a letter written at the time by Justice James BOOTH - "The Great Man stood upon the hearthstone and kissed the pretty girls - as was his wont." He not only kissed them at the hearthstone, but, according to another witness, renewed the salute at his departure, for he stood on the steps, cupped the bride's cheeks in his hands, and bestowed his parting kiss on her upturned face. Kensy Johns, Sr. is believed to have paid tribute to his bride with the lines:

> "Around her head ye angels constant vigil keep,
> And guard fair innocence her balmy sleep."

The lines have been scratched with a diamond upon the pane of the window of the bedroom at the left of the stairs on the second floor. The author's name is not signed, nor did he leave any hint that they were not original.

The chief rooms throughout the house contain wooden paneling on walls, with fireplaces, done in the same style as that of the music room. The woodwork of this paneling has survived remarkably well, and contains so-called secret panels.

The kitchen has been restored and furnished with utensils that, while suitable to the period of the house, would prove a puzzle to the modern housewife. In many of the other rooms are pieces of furniture, some crude and humble, some of finer workmanship, but all of early origin and associated with New Castle.

The house was owned from 1795 to 1832 by Joseph TATLOW and his family. In 1832 the property was bought by John MOODY and remained in the Moody and Burnham families until it was sold by John B. BURNHAM in 1904. The first known owner of the site was Richard REYNOLDS, who sold it to William HOUSTON in 1706. This deed, however, is not recorded. The first recorded deed is dated October 25, 1738, when the property was sold by the sheriff as the property of William GODDARD. It was purchased a week later by DR. FINNEY. The last occupants of the house were Professor and Mrs. Henry Hanby HAY and Mrs.Louise Rodney HOLCOMB. It was opened as an historical museum in 1929, and has since been maintained on that basis.

NOTE: The following item hand-written on the bottom of this writer's project: "Some of the data included taken from secondary sources is still to be checked." There is also a notation, hand-written on the margin of the fourth paragraph where he is speaking of the fact that no two windows in Amstel House are exactly alike - he has penciled in the words "how are they unlike?"

* * * * * * * * * *

ii. Robert Finney, s/o Robert & Dorothea - died @ 1782, unmarried

iii. William Finney b. 1700/10 Ire - d. 1750 Chester Co., Pa. - was a carpenter. His will is dated 12 Jan 1749 and he is buried Thunder Hill Cemetery. Married Jean STEPHENSON - and they had 11 children.

In the Name of God Amen. I William Finey of the township of
New London in Chester County being weak of body but of a sound Judgment &
Memory, & calling to mind my latter End do make & ordain this my last will &
Testament in the following Manner, first I recomend my soul to God who gave
it, & my body to the Earth to be buried in a christian like & decent manner not
doubting but if I shall receive ye same again at ye last day by ye mighty power
of God; & as touching such worldly Goods wherewith it has pleased God to bless
me I will & dispose of them in the following manner;

Imprimis: After the payment of all my debts, I order & appoint that my personal Estate be Equally divided between Jean my beloved wife & my children
if she marry & that she be alowd ye third of my Real Estate during her life; It is my
will & desire that she & they live together & that she take care to educate
& School the children by ye benefits of the Plantation & that there be no division
till they be come of age provided that she live unmarried; & at her death order that ye Plantation be sold & Equally divided among the children

Item I order that ye Lands I hold in Faggs mannor being about ninety acres be
sold if there be occasion to Enable them to pay debts or to Educate the children;

Lastly I ordain & Appoint Robert Finey of Thunder hill & Jean my wife to be
the Executors of this my last will & testament, & Francis Alison Clerk, to be
a Trustee or overseer & I do hereby revoke & disalow all other will & wills
& declare this & no other to be my last will & Testament, In witness
whereof I have hereunto set my hand & seal this twelth day of January
in the year of our Lord one thousand seven hundred & fourty eight nine,

Sealed Published & declared to be the last will & testament of William Finey before us —
note before signing ye ye words if she marry were marked on ye margin between ye tenth & ye Eleventh line

John [illegible]

John Patterson

Jean Stevenson

William Finey

Jan. 30th 2mo 1751

Inventory 1st of June 1757

a. James Finney, s/o William & Jean, b. 1726 Chester Co., Pa. - d. 2 Aug 1802 Allegheny Co., Pa. - m. 1747 Martha MAYES who d. 1805, d/o Thomas & Margaret. In Revolutionary War, will dated 19 May 1802, probated 30 Sep 1802. On 1 July 1784 he patented "Blooming Grove" in Allegheny Co., Pa. His grandson Robert and wife Margaret PATTERSON lived there.

31 Oct 1809 - Samuel Wylie, William Finney and Andrew Finney, executors of the estate of James Finney deceased, deeded to Robert Finney, son of said James, for $1,238.50, the undivided half of a 182½ acre tract called "Blooming Grove", located in Elizabeth Twp., formerly called Rostraver Twp., Westmoreland Co. Patented to James Finney April 4, 1791, on July 1, 1784, warrant.

1. Thomas Finney, s/o James - b. 1747/8, lvd. Dauphin Co., PA.- m. 12 June 1770 Margaret SWAN, d/o Alexander & Martha [Gilchrist] Swan.

   19 Mar 1785 - a tract of 265 acres called "Paxtang", warranted Feb. 10, 1785, surveyed for Thomas Finney on Mar. 19th, located on Pine Run, Dickenson Twp., and included in Allegheny Co. 1788. This tract adjoined lands owned by James Forsyther, McCoy claim, Elliot claim, McNulty, Benjamin Reed and Wm. McKee. Wits: George Wallace, James Finney. Rec'd Apr. 10, 1790, Book 2, p. 89, Allegheny Co. Deeds.

   Thomas evidently left Pennsylvania after selling his land to his brother Andrew in 1789. His children were:

   A,.James Finney - baptized 16 June 1771
   B. Sarah Finney
   C. Jennet Finney

2. James Finney, Jr - b. 1750 Lancaster Co., Pa. - d. 1 Sep 1829 Cadiz, Harrison Co., Oh - m [1] 20 Apr 1774 Martha CRUNKLETON - d. after 1791, d/o Robert, m [2] Elizabeth BRADEN - d. 1802 when son Walter B. born, m [3] Rebecca who d. 16 May 1837.

   A. Robert P. Finney - b. 1777 Fayette Co., Pa - to Harrison Co., Oh 1804 on flatboat, settled in Richland Co., Oh in 1820 - m @ 1800 to ?, m [2] 11 Dec 1844 Mary HITCHCOCK - b. 28 Mar 1825 - d. 14 Oct 1845, m [3] 8 Nov 1846 Lydia Ann JENKINS

      [1] John Finney - b. 1801 Fayette Co., Pa, famous Ohio abolitionist
      [2] James Finney
      [3] William Finney
      [4] Martha Finney
      [5] Mary Finney
      [6] Jane Finney

   B. Walter B. Finney - b. 1802
   C. Margaret Finney
   D. Martha Finney - b. 1780 - 1868 - m. Walter FRANCIS b. 1763-1849
   E. Elizabeth Finney - m. McMILLAN
   F. John Finney - m. 10 Dec 1846 Betsy CANNON
   G. Thomas Finney - m [1] 2 May 1847 Susanna COCHERAL, m [2] 14 May 1848 Margaret NASH
   H. James Finney
   I. Francis Finney

3. Andrew Finney, s/o James & Martha
4. Robert Finney - b. 1765 - 1850 - m. Polly PEDEN

   A. Robert Finney - 3 Oct 1817 - m [1] Nancy NEVIN, m [2] Margaret PATTERSON b. 15 Aug 1818 Allegheny Co., Pa, d/o James & Mary

      [1] Nancy Finney - died age 18 years
      [2] Sarah Jane Finney - b. 5 Sep 1848 - 13 Apr 1923 Allegheny Co. - m. Alexander McCLURE

         [a] Belle McClure - m. Melvin REYNOLDS
         [b] Martha McClure - m. Ed HARPER
         [c] Robert McClure - m. Sue SHARP

[3] William Finney, s/o Robert - b. Nov 1851 - m. 27 Dec 1876 Lizzie REYNOLDS b. 1 Jan 1856 - d. 1908

[a] Clyde Finney - b. 22 Sep 1877 - m. 8 Feb 1898 Sylvia RHODES b. 4 July 1880

i. Harold Rhodes Finney - b. 8 Mar 1900
ii. Mana Magetta Finney - b. 27 Sep 1904 Blythdale,Pa
iii. Mary Elizabeth Finney - 5 Jan 1907, lvd. Boston
iv. Viola Myrtle Finney - 21 Aug 1911
v. Reynolds Monroe Finney - 24 July 1911
vi. Vaughn LaRene Finney - 29 Sep 1919

[b] Lillie Finney - b. Aug 1879 - m. 25 Apr 1900 John SHALER b. 12 June 1878, lvd. Blythdale, Pa in 1930
[c] Alice Finney - b. 23 Dec 1881 - d. young
[d] David Finney - 23 Mar 1893 - m. 4 Oct 1917 Mabel WARRELL b. 5 Oct 1896

[4] David Finney, s/o Robert - b. 4 May 1855 - d. 31 May 1936 m.[1] 19 Oct 1881 Sarah PATTERSON b. Nov 1862 - 24 Nov 1889, m [2] 15 Dec 1892 Harriet WAY b. 28 Nov 1872

[a] Howard Patterson Finney - 31 May 1882 - m. 16 Feb 1922 Nancy gAMBLE
[b] Samuel Guy Finney - died young
[c] Frank Wylie Finney - 14 Apr 1884 - m. 11 Mar 1913 Susie LITTLEJOHN - lvd.N. Clymer, NY 1930,, in Mercer Pa. in 1946

i. Ellen Simpson Finney - Jan 1914 - m. 7 Jan 1936 Blaine Edward SHEASLEY b. 26 Aug 1913
ii. William David Finney - 23 Jan 1916 - m. 16 Sep 1939 Jean Florence MURDOCK b. 1 Nov 1920

a. Stephen David Finney - 24 July 1940 Glass-port, Pa
b. William Thomas Finney - 27 Aug 1941
c. Nancy Jean Finney - 20 Feb 1944

iii. Frank Wylie Finney - 30 Apr 1918 - m. 20 Oct 1939 Chloriene ANDERSON b. 9 June 1910
iv. Anna Margaret Finney - 7 Feb 1920 Glassport, Pa - m. Aug 1940 Robert Earl WHITE b. 16 Oct 1919

[d] Robert Colmore Finney - 22 Sep 1888 - m. 24 Aug 1915 Mary FERGUS b. 23 Oct 1891, lvd. Mercer, Pa.

i. Elinor Bell Finney
ii. Lois Marie Finney
iii. Ruth Norma Finney

[e] Zillah Finney - 21 Aug 1893 - m. 31 Apr 1918 Albert F. ROTH b. 29 June 1890
[f] Anna Margaret Finney - 24 Dec 1894, a trained nurse
[g] Porter Milroy Finney - 30 Mar 1896 - m. 18 Dec 1922 Edna HOUSEHOLDER, lvd. Glassport, Pa 1930

i. Harriet Jane Finney - 23 June 1925 Augusta, KS
ii. Robert David Finney - b. 19 Nov 1926
iii. Helen Virginia Finney

[h] Harold Charles Finney - b. 19 Nov 1926
[i] Iva Elberta Finney - 13 Feb 1901 - m. 9 June 1925 Colin L. FORSYTHE b. 31 Mar 1904
[j] Oliver Erhardt Finney - 6 Aug 1904 m. 31 May 1928 Margaret BADDERS

i. Richard David Finney - 18 Dec 1931

[k] Rebecca Ruth Finney - 15 Sep 1908 - m. 20 Mar 1927 Francis Aaron FOX - 15 Aug 1902 - lvd. Mercer, Pa.

[5] Robert Finney, s/o Robert & Nancy [Nevin]
[6] Joseph Finney
[7] Mary Finney - b. 1837 - 1903 Allegheny Co., Pa - m. 8 Apr 1867 John Musgrave WATT - 4 June 1842 - d. in Pennsylvania
[8] John A. Finney

B. James Finney, s/o Robert & Polly [Peden], lived Maryland
C. Thomas Finney - lived Illinois
D. John Peden Finney - b. 1790 - 1885, lvd Pa. & Ohio - m. Rebecca HITCHCOCK

[1] Robert Finney
[2] Charles Finney
[3] William Finney - b. 1839 - 1919, lvd. E. Liverpool, Oh - m. Emma RAYL

[a] Frank Finney - 1879 - 1921 - m. Louise JAMESON

i. Gladys Finney
ii. Ivan Finney - b. 1909, lived Wyandotte, Mich. - m. Gertrude BOTT

a. John Finney - b. 1946 m. Phyllis SCHALINSKE

iii. Ila Finney
iv. Margaret Finney
v. Ethel Finney

E. William Finney - lvd. Allegheny Co., Pa & West Newton, Pa - m. Lucinda NICHOLS

F. Jane Finney - m. Robert McCONNELL

G. Sarah Finney - m. Joseph B. WADDELL

5. Jean Finney, d/o James & Martha [Mayes] Finney
6. William Finney
7. Margaret Finney
8. John Wesley Finney
9. Mary Finney

b. Elizabeth Finney, d/o William & Jean - b. 1728 - 1816 Chester Co., Pa - m. Andrew HENDERSON - died 1762

c. Archibald Finney - b. 1730 - m. LOUGHEAD, d/o Robert

1. Elizabeth Finney - died before 1774

d. Thomas Finney - b. 1732 Chester Co., Pa - d. 1770/71 Dauphin Co., Pa - m. 15 Feb 1757 Susanna STEWART

Thomas was a soldier in French & Indian Wars - enlisted age 24, on 6 Mar 1756, made Corporal, with Major James Burd's Co., 1st Regiment, Province of Pa. [REF: Pennsylvania Archives, Series 5, Vol. 1, pg 60] He went to Lancaster Co., Pa. by 1756. Owned 73½ acres, surveyed to him 23 Oct 1765, located West Hanover Twp.,Lancaster Co., Pa. After his death Susanna married William BRANDON @ 1778. On 20 Mar 1778 an account on estate of Thomas Finney, deceased, was rendered by William Brandon & Susannah, his wife, late Susannah Finney, widow, and Samuel Stewart. Notes are dated 20 Mar 1778.

1. James Finney - b. 12 Mar 1758 - died infant
2. Agnes Finney - bapt.,27 May 1759 [Sometimes called Ann] - died 1813/17. Married James PATTERSON - bapt. 17 Dec 1751 - d. 1813

A. John Patterson - 1777/81 - d. before 1813, married, had 4 children

[1] Nancy Patterson
[2] Jane Patterson
[3] Mary Patterson
[4] James Patterson

B. Susanna Patterson - bapt. 26 Sep 1779 - 1849 - m. [cousin] William PATTERSON - lvd. Allegheny Co., Pa.

C. Thomas Patterson - b. 1781 - 7 Apr 1848, lvd Ohio Co., Va 1817, buried Washington Co., Pa. - m. Sarah cRAIG

D. William Patterson - b. 1782 - 1860 Hartstown, Crawford Co., Pa m. Sarah STEWART

E. James Patterson, s/o James & Agnes - b. 1784 - 1855 - m [1] Mary WATT who d. 1836/37, m [2] Mary SWANGLE b. 1809

[1] Nancy Agnes Patterson - 26 Nov 1813 - m. 24 Sep 1835 William WATT
[2] Jane Patterson - 5 Apr 1816 Allegheny Co., Pa - 26 Jan 1853 Mansfield, Oh - m. 5 May 1835 William Stewart FINNEY b. 18 Dec 1807 - d. 6 Dec 1877
[3] Margaret Patterson - b. 15 Aug 1818 - m. Robert FINNEY b. 3 Oct 1817
[4] Susanna Patterson
[5] John Watt Patterson - 9 Mar 1823 - 1909 - m. 1845 Susan SCOTT - b. 1825 - 1899 McKeesport, Pa.
[6] James S. Patterson - 11 Feb 1825 - 25 Dec 1895 - m. @ 1846 Sarah Ann VanKIRK - 1824 - 16 June 1892 - Westmoreland Co., Pa.
[7] Joseph Patterson - 28 May 1827 - 2 Jan 1889 - m. 26 Aug 1851 Rebecca SCOTT - 23 Mar 1822 - 10 May 1872
[8] Thomas Patterson - 19 Sep 1830 - 18 Nov 1894 - m. Martha Jane VanKIRK - b. 1835 - 26 Dec 1907, Allegheny Co., Pa.
[9] Finney C. Patterson - 5 July 1833 - 17 Nov 1865 - m. 2 Feb 1859 Caroline AYERS - 21 Feb 1829 - 12 July 1898 Haysville, Oh
[10] Mary Patterson - b. 5 July 1833
[11] Sarah Patterson - b. 1835

F. Margaret Patterson - b. 1787 - 1856, unmarried - Westmoreland Co., Pa.

G. Elijah Patterson - b. 1788 - 4 Oct 1876, unm. He made a home for his two unmarried sisters and for a brother as well as giving a home to his orphan nieces and nephew, children of his brother John.

H. Joseph Patterson - 1792 - 1855, unmarried
I. Samuel Patterson - b. 1794 - d. before 1875
J. Finney Henry Patterson - b. 1796, drowned
K. Robert Patterson - b. 1798 - 1845 Princeton, Ind. m. Rebecca WILSON
L. Nancy Agnes Patterson - b. 1802 - 1835, unmarried

RECORDS of ORPHANS COURT DOCKET, Book 1, Greensburg, Pa: Upon the petition of Agnes Patterson a minor under the age of fourteen years setting forth that her late father James Patterson deceased formerly of this county left among others the said Nancy and that she has no person appointed as guardian to take care of person and estate and praying the court to appoint some suitable person for the purposes aforesaid the court do appoint William Reynolds of South Huntington Twp. in same county and John Patterson of Fayette Co. Esq. guardian over the person and estate of the said Agnes Patterson until she shall attain the age of fourteen years.

Same book 1, page 129 - On petition of James Patterson administrator of James Patterson late of South Huntington Twp., Westmoreland Co., Pa. setting forth that James Patterson died intestate amongst other children left heirs children of John Patterson deceased, one of his sons who left four children - Nancy, Jane, Mary and James all under age of fourteen years who are entitled to a part of the estate of their grandfather James Patterson deceased who died intestate and praying the court to appoint Elijah Patterson of Rostraver Twp. to be their guardian for the purpose of receiving and settling that part of the estate they are entitled to from the estate of James Patterson their grandfather deceased. The Court do appoint Elijah Patterson guardian over the persons and estate of the above mentioned children until they severally shall attain the age of fourteen years.

3. Samuel Finney, s/o Thomas & Susannah - bapt. 22 Jan 1761 - 4 Dec 1823 Dauphin Co., Pa. In Revolutionary War - m. 11 Apr 1786 Ann CRAWFORD - b. 25 Aug 1763 - 6 Feb 1845

A. George W. Finney - 4 Apr 1804 - 6 Feb 1866 - m. 3 Mar 1831 Elspy SMITH - 2 Jan 1811 - d. 12 Jan 1899

[1] Thomas J. Finney

4. Thomas Finney - bapt. 4 Oct 1762 - in Revolutionary War
5. William Finney - bapt. 31 Jan 1764 Lancaster Co., Pa - d. 1821 Jefferson Co., Oh. - m. @ 1794 Margaret STEWART - b. 17 Aug 1774 - 17 Dec 1858. Left Pa. about 1798/99 - to Mt. Pleasant Twp.,Jefferson Co., Ohio

A. Thomas Finney, s/o William & Margaret [Stewart] Finney - b. 9 July 1795 - d. 26 May 1856, to Richland Co., Oh. 1830's - m. 4 Jan 1827 Nancy CULBERTSON - 29 Jan 1806 Guernsey Co., Oh - 11 Feb 1877

[1] Margaret Finney - 1826 OH - d. 1895 Goshen, Ind.
[2] Mary Finney - 1830 Oh - 1877 - m. POLLOCK
[3] James Culbertson Finney - 1833 Oh - 1908 Richland Co., Oh
[4] Agnes Finney - 20 Apr 1837 Oh - 1912 Fayetteville, Tenn. - m. 15 May 1860 William RALSTON b. 21 Dec 1824 Fayetteville, Tenn.
[5] Elizabeth Finney - b. 1840 - 1922 Goshen, Ind. - m. BIGGS
[6] Willian Shannon Finney - b. 1843 - d. 1884
[7] Joseph Stewart Finney - died WAbash, Ind.

B. Mary [Polly] Finney - b. 1796 - 31 Dec 1867 Richland Co., Oh, unmarried
C. Elijah Finney - b. 26 May 1799 Oh - 29 Oct 1870 Richland Co., Oh - m. 1827 Elizabeth CULBERTSON b. 1800 - 2 Oct 1839, m [2] 1 Mar 1841 Maria [Dougal] MARSHALL - 24 Feb 1807 - d. 29 May 1892

[1] William Patterson Finney - b. 1829 - d. 1916 Galion, Ohio
[2] Joseph Finney - died infant
[3] Abigail Ann Finney - b. 1833 - 1907 Lexington, Oh - m. GARRETT
[4] James Johnson Finney - b. 1837 - 1899 Richland Co., Oh
[5] Elijah Finney, Jr. b. 1839 - d. 1865 Richland Co., Oh
[6] Thomas Alexander Finney - b. 1842 - 1862 Richland Co., Oh
[7] Margaret E. Finney - b. 1845 - 21 May 1935Richland Co., Oh
[8] John Craig Finney - b. 1846 - 1929 Allegheny Co., Pa.
[9] Adalina M. Finney - b. 1846 - 28 May 1935 Richland Co., Oh

D. Susannah Finney b. 1801 - 25 May 1868 Richland Co., Oh, unmarried

E. James Finney - b. Jan 1805 - d. young, buried Mansfield, Ohio

F. William Stewart Finney - b. 18 Dec 1807 Jefferson Co., Oh - d. 6 Dec 1877 Mansfield, Oh - m. 5 May 1835 Jane PATTERSON - b. 5 Apr 1815 - 26 Jan 1853, m [2] 7 Nov 1853 Sarah [Thompson] STEWART - b. 7 Nov 1819 Fairview, Oh - d. 7 Sep 1896 [widow of Samuel Stewart who d. 15 Sep 1850]

"FINNEY FAMILY HISTORY" compiled by Minnehaha Finney: On the night of December 6, 1877 William Stewart Finney and his wife Sarah were sleeping in a downstairs bedroom of their farm home. In another downstairs room were James Finney, his wife and three children - upstairs were the hired man named Lindsay and two small boys. Hearing a noise about midnight in the room of the elderly couple, William and Sarah, James' wife Elizabeth, arose and started for the other bedroom. She had reached the door when she was struck over the head. Her husband was struck next and the assailant stood over the bed of 10-year-old Minnehaha. She pretended to be asleep but she recognized him as a black man named Cook's Darkey who worked on a neighboring farm. When he jumped out of the window his tracks in the light snow led toward his house. The grandfather, William, was so badly beaten with the assailant's gun that he died before medical aid could arrive and the grandmother was so badly injured she was unconscious for three days. The assailant, real name Edward Webb, was arrested, stolen articles found in his home. The gun had been stolen the previous fall. Webb was convicted on the murder charges and on 31 May 1878 was hanged at Mansfield, the only execution in the history of that city.

[1] James Patterson Finney - b. 27 Feb 1837 Jefferson Co., Oh - d. 16 Aug 1918 Beloit, Ks - lvd. Lawrence, Ks 1879 - m. 22 Mar 1865 Haysville, Oh Elizabeth SHORT - b. 8 May 1841 Ashland Co., Oh - 8 Dec 1916 Mitchell Co., Ks. She was a school teacher, is buried Elmwood Cemetery, d/o James & Margery Short. James was a minister and lived Riley Co.,Ks, to Adams Co., Oh 1871, to Richland Co., Oh, returned to Kansas 1877. In 1891 - 1905 in Tarkio, Mo., returned to Kansas.

[a] Minnehaha Finney - b. 24 Jan 1867 Pittsburgh, Ind. - d. 1946. She was a foreign missionary in Tanta, Egypt for 34 years, and compiled the "Finney Family History 1732 - 1946."

[b] William Herbert Finney - 21 Mar 1869 Riley Co., Ks - 2 May 1931 - m. 22 Oct 1902 Susanna BELL - 25 Aug 1883 Adair Co., Iowa - 17 Oct 1926 Mitchell Co., Ks.

i. Minette Elizabeth Finney - 29 July 1903 Ks - m. 10 June 1931 Raymond Edward HARROUFF b. 18 Nov 1898 Glava, Ks - lived Emporia, Ks.
ii. Helen Susannah Finney - 9 Nov 1904 Mitchell Co., Ks, unm.

Page 7.
Rev. James Patterson Finney B. Feb 27, 1837
near Mt. Pleasant, Jefferson Co., Ohio. His
parents were Wm Stewart Finney + Jane (Patterson)
Finney. He married Elizabeth Short of Ashland,
Ohio, Mar. 22, 1865. They left Ohio in 1879 with
5 little children. + came to Kansas. They had
Homestead is in Mitchell Co. Beloit, Ksc 67420
My Cousin John Charles Finney inherited it
from his parents Dwight McDill Finney
+ Wave (Wooster) Finney. John + his
family still live there. I have a book
"The Finney Family History (1732-1946)
Compiled by Minnehaha Finney (my Aunt)
Reprinted 1978.

Mr. + Mrs. Lynn D. Yocum
1303 Milan Way
Carrollton, Texas - 75006

Lynn is son of my cousin Nannie Elizabeth
Finney Yocum. Nannie is Sister of John
Charles Finney mentioned above.
The Patterson name is mentioned
frequently in this book.
I wish you "Happy Hunting" in
your search of your Ancestors.

Sincerely
Anabelle Jacobson.

X call 539-2027

My father was Wm Herbert Finney
+ my mother was Susannah (Beel) Finney.
He died in 1931. My mother died in 1926.
I've lived in Manhattan since 1928 but
one year returned to teach in Rural School 1929-30
I married Alva C. Jacobson 1931. He died 1961.

iii. Anabelle Finney, d/o William H. & Susanna [Bell] - b. 14 Oct 1906 Mitchell Co., Ks - m. 10 June 1931 Alva Clement JACOBSON - b. 14 Jan 1903 Riley Co., Ks - lvd. Manhattan, Ks

iv. Claire Finney - 8 Mar 1908 Mitchell Co - m. 10 June 1933 George Duncan CRUMBAKER - b. 14 Jan 1900 Onaga, Ks

v. William Herbert Finney - b. 17 Sep 1909 - 15 June 1943 Fort Collins, Colo. - electrocuted repairing "high line" - m. 9 June 1937 Evelyn EISLEE

a. Tommy Lee Finney - b. 2 Feb 1938 Lyons, Colo.
b. William Herbert Finney - 6 Apr 1943 Boulder, Colo.

vi. Esther Finney - 11 Sep 1912 - m. 3 May 1934 Woodrow M. KETHCART- b. 23 Mar 1913 Simpson, Ks.

vii. James Boyd Finney - 4 Sep 1914 - m. 20 June 1943 Neva GATEWOOD b. 3 Sep 1917 Emporia, Ks.

a. James Lee Finney - 24 July 1944 Amarillo, Texas

b. Roger Finney - b. 5 May 1947 Rantoul, Ill.

viii.Margaret Lorraine Finney - b. 7 Aug 1916 - m. 1 May 1936 Emporia, Ks Clarence Andrew WALKER - b. 24 Nov 1914

ix. Dwaine Lee Finney - b & d 16 May 1919

x. Justine Lillis Finney - 19 June 1925 - m. 9 Sep 1945 Manhattan, Ks to Harold OLSON - b. 6 Oct 1921 Lindsborg, Ks

[c] Roscoe Raitt Finney - b. 13 Aug 1871 Richland Co., Oh - 4 Feb 1885

[d] Sarah Jane Pearl Finney - 15 July 1873 Wheat, Adams Co., Oh - m.21 Dec 1898 Tarkio, Mo. Andrew Milton STEVENSON - b. 11 Feb 1871 Paoli, Ks - d. 7 Nov 1928 Middlesex, Pa, lvd Pretty Prairie, Ks.

[e] Dwight MacDill Finney - 27 May 1876 Adams Co., Oh - m. 4 June 1902 Salina, Ks to Wave Washington WOOSTER - b. 19 Aug 1882

i. James David Finney - 24 Apr 1903 Mitchell Co., Ks - m. 24 Apr 1924 Alma LANGE - b. 9 Apr 1903 Mitchell Co., Ks.

a. Neil Finney - b. 13 Nov 1927 Mitchell Co., Ks

ii. Nannie Elizabeth Finney - 17 Dec 1905 - m. 28 Apr 1926 William Ross YOCUM - b. 14 July 1903 Ks

a. Owen Oliver Yocum
b. David Lynn Yocum

iii. Julia Pearl Finney - 11 June 1908 - m. 28 Mar 1929 Carl Hershel BROADBENT - b. 4 Sep 1906 Mitchell Co., Ks

iv. Wave Wooster Finney - b. 16 Jan 1911 - m. 8 Aug 1931 Dr. James Lowell CREIGHTON - b. 23 July 1909 Goodland, Ks - a dental surgeon

v. Dwight MacDill Finney - b. 6 Oct 1916 - m. 27 May 1938 Charlotte Mae GATES - b. 28 Oct 1921

vi. John Charles Finney - b. 7 Nov 1920 - m. 22 oct 1942 Jane Ann POOLER - b. 26 Aug 1925

[2] William Finney, s/o William Stewart & Jane - b. 25 Jan 1839 Jefferson Co., Oh - d. 5 July 1853 Richland Co., Oh - killed by a horse

[3] Margaret Finney - b. 18 Dec 1840 Jefferson Co., Oh - 10 Feb 1883 Walton, Harvey Co., Ks - m. 16 Nov 1865 Hiram AYERS - b. 31 Aug 1833 - 3 Aug 1917

[4] Mary Jane Finney - 10 May 1843 Jefferson Co - 19 Feb 1923 Los Angeles, Calif. - m. 23 May 1870 Denny Burns SIMPSON b. 5 Mar 1836 - 11 Oct 1896

[5] Susanna Finney - b. 22 Dec 1846 Richland Co., Oh - 6 Mar 1851

[6] Sarah Agnes Finney - 16 Jan 1845 Richland Co., Oh - 30 Sep 1850

[7] Alphraetta Finney - 30 Dec 1838 Richland Co - 24 Sep 1928 Richland Co - m. 10 Mar 1875 John Kenny CROUCH - 29 Dec 1847 - d. 28 Nov 1884

[8] Martha Eunice Finney - 9 Jan 1851 Richland Co - d. 5 Jan 1853

[9] Samuel Philander Finney - 17 Jan 1853 - 11 Feb 1853

G. Samuel Finney, s/o William & Margaret - b. 1813 - 29 Aug 1876 Richland Co., Oh - m. 14 Oct 1849 Mary LOWRY b. 15 June 1821 - 10 May 1892 - in Jefferson Co., Oh until 1858, then Richland Co., Oh

[1] William Lowry Finney - b. 1850 Jeffrson Co - d. 1916
[2] Thomas Johnson Finney - b. 1852 - 1915 Alexandria, EGYPT
[3] Margaret Jane Finney - b. 1854 - d. 1938 - m. MARTIN
[4] Sarah Agnes Finney - b. 1856 - d. 1881 Richland Co,.Oh.
[5] Samuel Stewart Finney - 1858 Jefferson Co - 1933 Newark, Oh.
[6] James Patterson Finney - 1862 Jefferson Co - 1892 Richland Co., Oh

H. Nancy Finney - b. 1821 - 1861 Jefferson Co., Oh [Seceder Cem.] m. John McKEE who died 9 Oct 1872

[1] Joseph McKee - b. 1846 - 1920 Richland Co., Oh.
[2] William McKee - died in California
[3] John McKee - b. 1851 - d. 1864 Richland Co., Oh.

6. Agnes Finney, d/o Thomas & Susannah [Stewart] - bapt. 24 July 1764 - died infant
7. Elijah Finney - bapt. 20 Oct 1765 - d. Aug 1788. His will dated 19 Aug 1788. Heirs mentioned are his sisters Sarah and Jennet and his brother James, who was executor. Witnesses were Andrew Stewart, Sarah Stewart, Elijah Stewart.
8. James Finney - bapt. 1 Feb 1767 - m. Sarah STEWART. Orphans Court Docket 2-28, Dauphin Co., Pa. 2 Mar 1786 says James Finey a minor son of Thomas Finey late of West Hanover Twp., deceased, being above the age of 14 years comes into Court and chooses Richard SWAN of Paxton Twp. guardian over his estate.
9. Sarah Finney - bapt. 9 Oct 1768 - d. 1811 - m. 10 Mar 1789 Robert STEWART - b. 8 Mar 1765 Lancaster Co., Pa. - d. 1854 - Sarah and her sister Janet chose James BYERS of Paxton Twp. as their guardian
10. Janet [Jane] Finney - bapt. 22 Dec 1769 - d. 9 May 1830 - m. 27 Apr 1790 Thomas BARNETT - 13 Nov 1761 - d. 28 Mar 1836 Lancaster Co., Pa.
11. John Finney

e. William Finney, s/o Wm. & Jean [Stephenson] - b. 1734
f. Lazarus Finney - b. 1737 - d. young
g. Martha Finney - b. 1740 Chester Co., Pa - d. @ 1764 - in her will dated 1764 she left her children to be cared for by William Finney. She lived New Castle Co., Del. and married LAUGHRON
h. Robert Finney - b. 1742 Chester Co., Pa - 17 Apr 1827 Meadville, Crawford Co., Pa - was a lawyer, moved to Crawford Co. 1794, donated 10 acres of land to Allegheny College at Meadville in 1817. In 1781 on tax roll in Washington Co., Pa. He was Pvt. in Capt. Thomas STRAWBRIDGE's Co., Militia. commanded by Lt. Col. Evan EVANS, City of Philadelphia on Company Muster Roll Dec 5 - 25 1776 inclusive, 4th Battalion, Chester Co., Pa. militia. His will 1824 was witnessed by Thomas FREW and mentions old John FREW tract of land with Joseph FINNEY a tax payer in 1810. [Are Joseph and Thomas FREW both sons of Catherine SYMONTON Finney FREW??] Robert m [1] LAUGHEAD [d/o Robert], m [2] Jane ?

1. Jennet Finney - b. 1765/75 - m. David MEAD, founder of Meadville, Pa.
2. James Finney - b. 1787 Crawford Co., Pa - m [1] Mary MYERS, m [2] Sarah b. 1786 - lived Holmes Co., Oh. in 1850

A. Sarah Jane Finney
B. Robert Finney
C. Joseph Finney
D. Wilson Finney
E. Sarah Finney
F. David Mead Finney
G. Catharine Finney - b. 1833 Pa
H. Daniel Finney - b. 1834 Crawford Co., Pa - to Calif. m. Eliza Jane GRIFFITH [married Bryan, Ind], m [2] Clarissa FROATIE - b. Oh

[1] Daniel E. Finney
[2] Harlow H. Finney
[3] Eli W. Finney
[4] Mary Arvilla Finney
[5] George Bertice Finney

I. George Finney, s/o James [1787] - b. 1839 Pa - m. Margaret b. 1834 Oh, lvd Holmes Co., Oh. in 1870

[1] Olive Finney - b. 1862
[2] Margaret Finney - b. 1864
[3] Hannah Finney - b. 1866
[4] Daniel Finney - b. 1869

J. James Finney
K. Sarah Finney - b. 1840 Pa
L. Luisa Sue Ann Finney - b. 1853
M. Hiram Finney - b. 1845
N. Alexander Finney

3. Elizabeth Finney, d/o Robert Finney

i. John Finney, s/o Wm. & Jean [Stephenson] - b. 1745 - 1814 Chester Co., Pa - m. [cousin] Ann Dorothea FINNEY - was ruling elder in New London Presbyterian Church, lived many years in Londonderry Twp., Chester Co. Engaged in agricultural career, also Justice of Peace, commissioned 1 Feb 1806 - sworn in 20 May 1806 for 7th District, comprising London British, New London and Londonderry. Patented land Westmoreland Co., Pa. on 1 July 1784.

1. John Finney - b. 1777 - 8 June 1862 Washington Co., Pa - m. 1806 Jane BOOTH b. 1789 - d. 16 Apr 1846 Pittsburgh

A. Ann A. Finney - b. 29 Oct 1809 - Feb 1881 - m. 1845 James K. LOGAN
B. William Finney - b. 1812 - d. young
C. Catharine Finney b. 1814 - d. 20 Oct 1891, unmarried
D. Mary Finney b. 1816 - d. 1826
E. John Finney - b. 1819 - d. 1850
F. William Finney - b. 1822 - d. young
G. Walter Finney - b. 1810 - d. 1852 - m. Rebecca SLAWSON b. 1813 - 10 Nov 1895

[1] William Finney - b. 1841 - d. 1850
[2] John Finney
[3] Kate Finney - b. 15 Nov 1844 - d., 30 May 1874 - m. 1868 Clemens CLACIUS b. 1829 - d. 1886
[4] Walter Finney - b. 1849 - d. 1867
[5] Carrie Finney - b. 13 Feb 1851 - m. George BUTLER

H. Robert Finney - b. 1823 - m. 30 Oct 1845 Annie E. EMERSON b. 1826, - they lived Kittanning, Armstrong Co., Pa. Annie E., in her will, mentioned her brother John A. WILLS and her mother Mrs. Elizabeth EMERSON.

[1] Lillie Finney - 11 Sep 1846 - d. 21 Mar 1868
[2] Frank Finney - died in 1851 as a child
[3] Blanche Finney b. 23 Nov 1849 - m. 20 Sep 1871 Thomas M. KING
[4] Henry or Harry - b. 8 Aug 1852 - m. Jan 1878 Kate McELROY

[a] Anna C. Finney - b. 25 Nov 1878
[b] Jane E. Finney - b. 8 Mar 1880
[c] Josephine Finney - b. 8 Oct 1882

[5] Florence Finney b. 1854 - died young
[6] Brady W. Finney - b. 11 Feb 1855 - 22 Sep 1890 - m. June 1885 Lillian WARWICK - no children.
[7] May Finney - b. 8 Aug 1857 - m [1] Steven HERSCHBURGH, m [2] 21 June 1883 John C. TEMPLE
[8] Jennie Finney - b. 27 Aug 1859 - 25 Nov 1884 - m. 7 Nov 1883 Henry BISSELL
[9] Maud Finney - 15 July 1861 - m. 3 Dec 1884 William R. HERSPERGER, brother of Steven HERSPERGER of Herschburgh
[10] Robert Finney - b. 10 Aug 1863 - died unmarried
[11] Ann Dorothea Finney - 20 Aug 1866 - m. 16 Sep 1891 Dr. William Holden CHACE

j. Walter Finney - b. 1747 New London, Chester Co., Pa - d. 17 Sep 1820 Thunder Hill, Chester Co. - m. Mary O'HARA b. 1753 - d. 10 Aug 1823 Chester Co., Pa. Walter joined army as Lieutenant at beginning of Revolution and also participated in the Indian Wars. He was made Major on 10 Aug 1776 and was at the Battle of Brandywine. On one occasion he was wounded in the head by a "grape-shot'. Also held prisoner on New York Prison Ship where he almost starved to death before he was exchanged. He became a Justice and in 1790 was an associate judge of the court.

1. Son of Walter & Mary [O'Hara] - died age 13
2. William Finney - b. 10 Oct 1788 Chester Co., Pa - d. 1 July 1873 Hartford Co., MD Attended Princeton College, New Jersey 1806 - 1809 - m [1] 7 Sep 1815 Susan CORREY - b. 2 Aug 1791 - d. 22 June 1817, m [2] 10 Oct 1820 Margaret MILLER b. 12 Oct 1801 - d. 21 July 1865,d/o John & Margaret Miller

A. Walter Scott Finney - b. 30 Aug 1816 - d. 17 Feb 1817
B. Susan Finney b. 30 Jan 1822 - d. 29 July 1894, unmarried
C. John (Dr] Finney - b. 3 Sep 1823 - d. 25 June 1896, unmarried
D. Ebenezer Dickey Finney - b. 12 Sep 1825 Md - m [1] 25 Oct 1860 Annie L. PARKER b. 12 Aug 1835 - 17 Nov 1863 Natchez, Miss, m [2] 7 May 1874 Elizabeth McCORMICK b. 1845 - d. 1925

[1] William Parker Finney - b. 9 Sep 1861 Natchez, Miss m. 5 Oct 1887
[2] John M. T. Finney - b. 20 June 1863 - m. 20 Apr 1892 Mary Elizabeth GROSS b. 2 June 1868

[a] John M. Train Finney - b. 26 July 1894
[b] Eben Dickey Finney - b. 15 Jujn 1897
[c] George Gross Finney - 15 Dec 1899 Baltimore, Md - m. 20 Sep 1924 Josephine LURMAN STEWART

i. George Gross Finney
ii. Kate Latimre Finney
iii. Redmond Finney
iv. Conyngham Stewart Finney
v. Jervis Spencer Finney

[d] Mary Elizabeth Finney

[3] Mary Margaret Finney - b. 1 June 1875 -= d. 10 Oct 1875
[4] James Monroe Finney - 13 Nov 1877 - d. 23 June 1884

E. William Finney - b. 11 Sep 1827 - d. 11 Dec 1862 Calif., unmarried
F. Charles McL. Finney - b. 4 Oct 1829 - 13 July 1897, unmarried
G. George Jenkins Finney - b. 28 Aug 1830 - m. 25 Apr 1865 Louisa Lyon WEBSTER - b. 29 Jan 1839 - d. 1926

[1] Margaret Finney - died young
[2] Walter Finney - b. 20 Aug 1867 - m. 15 June 1901 Eva SMITH
[3] George Finney - b. 4 July 1870 - d. 10 July 1880
[4] Edwin Wabster Finney - b. 3 Apr 1874 - d. 1932
[5] John Clark Finney - b. 6 Aug 1882
[6] William Webster Finney - b. 7 Mar 1869 m. 26 Mar 1904 Eliza McCORMICK

[a] Mary McCormick Finney - b. 1905 Baltimore m. M. BARADA
[b] Louise Finney - b. 1906 MD.
[c] George J. Finney - b. 1908 - m. 5 July 1937 Suzanne B. MOREAU
[d] James McCormick Finney - b. 1915 Baltimore, MD.

3. Walter, Finney, s/o Walter & Mary - b. 27 Oct 1795 - d. 6 Oct 1809

k. Jane [Jean] Finney, d/o William & Jean - m. David HUNTER - lvd. Allegheny Co., Pa. & Pittsburgh, Pa.

iv. Thomas Finney, s/o Robert & Dorothea [French] = b. Ireland - d. 1767 New London, Chester Co., Pa. - m. 27 Oct 1736 Christ Church, Philadelphia, Pa. Mary CHESTER who died @ Nov 1791 Chester Co., Pa.

a. Robert Finney - died 10 Aug 1799 - m. Agnes STEPHENSON who died 17 Mar 1800

1. Robert Potts Finney - died 1843 - m. Phoebe FEW

A. Robert Thomas Finney - b. 20 Jan 1779 - d. 1843 m. 13 Mar 1806 Margaret GUTHRIE b. 11 Dec 1786, d/o Robert

[1] Amaria H. Finney - 14 Feb 1809, unmarried
[2] Joseph Finney - b. 24 Mar 1810 - 27 Feb 1887 m. 22 Dec 1842 Belmont Co., Oh. Elizabeth BROWNLEE who died 2 Feb 1891

[a] James Finney - b. 21 Mar 1844 - d. 28 May 1864
[b] Robert T. Finney - b. 29 Aug 1845 - d. 19 Apr 1869
[c] William H. Finney - 17 May 1847 - d. 15 May 1864

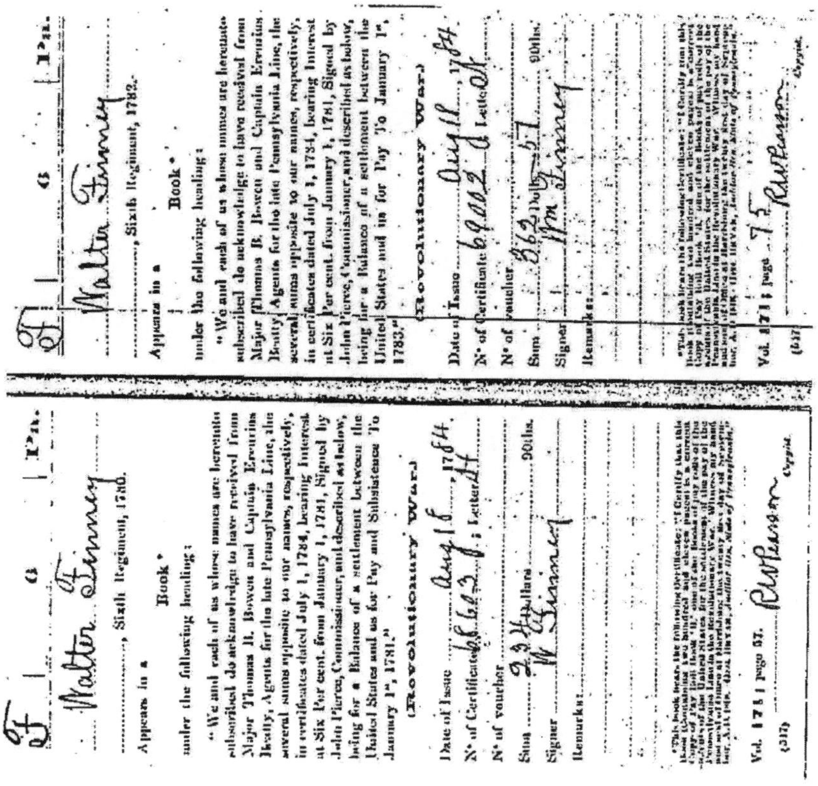

F | 6 | Pa.

Walter Finney

........................, Sixth Regiment, 1780.

Appears in a

Book *

under the following heading:

"We and each of us whose names are hereunto subscribed do acknowledge to have received from Major Thomas B. Bowen and Captain Erenius Beatty, Agents for the late Pennsylvania Line, the several sums opposite to our names, respectively, in certificates dated July 1, 1784, bearing Interest at Six Per cent. from January 1, 1781, Signed by John Pierce, Commissioner, and described as below, being for a Balance of a settlement between the United States and us for Pay and Subsistence To January 1st, 1781."

(Revolutionary War.)

Date of Issue Aug 18, 1784.

No of Certificate 68603 ; Letter H

No of voucher ....

Sum 234 Dollars .... 90ths.

Signer W Finney

Remarks: ....

*This book bears the following Certificate: "I Certify that this Book (Containing two hundred and eleven pages) is a correct Copy of Pay Roll Book 'B,' one of the Books of pay rolls of the [illegible] of the United States for the settlement of the pay of the Pennsylvania Line in the Revolutionary War." Witness my hand and seal of Office at Harrisburg the twenty first day of September, A.D. [illegible]. [illegible], Auditor Gen. State of Pennsylvania."

Vol. 171 ; page 57.

R W Pearson
Copyist.

(317)

F | 6 | Pa.

Walter Finney

........................, Sixth Regiment, 1782.

Appears in a

Book *

under the following heading:

"We and each of us whose names are hereunto subscribed do acknowledge to have received from Major Thomas B. Bowen and Captain Erenius Beatty, Agents for the late Pennsylvania Line, the several sums opposite to our names, respectively, in certificates dated July 1, 1784, bearing Interest at Six Per cent. from January 1, 1781, Signed by John Pierce, Commissioner, and described as below, being for a Balance of a settlement between the United States and us for Pay To January 1st, 1783."

(Revolutionary War.)

Date of Issue Aug 18, 1784

No of Certificate 69002 ; Letter H

No of voucher ....

Sum 362 Dolls 57 90ths.

Signer Wm Finney

Remarks: ....

*This book bears the following Certificate: "I Certify that this Book (Containing two hundred and eleven pages) is a correct Copy of Pay Roll Book 'B,' one of the Books of pay rolls of the [illegible] of the United States for the settlement of the pay of the Pennsylvania Line in the Revolutionary War." Witness my hand and seal of Office at Harrisburg the twenty first day of September, A.D. [illegible]. [illegible], Auditor Gen. State of Pennsylvania."

Vol. 171 ; page 75

R W Pearson
Copyist.

(517)

F | 6 | Pa.

Walter Finney

Capt , 6 Regiment Pa

(Revolutionary War.)

Appears in a book*

Compiled from Rolls

of the organization named above, under the head of, "State of Pennsylvania against United States for Depreciation on Pay of the Army."

Sum charged £109 12 6

Sum admitted

Remarks: Charged P. 39 No. 1563

*This book appears to have been compiled (from original rolls) in the Office of Army Accounts under the Paymaster General, U.S.A., who was authorized by Congress, July 4, 1783, to settle and finally adjust all accounts whatever between the United States and the officers and soldiers of the American army. (Journal American Congress, Vol. 4, page 237.)—R. & P. 436,784.

Vol. 7, page 38
No 1500

Hearst
Copyist.

(575)

F | 6 | Pa.

Walter Finney

Capt , 6 Regiment Pa

(Revolutionary War.)

Appears in a book*

Compiled from Rolls

of the organization named above, under the head of "State of Pennsylvania against United States for Depreciation on Pay of the Army."

Sum charged £591 1 6

Sum admitted

Remarks:

*This book appears to have been compiled (from original rolls) in the Office of Army Accounts under the Paymaster General, U.S.A., who was authorized by Congress, July 4, 1783, to settle and finally adjust all accounts whatever between the United States and the officers and soldiers of the American army. (Journal American Congress, Vol. 4, page 237.)—R. & P. 436,780.

Vol. 7, page 39
No 1563

Hearst
Copyist.

(575)

F | 6 | Pa.

Walter Finney

, Sixth Regiment.

Appears in a

Book*

under the following heading:

"We and each of us whose names are hereunto subscribed do acknowledge to have received from Major Thomas B. Bowen and Captain Erasmus Beatty, Agents for the late Pennsylvania Line, the several sums opposite to our names, respectively, in certificates dated July 1, 1784, bearing Interest at Six Per cent. from January 1, 1781, Signed by John Pierce, Commissioner, and described as below, being for a Balance of a settlement between the United States and us for Subsistence To August 1st, 1780."

(Revolutionary War.)

Date of Issue Aug 18, 1784

No of Certificate 68581 ; Letter R

No of voucher

Sum 108 Dolls. 82 90ths.

Signer W. Finney

Remarks:

*This book bears the following Certificate: "I Certify that this Book (Containing two hundred and eleven pages) is a correct Copy of Pay Roll Book 'H' one of the Books of pay rolls of the agents of the United States for the settlement of the pay of the Pennsylvania Line in the Revolutionary War. Witness my hand and seal of Office at Harrisburg the twenty first day of September, A.D. 1818.—Geo. Bryan, Auditor Gen. State of Pennsylvania."

Vol. 171; page 56.

RWPearson
Copyist.

(517)

F | 6 | Pa.

Walter Finney

, Sixth Regiment, 1781.

Appears in a

Book*

under the following heading:

"We and each of us whose names are hereunto subscribed do acknowledge to have received from Major Thomas B. Bowen and Captain Erasmus Beatty, Agents for the late Pennsylvania Line, the several sums opposite to our names, respectively, in certificates dated July 1, 1784, bearing Interest at Six Per cent. from January 1, 1781, Signed by John Pierce, Commissioner, and described as below, being for a Balance of a settlement between the United States and us for Pay & Subsistence To January 1st, 1782."

(Revolutionary War.)

Date of Issue Aug 18, 1784

No of Certificate 68785 ; Letter L

No of voucher

Sum 370 Dolls. 17 90ths.

Signer W. Finney

Remarks:

*This book bears the following Certificate: "I Certify that this Book (Containing two hundred and eleven pages) is a correct Copy of Pay Roll Book 'H' one of the Books of pay rolls of the agents of the United States for the settlement of the pay of the Pennsylvania Line in the Revolutionary War. Witness my hand and seal of Office at Harrisburg the twenty first day of September, A.D. 1818.—Geo. Bryan, Auditor Gen. State of Pennsylvania."

Vol. 171; page 65

RWEmmon
Copyist.

(517)

F | 6 | Pa.

Walter Finney
Capt 6" Regiment

Appears on a

List

under the following heading:

"Arrangement of the Pennsylvania Regiments"

(Revolutionary War.)

List dated Not dated, 17

Rank, Captain

Date of Commission, 13th July, 1776

Remarks:

11 J.Clauston Copyist.

F | 6 | Pa.

Walter Finney
Capt 3 Com'l 7 { 6th Pennsylvania Regiment, commanded by Lt. Col. Josiah Harmar.

(Revolutionary War.)

Appears on

Field and Staff Muster Roll

of the organization named above for the month of * Nov, 1778.

Roll dated Nov 14, 1778.

Appointed, 17

Commissioned, 17

Enlisted, 17

Term of enlistment

Time since last muster or enlistment

Alterations since last muster

Casualties

Remarks:

* Endorsement shows Roll to be for Oct 1778

(644) M. J. Sh[illegible] Copyist.

F | | Pa.

Walter Finney
Capt 6th Regiment

Appears on a

List

showing "Rank of Regiments & Officers in the Penns' Line 2nd Sept 1778"

(Revolutionary War.)

List dated Not dated, 17

Date of Commission, Aug, 1776.

Remarks:

9 (643m) J. B. Sitler Copyist.

F | 6 | Pa.

Walter Finney
Capt { Capt. Walter Finney's Co. of the 6th Pennsylvania Reg't commanded by Lieut. Col. Josiah Harmar.

(Revolutionary War.)

Appears on

Company Muster Roll

of the organization named above for the month of Oct, 1778.

Roll dated Nov. 16, 1778.

Appointed, 17

Commissioned, 17

Enlisted, 17

Term of enlistment

Time since last muster or enlistment

Alterations since last muster

Casualties

Remarks: On Furlough

(643) G. Day Copyist.

KNOW ALL MEN, BY THESE PRESENTS, THAT We John W Cunningham James Alexander Robert Graham and Joseph Strawbridge all of Chester County are held and firmly bound unto the Commonwealth of Pennsylvania, in the sum of Twenty Thousand Dollars, to be paid to the said Commonwealth, to the which payment well and truly to be made, we bind ourselves jointly and severally for and in the whole, our heirs, executors and administrators, firmly by these presents; sealed with our seals; dated the Second day of October in the year of our Lord, one thousand eight hundred and Twenty

THE CONDITION OF THIS OBLIGATION IS SUCH, THAT IF the above bounden John W Cunningham and James Alexander administrators of all and singular the goods and chattels, rights and credits of Walter Finney Esqr late of the township of New London deceased, which

deceased; DO make or cause to be made a true and perfect inventory of all and singular the goods, chattels and credits of the said Walter Finney Esqr which have or shall come to the hands, possession or knowledge of the said John W Cunningham and James Alexander or unto the hands or possession of any person or persons for them and the same so made,—Do exhibit or cause to be exhibited into the Register's Office, in the county of Chester, at or before the Second day of October next ensuing; and the same goods, chattels and credits, and all other the goods, chattels and credits of the said Walter Finney Esqr at the time of his death, which at any time after shall come to the hands or possession of the said John W Cunningham and James Alexander or unto the hands or possession of any person or persons for them do well and truly administer according to law, and further do make or cause to be made, a true and just account of their said administration, at or before the Second day of October one thousand eight hundred and twenty one and all the rest, residue and remainder of the said goods, chattels and credits which shall be found remaining upon the administration account, (the same being first examined and allowed of by the Orphans' Court of the said county) shall deliver and pay unto such person or persons respectively, as the said Orphans' Court, by their decree or sentence, pursuant to the true intent and meaning of the laws of this Commonwealth shall limit and appoint; and if it shall hereafter appear, that any last will and testament was made by the said deceased, and the executor or executors therein named, do exhibit the same into the said Register's Office, making request to have it allowed and approved accordingly, if the said John W Cunningham and James Alexander within bounden, being thereunto required, do render and deliver the said letters of administration, approbation of such testament being first had and made, in the said Register's Office, this obligation to be void and of none effect,—or else to be and remain in full force and virtue.

Sealed and delivered in the presence of

Wm J. Wersley

John W Cunningham (Seal)
James Alexander (Seal)
Robt Graham (Seal)
Joseph Strawbridge (Seal)

Newlondon October 2nd 1820 –

Jesse Sharp Esqr

Sir,

The undersigned, only son, & heir, of Walter Finney Esqr late of the township of Newlondon, deceased, who died ~~intestate~~, hereby relinquishes his right of administration on the estate of the said deceased, & desires that letters of administration may be granted to Jno M. Cunningham & James Alexander on the estate of said deceased.

William Finney

County of Chester ss

Before the Subscriber one of the Justices of the peace in and for said county personally came Robert Hodgson and John Hutchison who on their solemn oaths duly administered did depose and say ~~that~~ that the foregoing inventory and appraisement of the personal Estate of Walter Finney Esquire as far as Enumerated or exhibited to them the said Robt Hodgson and John Hutcheson is Just and true to the best of their knowledge and belief Witness my hand and Seal this 24th day of October 1820

John Finney [Seal]

in Inventory and Consceonable appraisement of the Goods and chattels Rights & credits which were of Walter Linney Esqr late of the Township of Newlondon deceased as far as exhibited to the subscribers the twelfth day of october 1820 Vizt

		Drs	
Wearing apparel		25	00
1 Silver Watch		8	00
Cash on hand		~~300~~	
Riding Horse Saddle & bridle (old)		15	00
1 Riding Chair		10	00
1 old bay mare		5	—
1 grey mare		25	—
4 cows a 11,25 ea		45	—
1 calf		3	00
5 hogs	3.00	15	—
22 Sheep	1.00	22	—
1 horse cart & gears		15	00
1 plough		5	—
1 Harrow		1	50
1 corn Harrow		1	00
a lot of Rakes forks grapes Hoes & sundries		2	00
Lot of plough gears		1	00
1 dutch fan		2	00
1 cutlery box		3	00
Hay in the Barn		50	—
Hay in the Stack		10	00
Wheat in the mow		30	—
Lot of corn in the ear		30	—
Lot of Lumber (boards scantling &c)		4	00
carried over	$	627	50

Item	$	¢
Amount brought forward	627	50
Lot of Rye in the Sheaf	5	00
Lot of Mattocks & Spades		50
Grindstone axes & Tools	2	00
1 Desk	10	—
1 Eight day clock	50	—
1 feather bed bedding & bedstead	20	—
1 do " "	20	—
1 do " "	20	—
1 do " "	20	—
1 do " "	20	—
1 under bed - do do	5	00
Library consisting of Divinity Law Physic History Maps &c	50	—
1 Mahogany dining table	4	—
1 Breakfast do - 1 Tea do & Stand	6	00
1 chest of drawers	4	00
4 looking glasses	15	00
a lot of coverlets blankets & quilts	30	—
1 doz old windsor chairs	5	00
a lot of trunks & chests	5	00
6 Rush bottomed chairs	2	50
1 Sett of Fire Irons Shovel & tongs	2	50
1 corner cupboard & furniture	12	00
Lot of table linnen Sheeting & unmade linnen	23	00
Kitchen furniture	15	00
Lot of Lumber in garrett & Kitchen loft	3	00
Casks &c in the cellar	1	00
Dr	985	00

Continued

Continued . . . . Dr	985	00
Balance of Mortgage from John McNaughton & wife a lien on land of Benj McDonald including Interest to octob 12th 1820	94	98
amount of Mortgage on Land of William Finney Assigned by John H Cunningham with Interest to same time	134	59
amount of Mortgage from John McMullan & wife with Interest to same time	217	15
amot of Mortgage on Land of William Finney given to deceased with Interest to same time . . .	403	46
amt of Mortgage from William Woodside & Wife with Interest to same time	172	88
amt of Mortgage Thomas Garrett & wife with Interest to same time . . .	3611	99
amt of Mortgage Patrick Harrah Lancaster County & Interest to same time . . .	1110	16
amt of Mortgage William Thrasher & Wife and Interest to same time which appears to have been taken without for the heirs of W William	1186	36
Balance due on Bond of Richd Boozer & Moore Falls and Interest to same time . . .	192	64
Bond of James Ford with Interest to same time	545	99½
Bond of Joseph Boothe Charles Boothe & Jonathan Boothe & Interest to same time . .	550	38
Due on note of Hand By Thomas Henderson Esqr Assigned by John Finney Esqr & Interest to same time	117	39
a note of Hand by Thomas Henderson Esqr assigned by Evan Jones . & Interest to same time . .	186.	57
amount of a Bond from Trustees of Newlondon Congregation ~~school~~ and Interest to same time . . .	94	15
Dr	9609	21½

carried forward

	$	
Brought forward . . . . $	9609	21½
Amount of due bill of Thomas Henderson Esq	21	
due from ditto on State accounts . .	52	
amount due on Bond of John Finney Esq deceased assigned by Andrew Henderson with Interest principal $37.57 due May 1st 1784 Interest 92.79	130	[illegible]
Do due on note of John Finney in fav John Ochiltree principal 6.51 Interest $10.53	17	0
Do due from John Finney Esq deceased being a payment made by Walter Finney Esq on a Bond due to David Hunter with Interest to this day	125	8
amt of note due by John Finney Jur Esq with Interest to this day	37	4
amt due from John Templeton of Armstrong Coy on three several obligations with Interest being the consideration for Land sold . . .	427	00
amt due from Jane Mellon on three several notes with Interest to this day . . .	326	17
amt due by J M Carlile on note with Interest from time	109	00
amt due by Do & Jas Hutcheson on three notes with Interest to same time . . .	964	67
amt due by John Hutcheson on note with Interest	56	50
amt due from William Streeper with Interest from time	237	20
amt due on Note of John Gamble with Interest . .	46	95
amt due on Note of J B McClenachan with Do . .	121.	50
amt due on two notes of William Carlile with Intt	96	25
amt due on note of Dennis Townsend with Do - -	32	66
amt due on note of Robt Armstrong with Do -	27	37
Continued $	12496	33

	Dollars	Cents
Continued . . . . . . Drs	12[illegible]	33
Amount of note due by John White & Interest	21	75
Amt of note due by Wm Fuller & B McDonald with Do	33	56
Amt due on note of James Thompson	20	—
Amt due on note of John Smith & Interest	18	81
Balance of a note due by John Ewing with Interest	10	57
Balance of a note due by Doct J Roberts with Interest	79	97
Balance due on a note by John Bakill		37
due on a note by William Finney with Interest	121	32
Twelve Shares of Stock in the Farmers & Mechanics Bank of Philadelphia Estimated at par (50 Drs p Share)	600	—
Amount of Bond due by John Menough with Interest	292	61
Amount due from William Finney Catharine Booth Saml B McElrath & Jell Carlile each 13.71 and from John Finney 3.71 being their part of the Expences of Building grave yard wall	58	55
Amount due from Estate of Susanna Mean decd (an account against deceased)	69	01½
Amount due from the Estate of John Finney Esq deceased as p. acct Exhibited	1078	29
Due from the Estate of Doct Finney on account of a Legacy bequeathed to the congregation of Newlondon over and above the amount Secured by William Finney	142	89
Due from Ann Jane Finney	98	50
$	15148	03½

Robert Hodgson

John Hutchison

...m Cunningham & James Alexander administrators
Walter Finney Esq late of Newlondon Township Deceased — Cr.

And the said accountants crave an allowance for the following payments & disbursements made out of the said proceeds as per vouchers & receipts herewith submitted

No.		
1	By cash paid David Willson (one of the heirs of William Willson dec.) of whom the deceased was guardian . . . as per receipts in full	221 87
2	By cash paid Charlotte Morrison one of the Legatees of Ephraim Morrison dec.^d (of whose Estate the dec.^d was the acting Executor) one year annuity agreeably to Will as per receipt	5 33
3	By cash paid Joseph Willson attorney of Phebe Willson One year Interest upon her Dower included in the mortgage of H Stewart per receipt	39 42
4.	By cash paid John M. Carlile amount p. receipt	9 52
	By cash retained in the hands of these accountants as a principal sum, the Interest of which is to enable them to discharge the annuity annually payable to Charlotte Morrison (above mentioned) one of the Legatees of Ephraim Morrison dec.^d which appears to have been under the control of the deceased — the said principal at her decease to be considered as a part of the Estate of the said Ephraim Morrison — to be disposed of accordingly . . . $ 89.00 and also 1 years Interest upon the same - 5 33	94 33
	By cash paid John Duer Esq professional services —	5 00
	By cash paid Register for examining & passing this acct. Copy - Notices &c	6 31
	By cash paid Clerk of the orphans' Court —	1 00
	By commissions on $ 6556 - 17 - @ 6 per cent	393 36
		776 14
	Balance —	13148 40
		13924 54

and also these accountants would again bring into view the Balance remaining due and unpaid upon the Mortgage of the said Thomas Garrett & Wife — not because they have received the amount thereof but because they intend to effect such an arrangement as will enable the Heir of this Estate to receive the money himself & discharge these accountants from Responsibility

Balance of Principal & Interest due to April 1. 1825 — 3238.75

Dolls 13924 54

E Excepted

John M Cuningham

James Alexander — admrs

Township of Newlondon deceased

Said accountants crave an allowance for the following payments and disbursements made out of said Estate as per vouchers accompanying the account by the

1.	By cash paid Register Fees letters	3 12	
•	By Do paid Do for 2 certificates of Do	1 20	4 32
2	By cash paid John M Cuningham Funeral Expense	23 42½	
3	By Do pd James Alexander Do	3 92	27 34½
4	By Do pd Mark Hall for coffin		7 00
5	By Do pd R M Waugh Esq fees in acknowledgm power of aty		25
6	By Do paid Samuel Moore attorney for Sarah Moore		150.28
7	By Do paid Pewrent Newlondon church		6 50
8	By Do paid R M Waugh Esq Adm Powers Road Tax		2 18
9	By Do paid Robt Hodgson County Rates		2 58
10	By Do paid Charles Menen advertising		1 00
11	By Do paid — Marshall Do		1 00

12 By Do paid Nath. Hudden p receipt . . . 18 55

13 By Do paid Jane Miller an acct . 77 66

14 By Do p . Do a note 56 47½ 134 13½

15 By Do paid Frothy Recording Judgment v. Silleway 1.00

16 By Do paid Joseph Willson Attorney for Phebe Willson 30 —

48 44

17 By Do paid Ditto 39 42

18 By Do paid Ditto . . . .

19 By Do paid David Willson of whom the deceased was Guardian (Interest due) 49 7

20 By Do paid Jesse Sharp Sheriff his bill of costs in Levying upon and selling the Estate of John McMullen for a debt due this Estate . . . 26 56

21 By Do paid R. McWaugh Esqr costs incurred by him in administering upon the Estate of John McMullen decd at the instance of these accountants . . 3 747

22 By cash paid Mary Coltt surviving admr of the Estate of Henry Coltt Decd. of whose Estate Judge Finney was Co administrator . . . 28 66

23 By Do paid Charlotte Morrison her annuity due by Will of Ephm Morrison decd — this deceased being one of Morrisons Executors . 5 33

. . . . . . - attorney & the)

per appraisement 23 25

25 By Sundry accounts and Errors settled & arranged with William Strupper being principally money which the deceased had received & not credited 143 92

26 By Cash paid John H Cunningham an acct 99

27 By Do paid John Duer Esqr Counsel fees . . . 5 00

Said accountant also crave a dis count for the following debts due to said Estate as appraised for the reasons given by

amount due on a note of John White he having absconded before the death of deceased	21 75	
amount due on note of John Smith there being no such person known to adm	12 —	
Balance due on note of John Ewing the same having been paid to deceased in his life time (see deposition)	10 57	51 13

and also for the following debts yet outstanding & due to said Estate as per appraisement Viz

Mortgage of William Finney assigned by John W Cunningham	139.59		
Mortgage on land of William Finney Executed to deceased	403 96		
[illegible] Finney	121 32		
Judgment Estate Doct Finney	142 89		
Due per Ann Jane Finney	98 50	906 26	
Mortgage by Thomas Garrett & wife		3611 99	
Part of Mortgage William [illegible] & wife		347 55	
Bond of James Ford deceased		545 99½	
Due on note of Thos Henderson Esq	117 39		
Due on do assigned by Evan Jones	186 57		
Amt due bill T Henderson	28 56		
Amt due on Stated acct	52 33		
Amt Due from Est Susanna [illegible]	69.01½	453.86	
Balance due on note by Doct L Roberts		79 97	
Balance due by John Bechtel		87	
Expence of Walling Grave yard by Sundries 5505.04		58 55	6505.04

By Commissions on $ 9657.68 @ 6 per cent — 579 10

The accountants charge themselves with the amount of the appraisement of the personal Estate of said deceased as per Inventory Exhibited to and remaining of file in the Registers office amounting to . . . . . Dolls 15.148 03½

also	
To cash received Dividend upon Bank Stock . . .	18 00
To Ditto rec^d at State Treasury balance of Judges Salary	78 70
To D^o Rec^d of J.M Carlile Interest accrued Since appraisement	2 43
To D^o Rec^d of William Carlile - D^o — D^o .	1 90
To D^o Rec^d of Richard Boyer D^o - D^o .	5 23
To D^o Rec^d of John Hutchison D^o — D^o .	1.31
To D^o Rec^d of Jane Miller - D^o D^o	6 87
To D^o Rec^d of Thomas Garrett D^o D^o (on Bonds)	49 00
To D^o Rec^d of Isaac Booth D^o — D^o - —	57 87
To D^o Rec^d of James and Davis Hutchison D^o. D^o .	28 05
To D^o Rec^d Dividend on Bank Stock D^o D^o	18 00
To D^o - Rec^d of Thomas Garrett . D^o. D^o (Bond No 2)	49 00
To D^o Rec^d of Anth^y Taylor on Wm Streeper Mortgage Interest for Phoebe Willson Dower accrued Since appraisement	57 8.
To D^o Rec^d of Thomas Garrett Interest on two Bonds D^o D^o	210 0
To D^o Rec^d of Trustees of New London Congregation D^o D^o	11 9
To D^o Rec^d of Anth^y Taylor (Phoebe Willson Dower)	39 4
To D^o Rec^d of John Menough Interest accrued Since app^t	41 6.
To D^o Rec^d of Dennis Connord D^o D^o . .	3 6
To D^o Rec^d of Thomas Garrett Interest on two Bonds D^o D^o	210 .
To D^o Rec^d of William Streeper Interest &c on addition to appraisement —	86 6
To D^o Rec^d of Edwd Ford adm^r Estate James Ford Interest	50
To D^o Rec^d of Sales of McMullin Lot in addition to the Sum appraised -	33 :
	16207 :

... [illegible] were

... the accountants charge themselves with the balance appearing to remain in their hands as per account Exhibited into & remaining of file in the Register office $. 1093 69½

Also

To cash received of Anthy Taylor Interest due to Phebe Willson upon her dower included in Sheapers mortgage } 39 42

And Further. with the following debts & parts of debts numbered 1 to 6 inclusive for which an allowance was made (as outstanding) by the Register in the settlement of former account Viz^t

No. 1. To cash received of William Strcapen in part of his mortgage being so much thereof as remained due to David Willson (a minor) one of the heirs of William Willson Dec^d of whom this deceased was Guardian } 221 87

2 To amount of claims against the Estate of Thos Hendasfen Esq deceased (after allowing the claims of said Estate against the Estate of this deceased – including and amount against the Estate of Susanna Mears Dec^d of whom they were Co Executors and also their connexion with the Estate of Ephraim Morrison deceased of whom they were also Co Executors) By award of arbitrators amicably chosen . . . } 301 01

3 To amount of Mortgages and other debts due by William Finney – a Judgment against the Estate of Doct R Finney and an acct against Ann Jane Finney . . . } 906 26

4 To amount of Sales of the Estate of James Ford in discharge of the claim upon his Estate Including Interest since acc^t } 624 05½

5 To cash rec^d of S Bell Blenagher Catharine Boothe & John McCarlile in part of Grave yard Expenses } 28 23

6 To Cash rec^d of Thomas Garrett in part of the principal & Interest due by Mortgage . . . . } 47 25

[d] Oscar Finney, s/o Robert T - 27 Feb 1849 - d. 21 Mar 1853
[e] Margaret Finney - b. 7 Jan 1851 - d. 31 Mar 1853
[f] John Finney - b. 27 Feb 1853 - d. 25 Dec 1900 California
[g] Wilfred E. Finney - b. 3 Apr 1855 Oh - m. Lottie - lvd. Jacksonville, Oregon 1935

i. Mark Albert Finney - b. 1884 - d. 1926 Oregon
ii. Robert N. Finney - b. 20 Feb 1895

[h] David A. Finney - b. 31 Dec 1856 - d.21 May 1932 Harrison Co., Oh. - m. 29 Oct 1883 Alice IRWIN who d. 8 Feb 1899

i. Blanche Finney - b. 27 Feb 1885
ii. Lena May Finney - b. 15 Aug 1888 m. Maurice FINK
iii. Grace Olga Finney - b. 7 Feb 1892 - m. H. L. MILLER
iv. Frank Finney - b. 22 Oct 1895 - d. 2 Apr 1897

[i] George Chandler Finney - b. 1 Mar 1858 - 15 Apr 1931 Lloydsville, Oh - m. Mary Elizabeth

i. Charles W. Finney - b. 1884 - 1924 m. Nellie B. - had son Kenneth A.
ii. William Albert Finney - 1 Jan 1888 - m. Lela Alice b. 4 Apr 1889

a. Richard Robert Finney b. 5 Nov 1904 Pittsburgh, Pa - m. Anna Virginia

1. Richard Robert Finney b. 5 July 1935 Wheeling, W. Va.

b. George Charles Finney - b. 2 May 1913
c. William Robb Finney - b. 4 Feb 1916 Akron, Oh - d. 24 Dec 1918
d. Jeanette Rose Finney - b. 19 Jan 1922
e. Lois Jacqueline Finney - b. 2 Sep 1926 Hutchinson, KS

[3] Jane C. Finney, d/o Robert T. b. 1 Jan 1812 - m. 25 Jan 1847 Samuel CARNAHAN
[4] Robert Potts Finney - b. 1 Mar 1814 - m [1] 29 Nov 1844 Mary HITCHCOCK, m [2] 7 Nov 1846 Lydia Ann JENKINS
[5] David A. Finney - b. 18 Nov 1815
[6] Sarah K. Finney - b. 17 Aug 1822
[7] James Finney - b. 12 July 1825
[8] William Guthrie Finney - 5 Sep 1818 Oh - d. 3 May 1904 Washington, D.C. m. 28 Dec 1842 Margaret CARNAHAN b. 18 Aug 1816 - 1895

[a] George Carnahan Finney - b. 17 Feb 1844 Oh - 19 Oct 1885 Chicago, unm.
[b] James Rea Finney - 25 Feb 1846 - 19 Feb 1932 - m. 7 Dec 1875 Sally BRINDLE

i. Valentine Cowan Finney - b. 27 Feb 1877 Oh - m. Elizabeth REED b. 23 June 1876
ii. Mary Bell Finney - b. 7 June 1881

[c] Argyle Finney - 23 Nov 1848 - 5 June 1898 NYC - m. 1872 Molly Julia NORWOOD 1857 - 1927

i. Charles Leander Finney - b. 1877 Wash., D.C. - m. Lillian HOSNER
ii. Guy Woodward Finney - b. 1879 - m. Carolyn Edna MACY b. 1890 NJ
iii. William Finney - died young

[d] David Craig Finney - b. 19 Mar 1850 - 21 Nov 1925 Washington
[e] Leroy R. Finney - b. 4 Nov 1851 Oh - 1915 Phoenix, Ariz. - m. 27 Sep 1887 Linnie GEE
[f] Mary M. Finney - adopted 1 Oct 1859
[g] Margaret I. Finney - 1 Oct 1859 - 1922 Washington - m. 8 June 1880 George B. PHELPS b. 10 May 1857 Mass.
[h] Mary Bell Finney b. 1 Mar 1860 [?] - d. 29 Aug 1864

B. Sarah Finney, d/o Robert & Phebe - m. GILLESPIE

C. Hannah Finney - m.John ARTHUR

D. Mary Finney - m. James SCOTT

E. Dorothea Finney

F. Nancy Finney - m. CUNNINGHAM

2. William Finney, s/o Robert & Agnes - b. 1777 - d. 2 Dec 1840 m. 1823 Margaret HARPER b. 18 Aug 1803 - d. 7 Mar 1872

   A. Robert Stevenson Finney - b. 4 Oct 1823 - m. 4 July 1865 Christiana MURYON who died Dec 1893
   B. James Harper Finney - b. 1 Feb 1826 - d. 2 Mar 1871
   C. Mary Ann Finney - b. 3 Mar 1828 - 15 Aug 1877 - m. 25 Dec 1849 Thomas MINARY
   D. William Finney - b. 15 Dec 1830
   E. Zipporah Finney - b. 15 Dec 1835 - d. 10 May 1868 m. 1863 John AUMACHER

3. Dorothea Finney - b. 1778 - d. 16 Feb 1840 unmarried
4. Ann Finney - middle name Jean - b. 1780 - d. 6 May 1856

b. Dorothea Finney, d/o Thomas & Mary [Chester] - died unmarried

c. Ann Finney - died unmarried

In the Name of God amen ye Twenty first day of June
in ye year of our Lord one Thousand Seven Hundred & Forty
Six, I Thomas Finney of ye Township of New London in ye
County of Chester & Province of Pensylva Yeoman being
of a Sound & disposing Mind, doe make & ordain this my last
will & Testament in manner following Vizt, Imprimis I
commend my Soul to Almighty God who gave it, & my Body
to be decently interred at ye discretion of my Executor here
in after named, & as to such Estate Real & Personal as I
shall dye possess of, I Devise & bequeath ye same in
manner following, Item. I order all my just debts to be first
paid, Item. I bequeath to my Dearly beloved Wife Mary
Finney, whom I ordain & appoint to be my only & Sole
Executrix of this my last will & Testament, the third of all my
personal Estate & further I allow her ye use of my Dwelling
House & ye profits of ye land or Plantation during her
Widowhood, this for her Suport & ye Suporting my Two
Daughters Ann Finney & Dorothea Finney while
they live with their Mother as usual, but in case my dear
wife should Marry, than I order that all my personal
Estat, be properly prized, or sold & division made, first
ye third of all to my wife Mary Finney & ye remaining
part to be divided in three Equal parts between my
Son Robert Finney's Children, and my Two Daughters
Ann and Dorothea Finney. to Each of ym an Equal part
Item I bequeath to my Son Robt Finney ye Sum of three
pound and all my wearing Apparel, and, after ye Death
of my beloved wife, I order that all my real Estate
be divided Equally into three parts, between my
Two Daughters Ann & Dorothea Finney, & my Son
Robts Children as above, to them their heirs &
assigns for Ever and its my desire that my friend
Patrick Ewing be assistant to my beloved wife
And I

in ye Year of our Lord, one thousand Seven hundred & sixty
six, I Thomas Finney of ye Township of Nelolondon, in ye
County of Chester & Province of Pensylva. Yeoman, being
of a sound & disposing Mind, doe make & ordain this my last
will & Testament in manner following, Vizt., Imprimis I
commend my Soul to Almighty God who gave it, & my Body
to be decently interred at ye discretion of my Executor here
in after named, & as to such Estate Real & Personal, as I
shall dye possessed of, I Devise & bequeath ye Same in
manner following, Item. I order all my just debts to be first
paid, Item. I bequeath to my Dearly beloved Wife Mary
Finney, whom I ordain & appoint to be my only & Sole
Executor of this my last will & Testament, the third of all my
personal Estate, & further I allow her ye use of my Dwelling
House & ye profits of ye land or Plantation during her
Widowhood, this for her support & ye supporting my Two
Daughters Ann Finney & Dorothie Finney while
they live with their Mother as usual, but in case my dear
wife should Marry, than I order that all my personal
Estate be properly prized or sold & division made, first
ye third of all to my wife Mary Finney, & ye remaining
part to be divided in three Equal parts between my
Son Roberts Finneys Children and my two Daughters
Ann and Dorothie Finney, to Each of ym an Equal part.
Item I bequeath to my Son Robt. Finney ye Sum of three
pound and all my wearing Apparel, and, after ye Death
of my beloved wife, I order that all my real Estate
be divided Equally into three parts between my
two Daughters Ann & Dorothie Finney, & my Son
Robts. Children as above, to them their heirs &
assigns for Ever, and its my desire that my Friend
Patrick Ewing be assistant to my beloved wife
And I

And I ordain & make this & no other to be my
last will & Testament. Witness my hand & Seal
The day & Year above writen

Signed Sealed published
and declard by ye sd Thomas
Finney as his last will
and Testament in ye pres=
ence of us ye Subscribers

Davis Hunter
John Finney
his
John X Laste

Thomas Finney

[illegible] 25 Nov. 1767 [illegible] 25 Dec. [illegible]

KNOW all Men by these Presents, That we Robert Finney, George Campbell & William Finney of the County of Chester — " — " — " — " — " — " —

— " — " — are held and firmly bound unto PERSIFOR FRAZER, Esquire, Register for the Probate of Wills, and granting Letters of Administration, in and for the County of Chester, in the Commonwealth of *Pennsylvania*, in the Sum of Two hundreds — Pounds, to be paid to the said *Persifor Frazer*, his Successors, Administrators or Assigns: To the which Payment well and truely to be made, we bind ourselves, jointly and severally, for and in the whole, ours Heirs, Executors and Administrators, firmly by these Presents. Sealed with our Seals. Dated the Eighth - day of Novem^{r} in the year of our Lord one thousand seven hundred and ~~eighty~~ ninety one

THE Condition of this Obligation is such, That if the above bounden Robert Finney — " — " — " — " — Administrator of all and singular the Goods, Chattels and Credits of Mary Finney late of New London — deceased, do make, or cause to be made, a true and perfect Inventory of all and singular the Goods, Chattels and Credits of the said Deceased, which have or shall come to the Hands, Possession or Knowledge of him the said Robert Finney — " — " — or unto the Hands and Possession of any other Person or Persons for him and the same so made do exhibit, or cause to be exhibited, into the Register's Office, in the County of *Chester*, at or before the eighth — " — day of December next ensuing; and the same Goods, Chattels and Credits, and all other the Goods, Chattels and Credits of the said Deceased at the Time of her Death, which at any Time after shall come to the Hands or Possession of the said Robert Finney — " — " — or unto the Hands and Possession of any other Person or Persons for him do well and truly Administer according to Law. And further do make, or cause to be made, a true and just Account of his said Administration, at or before the eighth — day of Novem^{r} 1792 And all the Rest and Residue of the said Goods, Chattels and Credits, which shall be found remaining upon the said Administrator's Account (the same being first examined and allowed of by the Orphans Court of the County of *Chester*) shall deliver and pay unto such Person or Persons respectively, as the said Orphans Court by their Decree of Sentence, pursuant to the true Intent and Meaning of the several Laws now in force in this Commonwealth, shall limit and appoint. And if it shall hereafter appear, that any Last Will and Testament was made by the said Deceased, and the Executor or Executors therein named do exhibit the same into the said Register's Office, making Request to have it allowed and approved accordingly: And if then the above bounden Robert Finney — " — " —

being thereunto required, do render and deliver the said Letters of Administration (Approbation of such Testament being first had and made in the said Register's Office) then this Obligation to be void and of none effect, or else to remain full Force and Virtue.

Sealed and delivered in the Presence of

John Kinnard

Jonathan Vernon

to present at the time of William Finney's signing of this Bonds

Matthew ... Kinnard

Robt Finney (L.S.)

George Campbell (L.S.)

William Finney (L.S.)

v. Ann Finney,d/o Robert [1667] - b. Londonderry, Ireland - d. after 1778 Chester Co., PA Buried at Thunder Hill - m. John McCLENAHAN who d. after 1778

a. Elijah McClenahan - b. 3 Nov 1728 - 23 Feb 1810 New London, Pa - m. Mary b. 1737 - d. 30 Apr 1780

1. Samuel Blair McClenahan - 1 May 1775 - 11 Sep 1851 - m [1] Amay CHARLTON, m [2] Sarah JOHNSON

vi. James Finney, s/o Robert - died 1774 Hanover Twp., Lancaster Co., Pa. - m. Jean [Jane]

a. Thomas Finney b. 1740/41 - d. Sep 1784 Dauphin Co., Pa. m. Isabella. In 1759 he was assessed a tax in Hanover, Pa. for use in war with the Indians. He also petitioned against the division of Hanover Twp. in 1769. In 1779 he was listed as tax payer on 110 acres and again in 1783.

1. Margaret [Peggy] Finney
2. Effy Finney - died @ 1803 - will dated 30 Aug 1803 Dauphin Co., Pa. File 1 - 6 Office of Register of Wills, Harrisburg, Pa. She left her property to be equally divided between her sisters Jean, Margaret, Martha HARBISON, Mary and brothers John and Hervey.
3. Martha Finney - m. 14 Mar 1796 Dauphin Co. Adam HARBISON
4. Jane [Jean] Finney
5. Isabelle Finney - d. @ 1803 - left in her will to John, Harvey and Martha each 7s-6d and the remaining portion of the estate among her four sisters Jean, Margaret, Mary and Effey.
6. Hervey Finney
7. John Finney - b. @ 1781 Pa - d. 19 Oct 1862 Xenia, Green Co., Oh. He lived there as early as 1820 census, there 1850 when he applied on 29 Nov 1850 for bounty land. Believed he moved to Ohio in 1811, member of Paxtang, Pa. church in 1808 - m [1] Isabell McDOWELL b. 1783 - 1838, d/o Archibald, m [2] 3 Apr 1845 at Xenia, Oh Eleanor [Ellen] HARPER b. 1810 Va

John & Eleanor were living in Xenia, Oh 1860 and her sister Sophia R. HARPER b. 1803 Va was with them. John was Pvt. Volunteer Rifle Co., commanded by Capt. John ROBISON, Ohio Militia, commanded by Col. James FINLEY in War of 1812. He, John Finney, volunteered in Butler, Co., Oh. on or about 20 Apr 1812 for a term of one year. He was immediately mustered into service. On 16 Aug 1812 he was surrendered by Gen HULL at Detroit, Michigan and was a Prisoner of War on board the brig ADAMS for 17 days, detained until on or about 4 Sep 1812 when he was set at large upon parole, and was still considered a prisoner until he was exchanged in July 1814. Above information is contained in his accompanying application for Bounty Land on 29 Nov 1850. He purchased land in Greene Co., Oh. 1814, 1816, 1822 and 1829.

A. Thomas Finney
B. Jane Finney
C. Sarah Ann Finney
D. Susan Armstrong Finney - b. 1814 Oh - m. 22 Mar 1843 Austin McDOWELL - b. 1815 Pa, lvd Greene Co, a lumber merchant in 1860

[1] Charlotte J. McDowell - b. 1846
[2] Sarah J. McDowell - b. 1850
[3] Hugh H. McDowell - b. 1857
[4] Sarah McDowell - b. 1853
[5] Margaret B. McDowell - b. 1858

E. Isabella Finney
F. Louisa Finney - middle name Ann
G. John Finney
H. Julia Ann Finney

b. Jane Finney,m d/o James & Jean - m. RITCHLEDGE
c. Mary Finney - m. McGUIRE
d. Rebecca Finney - m. David CALDWELL
e. Effie Finney - b. 1735 - 28 Dec 1765, buried Old Hanover Church, Lancaster Co., Pa m [1] 1750 Thomas ROBINSON b. 1729 - Aug 1758, m [2] 1760 Colonel Timothy GREEN - b. 1733 Dauphin Co., Pa - d. 27 Feb 1812

1. Jane Robinson - b. 1751 - m. Robert STURGEON
2. Mary Robinson - b. 1753
3. Elizabeth Robinson - b. 1756
4. Joseph Green - b. 27 Mar 1761
5. Rebecca Green - 1763 - 30 July 1837 - m. Col. William ALLEN
6. Timothy Green - b. 7 Sep 1765 - in Revolutionary War - m. 25 Feb 1783 Sarah AWL b. 24 Feb 1764 Dauphin Co., Pa - d. 1835 Chillicothe, Ohio

F | 2 (Findlay's.) | Ohio Vols. and Mil.

John Finney,

Pvt., { Capt. John Robison's Company of Volunteer Riflemen in Regiment of Ohio Volunteers and Militia commanded by Col. James Findlay.

(War of 1812.)

Appears on

Company Muster Roll

for June 30 to Dec 31, 1812.

Roll dated Not Dated

............, 181 .

Date of appointment or enlistment, } Apl 27, 1812.

Date of appointment or commencement of service, } ...., 181 .

To what time engaged or expiration of service, } ...., 181 .

For what time engaged, One Year.

Present or absent, Present.

To what period paid, ..., 181 .

Remarks and alterations since last muster: ....

(669) Huxley Copyist.

F | 2 (Findlay's.) | Ohio Vols. and Mil.

John Finney.

Pvt., { Capt. John Robison's Company of Volunteer Riflemen, in Regiment of Ohio Volunteers and Militia commanded by Col. James Findlay.

(War of 1812.)

Appears on

Company Muster Roll

for Apl 27 to June 30, 1812.

Roll dated ....

June 30, 1812.

Date of appointment or enlistment, } Apl 27, 1812.

Date of appointment or commencement of service, } ...., 181 .

To what time engaged or expiration of service, } ...., 181 .

For what time engaged, One year

Present or absent, Present.

To what period paid, ..., 181 .

Remarks and alterations since last muster: ....

(669) Huxley Copyist.

F | 2 (Findlay's.) | Ohio Vols. and Mil.

John Finney.

Pvt., { Capt. John Robison's Company of Volunteer Riflemen, in Regiment of Ohio Volunteers and Militia commanded by Col. James Findlay.

(War of 1812.)

Appears on

Company Muster Roll

for Apl 27 to May 31, 1812

Roll dated ....

May 31, 1812.

Date of appointment or enlistment, } ...., 181 .

Date of appointment or commencement of service, } Apl 27 1812.

To what time engaged or expiration of service, } Apl 27 1813.

For what time engaged, ...

Present or absent, Present

To what period paid, ..., 181 .

Remarks and alterations since last muster: ....

(669) Huxley Copyist.

F | 2 (Findlay's.) | Ohio Vols. and Mil.

John Finney.

Pri., Capt. John Robison's Co., 2 Reg't Ohio Volunteers and Militia.

(War of 1812.)

Appears on

Company Pay Roll

for Jan 1 to Apl 26, 1813.

Roll dated Not dated, 181 .

Commencement of service, or of this settlement, Jan. 1, 1813.

Expiration of service, or of this settlement, Apl 26, 1813.

Term of service charged, 3 months 26 days.

Pay per month, 5 dollars .... cents.

Amount of pay, 19 dollars 33 1/3 cents.

Signer's name ....

Remarks: ....

[672] Hensley Copyist.

F | 2 (Findlay's.) | Ohio Vols. and Mil.

John Finney.

Pri., Capt. John Robison's Co., 2 Reg't Ohio Volunteers and Militia.

(War of 1812.)

Appears on

Company Pay Roll

for July 1 to Dec 31, 1812

Roll dated Not dated, 181 .

Commencement of service, or of this settlement, July 1, 1812

Expiration of service, or of this settlement, Dec 31, 1812

Term of service charged, 6 months, ... days.

Pay per month, 5 dollars, ... cents.

Amount of pay, 30 dollars, ... cents.

Signer's name, ...

Remarks: ....

[672] Hensley Copyist.

F | 2 (Findlay's.) | Ohio Vols. and Mil.

John Finney.

Pri., Capt. John Robison's Company of Riflemen, 2 Reg't Ohio Vols.

(War of 1812.)

Appears on

Company Pay Roll

for July to Dec, 1812

Roll dated Not dated, 181 .

Commencement of service, or of this settlement, July 1, 1812

Expiration of service, or of this settlement, Dec 31, 1812

Term of service charged, 6 months, ... days.

Pay per month, 5 dollars, ... cents.

Amount of pay, 30 dollars, ... cents.

Signer's name, ...

Remarks: ....

[672] Hensley Copyist.

F	2 (Findlay's.)	Ohio Vols. and Mil.

John Finny,

Pri., Capt. John Robison's Company of Volunteer Riflemen, 2 Regiment Volunteers, State of Ohio.

(War of 1812.)

Appears on

Company Muster Roll

for Apl 27 to, 1812

Roll dated

Apl 27, 1812

Date of appointment or enlistment, Apl 27 1812

Date of appointment or commencement of service, 181

To what time engaged or expiration of service, Apl 27 1813.

To what time engaged or enlisted, 181

Present or absent Present

To what period paid, 181

Remarks and alterations since last muster:

On Duty.

(669) Hinxley Copyist.

The State of Ohio Greene County ss

On this 29 day of November one thousand Eight hundred and fifty, Personally appeared before me a Notary Public within and for the County and State aforesaid John Finney aged sixty nine years a resident of Greene County and State of Ohio who being duly sworn according to Law, Declares that he is the identical John Finney who was a private in the volunteer rifle company commanded by captain John Robeson in the first regiment of Ohio Militia Commanded by Colonel James Finley in the war with Great Britain declared by the United States on the 18th day of June AD 1812. That he volunteered in Butler County Ohio on or about the 20th day of April AD 1812 for the term of one year and was immediately mustered into the service, and that he continued in actual service untill the 16th day of August AD 1812, That he was in the American Army at and was surrendered by General Hull at Detroit, That he remained a prisoner of war on bord the brig Adams, Seventeen days Being detained in captivity untill the on or about the 4th day of September AD 1812, when he was set at large upon parole that he was still considered a prisoner of war, untill he was exchanged which he thinks was in July 1814.

He makes this statement for the purpose of obtaining the Bounty Lands to which he may be entitled, under the Act Granting Bounty Lands to certain officers and soldiers who have been engaged in the military service of the United States

passed September 28th 1850 — John Finney

Sworn to and subscribed before me this day and year above written and I do further certify that I believe the said John Finny is the Identicall man who served as aforesaid and that he is of the age above stated

In testimony whereof I have here unto set my hand and affixed my seal Notarial this 29th day of November 1856

David Torrence N.P.

The State of Ohio
Greene County ss

Personally appeared before me a Notary Public within and for said County Samuel Stewart a resident of Clark County and state aforesaid, who is of full age and entitled to credit, who being by me duly sworn deposeth, that he is personally acquainted with the forementioned John Finney that he saw him sign the foregoing affidavit and application for bounty Lands, That he knew the said John Kinney to serve as he there claims to have served. That he frequently saw said Kinney in the service between the 26th day of April AD 1812 and the 16th day of August 1812, But that after the surrender he saw no more of him while in the army, and further this deponent saith not

Samuel Stewart

Sworn to and Subscribed before me this 29th day of November 1850 in Testimony whereof I have hereunto set my hand and affixed my seal Notarial day and date above written

David Lorrence N P

The State of Ohio }
Greene County ss } I James J Winans Clerk of the Court of Common Pleas within and for the said County of Greene do Certify that David Lorrence Esq was at the date of the foregoing declaration and the above affidavit and state is a Notary Public within and for the said County duly Commissioned and Qualified, and authorized to administer oaths for general purposes, and that his signatures to the Certificates to said declaration and affidavit are genuine

In testimony whereof I have hereunto set my hand and affixed the seal of said Court at Xenia the 9 day of Dect. AD 1850. James J Winans Clerk

State of Ohio County of Greene SS.

On this 14 day of August A.D. One thousand Eight hundred and ninety one, personally appeared before me Clerk of the Common Pleas Court a Court of record in and for the County and State aforesaid.

Ellen F. Cassel aged 81 years a resident of Xenia County of Greene and State of Ohio who being duly sworn according to Law declares that she is the former widow of John Finney who served the full period of Sixty days in the Military Service of the United States in the war of 1812 and who was the identical John Finney who enlisted in Captain Robinson's Company.

division Commander General William H. Harrison 1812 and was honorabled discharged in 1812

That she was married under the name of Ellen W. Harper to said John Limney on the 3 day of April A.D. 1845 by Rev. Samuel Wilson D.D. at Xenia Ohio there being no Legal Barrier to such Marriage. That her said Husband died at Xenia Ohio on the 19 day of October A.D. 1862. That she has re-married since his death.

That she married Robert Cassel at Xenia Ohio April 28 A.D. 1871.

That at no time during the late rebellion against the authority of the United States did she or her said husband adhere to the cause of the Enemies of the Government giving them aid or comfort or exercise the functions of any Office whatever, under any authority or pretended authority in hostility to the United States:- that she is not in receipt of a Pension under any previous Act:- That she makes this Declaration for the purpose of

being placed on the Pension Roll
of the United States under the provisions
of the act approved February 14 1871 -
and hereby constitutes and appoints
with full power of substitution and
revocation J. S. Armstrong & Son
of Xenia Ohio her true and
Lawful Attorneys to prosecute her
Claim and procure the issuance
of a Pension Certificate to her -
That her Post office address is
No 317 E. Second Street, Xenia
Greene County Ohio. That
her domicil or place of abode
is No 317 E. Second street Xenia Ohio

Witnesses
E E Armstrong   x Ellen W Rarsill
W P Lauman

Also personally appeared E. E.
Armstrong and W. P. Lauman
residing at No : St :
Xenia Ohio. persons whom I certify
to be respectable and entitled to credit
and who being by me duly sworn
say that they were present and saw

Ellen W. Cassil the Claimant
sign her name (or make her mark)
to the foregoing declaration. That they have
every reason to believe from the appearance
of said Claimant and their acquaintance
with her, that she is the identical person
she represents herself to be and at no
time during the late rebellion against
the Authority of the United States did
she or her husband adhere to the
Cause of the Enemies of the
Government or give them aid or
Comfort: That they have no interest
in the prosecution of this
Claim.

E E Armstrong
W F Lamman

Sworn to and subscribed before me this
day of Aug. AD 1891. and I hereby certify
that the contents of the above declaration were
fully made known and explained to the Applicant
and Witnesses before swearing. That I have no
interest direct or indirect in the prosecution
of this Claim. J F Haverstick

Clerk Court Greene Co.
Ohio

3—1321

Claim No. 45819

Act of Mch 9"78

Cert. No.

Original Case.

Reopened from

Act of

SERVICE PENSION,

War of 1812.

WIDOW'S BRIEF.

Ellen W. Karsell former, widow of

John Finney

REJECTED

Rank: Private

Captain John Robinson

Regiment: Militia Ohio

317 E. 2' St.

Post Office: Xenia, County of Greene, State of Ohio

Attorney: J. S. Armstrong Son P.O. Xenia

County, State of Ohio, Fee 5, Contract

Application filed Aug 17 1891.

Alleged service. Capt. Robinson War 1812.

Record evidence of service. In B.L.Wt. 75893-160.50. 3' and reports service from Apl 27/12 to Apl 27/13.

Parol evidence of service.

Length of service 1 Year. Days

Proof of identity. Rejected by reason of re-marriage after soldiers death.

Proof of loyalty. married to Robt Cansel or Russell Apl. 28th 1871.

Rejected Oct. 23, 1891, to a pension of EIGHT DOLLARS per month

from .... the date of ....

No other pension previously applied for

Frank Shapley
Pension Searcher

Bounty Land claim 7523-160-50

Frank Shapley
Bounty Land Searcher

[illegible]
Examiner.

MB. APPROVED for rej. Dec 3, 1891.

J. [illegible]
Reviewer.

(OVER.)

1st DIVISION.—(To be filled by Ex'r.)

No. 44.719 Invalid J. Fennessy

Filed 18 91 Apl 27, 1862 — Service term'd by M. O. Disability. Desertion. Death.

1st ser. ... Co. ... Ohio, Reg't Mil., from Apl 27, 1861

Ship (if Navy) ....

2d ser. ... Co. ..., Reg't X, from ..., 18.. to ..., 18.. — Service term'd by M. O. Disability. Desertion. Death.

Ship (if Navy) ....

Date of invalid's death (if after service) Oct 19, 1862

Did invalid apply for pension? no

Was invalid a pensioner? no His Cert. No. ....

Claim NOT made under act of June 27, 1890.

2d DIVISION.—(To be filled by Rev'r.)

Did invalid die of pensioned disability? ....

If not, cause of death ....

Number of minor children pensionable ....

Claim allowed ...., 18.... Rates $ .... from ...., 18....

$ ...... from ...., 18....

If pension terminates, date ...., 18.... Cause: ....

3d DIVISION.—(To be filled by Cert. Div.)

Cert. No. .... Value of issue at date, $ ....

Dated ...., 189

4th DIVISION.—Rejection.—(To be filled by Ex'r.)

Date, ..., 18.... Cause: Death cause not in line of duty. Death cause since service. Service not legal. Not legal widow. Unable to file necessary evidence. If other cause, state it ....

Court House, Lancaster Co.,Pa. - JAMES FINNEY - 26th July 1770

I James Finney of Hanover Township, Lancaster Co., and Province of Pennsylvania etc. etc. and as touching my worldly estate which it pleases God to endow me with, I do bequeath in manner following:

I give and bequeath to my wife Jane Finney the 1/3 part of all my movable estate etc. etc. also I give and bequeath to my son Thomas Finney 2/3's of my Real Estate and at his mother's death the other 1/3 of my said Real Estate, also I give and bequeath to my said son Thomas the 2/3's of all my moveable estate, out of which he is to pay the following bequeathments -

I give to my daughter Jan Ritchledge ten pounds, also I give to my daughter Mary McGuire twenty pounds, also I give and bequeath to my daughter Rebecca Caldwell eight pounds, also I give to Jane Sturgeon twenty shillings and also I give to Mary Robinson twenty shillings, and also I give to Rebecca Green twenty shillings -

The above to be paid in two years after my decease and I do appoint my wife Jane Finney and my son Thomas Finney my executors, etc. etc. etc.

Witness my hand and seal the 26th of July 1770

James Finney [Seal]

Signed, sealed and delivered in Presence of Witnesses

Benj. Wallace

Mich. Wallace

State of Pennsylvania]
County of Lancaster] SS

Etc. etc. etc. - duly sworn May 4th 1774 and among files of records in Register's Office of Lancaster County.

NOTE: Thewill inventory showed "one plantation of about 100 acres of watered land" valued at 400 pounds.

* * * * *

Harrisburg, Pa. - Dauphin Co., Office of Register of Wills - Book A - 45

15th Sept 1784 - Thomas Finney and wife Isabella

This 15th day of September 1784 I Thomas Finney of the Township of Hanover, Lancaster Co., Pa. etc. etc. etc. I will and bequeath to my wife Isabelle Finney 1/3 of the whole of my Real Estate - etc. I will and bequeath to my son John Finney my lower plantation. I will and bequeath to my son Hervey Finney the plantation that I now live on. I will and bequeath to my wife Isabelle Finney the one full 1/3 of the whole of my Personal Estate, etc. etc.

I give and bequeath to my daughters Martha, Mary, Jane, Isabelle, Margaret and Effy, etc. etc.

It is my will and I allow that John, Jane, Isabella, Margaret, Hervey and Effy be schooled and maintained off the whole Head until they arrive to maturity, etc. etc. etc.

Signed Thos. Finney [Seal]

Witnesses: John Cuper
Samuel Sturgeon
Jos. Green

22 Mar 1786 - This 22nd day of March 1786 came John Cuper and Samuel Sturgeon two of the subscribing witnesses to foregoing will - and being duly sworn according to law doth depose and say they were present and heard and saw Thos. Finney sign, seal will, etc. etc.

Signed Jos. Montgomery
Register

* * * * *

Dauphin Co., Pa, Orphans Court Docket A-28 - Session held March 22, 1786

James Finney, a minor son of Thos. Finney late of West Hanover Township, deceased, being above the age of 14 years, comes into Court and chooses Richard Snow of Paxton Township guardian over his Estate during his minority and Court approves of and appoints said Richard Snow his guardian accordingly.

And Sarah Finney and Jennet Finney, minor children of same Thomas Finney deceased being above the age of 14 years come into Court and choose James Byers of Paxton Township guardian over their Estate during their minority and Court approves of and appoints said James Byers their guardian accordingly.

Session held Jan 16th, 1799 - Court Docket - B - 78 - Peggy Finney, a minor daughter, above the age of 14 years of Thos. Finney, late of W. Hanover Twp., deceased, came into Court and chooses Benjamin Wallace Guardian of her person and Estate during her minority and Court approves of and appoints said Benjamin Wallace her Guardian accordingly.

DAUPHIN CO., PA. Court Docket - B - 79

Harvey Finney and Effey Finney minor children above the age of 14 years of Thos. Finney, late of West Hanover Twp., deceased, came into Court and choose Timothy Greene of same Township Guardian of their person and estate during their minority and the Court approve of and appoint the said Timothy Greene their Guardian accordingly.

vii. Letitia [Leticia] Finney, d/o Robert & Dorothea - died 1742 Chester Co., Pa - m. 1731 William McKEAN - b. 1707 Londonderry, Ire. - d. 18 Nov 1769, s/o William & Susannah. William was a grandson of an Argyleshire Scot who had gone to Ireland. William came to Pennsylvania as a child with his parents. The name is sometimes spelled McCane. William had a tavern known as "Chatham" in New London till 1741. He moved to Londongrove, an adjoining township; in 1745 to Londonderry.

a. Thomas McKean, Sr. - b. 9 Mar 1734 Chester Co., Pa. - d. 24 June 1817 Philadelphia, Pa. He was the youngest signer of the Declaration of Independence. Married [1] July 1763 Mary BORDEN, d/o Joseph of Bordentown, NJ - b. 21 July 1744 - d. 13 Mar 1773 - m [2] 2 Sep 1774 Sarah ARMITAGE, d/o James and his 2nd wife Frances Land - b. 19 Dec 1746 New Castle, Del. - d. 6 May 1820

1. Thomas McKean, Jr. - b. 20 Nov 1770 - 5 May 1852 - m. 14 Sep 1809 Sarah Clementina PRATT - b. 1781 - d. 31 Dec 1836

A. Henry Pratt McKean - b. 3 May 1810 - m. 8 July 1841 Phebe Elizabeth WARREN

[1] Thomas McKean - b. 28 Nov 1842 Philadelphia - m. 24 Sep 1863 Elizabeth WHARTON - b. 15 Dec 1844

[a] Henry Pratt McKean, Jr.
[b] Thomas McKean - b. 29 Apr 1869 Philadelphia - m. 25 Nov 1896 Katherine JOHNSTONE

i. Nancy B. McKean - b. 17 July 1901
ii. Thomas McKean - b. 16 Mar 1909 Paris, France

[c] Maria Wharton McKean
[d] George Wharton McKean
[e] Phebe Warren McKean - m. Morton DOWNS, M. D.

B. Sarah Ann McKean - m. George TROTT

C. Elizabeth Dunds McKean - m. Adolphe E. BORIE

D. Clementina Sophia McKean - m. Charles Louis BORIE

2. Joseph Borden McKean - 29 Nov 1768 Philadelphia - 13 Dec 1822 in Tennessee, a lawyer and judge - m. 13 May 1796 Maria Pearson CLUNN - b. 28 Jan 1775 - d. 29 Mar 1819 Tennessee

A. John Clunn McKean - 20 Feb 1797 - 18 July 1880 Prairie Lee, Texas. Born Wheeling, W. Va - m. 29 Sep 1819 Margaret F. KEARNEY b. 7 Oct 1801 - 11 Mar 1833 Tenn - m. Maury Co., Tenn.

[1] Lucy Ellen McKean - 20 May 1824 Tenn - 25 Oct 1908 Texas - m [1] 18 May 1843 John BLACKBURN, m [2] 19 May 1853 Edward MALLOCH

3. Sarah Maris Theresa McKean - died ? - her will dated 1840 - m. Senor Don Carlos Martinez de Yruro - minister of ?pain to the United States

A. Narcissa Maria Louisa Martinez de Yruro - m. Don Blas Santiago de Pierrard, Knight of John of Jeruselum, Commander of Order of Charles III of order of Isabella, who was decorated for military deeds of daring. Her will dated 13 Sep 1876. She was lady in waiting to Queen Maria Louisa of Spain and resided at her Court.
B. Narcisa Escano Martinez de Yruro
C. [Step-dau] Duchess of Soto Myers

4. Robert McKean - died 8 June 1802 Philadelphia
5. Elizabeth McKean - m. 8 Dec 1791 Andrew Pettit
6. Mary McKean - died young
7. Letitia McKean - m. 10 June 1789 Philadelphia Dr. George BUCHANAN

b. Dr. Robert McKean - 13 July 1732 - 17 Oct 1767 Perth Amboy, NJ - m. 19 Feb 1766 Isabel Graham ANTILL, d/o Edward - married Shrewsbury, New Jersey

c. Dorothea McKean,d/o William & Leticia - m. John THOMPSON - had son Thomas McKean Thompson

d. William McKean - died 2 Jan 1782 - m. Elizabeth b. 1748 - d. 8 July 1792 Boston, Mass.

THOMAS McKEAN - b. 9 Mar 1734 Chester Co., Pa. was the youngest, age 42 years, of the three delagates who signed the declaration of Independence. He became a conspicuous and also a controversial public figure. At the time of the signing of the Declaration he lived at new Castle, Delaware but had legal practices not only in the Lower Counties but in New Jersey and Pennsylvania as well. In later phases of his career he was identified with Pennsylvania. He was a man of vigorous personality. In Delaware he was a perennial member of the Assembly from young manhood and became noted as a champion of the Colonial cause. Except for about a year he represented Delaware in the Continental Congress continuously from 1774 to 1783. His family connections were invaluable in securing a successful career. In 1752 at age 18 he became a prothonotary's clerk, then a deputy of prothonotary and recorder of wills. In 1756 he was deputy attorney general, age 22, and helped revise the state assembly laws.

His first wife, Mary BORDEN, was the daughter of Joseph Borden and Thomas and Mary had six children. His second wife, Sarah ARMITAGE, had five children. After the death of Mary Borden in 1773 he married Sarah in 1774 and moved to the city of Philadelphia, Pa. All of his children are not known.

The Delaware Constitution has been credited to him also, and for a short time he was acting president of Delaware. His career is confusing because he held office in two of the commonwealths at the same time. He was appointed Chief Justice of Pennsylvania in 1777, at age 43. He occupied that post for 22 years and as time went by he became increasingly identified with that state. He had been regarded as a radical Whig, but opposed the Pennsylvania Constitution of 1776 and was active in that convention that adopted the more conservative document of 1790. He strongly supported the new Federal Constitution but in the party struggles of the 1790's he became a Republican against the Federalists. His election as Governor of Pennsylvania in 1799 was an important political event, and he served three terms of three years each in that office. While Governor, he appointed his son, Joseph Borden McKean, as attorney general, and this action aroused remarks about the "heir apparent" and "royal family." This son was a lawyer of ability, however, and afterward held high judicial offices. Part of Thomas' difficulties arose from his personality. This tall and stately man of unquestionable ability and honesty was cold in manner, was vain, and tactless, and he gained a host of enemies as well as admirers. His terms as governor were extremely tumultuous and he was accused of nepotism, constitutional violation, and abuse of office. Although impeachment proceedings were begun, they were later dropped and he ended his second term peacefully and served one more term. He amassed a very great estate and after his retirement he remained an impressive figure in Philadelphia until his death in 1817 at the age of 83 years.

State of Pennsylvania } ss
Columbia County }

On the eleventh day of June in the year one thousand eight hundred and thirty three, Personally come before me the Subscriber one of the Justices of the Peace in and for the County of Columbia James Loughead Esquire Post Master of Danville Penn.a in the county aforesaid aged in the 69th year, who after being duly Sworn according to Law, Deponant Says that he seen Lazarus Finney in city of Philadelphia on his way, at Deponants fathers house, to camp in the Charater of an Ensign Deponant thinks in the year 1776 or 1777 Deponant was then thinks he was then 12 or 13 years of age, the circumstance that leads to the above that Lazarus Finney was a Relation of Deponants mother who was then living and that Mr. Finney was frequaintly at Deponants fathers house Deponant further Says that he remembers that Mr Finney went on the second Service he thinks in fall of the Same year of the first Service

Sworn and Subscribed the day and year aforesaid before Me } James Loughead

Rudolph Seckler J. P.

I do hereby certify that the above named deponant James Loughead, is a person of credibility and that full confidance may be placed in his Testimony In testimony whereof I have hereunto set my hand the 11th day of June 1833.

Rudolph Seckler (Seal)

Declaration in order to obtain the benefit of the act of Congress passed June 7. 1832.

State of Pennsylvania }
Union county } ss.

On this eighth day of June in the year of our Lord one thousand eight hundred and thirty three, personally appeared before the subscriber Hugh Wilson, Esquire, one of the judges of the court of common Pleas, in and for the county of Union aforesaid, in vacation, Lazarus Finney a resident of the Penn Township, in the county of Union and State of Pennsylvania, aged eighty one years, who being first duly sworn according to Law, doth, on his oath make the following declaration, in order to obtain the benefit of the act of Congress passed June 7. 1832.

That he entered the service of the United States under the following named officers, and served as herein stated.

That he lived in New London Township, in the county of Chester and State of Pennsylvania, when he was called into service the first, as well as every succeeding time; that the first time was in the month of July 1776 when he was draughted and marched, as Ensign, in Captain John McDowell's company of Col. William Montgomery's Regiment of Pennsylvania militia, to Philadelphia, where he got his commission as Ensign aforesaid; thus from Philadelphia they crossed the river Delaware, and marched through Trenton in the state of New Jersey to a place called the "Blazing Star," which was on the sound between Jersey and Staten Island, where they lay, guarding the sound, and the term for which they had been draughted, which was two months, having expired; that at the expiration thereof they were required to make up a certain quota of men for the Flying Camp, which was accordingly done and their Colonel became Colonel in the Flying camp; but that for his part he was discharged, and returned home in September 1776.

That the second time he was called out, was in the month of November in the same year; that he was again draughted and marched as Ensign, in Captain John McDowell's company of Pennsylvania militia, then attached to a Regiment commanded by Col. Evan Evans, to Philadelphia, where they remained and served as city guard for the space of three or four weeks; that between Christmas and New Year, they were ordered to Trenton in New Jersey; that the day after they had reached that, the cannonade of Trenton took place, in which he was; that Genl Washington was there, and the same night took a circuitous route to Princeton, where he fought the British the next day, and defeated them; that British then retired to Brunswick and Washington to Morristown; there they lay at Morristown untill about the 1st February 1777, where they were discharged, having again served two months, the term for which they had been draughted.

That he was draughted a third time in the month of September 1777; that previous to this time, the Law had been altered and the were all classed, which changed their officers, each one being obliged to go with a particular class; that he was again draughted but in consequence of the arrangements effected by the new Law, he was thrown into Captain Ephraim Blackburn's company in Col. Bull's Regiment militia; that he again marched as Ensign of said company; that they marched from New London Township aforesaid to the Yellow Springs, thence across the river Schuylkill, eighteen miles above Germantown where they joined General Irwin's Division which lay near the army commanded by General Washington; that they remained there till about the 1st October, when they had the battle at Germantown in which battle he was; that after the battle they retreated to Skippack creek where they lay untill their term of service, which was two months, had expired when they were discharged, and he returned home in the month of November.

That he was draughted and marched a fourth time in May or June 1781, in Captain Robert Corry's company of Penn Militia to Philadelphia, and from there to Trenton, when they lay they were discharged which was one months and upwards; that he received one months pay when he was discharged; that he was still Ensign and served as such in Capt. Corry's Company. don't remember the Cols name

That the whole period of his service was seven months and upwards; that he has no documentary evidence of his service and that from the lapse of time, and change of residence, he knows of no person, whose testimony he can procure, who can testify to it except James Laughhead of Danville, Columbia county Pennsylvania that from bodily infirmity he is unable to attend the court of said county to make the above declaration.

1 I was born in New London Township, in the county of Chester, State of Pennsylvania, on the 9th day of September 1751 old style.

2 I have my age recorded in my family Bible.

3 I was living in New London Township, Chester county, Penna. I was first called into service, and during the whole of the revolutionary war & untill six years after it, when I moved to White Deer Township then Northumberland county) now Union, where I now live.

4 This I have answered in my general declaration

5. this I have also answered as far as my recollection serves me

6. I received a commission as Ensign, & served as such during the whole of my service, but I can not recollect positively by whom it was signed, but think, John Hancock. I have lost it by some means, but how I can not now say.

Dan Caldwell Esq., Andrew McLanahan Esq; Rev. Thomas Hood Thomas Howard, Matthew Laird and many others in my neighborhood can testify as to my character for veracity & their belief of my services as a soldier of the revolution.

I hereby relinquishes every claim whatever to a pension or annuity except the present, and declares that his name is not on the pension roll of the agency of any state

Lazarus Finney

Sworn & subscribed this day & year aforesaid.

Hugh Wilson

I do hereby certify that the above named Lazarus Finney can not from bodily infirmity attend the court of this county in order to make the above declaration in open court. — Hugh Wilson

January 17, 1938

Lazarus Finney
S. 13032
Robert Foster
S. 2220
RA-J/AWY

Mrs. Edward L. Evereitt
3034 Wisconsin Avenue, N.W.
Washington, D. C.

Dear Madam:

In complainoe with your request of recent date, you are furnished the Revolutionary War record of Lazarus Finney, pension, claim, S. 13032, and the Revolutionary War record of Robert Foster, pension claim, S. 2220.

Lazarus Finney - S. 13032

The data furnished herein concerning Lazarus Finney were obtained from papers on file in pension claim, S. 13032, based upon his service in the War of the Revolution.

Lazarus Finney was born September 9, 1751 (Old Style) in New London Township, Chester County, Pennsylvania. The names of his parents were not given. While residing in New London Township, Lazarus Finney served in the Pennsylvania militia as an Ensign, as follows:

In the summer of 1776, two months in Captain John McDowell's company, Colonel William Montgomery's regiment; from sometime in November 1776, two months in Captain John McDowell's company, Colonel Evan Evans' regiment and was in the battles of Trenton and Princeton; from sometime in September 1777, two months in Captain Ephraim Blackburn's company, Colonel Bull's regiment and was in the battle of Germantown; in the spring of 1781, one month in Captain Robert Correy's company.

Lazarus Finney, about six years after the close of the Revolution, moved from New London Township, Pennsylvania, to White Deer Township, Union County, Pennsylvania. He was allowed pension on his application executed June 8, 1833, then a resident of White Deer Township, Pennsylvania. The papers on file in this claim contain no reference to wife or children.

James Longhead or Laughead who in 1833 was then about sixty-eight years of age and the Postmaster at Danville, Pennsylvania, stated that the soldier, Lazarus Finney, was a relative of his mother; he did not give his mother's name.

In order to obtain the date of last payment of pension, name and address of person paid, and possibly the date of death of this pensioner, you should apply to the Comptroller General, General Accounting Office, Records Division, Washington, D. C. and furnish the following data:

Lazarus Finney, Certificate # 11914, issued July 12, 1833
Rate $70.00 per annum, Commenced March 4, 1831
Act of June 7, 1832
Pennsylvania Agency.

Robert Foster - S. 2220 - the data which follows relative to Robert Foster were obtained from papers on file in pension claim S. 2220

State of Pennsylvania } Ss
Columbia County }

On the eleventh day of June in the year one thousand eight hundred and thirty three, Personally
came before me the Subscriber one of the Justices
of the Peace in and for the County of Columbia
James Loughead Esquire Post Master of
Danville Penn^a in the county aforesaid aged
in the 69th year, who after being duly sworn accor-
-ding to Law, Deponant says that he seen Lazarus Kinney in city of Philadelphia on his
way, at Deponants fathers house, to Camp in the
Character of an Ensign. Deponant thinks in the
year 1776 or 1777. Deponents was then, thinks he
was then 12 or 13 years of age, the circumstance
that leads to the above that Lazarus Kinney
was a Relation of Deponants mother who was
then living, and that Mr Kinney was frequently
at Deponants fathers house. Deponant further
says that he remembers that Mr Kinney went
on the Second Service he thinks in fall of the
Same year of the first Service

Sworn and Subscribed } James Loughead
the day and year aforesaid }
before Me }
Rudolph Seckler J. P.

I do hereby certify that the above named deponant
James Loughead, is a person of credibility, and
that full confidence may be placed in his testimony
In testimony whereof I have hereunto set
my hand the 11th day of June, 1833.
Rudolph Seckler {Seal}

Declaration in order to obtain the benefit of the act of Congress passed June 7. 1832.

State of Pennsylvania }
Union county } ss.

On this eighth day of June, in the year of our Lord one thousand eight hundred and thirty three, personally appeared before the [illegible] Wilson, Esquire, one of the Judges of the court of common Pleas, in and for the county of Union aforesaid, in vacation, Lazarus Finney, a resident of [illegible] Township, in the county of Union and State of Pennsylvania, aged [illegible] years, who being first duly sworn according to law, doth, on his [illegible] make the following declaration, in order to obtain the benefit of the act [of] Congress passed June 7. 1832.

That he entered the service of the United States under the following [named] officers, and served as herein stated.

That he lived in New London Township, in the county of Chester, State of Pennsylvania, when he was called into service the first, as well as every succeeding time; that the first time was in the month of July 177[6] when he was draughted and marched, as Ensign, in Captain John McDowell's company, of Col. William Montgomery's Regiment of Pennsylvania militia, to Philadelphia, where he got his commission as Ensign aforesaid; that from Philadelphia they crossed the river Delaware, and marched through Trenton in the state of New Jersey, to a place called the "Blazing Star," which was on the [line] between Jersey and Staten Island, where they lay, guarding the sound, and the term for which they had been draughted, which was two months, had ~~[illegible]~~, that at the expiration thereof they were required to make up a certain quota of men for the Flying Camp, which was accordingly [done] and their Colonel became colonel in the Flying camp; but that for his part he was discharged, and returned home in September 1776.

That the second time he was called out, was in the month of November in the same year; that he was again draughted and marched, as Ensign, in the Captain John McDowell's company of Pennsylvania militia, then attached to a Fly[ing camp] commanded by Col. Evan Evans, to Philadelphia, where they remained and served as city guard for the space of three or four weeks; that between Christmas and New Year, they were ordered to Trenton in New Jersey; that the day after they had reached that, the command of Trenton took place, in which he was; that Genl Washington was there, and the same night took a circuitous route to Princeton, where he fought the British the next day, and defeated them; that British then retired ~~[illegible]~~ to Brunswick, and Washington to Morristown; there they lay at Morristown untill about the 1st February 1777, when they were discharged, having again served two months, the term for which they had been draughted.

That he was draughted a third time in the month of Sept 1777; that, previous to this time, the law had been altered, and the men were all classed, which changed their officers each one being obliged to go with a particular class; that he was again draughted, but in consequence of the arrangements affected by the new law, he was thrown in Captain Ephraim Blackburn company in Col. Bull's Regiment of militia: that he again marched on Ensign said company; that marched from New London Township aforesaid to the Yellow Springs, thence across the river Schuylkill, eighteen miles above Germantown where they joined General Irwin's Division which lay with the army commanded by General Washington; that they remained there till about the 1st October, when they had the battle at Germantown in which battle he was; that after the battle they retreated to Skippack creek where they lay until their term of service, which was two months, had expired, when they were discharged, and he returned home in the month of November.

That he was draughted and marched a fourth time in May or June 1781, in Captain Robert Corry's company of Penna Militia to Philadelphia, and from there to Trenton, where they lay [illegible] were discharged, which was two months and upwards; that he received one month pay when he was discharged; that he was still Ensign, and served as such in Capt. Corry's Company. [illegible]

That the whole period of his service was seven months and upwards; that he has no documentary evidence of his services and that from the lapse of time, and change of residence, he knows of no person, whose testimony he can procure, who can testify to it except James Laughhead of Danville, Columbia county Pennsylvania. that from bodily infirmity he is unable to attend the court of said county to make the above declaration.

1. I was born in New London Township, in the county of Chester, State of Pennsylvania, on the 9th day of September 1751 old style.

2. I have my age recorded in my family Bible.

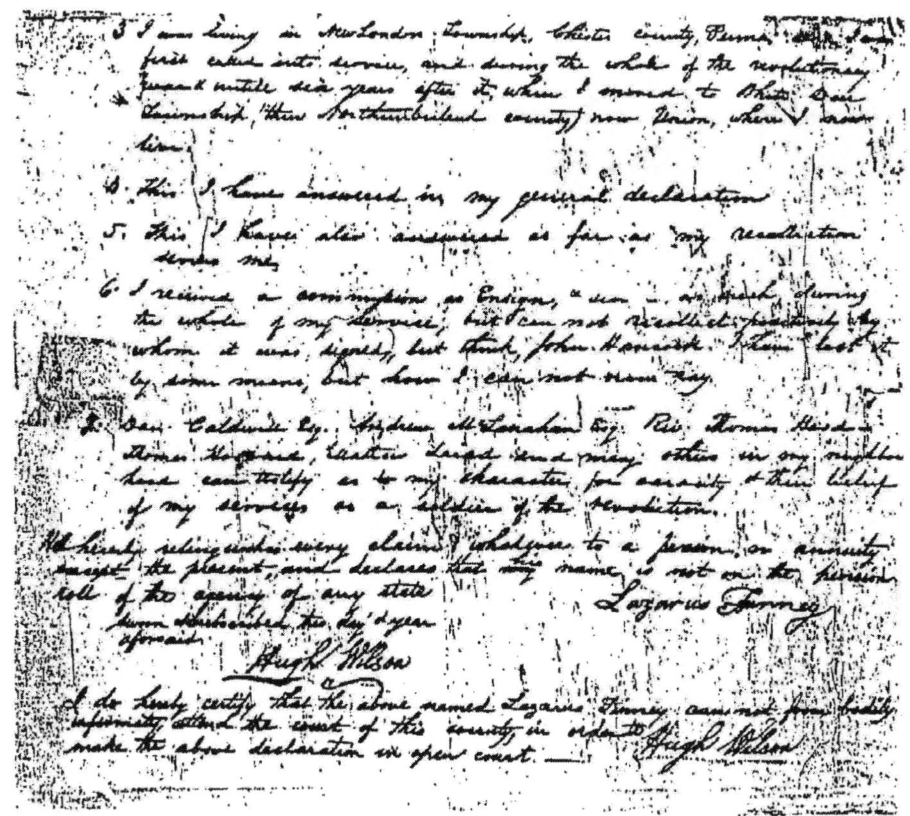

3 I am living in New London Township, Chester county, Penna [illegible] I was first called into service, and during the whole of the revolutionary [illegible] until six years after it, when I moved to White Deer Township, then Northumberland county, now Union, where I now live.

4. This I have answered in my general declaration

5. This I have also answered as far as my recollection serves me.

6. I received a commission as Ensign, [illegible] during the whole of my service, but I can not recollect [illegible] by whom it was signed, but think, John Hancock. I have lost it by some means, but how I can not now say.

7. [illegible] Caldwell Esq. Andrew McLanahan Esq. Rev. Thomas Hood, Thomas [illegible], [illegible] and many others in my neighborhood can testify as to my character for veracity & their belief of my services as a soldier of the revolution.

He hereby relinquishes every claim whatever to a pension or annuity except the present, and declares that his name is not on the pension roll of the agency of any state

Sworn & subscribed the day & year aforesaid.

Hugh Wilson

Lazarus Finney

I do hereby certify that the above named Lazarus Finney cannot from bodily infirmity attend the court of this county in order to make the above declaration in open court. — Hugh Wilson

N: 11,914

Pennsylvania

Lazarus Finney

of Union in the State of Penna.

who was an Ensign in the company commanded by Captain McDowell of the Regt. commanded by Col. Evans in the Penna. Militia for 7 months

Inscribed on the Roll of Pennsylvania at the rate of 70 Dollars —— Cents per annum, to commence on the 4th day of March, 1831.

Certificate of Pension issued the 12 day of July 1833 and sent to Hon. L. Dewart, Sunbury Pa.

Arrears to the 4th of March 1833 140.00

Semi-anl. allowance ending 4 Sep. 1833 35.00

$175.00

Revolutionary Claim, Act June 7, 1832.

Recorded by D. Brown Clerk

Book E. Vol. 5 Page 19,

Date of death not given.

viii. Lazarus Finney, s/o Robert & Dorothea - b. Ireland - d. 1740 Chester Co., Pa - kept tavern at New London Crossroad, Pa., buried Thunder Hill - m. Catherine SYMONTON - she m. [2] John FREW

a. Robert Finney - b. 1727 New London, Pa - 29 Oct 1822 Northumberland Co., Pa [now part of Union Co.] - m. Sep 1746 Diana SPENCER who died 5 Aug 1815

1. Lazarus Finney - b. 9 Sep 1751 New London, Pa. - d. 3 Oct 1833 m. Elizabeth FULTON, m [2] Elizabeth OCHELTREE b. 5 Dec 1761 - 18 Feb 1826. To Union Co., Pa., White Deer Twp. @ 1787, died there.

A. John Finney - b. 27 Feb 1783 - d. 27 Mar 1784
B. Robert Finney - b. 28 Oct 1784 - d. 28 Nov 1786
C. Samuel Finney - b. 4 Jan 1787 - 25 Mar 1854 - m. 15 Feb 1827 Susan BAUSH who died 22 Sep 1866

[1] David A. Finney - 27 Aug 1834 - 16 Dec 1876 - m. 16 May 1861 Margaretta GERRINGER

[a] Nora Finney - b. 12 May 1867 - m. Lloyd P. STERNER

[2] James Finney - m. Elizabeth JOHNSON

[a] James Robert Finney - b. 1847 - m.1865 Anne M. ELINGAM b. 1848

i. May Scott Finney - m. Frank E. MARCY

[3] Mary Jane Finney - b. 29 Sep 1827 - 26 Oct 1870 - m. Ephraim HILLARD
[4] John L. Finney - b. 2 Feb 1829 - d. 10 Aug 1849, unmarried
[5] Elizabeth Finney - b. 6 Feb 1831 - 12 Jan 1856 - m. 10 Feb 1853 George W. NICELY b. 12 Feb 1828
[6] William Finney - b. 19 Nov 1832
[7] Adam Baush Finney - 23 July 1836 - m. Margaret I. BURROWS

[a] Samuel Finney - 20 Oct 1861 - 15 July 1864
[b] Grace Burrows Finney - 11 July 1865 Jersey Shore, Pa.
[c] Horace B. Finney - 14 Aug 1867

[8] Sarah Finney - 10 Jan 1839 - m. 23 Aug 1866 John GILBERT
[9] James Fulton Finney - 10 Jan 1841 - 23 May 1877
[10] Samuel Finney - 19 Nov 1843 - d. 1868
[11] George Carey Finney - 22 Mar 1847 - d. 31 May 1913 Laramire, Wyo. - m. Caroline R. HAYES - 17 June 1849 - d. 10 Feb 1916

[a] Dr. Harry Silby Finney - 4 Apr 1876 Des Moines - m. Helen M.

D. Mary Finney - b. 20 Oct 1790 - d. 1 Nov 1866
E. Nancy Finney - b. 15 June 1792 - d. 14 Aug 1866
F. Robert I. Finney - b. 25 June 1794 - 8 Sep 1870 - m. 1820 Elnor GRAHAM - b. 1 Apr 1799 - 1 Sep 1881 Warrior Run, Northumberland Co., Pa., d/o Henry & Elizabeth [Ferguson] Graham

[1] Eliza Finney - 1 Nov 1821 - 18 Dec 1880 m. 13 May 1845 Oliver Perry PEIPER who died 1847
[2] Jane Graham Finney - 20 Aug 1827 - m. 22 Apr 1851 James R. CALDWELL b. 10 Jan 1822 - lvd Laurenville, NJ
[3] Spencer I. Finney - b. 24 Sep 1825 - 9 Dec 1885 Rye, NY - m. 27 Apr 1853 Isabella R. MATTHEWS b. 26 Sep 1829 - 26 Apr 1893 - in 1881 he had the deed & Patent for Thunder Hill estate and other family papers

[a] Eleanor C. Finney - b. 24 Apr 1854
[b] William M. Finney - b. 17 Nov 1855
[c] Isabelle R. Finney - b. 15 Oct 1857 - m. Phillip A. P. LLOYD
[d] Mary M. Finney - b. 7 Apr 1859 - d. 8 May 1861
[e] Robert S. Finney - 8 May 1861 - m. 24 Feb 1888 Carrie Gold SCHMIDT b. 22 Aug 1866
[f] Henry M. Finney - b. 13 Dec 1862 - d. 19 July 1863
[g] Elizabeth Finney - b. 20 Dec 1865
[h] Jane Finney - b. 9 Aug 1867 - 27 Sep 1879
[i] James Finney - 25 Oct 1868 - 1 Apr 1869
[j] Gertrude Finney - b. 8 Apr 1870 - 1 Mar 1884
[k] John Finney - b. 30 Sep 1872 - 27 July 1873

[4] Mary Agnes Finney, d/o Robert & Elenor - died 14 Dec 1870 - m. 21 May 1854 John Edward HACKENBURG, lawyer in Philadelphia

[5] Henry Graham Finney - b. 10 Sep 1830 - 1910 Pa - m. 9 June 1863 Sallie Jane GARDNER b. 25 Aug 1839

[a] Bertha G. Finney - b. 18 Apr 1864 - 1932 m. 5 Jan 1887 William Lyon LOWRE
[b] William Graham Finney - b. 21 Sep 1867
[c] Florence G. Finney - b. 2 July 1872
[d] Eleanor May Finney - b. 11 Mar 1874

[6] Eleanor G. Finney - b. 9 Nov 1833 - m. 22 Oct 1856 William MATTHEWS

[7] Hadessa Finney - 31 Mar 1837 - lvd. Winchester, Va. - m. 22 July 1885 Samuel P. HERRON

[8] Robert Bines Finney - b. 16 July 1839, unmarried, lvd. Winchester, VA

G. Lazarus J. Finney, s/o Lazarus & Elizabeth - b. 14 May 1797 - 3 Sep 1807

H. John S. Finney - b. 5 Nov 1799 - 3 July 1877 m. Jan 1829 Ellen MOORE b. 13 Feb 1801 - d. Jan 1835

[1] Matilda J. Finney - b. Feb 1831 - 23 May 1896 m. 21 Nov 1867 Samuel TEAS b. 2 Sep 1811 - d. 1887
[2] Elizabeth O. Finney - b. 7 May 1833 - 1888 - m. William CLINGAN b. 18 June 1826

I. James Finney - 25 June 1801 - d. 11 Dec 1876 Milton, Pa - m. 1824 Elizabeth JOHNSON who died 1872

[1] Elizabeth Finney - b. 16 June 1827 - m. 15 Jan 1845 John S. LAWSON b.,20 Nov 1819 - d. 1 Apr 1891
[2] Mary M. Finney - b. 13 June 1829 - unmarried
[3] Margaret S. Finney - 29 Aug 1831 - m.Jan 1869 Hunter HAYNES
[4] Spencer L. Finney - b. 16 Feb 1834 - m. 8 Sep 1856 Sarah WERTMAN - b. 30 Sep 1838
[5] Eleanor Finney - 3 Apr 1836 - m. 26 Apr 1866 Berryhill YOUNG
[6] Nancy Jane Finney - m.14 Feb 1884 James LAWSON - b. 14 Nov 1823
[7] James Robert Finney - b. 1847 - m. 30 Nov 1865 Anna Mary CLINGAN - b. 15 July 1838 - at one time lvd. Lawrence, KS

[a] Edward Clingan Finney - 12 Nov 1869 m. 23 Aug 1892 Jean STEELE

i. Bernice J. Finney - m. SCOGEN
ii. Jean Finney
iii. Edith Finney - m. RYLAND
iv. Elizabeth Finney

[b] Isaac H. Finney
[c] Mary Scott Finney - m. 25 Dec 1901 Ks to Frank Earl MARCY

J. Elizabeth Finney - b. 8 Aug 1803 - 25 July 1863 - m. James REZNER b. 29 Nov 1797 - d. 31 May 1836

[1] Sarah A. Rezner - m. Dr. Jacob SCHUYLAR

b. John Finney, s/o Lazarus & Catherine - b. 1730 Chester Co., Pa. - d. 5 July 1783 New Castle, Del. - m. 9 Jan 1758 Ruth LLOYD, d/o Joseph. Married in Old Swedes Holy Trinity Church, Wilmington, Del., built 1698. Buried church cemetery.

1. James Finney b. 1768 - to Gibson Co., IND. after 1800 - m [1] Mary COGHORN, m [2] 21 Dec 1837 in Ind. to Sarah Jean MAKEMSON

A. Polly Ann Finney - b. 19 Oct 1803
B. Jane Finney - b. 27 Nov 1805
C. Thomas M. Finney - b. Jan 1808
D. James W. Finney - b.19 Apr 1809
E. Joseph Alexander Finney - b. 2 Feb 1813
F. John Kell Finney - 12 Apr 1815 - m. Laura MORGAN

[1] Nancy J. Finney - m. Robert Milton MUNFORD b. 21 Sep 1832 - 2 Feb 1902 Ind
[2] Sallie Finney - m. John Riley ERVIN
[3] Mattie Finney - m. Robert McCLERKIN
[4] Minerva Finney - m. George SHULL

CONTROVERSY!

This contains a **correction to information about John and Robert Finney** on pages 66 and 67.

From Lynn Finney Stuter

John Finney did not die in 1783 and he's not buried at Old Swedes. This came out of that book, Finney/Phinney Family in America and it's incorrect.

> b. John Finney, s/o Lazarus & Catherine - b. 1730 Chester CO., Pa. - d. 5 July 1783 New Castle, Del. - m. 9 Jan 1758 Ruth LLOYD, d/o Joseph. Married in Old Swedes Holy Trinity Church, Wilmington, Del., built 1698. Buried church cemetery.

See the death date listed here? I contacted Old Swedes Holy Trinity Church, asked if there was a John Finney buried there. Their response was "there is no record of John Finney's burial in the cemetery of Holy Trinity (Old Swedes) Church. But that does not mean he is not buried here. Our records begin in 1713, but very few burials were recorded until the 1750 period, and there are large gaps between 1765 and 1815. Most of our early burial records were checked but we found no mention of John Finney and his wife Ruth Lloyd. It is probable they were just married at the church, as many people were and were not members."

Her genealogy also lists (page **67**) Robert Finney, born 1783, as the son of Joseph and Ruth. He was not. He was the son of Ann Finney. He took his mother's name. I have the will of Joseph Finney and it clearly states that Robert is his grandson, son of his daughter, Ann.

Page 67 states the second child of John Finney and Ruth Lloyd was:

> Robert Finney, s/o John & Ruth - b. 8 Dec 1783 Grayson CO., Va. - d. 10 July 1866 West Milton, Miami CO., Ch - m. Wilkes CO;, NC 7 Apr 1805 Hannah HICKMAN b. 19 June 1785 - 2 Jan 1869 - lvd. Wilkes CO., NC 1810, in Miami CO, Ch. in 1850. In War of 1812 with Kentucky Militia

Robert Finney, in fact, was the son of Ann Finney. These two entries come straight out of that book Finney/Phinney Families in America by Howard Finney. Where they came up with this, I have no clue. But every time I request proof of this, I invariably get referred to that book.

These misrepresentations have been repeated so often that they have been accepted as fact. I find these in practically every genealogy done of my (Finney) family, and the source is *Finney/Phinney Family in America.*

From Cousette Copeland

PLEASE SEE "CONTROVERSY, SCIENCE, AND REVELATION" IN PART TWO OF THIS BOOK FOR EVIDENCE THAT CONTRADICTS PREVIOUSLY PUBLISHED FINNEY GENEALOGIES AND ACCEPTED "FACTS!"

Marth Finney, Zanesville, OH

I could not find her in my research but I did find this photo online. Perhaps it will be useful to a Finney researcher.

[a] Mary Finney - b. 11 July 1865 Millersburg, Oh - m. Newton DICKINSON - b. 3 May 1865 Ill
[b] Christiana Finney - b. 6 May 1867 Holmes Co., Oh - m. John C. MADDEN - b. 20 July 1867
[c] Hallie Finney - b. 25 May 1870 Tecumseh, KS - m. Robert B. FERGUSON - b. 9 Apr 1859
[d] John Edgar Finney - b. 14 Feb 1872 Paxico, Ks - 1951 - m. Olive DICKINSON - 28 July 1872 Ill - 20 June 1958

i. Whitham D. Finney - b. 17 Sep 1898 Wabaunsee Co, Ks - m. Irma WRAY

a. Whitham Wray Finney

ii. William F. Finney - b. 19 Feb 1901 - m. Dorothy CLIBORNE

a. William C. Finney b. 1929 Okla
b. James H. Finney - b. 9 Jan 1935

[e] William Albert Finney - b. 5 Mar 1874 Wabaunsee Co, Ks - drowned 25 June 1884
[f] Thomas Arthur Finney - b. 30 Dec 1878
[g] James Garfield Finney - b. 30 Dec 1879
[h] Susan Albertine Finney - b. 17 Nov 1881
[i] Jessie Elizabeth Finney - b. 11 Aug 1884
[j] Louise Rebecca Finney - b. 18 Jan 1887
[k] Horace David Finney - 10 Aug 1890 - d. 31 July 1892

[6] Rebecca Finney, d/o John French - b. 9 July 1842 Oh - d. 25 Dec 1874
[7] George Gordon Finney - b. 25 Apr 1845 Oh - m. Mary Jane ARMSTRONG

[a] Walter Scott Finney - m. Anna McGILLWOOD

i. Cecil Gordon Finney - b. 25 Nov 1907 Okla City - m. Gladys BOSWELL

a. Della Lee Finney - b. 5 Mar 1928 Okla City
b. Sylvia M. Finney - b. 22 Sep 1933

ii. Alice V. Finney - b. 3 Feb 1910

[b] Carrydon Finney
[c] Alice Finney
[d] Ollie Olive Finney
[e] Lillian Finney
[f] Lulu Finney

[8] William Finney - b. 3 Apr 1832 - d. 1 Sep 1836

B. David Thompson Finney, s/o David Thompson - 1 27 Nov 1799 Del - 13 Sep 1881 m. 10 Jan 1827 Hannah BUTLER b. 1 Feb 1804 Oh - 30 July 1884 - lvd. Holmes Co., Oh. 1850

[1] Sarah Finney - b. 17 Dec 1828 Oh - m. 22 Dec 1851 REv. Milton W. BROWN
[2] John Finney - b. 10 Aug 1830 - d. 11 Sep 1839
[3] Mary Finney - b. 19 Sep 1832 - d. 8 Dec 1836
[4] James McKenna Finney - b. 20 Jan 1834 Oh - m. Mary E. PHILLIPS b. 1848

[a] Louis C. Finney - b. 20 Aug 1871
[b] Bessie Finney - b. 29 Aug 1875
[c] Bertie Finney - b. 12 June 1882

[5] Rebecca Finney - b. 2 Apr 1837 - 12 Sep 1839
[6] Ann Dora Finney - b. 13 Feb 1840 Oh - m [1] 24 Feb 1864 Ephraim CRIST - died 24 Oct 1873, m [2] William HAGUE
[7] Jane Finney - b. 4 July 1842 Oh - m. 11 Mar 1864 Milton F. LAW
[8] Lucretia Finney - 1 Jan 1844 Holmes Co., Oh - m. 13 Oct 1870 William McCAUGHEY

SUSPENDED BOUNTY LAND CLAIM RE-EXAMINED.

No. 177581 }
34790 }

Treasury Department,
THIRD AUDITOR'S OFFICE,
August 1. 1856.

Robert Linney, a Private served in Captain Joseph McClosky's Company Kentucky Militia from the 17 August 1812 (the day) to the 28 Dec 1812, when Co was discharged.

R. Graham
for Third Auditor.

COMMISSIONER OF PENSIONS,
Department of the Interior.

Schrimer

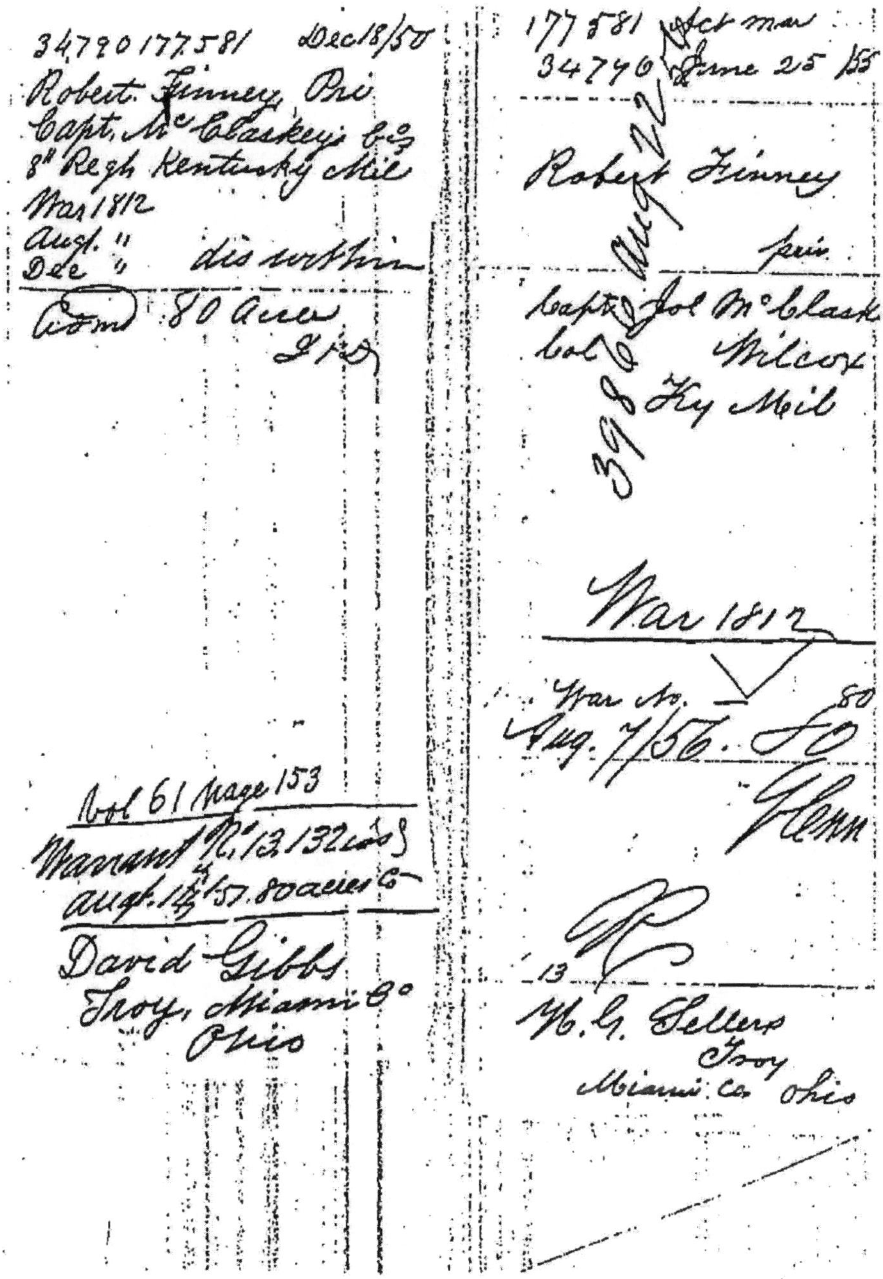

34790 177581 Dec 18/50
Robert Finney Pri
Capt. McClaskey's Co
8th Regt Kentucky Mil
War 1812
Aug. "
Dec " dis within
Adm 80 Acre
I.R.D.

Vol 61 Page 153
Warrant No 13132 cos
Aug. 14/57. 80 acres Co
David Gibbs
Troy, Miami Co
Ohio

177581 Act mar
34790 June 25 /55
Aug 22
Robert Finney
pri
Capt Jol McClask
Col Milcox
398 8 Ky Mil

War 1812

War No. 80
Aug. 7/56. SO
Glenn

R
13
M. G. Sellers
Troy
Miami Co Ohio

Troy Miami County Ohio 20th Jan 1855

Sir

Enclosed please find application of Robert Finney for additional bounty land.

Respectfully yours
H G Sellers

The State of Ohio
County of Miami ss } On this twelfth day of December A.D. One thousand eight hundred and fifty personally appeared before me a Notary Public within and for the County and State aforesaid Robert Finney aged Sixty Seven years a resident of Union Township Miami County Ohio, who being duly sworn according to law, declares, that he is the identical Robert Finney who was a private soldier in the Company commanded by Captain Joseph McClaskey in the 8th Regiment of Kentucky Militia commanded by Col. George Millory in the War with Great Britain declared by the United States on the 18th day of June 1812; that he was drafted at in Nelson County in the State of Kentucky (near Bairdstown) on or about the 17th day of August 1812, for the term of Six months, and continued in actual service in said war for the term of four months seven days - and was honorably discharged at Louisville in the State (Bairdstown aforesaid) on the 26th day of December AD 1812 as will appear by his original certificate of discharge herewith presented or by the muster rolls of said company.

He makes this declaration for the purpose of obtaining the bounty land to which he may be entitled under the "act granting bounty land to certain officers and soldiers who have been engaged in the military service of the United States" passed September 28th 1850

Robert Finney

Sworn to and Subscribed before me the day and year above written
And I hereby certify that I believe the said Robert Finney to be
the identical man who served as aforesaid, and that he is of the age
above stated

In testimony whereof I have hereunto set my
hand and Notarial Seal at Troy on the day
and year first above written
David Gibbs
Notary Public

The State of Ohio
Miami County ss } I John G. Telford Clerk of the
Court of Common Pleas for said County
hereby Certify that David Gibbs, before whom the foregoing Declaration was made was at the date thereof and
now is an Acting Notary Public of said County duly commissioned and qualified, and authorized by the Laws of
said State of Ohio to administer oaths for general purposes
and that the signature thereto is genuine

In testimony whereof I have hereunto
subscribed my name and affixed
the seal of said Court at Troy
5th day of December A.D. 18[illegible]
J. G. Telford Clerk
Per R. Gibbs Dept Clerk

State of Ohio }
County of Miami } ss.

On this 20th day of June AD One thousand Eight hundred and fifty-five personally appeared before me a Justice of the Peace within and for said County & State aforesaid Robert Finney aged Seventy One years a Resident of Miami County in the State of Ohio who being duly sworn according to law, declares that he is the identical Robert Finney who was a private in the Company Comm=anded by Captain Joseph McClasky in the Regiment of Kentucky Militia Commanded by Col. Wilcox in the war with Great Britain, declared by the United States on the 18th day of June, 1812 for the term of Six Months and Continued in actual service in said war for fourteen days and more; that he has hereto=fore made application for bounty land, under the act of Sept 28, 1850 and received a land warrant for Eighty acres the No of which he does not now remember and which he has since legally disposed of and Cannot now return. His original Certificate of discharge he sent to department at Washington on his former application

He makes this declaration for the purpose of obtaining the additional bounty land to which he may be entitled under the act approved the 3d day of March, 1855. He also declares that he has never applied for nor received, under this nor any other act of Congress, any bounty land warrant except the one above mentioned

Robert Finney

We Menalcus Crew and W. H. Ross Residents of Miami County in the State of Ohio upon our oaths declare that the foregoing declaration was signed and acknowledged by Robert Finney in our presence and that we believe from the appearance and statements of the applicant that he is the identical person he represents himself to be.

W. H. Ross

Menalcus Crew

The foregoing declaration and affidavit were sworn to and subscribed before me on the day and year above written, and I certify that I know the affiants to be credible persons, that the claimant is the person he represents himself to be and that I have no interest in this claim.

H. J. Pettit J.P.

The State of Ohio }
Miami County ss }

I, B. W. Leavell Clerk of the Court of Common Pleas within and for said County do hereby certify that H. J. Pettit Esqr, before whom the foregoing declaration and affidavits were made was on the 20th day of June AD 1855 an acting Justice of the Peace within and for the County aforesaid duly commissioned and qualified; and that I have no interest in the above claim.

In testimony whereof I have hereunto set my hand and affixed the seal of said Court at Troy this 20th day of June AD 1855

B. W. Leavell Clerk

By C. V. Rogers Deputy

F | 8 (Wilcox's) | Ky. Militia.

Robert Finney

Pvt., Capt. Joseph McClaskey's Co. of Infantry, 8 Reg't Kentucky Detached Militia.

(War of 1812.)

Appears on

Company Pay Roll

for Aug 17 to Dec 28, 1812.

Roll dated not dated, 181

Commencement of service, Aug 17, 1812.

Expiration of service, Dec 30, 1812.

Term of service charged, 4 months, 16 days.

Pay per month, 6.66 dollars, ... cents.

Amount of pay, 20 dollars, 19 cents.

Remark: Commissioned officers drew one month's pay, Sergeants sixteen dollars, Corporals twelve dollars and Privates ten dollars, each in advance.

Remarks:

Patterson, Copyist.

F | 8 (Wilcox's) | Ky. Militia.

Robert Finney

Pvt., Captain Joseph McClaskey's Co., 8 Reg't Kentucky Detached Mil.

(War of 1812.)

Appears on

Company Muster Roll

for Aug 17 to Dec 28, 1812.

Roll dated Louisville Ky

Dec 28, 1812.

Commencement of service, Aug 17, 1812.

Expiration of service, Dec 27, 1812.

Distance from place of residence to place of rendezvous, 30 miles.

Distance from place of discharge to place of residence, 30 miles.

Present or absent, Present

Remarks:

Patterson, Copyist.

I DO CERTIFY that the bearer hereof Robert Finney Soldier in a company of *Kentucky Militia* under my command having been in the service of the United States under a requisition of the Secretary of War, [illegible] to his Excellency the Governor of Kentucky, authorised by an act of Congress [bearing] date the 10th day of April, 1812, and that the said Finney [enter]ed the service on the 17 day of august 1812, and by virtue of an order from *Major General* SAMUEL HOPKINS, bearing date the 10th day of December, 1812, is hereby discharged. Joseph McClaskey Capt

28 day of Decr 1812 Jo. Wilcox Colo Comdt 8 Regt Ky

5. Joseph Finney, s/o John & Ruth - b. 2 Apr 1765 New Castle, Del - d. 22 Mar 1837 Parke Co., Ind. Buried Rawlins Cemetery, e. of Annapolis, Ind. M [1] 13 Dec 1783 Orange Co., N.C. Rachel BARKLEY who died 1795 Surry Co., N.C. - m [2] @ 1800 Ann KESSTER [or Rector?] b. 9 Jan 1774 NC - 15 Mar 1853 Park Co., Ind., d/o John

A. Joseph Finney - b. 18 Sep 1784 Orange Co., NC - d. 8 Mar 1867 Parke Co., Ind. m. 10 Sep 1805 Green Co., Tenn. Mary [Polly] LONG b. 2 Apr 1786 Grayson Co., Va. - 27 Sep 1872 Parke Co. He served in War of 1812 - lvd. Lawrence Co., Ind. 1817 - to Parke Co. in 1826

[1] Robert Finney - 23 Aug 1806 Green Co., Tenn - 9 Mar 1861 Parke Co. He died Parke Co. but was later buried at Tuscola, Douglas Co., Ill - m. 10 Mar 1835 Malinda HUNT b. 20 Sep 1815 Guilford Co., NC - d. 16 Oct 1896 d/o Zimri & Mary [Dicks] Hunt

[a] Elijah Cook Finney - b. 4 Apr 1836 Parke Co., Ind. - d. 24 Jan 1917 Douglas Co., Ill. * Unmarried. Held extensive land holdings, a grain dealer and a merchant. Elijah signed the autograph book of DANIEL WEBSTER FINNEY in the year 1894, lived Tuscola, Ill.

[b] Daniel William Finney - b. 8 Oct 1837 Parke Co - 17 June 1905 Vermillion Co., Ind - m. Gilla HUFFMAN - b. 1840 Ind, d/o Lawson

i. Cora E. Finney
ii. Alice M. Finney
iii. Annis Finney
iv. William P. Finney
v. Maude Finney
vi. Edgar F. Finney - died age 4 years

[c] David Wesley Finney - b. 22 Aug 1839 Parke Co, Ind - 1 Nov 1916 in Emporia, KS - m. 1869 Helen Hester McCONNELL b. 1845 - d. 1931, d/o Hiram. Enlisted 1862 Pvt. 85th Indiana Volunteer Inf. - discharged June 1865. Attended Waveland Collegiate Institute, Parke Co., Ind. To Neosho Falls, Woodson Co., Ks. 1866 in a wagon with a large American flag painted on the side. Opened a general store, operated a mill, invested in farmland. Served many terms in Kansas Senate and Legislature - two terms as Lt. Governor 1881 - 1886. During period Finney Co., Ks. was named for him by an act of legislature. He served as State Railroad Commissioner. After being Governor he retired from public office.

i. Warren Wesley Finney - b. 3 Apr 1874 Woodson Co., Ks - d. 5 June 1935, a suicide as result of bank scandal - m. 1897 to Mabel TUCKER, d/o Edwin who died Dec 1947 California. In 1896 he was elected to the Kansas House. Previous to this he attended Washburn College in Topeka - then joined his father in the milling business. He organized the Neosho Falls Telephone Co., bought another in Emporia, then more, until he owned 20 and was the largest independent telephone owner in Kansas in the 1920's. He sold all of them in 1930 to a Salina group who went bankrupt. In 1905 he moved to Emporia. About 1920 he went into banking business and in 1921 built an English Tudor style 25-room mansion in Emporia. He was a close friend of William Allen White, editor and Alfred Landon, Governor of Kansas. [See accompanying article.]

a. Ronald Tucker Finney - b. 18 Sep 1898 Woodson Co - d. 1 Oct 1961 Florida - graduated from Cornell University 1921, became a banker Neosho Falls, Ks - m. 21 Apr 1923 Winifred WIGGAM b. 1900. About 1927 he went to work for Kansas City Life Insurance and was highly successful, moved to Emporia about 1930.

i. Daughter b. 1926 - no information
ii. Son - b. 1929 - No information

His wife and children moved to California while he was in prison. He was 35 years old when he entered prison and 46 when he was released on 18 Feb 1945. He also went to California and he and his wife were divorced in 1948. He m [2] Selma ? and in 1950's bought a home in Florida.

b. Mary Jane Finney - b. 1914 - no information

Did the Finneys worship with the Quakers or United Brethren?

It was not unusual for Quakers to convert to another religion, to formally or informally distance themselves from the Society of Friends, or to be disowned by their Friends Meeting.

Wesley Finney's parents (Joseph and Mary Polly Long) were Quakers, but Wesley was United Brethren. He married Mary Matilda Hinshaw, who was also United Brethren. Mary's parents were Jesse Hinshaw and Hannah Moon.

On 7-4-1818 at Cane Creek Monthly Meeting in Chatham County, North Carolina, "Jesse Finney Jr." was disowned for being "married out of unity (to first cousin)". On 10-3-1818, "Hannah Hinshaw" was also similarly disowned for marrying a first cousin. Hannah was the daughter of Ruth (Hinshaw) Moon, Jesse's Aunt (sister of Jesse's father, Jesse), so they were indeed first cousins.[1]

Quaker Roots

"The Religious Society of Friends is a movement that began in England in the 17th century. Members of this movement are informally known as *Quakers*, a word that means, "To tremble in the way of the Lord."

Persecution in the New World

Quakers faced persecution in Puritan Massachusetts. In 1656 Mary Fisher and Ann Austin began preaching in Boston. They were considered heretics because of their insistence on individual obedience to the Inner Light. They were imprisoned and banished by the Massachusetts Bay Colony. Their books were burned, and most of their property was confiscated. They were imprisoned in terrible conditions, then deported.

Some Quakers in New England were only imprisoned or banished. A few were also whipped or branded. Christopher Holder, for example, had his ear cut off. A few were executed by the Puritan leaders, usually for ignoring and defying orders of banishment. Mary Dyer was thus executed in 1660.[2]

Quakers and United Brethren

Quakers and United Brethren had different roots, but followed similar principles, such as pacifism and anti-slavery.

---

[1] http://familytreemaker.genealogy.com/users/o/k/a/Joey-Okamoto/WEBSITE-0001/UHP-0044.html

[2] http://en.wikipedia.org/wiki/History_of_the_Religious_Society_of_Friends

Top of page 75.

5. Joseph Finney + Rachel Barkley

A. Joseph Finney + Mary Polly Long

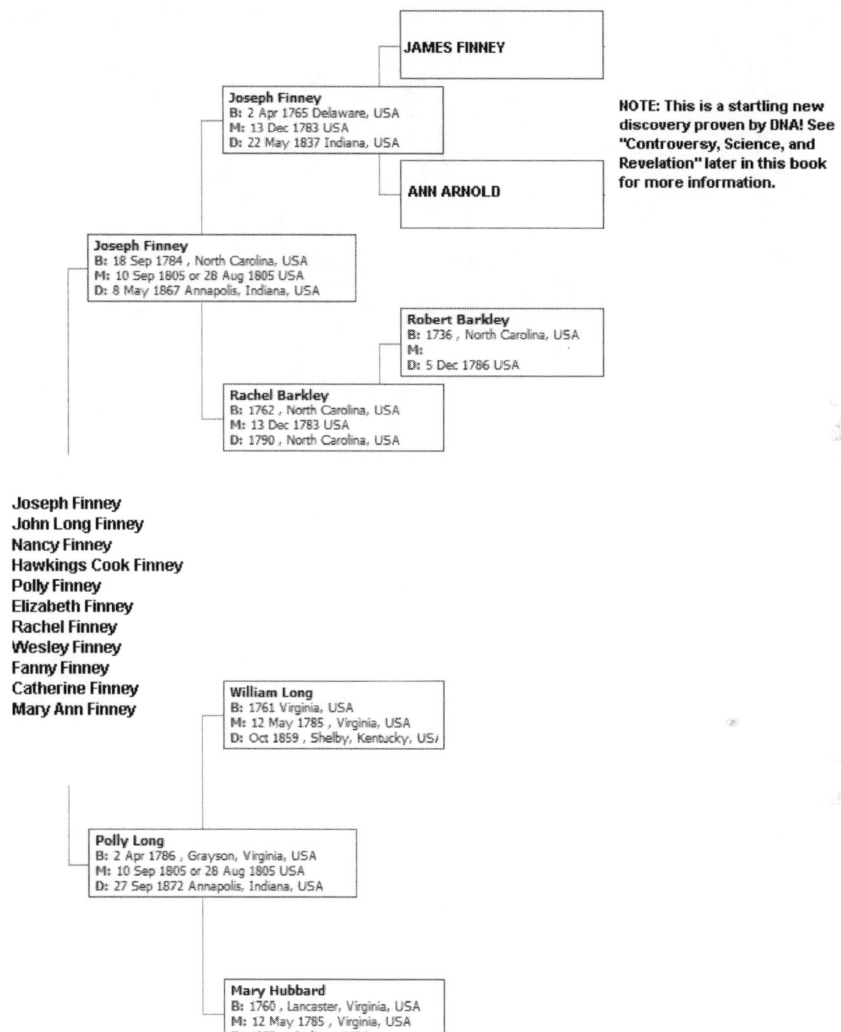

Family tree for Joseph and Mary Polly (Long) Finney and their children

Joseph and Mary Polly (Long) Finney tintype photos

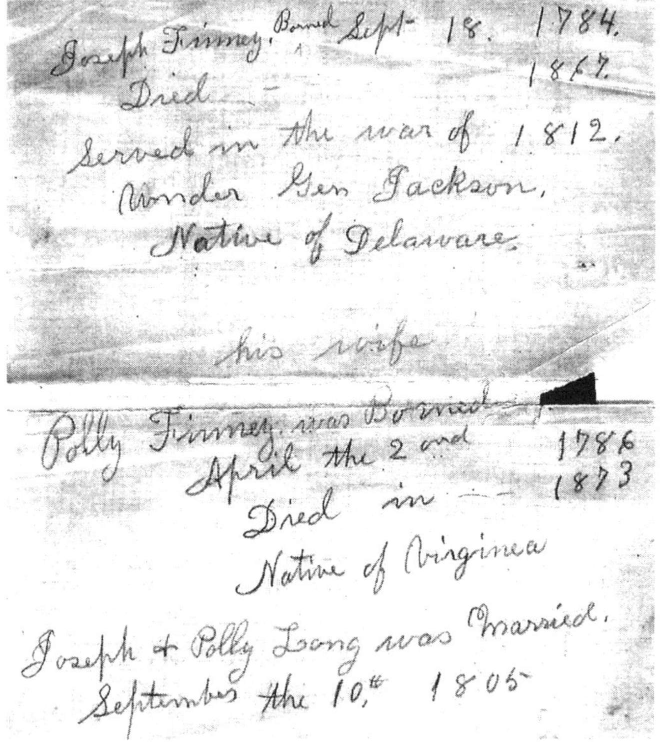

Joseph Finney Borned Sept 18. 1784.
Died — 1867.
Served in the war of 1812.
Under Gen Jackson.
Native of Delaware.

his wife

Polly Finney was Borned
April the 2nd 1786
Died in — 1873
Native of Virginea

Joseph + Polly Long was Married.
September the 10th 1805

Info on the back of the tintypes that are kept by George Copeland

Mary Polly Long was a Cherokee Indian. Her parents died in the Trail of Tears March. She was adopted by Quakers William and Mary (Hubbard) Long, who had no other children. She married Joseph Finney, who was also a Quaker.

Home of Joseph and Mary Polly (Long) Finney in Parke County, Indiana

DIED.—At the residence of Wesley Finney, near Annapolis, on Friday, the 27th ult., Mrs. Polly Finney; aged 87 years, 5 months and 25 days.

Mary Polly (Long) Finney obituary – died 27 Sept. 1872

Middle of page 75.

c. David Wesley Finney

From Lynn M. Stuter

David Wesley Finney who was the brother of my g-grandfather, Zimri Dix Finney. David Wesley also fought in the Civil War (Union Army) as did a first cousin, Josiah Ephlin. They were all in the same company; all spent time in Libby Prison. They all participated in Sherman's March to the Sea. David Wesley went on to become the Lt Gov of Kansas. Finney County, Kansas is name after him. (Recently, a Joan Finney was the governor of Kansas. I don't know if she descends from David Wesley or belongs to one of the other Finney lineages.)

***

i. Warren Wesley Finney

a. Robert Tucker Finney

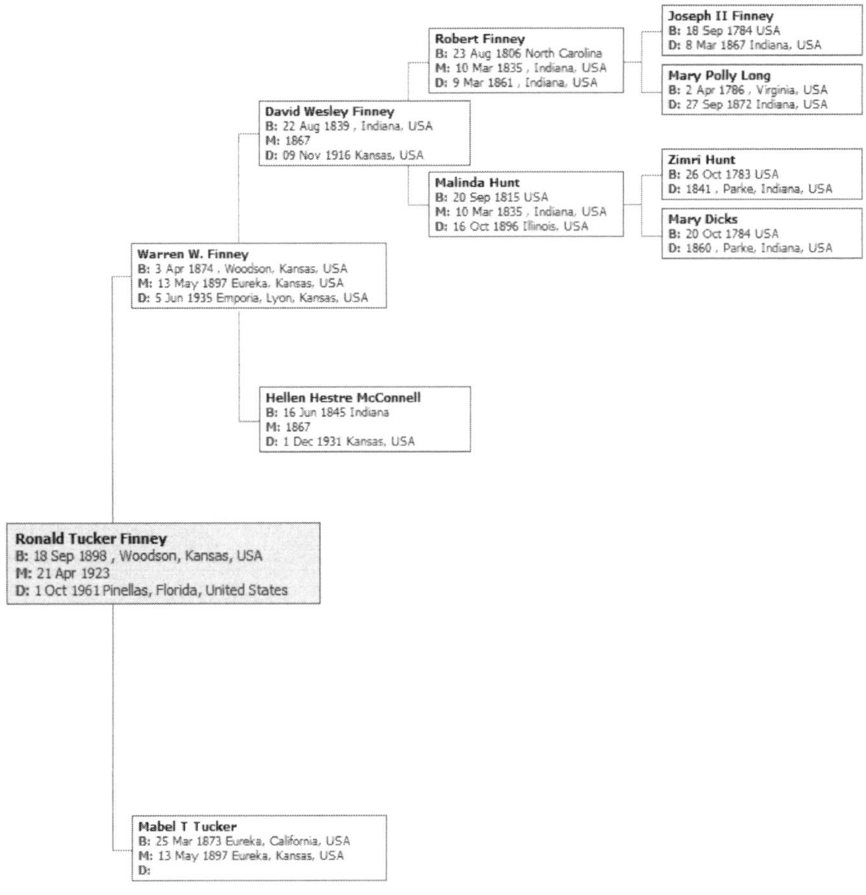

Ronald Finney's family tree

Birth:	Aug. 22, 1839 Annapolis Parke County Indiana, USA
Death:	Nov. 1, 1916 Emporia Lyon County Kansas, USA

Civil War:
Company A.
85th Regiment Indiana Infantry

He enlisted as a private in the Union Army in July, 1862 and was mustered in on Sept. 2, 1862 at Terra Haute, Ind. and assigned to Co. A, 88th Indiana Volunteer Infantry; served the first winter in Kentucky in repelling the rebel invasion. In the spring of 1863 was transferred to Tennessee and took part in clearing the country of rebels from Nashville to Franklin. On March 2nd was a part of the command under Col. Coburn in the hard fought battle of Thompson's Station, Tenn., where a part of the brigade fought all day against the combined forces of Van Dorn, Forrest and Wheeler, and were forced to surrender about 4 o'clock p. m., their ammunition being entirely exhausted. He was taken to Richmond, Va. via Columbia, Tullahoma, Chattanooga and Knoxville, Tenn. and Lynchburg, Va.; was confined in Libby prison for about 2 months, and then exchanged and was back at Franklin, Tenn. in June 1863, ready for the forward march to Chattanooga and Atlanta; took part in most of the engagements during the first Union guard on the streets of Atlanta, marched with Sherman to the sea, and from Savannah, Ga. Through the Carolinas to Richmond, Va.

Added by: Becky Doan

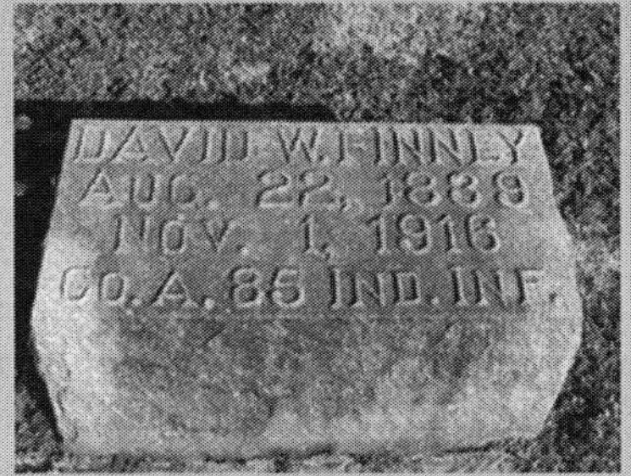

Added by: robin hixon

Added by: robin hixon

The war being over, Sherman's army joined that of Grant at Washington in the Grand Review. Thence back to Indianapolis, Ind., where he was honorably discharged. He enlisted as a private, appointed as 8th Corporal and after the battle of Averysboro was promoted to the rank of 1st Sergeant.

After the close of the war attended a six month's term of school at Waveland Academy.

Family links:
Spouse:
Hellen Hester *McConnell* Finney (1845 - 1931)*

Children:
Warren Wesley Finney (1874 - 1935)*
Glen David Finney (1880 - 1972)*

*Point here for explanation

Burial:
Cedarvale Cemetery
Neosho Falls
Woodson County
Kansas, USA

Edit Virtual Cemetery info [?]

Created by: Judy Mayfield
Record added: Feb 05, 2007
Find A Grave Memorial# 17817044

David Wesley Finney info[1]

[1] http://www.findagrave.com/cgi-bin/fg.cgi?page=gr&GRid=17817044

Birth: Apr. 3, 1874
Death: Jun. 6, 1935

Son of Hellen McConnell and David Finney. When Mr. Finney was 16, he enrolled in the prep class at Washburn Academy, a Congregational institution in Topeka, KS. The following year he was admitted to Washburn College where he became a full-time liberal arts student for the next three years. E was elected president of Gamma Sigma, a literary society. Though he had enough credits to graduate, his transcript shows that he last attended school in 1894 without graduating. After completing his studies at Washburn, Finney joined his father in the milling business in Neosho Falls. Shortly thereafter, he became interested in the telephone business, and organized the Neosho Falls Telephone Company in 1895.

In 1897, he married Mabel Tucker. They met at Washburn. Mr. Finney became a leading citizen of Neosho Falls, serving terms as mayor and as Sunday School superintendent of the Congregational Church. In 1905, Finney sold the Neosho Falls Telephone Company and purchased the Independent telephone Company at Emporia, KS, and subsequently moved to Emporia. A few years after he moved to Emporia, he borrowed heavily to acquire an extensive series of small phone companies in eastern Kansas (Yates Center, Burlington, Sabetha, Paola, Fredonia, Altoona, and others), over twenty in all by the early 1920's.

After becoming well established as one of the state's leading utilities powers, Finney decided to go into banking, a fateful decision that would ultimately lead to his downfall. He bought controlling interest in the Farmers State Bank at Neosho Falls about 1920 and soon consolidated it with the rival Neosho Falls State Bank, a very costly acquisition. He purchased and reorganized the Fidelity State and Savings Bank at Emporia in 1924.

Added by: Becky Doan

Added by: Becky Doan

Warren and Mabel Finney were active in the civic, social and religious life of Emporia soon after their arrival. They joined a host of civic organizations, becoming members of the Emporia Country Club and the Good Road Boosters and were official welcomers to visiting dignitaries. They moved into a 25-room mansion which allowed them to entertain extensively. From the time that automobiles first became available to the public, Finney possessed the largest, most conspicuous cars in Emporia. By the end of the 1920's, Finney owned several farms stocked with prize cattle as well as extensive oil well interests in the Flint Hills.

Added by: Becky Doan

As a 22-year-old, he ran for the state legislature and was elected to the same House seat that his father had held 30 years earlier. He never again ran for political office after his term as Representative, but he remained a lively interest in politics throughout his life. He served his alma mater, Washburn, on its Board of Trustees from 1917 until his abrupt resignation in the fall of 1933. He also became a lay leader in the Congregational Church, whose board of trustees he headed up for several years.

On November 9, 1992, Mr. Finney was found guilty of extensive embezzlement charges. His banking practices were linked to his son's security bond scandal. Mr. Finney was sentence to 36 to 600 years in the Kansas State Penitentiary for 12 embezzlement charges. The sentence was sent to the Kansas Supreme Court for appeal, but on January 26, 1935, it upheld the prosecution on all counts. His attorneys attempted to file a motion for rehearing to give Finney time to decide whether or not he wanted to appeal to the United States Supreme Court. On June 5, 1935, the Kansas Supreme Court announced that it had mailed a mandate to the Lyon County Court for execution of the court order; all avenues of appeal had been exhausted. The following day, the Lyon County Sheriff went to Mr. Finney's home. He left, allowing Mr. Finney one hour to spend time with his family to say their goodbyes. When he returned, Mr. Finney had left the home, travelling to his cabin 5 miles east of Emporia. The phone then rang in the Finney home announcing that Mr. Finney had been found at the cabin with a gunshot to his head. He had been found by a friend who happened to drop by to discuss business. Mr. Finney died later at 7:40 PM at an Emporia Hospital.

Family links:
Parents:
David Wesley Finney (1839 - 1916)
Hellen Hester *McConnell* Finney (1845 - 1931)

Spouse:
Mabel *Tucker* Finney (1872 - 1947)*

Children:
Ronald Tucker Finney (1898 - 1961)*

*Point here for explanation

Burial:
Cedarvale Cemetery
Neosho Falls
Woodson County
Kansas, USA

Edit Virtual Cemetery info [?]

Maintained by: Becky Doan
Originally Created by: robin hixon
Record added: Apr 06, 2010
Find A Grave Memorial# 50753713

Warren Wesley Finney info[2]

[2]http://www.findagrave.com/cgi-bin/fg.cgi?page=gr&GSln=finney&GSfn=warren&GSmn=w&GSbyrel=all&GSdyrel=in&GSst=18&GScntry=4&GSob=n&GRid=50753713&df=all&

Birth: Sep. 18, 1898
Woodson County
Kansas, USA

Death: Oct. 1, 1961
Saint Petersburg
Pinellas County
Florida, USA

Son of Mabel Tucker and Warren Wesley Finney. 1m to Winifred Wiggam on 21 Apr 1923. Two children.

Mr. Finney was the primary instigator of the Kansas Bond Scandal in 1933. His operation generated nearly $1.35 million in bogus securities. This occurred during the Great Depression when nearly a third of the US population was unemployed or underemployed. The Bond Scandal impacted others such as Gov. Alf Landon and the Emporia Gazette newspaper editor William Allen White. Mr. Finney and several coconspirators were convicted and imprisoned at Lansing State Penitentiary. Altogether, there were four criminal convictions, two state officers were impeached, and six federal indictments were brought against seven defendants (including his father, a bank president, who committed suicide). He was sentenced to serve the state's second-longest prison sentence at the time, 31 to 635 years. However, his sentence was later commuted to 18 to 36 years, and he was released from prison on February 18, 1945, and moved to Southern California where his wife and children had moved. In November 1949, he applied for a full pardon. Gov. Carlson commuted his sentence to 24 years, and then granted him a citizen pardon in December 1949.

Added by: Becky Doan

Added by: Becky Doan

While Mr. Finney was imprisoned, he enrolled in an extension course through KU entitled "The Short Story" in 1938. He began to write well enough that his stories published. Over the next three years he took several other courses. His writing transformed into creating articles for trade magazines, and the income he received was sent to his wife to support his family. About one year later, the Finneys were divorced. Winifred then married her high school sweetheart, and Ronald married a woman named Selma whom he had hired while in prison as a journalistic researcher for his writing. They lived in a cabin on a lake in Oregon during the summers, and in the winter they lived in Florida. Mr. Finney continued to make a legitimate income through writing for trade journals.

Mr. Finney died at a St. Petersburg, FL hospital as a result of acute bronchitis which complicated by pulmonary emphysema. He was 63.

Two books have been written about the bond scandal. The first was published in the spring of 1938, written by W.L. White. "What People Said" was Ronald Finney's story, but it was disguised as a fictional novel with all of the names of the characters changed. In 1982, another more factual book was published, "The Great Kansas Bond Scandal," by Robert Smith Bader.

Family links:
Parents:
Warren Wesley Finney (1874 - 1935)
Mabel *Tucker* Finney (1872 - 1947)

Burial:
Unknown

Edit Virtual Cemetery info [?]

Created by: Becky Doan
Record added: Oct 06, 2010
Find A Grave Memorial# 59672757

Ronald Tucker Finney info[3]

About the great bank scandal of 1962. Read more in this book: *The Great Kansas Bond Scandal*, by Robert Smith Bader, University Press of Kansas 1982: "In the midst of Depression, banker and confidence man Ronald Finney bilked the state of Kansas in addition to individual banks and depositors in excess of one million dollars. In what has become known as the "Great Bond Scandal" the author explores the genesis of the affair and the subsequent trial and aftermath. While outlining the scandal and fallout, the author offers a fascinating image of Kansas in the 1930s."

In modern times, both Mr. Finneys would have served time in a white collar prison, got out and made millions from book/tv/movie deals.

[3] http://www.findagrave.com/cgi-bin/fg.cgi?page=gr&GRid=59672757

The Kansas City Times Tuesday, November 9, 1982

Finney's scam drove state mad

LAWRENCE, Kan. — White-collar crime stories are so common these days that they often wind up on a newspaper's back page. They include the Equity Funding Corp., I.O.S. Securities ("The Mutual Fund of Mutual Funds) and Gary Lewellyn, the Iowa banker who claims he was insane when he embezzled $13.5 million recently.

The crimes involve tens of millions of dollars as well as prison sentences at some minimum-security facility, usually of no more than five to seven years. A slap on the wrist.

It didn't used be that way, at least in Kansas.

In the early 1930s, affable Ronald Finney bilked Kansas out of $1.2 million with forged bonds and warrants, which is equal to about $10 million today, barely a misdemeanor in light of the Equity Funding and I.O.S. scams.

But reaction then was swift. The judge sentenced Mr. Finney to 31 to 630 years at hard labor in the Kansas State Penitentiary. And hard labor meant hard labor. Mr. Finney, 34, soon was digging coal by hand in the mine 720 feet below the prison.

Mr. Finney's father, Warren W. Finney, called "the very quintessence of what a successful country-town businessman should be and do," got 40 to 600 years in prison. He went home and shot himself. Mr. Finney's chief lieutenant got 40 to 800 years and went to prison.

Largely ignored in Kansas history, the rapacious events of the early 1930s and Kansans' outraged responses have been brought back in *The Great Kansas Bond Scandal*, to be published next week by the University Press of Kansas. The author is Robert Smith Bader, a Kansas native who trained as a biologist and is dean of the College of Arts and Sciences at the University of Missouri-St. Louis.

"I'd heard about it (the scandal) all my life," said Mr. Bader, who grew up in Le Roy, not far from Neosho Falls, where one of the Finney family banks was.

Yet literature on the scandal was scant despite the fact that the event convulsed Kansas, a state militantly and assertively virtuous, known outside its borders as a national censor (prohibition and laws against smoking cigarettes) and common scolds (including the "What's the Matter with Kansas?" editorial by William Allen White).

In 1979 Mr. Bader took a year's sabbatical, then found copious written material and all sorts of Kansans, many of them in their 70s, 80s and 90s, who remembered the event. Most passions had cooled; only one person refused to talk to Mr. Bader about those days, ones fraught with such emotion that a letter writer from southeast Kansas suggested to Gov. Alf Landon that the culprits be manacled and "thrown in the Neosho River to drown like a litter of blind pups."

What Mr. Finney and his minions did was simple.

First, after years of running the Finneys' Neosho Falls bank, Mr. Finney became a bond broker, willing and able to help the state buy and sell its securities. Ronald was a born salesman, the true ice-box-to-an-Eskimo type.

Mr. Finney's original prey was the Kansas School Fund Commission which had first refusal rights on all municipal, school district and county bonds. It was the Depression and poverty-stricken school districts would offer bonds to the commission. The commission would turn them down because of the "financial embarrassment" of the district or its shortage of ready cash. The board members would be faced with the task of telling home folks there was no market for their bonds and any dreams for their childrens' education would have to wait.

Then, lo and behold, who would apppear but friendly, round-faced Ronald Finney or one of his associates.

They would buy the bonds from the eager school district at a discount or market them to a "mysterious customer," in reality the School Fund Commission. The commission, several of whose members were in thrall to Mr. Finney because of "his tips on the market" (a cruder word is bribe), just loved to buy bonds presented by Mr. Finney. Mr. Finney, in turn, would get a tidy commission.

In the early 1930s, however, Mr. Finney found his style cramped and the bond brokerage business limiting his income. So he started forging bonds, simple enough since he had the run of the state treasurer's office and knew what and where the bonds were.

Friendly printers reproduced bonds exactly — the originals had a few typographical errors, Mr. Finney would tell them — and the legitimacy of the bonds was unquestioned because Mr. Finney and his associates were embossing them with the genuine Great Seal of the State of Kansas.

Of course it eventually all came out and Kansas, as it is wont to do occasionally, went slightly insane.

Residents of Finney County (named after Mr. Finney's grandfather) asked that the name of their county be changed; the elder Finney committed suicide; Mr. Finney and a couple of others went to jail; two state officers were impeached; a Chicago brokerage firm went bankrupt; and three Kansas banks closed.

The civil suits dragged on for years, almost until 1945 when Mr. Finney was paroled. He led a prosaic life after that as a freelance writer and died in 1961 of acute bronchitis in a Florida hospital.

Eventually the case faded into the mists of time, resurrected only now by Mr. Bader who found not only the specific facts of the event fascinating, but also the reaction of his fellow Kansans to it.

Early in the investigation, when authorities were searching to find just what bonds were missing, they tested the burglar alarm in the treasury vault. It worked.

A man in the corridor exclaimed, "Ain't it a shame that thing didn't go off three or four years ago."

[d] Pamela Ann Finney, d/o Robert & Malinda - b. 1 Jan 1841 - 3 Mar 1843
[e] Zimri Dix Finney - 18 Mar 1842 Parke Co., Ind - 14 Jan 1876 Neosho Falls, Woodson Co., Ks - m. Rachel STEWART, d/o Abraham & Mary - Zimri served in the Civil War.
[f] Robert Johnson Finney - 10 Dec 1844 Parke Co - 11 Dec 1912 Rockville, Parke Co., Ind - m [1] 8 July 1867 Melissa Dickinson THOMPSON b. 9 Feb 1845 Parke Co - 4 Sep 1909, d/o Morris & Sally [Timberman] - m [2] 1 Dec 1910 Rockville, Ind to Gertrude May ATKINSON - b. 27 Apr 1883 - 1960, d/o Simon. She is buried Bloomingdale Cemetery,. Parke Co., Ind. Robert was in Civil War, Co. C. 149th Regiment Ind. Vol. Infantry, was railway mail clerk and merchant. He was also constable in Douglas Co., Ill [1880 census] and sheriff Parke Co., Ind. in 1912

i. Charles Edward Finney - b. 29 Apr 1869 Tuscola, Ill - m. 20 June 1895 Indianapolis,Ind. to Jessie GROSE b. 30 Nov 1871 in Newcastle, Ind, d/o Madisonn & Mary Jane [Rader] - lvd. in Tucson, Arizona in 1940

a. Dorothy Mildred Finney - b & d 11 June 1898, buried Friends Cemetery, Bloomingdale, Parke Co., Ind.

b. Charles Wesley Finney - b. 30 Nov 1899 Marion Co., Ind., lvd. Oklahoma City 1940 - m [1] 10 Mar 1921 Gladys CLINE - b. Apr 1898 Goshen, Ind, m [2] 30 June 1928 Fullerton, Calif. to Beulah Blanche BIRDEN b. 23 Apr 1906 Hydro, Ok.

He attended the University of Arizona, was a Mason, Methodist and a newspaper man. City editor of the Arizona Republic in Phoenix; news editor Pasadena, Calif., Star News; acting & assistant managing editor New Bedford, Mass. Standard Times; on editorial staff Daily Oklahoman in 1940.

c. Marion Finney - b. 25 Feb 1905 - d. 26 Feb 1905

ii. Robert Johnson Finney - b. 28 Sep 1911 Parke Co., Ind - m. Doris - no children, lvd. Chesterton, Ind. 1940

[g] Mary Elizabeth Finney - 10 June 1847 Parke Co - 1929 Tuscola, Douglas Co., Ill - m. William Palmer MILLER - b. 1843 Oh, a dry goods merchant

i. Ethel Miller - b. 1873 Douglas Co., Ill.

[h] Joseph Harrison Finney - 19 Jan 1849 Parke Co - 9 Sep 1897 Newman, Douglas Co., Ill - m [1] Catharine Alice PORTER, m [2] Sarah Agnes VALODIN

i. Porter Finney
ii. Everett Finney
iii. Daughter who m. W. P. MILLER
iv. Daughter who m. W. G. GOLDMAN

[i] Malinda Catherine Finney - b. 4 Feb 1855 Parke Co - alive 1940 in Tuscola, Ill - m. William David GOLDMAN b. 1848 Ind, s/o George & Elizabeth [Tucker] - William was merchant in Douglas Co. 1880

i. Edna Goldman - b. 1875 Douglas Co., Ill.
ii. Burt Goldman - b. 1876
iii. Odie Goldman - b. 1879
iv. Dada Goldman - b. Mar 1880 Douglas Co.,Ill.

[2] Joseph Finney - 19 Dec 1808 Green Co., Tenn - 4 May 1854 Clinton Co., Ind. - m. Lorena MORGAN, d/o Kenahen & Sarah

[3] John Long Finney - 16 Dec 1810 Surry Co., NC - d.before 1903 Ks, - m [1] 13 Nov 1832 Elizabeth CAMPBELL who d. 6 Nov 1836, m [2] 2 Feb 1840 Parke Delaney HUNT

[a] Mary Jane Finney - b. 29 Jan 1834
[b] Elizabeth Finney - b. 29 Aug 1836 - 1 Dec 1837

Zimri Dix Finney

Finney descendancy continues with the Zimri Finney family from the top of page 77.

e. Zimri Dix Finney - 18 Mar 1842 Parke Co., Ind - 14 Jan 1876 Neosho Falls, Woodson Co., Ks - m. Rachel STEWART b. 6 Dec 1849 Rockford, Winebago, IL, d. 25 Nov 1890 Moscow, Latah, ID, d/o Abraham & Mary (Mitchell) Stewart

Zimri served in the Civil War. Zimri served in the Union Army, enlisted 7 Aug 1862 in Company A, 85th Infantry Regiment Indiana, and mustered out on 12 Jun 1865 in Washington, DC.

Zimri Dix Finney and Rachel (Stewart) Finney

From Lynn Stuter:

Zimri served in the Civil War, enlisting 7 Aug 1862. He served in Company A, 85th Infantry Regiment, Indiana, and mustered out on 12 Jun 1865 in Washington, DC.

Zimri's brother David Wesley Finney also fought in the Civil War as did a first cousin, Josiah Ephlin. They were all in the same company; all spent time in Libby Prison after their capture at Thompson Station, Tennessee. They all participated in Sherman's March to the Sea.

David Wesley went on to become the Lt Gov of Kansas. Finney County, Kansas is named for him.

Zimri Dix Finney is buried in Neosho Falls, Woodson County, Kansas. His wife, Rachel (Stewart) Finney, is buried at Moscow, Idaho.

They had four children but only three survived to adulthood – Mary Malinda (1869), Frank Abraham (1871), George Washington (1872). A fourth child, John, was born and died in 1876.

Zimri's untimely death in 1876 was the result of wounds incurred in the Civil War and his incarceration at Libby Prison. After his death, Rachel and her three surviving children removed to Moscow, Idaho via Oregon where they resided near her parents. Her parents, Abraham and Mary Ann (Mitchell) Stewart, are also buried at Moscow.

***

i. Mary Malinda Finney b. 10 Oct 1869 Woodson, KS, d. 10 Feb 1933 Westport, Grays Harbor, WA; m. Frank D. Roberts b. 1872 Kentucky

a. Trula Maxine Roberts b. 19 Feb 1914, d. 30 Dec 1914, bur. Woodland Cemetery, Idaho County, ID.

ii. Frank Abraham Finney b. 10 May 1871 Woodson, KS, d. 31 Dec. 1941 Woodland, ID; m. Mabel Lily George b. Nov. 1883 Nebraska, d. 28 Jul 1935, Woodland, ID, d/o Austin Sherman and Sarah Jeanette (Haskins) George; bur. Woodland Cemetery, Idaho County, ID.

Frank Abraham Finney, Mary Melinda Finney and George Washington Finney

Frank and Mabel Finney

a. Florence Jeanette Finney, b. 3 Oct 1903, d. 15 Sept 1968, bur. Woodland Cemetery, Idaho County, ID; m. James Patterson, div.

b. George Austin Finney, b. 26 Apr 1905, d. 20 Aug 1957; m. Mildred Speer; bur. Memorial Gardens, Lewiston, Nez Perce County, ID.

c. Minnie Ora Finney, b. 4 Jun 1908, d. 12 Mar 2002, m. Albert John Schroeder, bur. Woodland Cemetery, Idaho County, ID.

d. Floyd Albert Finney, b. 10 Sept 1910, d. 11 Oct 1996, m. Evelyn Carol Skeels, bur. Woodland Cemetery, Idaho County, ID.

e. Avaril Estella Finney, b. 28 Jan 1914, d. 18 Dec 1990, m. Clifford Vance Caldwell, bur. Woodland Cemetery, Idaho County, ID.

f. Francis Mary Finney, b. 13 Apr 1915, d. 7 Oct 1989, m. Harold Joseph Knight, bur. Woodland Cemetery, Idaho County, ID.

g. Charles Everett Finney, b. 3 Jan 1924, Kamiah, Lewis County, ID; m. Nadine Thomsen b. 20 Feb 1926 Iowa (Living).

   Charles Finney served in the Navy, Pacific Theater, World War II. He served aboard the USS Sea Cat SS-399. He was aboard the Sea Cat when it was ordered to Tokyo Bay for the surrender of Japan on 2 Sept 1945.

   (1) Lee Dee Finney

   (2) Cheryl Sue Finney, b. 7 Dec 1948, Cottonwood, Idaho County, ID; d. 8 Dec 1948, bur. Woodland Cemetery, Woodland, Idaho County, ID.

   (3) Chris Everett Finney

   (4) Julie Nadine Finney

   (5) Lynn Marie Finney; m. Byrd C Stuter

      1. Michelle Renee Stuter, m Josepheus Joyner.

      2. Monica Lynn Stuter, m Jeremy Yeager.

iii. George Washington Finney b. 9 Sept. 1872 Woodson, KS, d. 5 Dec. 1927 when his horse lost his footing while crossing the Lolo Creek railroad trestle; George was thrown into Lolo Creek and drowned; bur. Woodland Cemetery, Idaho County, ID; m. Rose M. Dunn b. 1891 Wisconsin.

a. Thomas Arthur Finney, b. 19 Apr 1923, d 7 Aug 1963, m. Selma Suzanne (Sally) Hannula; bur. Woodland Cemetery, Idaho County, ID

b. Rose Mary Finney, b. 19 Oct 1924, d. 19 Jan 1986, m. Richard P. Janes, bur. Haywood, CA.

c. Patrick James Finney, b. 29 Sept 1925, d. 12 May 1995, bur. Kooskia, Idaho County, ID.

iv. John Finney b. 1876 Woodson KS, d. 1876 Neosho Falls KS

Update to page 78.

[6] Polly Finney m. Alexander P. Ephlin

[a] Josiah M. Ephlin (Joe) m. Anna Jane Tenbrook

i. Adeline (Addie) Ephlin

ii. William Tenbrook (Willie) Ephlin

iii. Theodosia (Dosia) Ephlin

Alexander Ephlin

Anna Jane (Tenbrook) and Josiah Ephlin; Josiah Ephlin

Adeline, William, and Theodosia Ephlin

[c] John Wesley Finney - 23 Dec 1844 - d. Penrose, Colo. - m. to Margaret VENEMAN

i. Neil Finney - 27 Jan 1866 - 14 Jan 1920 m. Minnie MINDERHAUT
ii. John Martin Finney - 26 Mar 1867 m. Jessie MILLER
iii. Iva Isadora Finney b. 6 Apr 1872 m. Arthur BALL
iv. Wilbert Finney - 27 June 1876 m. Hattie ABEL
v. Mary Finney - b. 13 Nov 1878 - m. George SHIPMAN
vi. Reuben Finney - 28 May 1881 m. Mable WATTS b.12 May 1888
vii. Nettie Finney - 5 Feb 1883 m. William GRAHAM
viii. Carl Finney - b. 31 Aug 1888
ix. Jane Finney - 19 July 1891 - m. Aubrey MOBERLY - d. 1933

[4] Nancy Finney - b. 16 Oct 1812 Surry Co., NC - d. Ind - m. 27 Sep 1838 Thomas B. WADE

[a] George Pickett Wade - b. 12 July 1839

[5] Hawkins Cook Finney - 28 Aug 1815 E. Tenn - d. 1 Jan 1889 Clinton Co., Ind. - m [1] 16 Nov 1837 Martha COUNTS, m [2] Mrs. Sarah E. [Wiley] WALTERS, m [3] Mary E. GOSSETT

[a]. John V. Finney - 18 Oct 1837 Ill - m [1] 1 Nov 1864 Mary RANSOPHER, m [2] 1 Apr 1877 Priscilla LOWRY

i. Savannah Finney
ii. James H. Finney
iii. Stephen V. Finney
iv. Samantha Finney
v. Dillie Finney
vi. Mattie Finney
vii. Priscilla Finney
viii. John Finney
ix. Clinton Finney
x. Omera Finney

[b]. David Finney - m. Catherine ORR - had son Matthew
[c]. Esquire D. Finney
[d]. Wesley Finney
[e]. Joseph Finney

[6] Polly Finney - 21 Jan 1818 Ind - 21 June 1896 Parke Co - m. 10 July 1839 Parke Co., Ind. Alexander P. EPHLIN. They are shown on Parke Co.,Ind. Tax List 1851, *also in* Reserve Twp., Parke Co. census 1860 and 1880. Alexander b. Feb 1821 NC - d. 12 Aug 1882

[a] Josiah M. Ephlin - 4 May 1840 - 14 July 1924 Parke Co - m. 2 Oct 1867 Annapolis,Ind. Anna Jane TENBROOK b. 26 Jan 1838 Ind -d. 12 Mar 1901 - on 1880 Parke Co., Ind. census

INSERT: See above Carl Finney, s/o John Wesley - m. Ruth MILLER b. 26 Feb 1894 - lived Orleans, Nebraska - had daughter Margaret Finney b. 3 May 1914 Colorado Springs, daughter Ethel Louise Finney b. 7 Aug 1917 - d.12 Jan 1927 Penrose, Colo, son Orville C. Finney b. 22 Oct 1918 Colorado Springs and daughter Ruth Ellen Finney - b. 29 Apr 1922

i. Adeline Ephlin - d/o Josiah - b. July 1868 Ind - 1940
ii. William T. Ephlin - b. Sep 1869 Ind - 1945 Parke Co., Ind.
iii. Theodosia Ephlin - b. July 1872 - d. 1957

Josiah Ephlin was in Civil War - Co. A., 85th Reg't. Ind. Vol. Infantry - enlisted 1 Aug 1862 at Annapolis, Parke Co., Ind. Discharged Washington, D. C. 12 June 1865. See Army papers on following pages.

Addie, Willie, and Dosia Ephlin

#366,220
71 P. G.

War Department,

ADJUTANT GENERAL'S OFFICE,

Washington, July 17, 1882.

Respectfully returned to the Commissioner of Pensions.

Josiah N. Ephlin, a Pvte of Company A, 85 Regiment Indiana Volunteers, was enrolled on the 1 day of August, 1862, at Annapolis for 3 yrs, and is reported: on Muster Roll for Jan & Feb 63 Josiah M. Ephlin present. Mch & Apl 63 Captured at Thompsons Station Tenn Mch 5/63 Co was in Action said time & place. May & June 63 present the same to Apl 30/64. May & June 64 absent sick in Hospl Madison Ind. July & Aug 64 present. Sept & Oct 64 absent Det. Oct 1/64 Brig Guard same to Apl 30/65. Mustered out with Co June 12/65. Does not appear on Det. Rolls.

Prisoner of War Records show him captured at Thompsons Sta. Tenn. Mar 5. 63. Confined at Richmond Va. Mar 22. 63. paroled at City Point Va. Mar 31. 63. reported at Camp Parole Md. April 1. 63 and sent to Camp Chase O. April 6. 63 where he arrived between April 10 & 12. 63 present April 13. 63. No evidence of disability and no further information on said records. Records of this Office furnish no evidence of alleged disability. Nature of sickness reported on Roll for May & June 1864, not stated. Regtl Hospl Records are not on file.

R. C. Corbin
Assistant Adjutant General.
by [illegible]

E | 85 | Ind.

Josiah McEphlin

, Co. A, 85 Reg't Indiana Infantry.

Appears on

Company Descriptive Book

of the organization named above.

DESCRIPTION.

Age 22 years; height 5 feet 5½ inches.

Complexion fair

Eyes dark; hair dark

Where born Parke Co. Ind.

Occupation farmer

ENLISTMENT.

When Aug 1, 186

Where Parke Co.

By whom Capt. A. Floyd; term 3 y'rs.

Remarks:

Book mark:

Cass
Copyist.

(358₁)

E | 85 | Ind.

Josiah N. Ephlin

Pvt, Capt. Floyd's Co., 85 Reg't Indiana Inf.*

Age 22 years.

Appears on

Company Muster-in Roll

of the organization named above. Roll dated

Terre Haute Ind. Sept 2, 1862.

Muster-in to date Sept 2, 1862.

Joined for duty and enrolled:

When Aug 1, 1862

Where Annapolis

Period 3 years.

Bounty paid $ 27 100; due $ 100

Remarks:

*This organization subsequently became Co. A, 85 Reg't Ind. Inf.

Book mark:

Brody
Copyist.

(358)

Josiah McEphlin

Pvt, Co. A, 85 Reg't Indiana Infantry.

Appears on

Company Muster Roll

for Sept 2 to Oct 31, 1862.

Present or absent Present

Stoppage, $ 100 for

Due Gov't $ 100 for

Remarks:

Book mark:

Brody
Copyist.

(358)

E | 85 | Ind.

Josiah McEphlin

Pvt, Co. A, 85 Reg't Indiana Infantry.

Appears on

Company Muster Roll

for Nov & Dec, 1862

Present or absent Present

Stoppage, $ 100 for

Due Gov't $ 100 for

Remarks:

Book mark:

Brodey
Copyist.

(358)

E | 85 | Ind.

Josiah McEphlin

Pvt, Co. A, 85 Reg't Indiana Infantry.

Appears on

Company Muster Roll

for Jan & Feby, 1863.

Present or absent Present

Stoppage, $ 100 for

Due Gov't $ 100 for

Remarks:

Book mark:

Brody
Copyist.

(358)

E | 85 | Ind.

Josiah McEphlin

Pvt, Co. A, 85 Reg't Indiana Infantry.

Appears on

Company Muster Roll

for Mar & April, 1863.

Present or absent Absent

Stoppage, $ 100 for

Due Gov't $ 100 for

Remarks: Captured at Thompson's Station Tenn. Mar. 5 1863

From Second Auditor's Roll.

Book mark:

Brody
Copyist.

(358)

E | 85 | Ind.

Josiah M. Ephlin
Pvt. 85 Reg't Ind Inf.

Appears on
Muster and Descriptive Roll
of a detachment of U.S. Paroled Forces forwarded from Annapolis, Md., to Camp Chase, Ohio, assigned to Co. D, 4 Reg't Paroled Infantry.* Received April 10, 11 and 12, 1863. Roll dated
Camp Chase Ohio April 13, 1863.
Where born Parke Co. Ind.
Age 23 y'rs; occupation Farmer
When enlisted Aug 1, 1862
Where enlisted Annapolis Ind
For what period enlisted 3 years.
Eyes Hazel; hair Dark
Complexion Fair; height 5 ft 5 in.
Bounty paid $....100; due $....100
Date of first muster ...., 186 .
Company to which assigned D.
Remarks:

*This organization was formed from paroled prisoners of war for duty compatible with their parole by G. O. No. 72, A. G. O., of June 28, 1862, and the members were returned to their commands, from time to time, by G. O. No. 10, A. G. O., of January 10, 1863, and subsequent orders from the A. G. O., declaring the exchange of paroled prisoners and directing their return to their commands.—R. and P. 399,213.

Book mark:

(358a) Park, Copyist.

E | 85 | Ind.

Josiah M Ephlin
Pvt, Co. A, 85 Reg't Indiana Infantry.

Appears on
Company Muster Roll
for May & June, 1863.
Present or absent Present
Stoppage, $....100 for....
Due Gov't $....100 for....
Remarks:

Book mark:

(358) Boody, Copyist.

E | 85 | Ind.

× Josiah M. Ephlin
Pvt, Co. A, 85 Reg't Indiana Infantry.

Appears on
Company Muster Roll
for July & Aug, 1863.
Present or absent Present
Stoppage, $....100 for....
Due Gov't $....100 for....
Remarks: × Name appears in present column as "Eplin"

Book mark:

(358) Simmons, Copyist.

E | 85 | Ind.

Josiah M Ephlin
Pvt, Co. A, 85 Reg't Indiana Infantry.

Appears on
Company Muster Roll
for Sept & Oct, 1863
Present or absent Present
Stoppage, $....100 for....
Due Gov't $....100 for....
Remarks:

Book mark:

(358) Simmons, Copyist.

E | 85 | Ind.

Josiah M Ephlin
Pvt, Co. A, 85 Reg't Indiana Infantry.

Appears on
Company Muster Roll
for Nov & Dec, 1863.
Present or absent Present
Stoppage, $....100 for....
Due Gov't $....100 for....
Remarks:

Book mark:

(358) Simmons, Copyist.

E | 85 | Ind.

Josiah M Ephlin
Pvt, Co. A, 85 Reg't Indiana Infantry.

Appears on
Company Muster Roll
for Jan & Feb, 1864
Present or absent Present
Stoppage, $....100 for....
Due Gov't $....100 for....
Remarks:

Book mark:

(358) Simmons, Copyist.

E. | 85 | Ind.

Josiah M Ephlin
Priv., Co. A, 85 Reg't Indiana Infantry.

Appears on
Company Muster Roll
for Mch & Apl, 1864.
Present or absent: Present
Stoppage, $ 100 for
Due Gov't $ 100 for
Remarks:

Book mark:

Simms
(853) Copyist.

E | 85 | Ind

Josiah M Ephlin
Pt., Co. A, 85 Reg't Ind Inf.

Appears on
Hospital Muster Roll
of U. S. A. General Hospital,
at Madison, Ind.,
for May & June, 1864
Attached to hospital:
When, 186
How employed
Last paid by Maj.
to, 186
Bounty paid $ 100; due $ 100
Present or absent: Present
Remarks:

Book mark:

Burnham
(848) Copyist.

E. | 85 | Ind.

Josiah M Ephlin
Priv. Co. A, 85 Reg't Indiana Infantry.

Appears on
Company Muster Roll
for May & June, 1864
Present or absent: Absent
Stoppage, $ 100 for
Due Gov't $ 100 for
Remarks: Sick in Hospital, Maddison Ind.

Book mark:

Simms
(853) Copyist.

E | 85 | Ind.

Josiah M. Ephlin
Pvt., Co. A, 85 Reg't Indiana Infantry.

Appears on Returns as follows:
May June 1864. Absent sick Hosp. Jeffersonville Ind.
Nov 1864 to Jany 1865: Absent on Det. service Brig. Guard
Mch to May 1865: Absent on Det. service Brig. Hd. Qrs. Prov. Guard

Book mark:

Kemp
(846) Copyist.

E | 85 | Ind.

Josiah M. Ephlin
Pvt., Co. A, 85 Reg't Indiana Infantry.

Appears on
Company Muster Roll
for July & Aug, 1864.
Present or absent: Present
Stoppage, $ 100 for
Due Gov't $ 100 for
Remarks:

Book mark:

Wm Kennedy
(858) Copyist.

E | 85 | Ind.

Josiah M. Ephlin
Pvt, Co. A, 85 Reg't Indiana Infantry.

Appears on
Company Muster Roll
for Sept. & Oct., 1864.
Present or absent: Absent
Stoppage, $ 100 for
Due Gov't $ 100 for
Remarks: Detached Brigade Provost Guard Oct 1st 1864 by order Lt Col Bloodgood Com Brig.

Book mark:

Wm Kennedy
(858) Copyist.

E | 85 | Ind.

Josiah M. Ephlin
Pvt., Co. A, 85 Reg't Indiana Infantry.
Appears on
Company Muster Roll
for Nov. & Dec., 1864.
Present or absent: Absent
Stoppage, $ 100 for
Due Gov't $ 100 for
Remarks: Detached as Brig Provo Guard Oct. 1st 64 by order Lt. Col. Bloodgood
Book mark:
W M Kennedy, Copyist.
(358)

E | 85 | Ind.

Josiah M. Eplin
Pvt., Co. A, 85 Reg't Indiana Infantry.
Appears on
Company Muster Roll
for Jan. & Feb., 1865.
Present or absent: Absent
Stoppage, $ 100 for
Due Gov't $ 100 for
Remarks: Detached as Brig Provost Guard.
Book mark:
W M Kennedy, Copyist.
(358)

E | 85 | Ind.

Josiah M. Ephlin
Pvt., Co. A, 85 Reg't Indiana Infantry.
Appears on
Company Muster Roll
for Mch. & Apl, 1865.
Present or absent: Absent
Stoppage, $ 100 for
Due Gov't $ 100 for
Remarks: Detached Brigade Provost Guard
Book mark:
W M Kennedy, Copyist.
(358)

E | 85 | Ind.

Josiah M. Ephlin
Pvt., Co. A, 85 Reg't Indiana Infantry.
Age 22 years.
Appears on Co. Muster-out Roll, dated Washington D.C. June 12, 1865.
Muster-out to date June 12, 1865.
Last paid to Aug 31, 1864.
Clothing account:
Last settled Aug 31, 1864; drawn since $ 56 04/100
Due soldier $ 100; due U.S. $ 100
Am't for cloth'g in kind or money adv'd $ 100
Due U.S. for arms, equipments, &c., $ 100
Bounty paid $ 25 100; due $ 75 100
Remarks:
Book mark:
W M Kennedy, Copyist.
(361)

JOSIAH M EPHLIN
BLOOMINGDALE IND
301926 ACT MAY

DROP REPORT—PENSIONER

INVALID Cert. No.
Pensioner
Soldier
Service
Class SECTION I

LAW DIVISION

, 192

In the above-described case a declaration filed in this Division indicates that said pensioner died , 19

Per Chief, Law Division.

FINANCE DIVISION
AUG 8 1924, 192

The name of the above-described pensioner who was last paid at the rate of $ 50 per month to July 4 1924, has this day been dropped from the roll because of Death July 13, 1924.

O. J. Randall
Chief, Finance Division.

WAR OF 1861.

Declaration for Invalid Army Pension.

STATE OF Indiana, COUNTY OF Parke, ss:

On this 27" day of April One Thousand Eight Hundred and Eighty personally appeared before me, David Strouse Clerk of the Circuit Court within and for the County and State aforesaid, Josiah M. Ephlin aged 39 years, and a resident of Annapolis County of Parke and State of Ind who being duly sworn according to law, declares that he is the identical Josiah M Ephlin who enlisted in the service of the United States at Annapolis County of Parke and State of Ind on the 1st day of Aug 1862, as a Private in Company A commanded by Captain Abner Floyd in the 85th Regiment of Ind Volunteers in the War of 1861, and honorably discharged at Washington State of D.C. on the 12th day of June 1865 That while in the service aforesaid and in the line of duty as a soldier at or near a place called Libby Prison State of Va from the 5" of March to 17 of April 1863,

Through hardships exposure and Starvation contracted Chronic Diarrhoea which still affects him Disabling him at times for the performance of Manual labor.

For which he prays a pension!

Received Hospital treatment, as follows: 1st on the field by Regimental Surgeon was not in Hospital for above disease

Since leaving the service he resided mostly at or near Annapolis Ind

His occupation has been Farming When enrolled he was a Farming And for the purpose of prosecuting his claim he hereby appoints P. H. FITZGERALD & CO., of Indianapolis, Indiana, his attorneys in fact, with full power of substitution.

His post office address is Annapolis County of Parke State of Ind

If mark is made, have two witnesses sign here.

Noval H. Cummings

David Strouse

Josiah M. Ephlin
Signature of Claimant.

SEE FOOT NOTE.

State of Indiana } SS:
County of Parke

In the claim of Josiah Wm Eplin

on this 20th day of January, 1885, personally appeared before me, a Notary Public in and for the County and State aforesaid, Josiah M Ephlin of Annapolis P. O., in the County of Parke and State of Indiana, who, being duly sworn according to law, on oath declare as follows: That he was late member of Company A 85th Reg't Indiana Vols., and ranked as Private, and that ~~said~~ ~~was a member of said organization, and who, while in the said service and line of duty as a soldier, at or near a place called~~

~~State of~~ ~~on or about the~~ ~~day of~~ ~~18~~

he cannot get a Doctors affidavit for the following reasons, viz, That I treated myself with medicine purchased from drug store and roots & barks procured from the woods. with the exception of a few doses of medicine taken from the doctor that was paid for at the time and no record being kept by him as I did not employ him to treat my case regularly.

and he further say that knowledge of the above facts is obtained from the following source, viz:

and that he has ~~no~~ interest and ~~nor~~ concern in this matter.

(If the person making the affidavit signs by mark have two witnesses sign here.)

Josiah Wm Ephlin

Subscribed and sworn to before me this 20th day of January, 1885 and I certify that the party whose name appear signed to the foregoing affidavit is the person he represents ~~himself~~ to be, and is good and credible witness, and that the contents of the foregoing affidavit were duly read and fully made known to affiant before making oath to the same, and that I have no interest in the matter.

Official Signature Joseph C. Vickory
Notary Public

PENSION OFFICE JAN 21 1885

It is always preferable that this should be executed before Clerk of Court; but if before Justice of the Peace or Notary Public have Clerk of Court attach Certificate of official capacity of such J. P. or N. P. in all cases. When complete return...

WAR DEPARTMENT,

SURGEON GENERAL'S OFFICE.

Washington, D. C., May 25, 1885.

To the Adjutant General, U. S. Army.

Sir: I have the honor to return herewith the papers received from your office in pension claim No. 366230., *with such information as is furnished by records filed in this Office, viz: that* Pvt Josiah M. Epkins, Co. A 85th Ind. Inf. was admitted to Cumberland G.H. Nashville, Tenn. May 14/64 with Ulcer, and transferred May 19/64. Entered Jefferson G.H. Jeffersonville, Ind., May 21/64 with Ulceration from Vaccination, and was transfd. June 28/64, and that he entered G.H. Madison, Ind. June 29/64 diagnosis: "Suppure vaccination", and returned to duty July 12/64.

The records of Camp Parole, Md Apr 1 to 6/63, and of Camp Chase, Ohio Apr 1 to 21/63 furnish no evidence in the case.

No Medical records of the Regiment on file, nor records of Camp Morton, Ind. prior to Aug 5/63.

By order of the Surgeon General:

B F Pope
Assistant Surgeon, U. S. Army.

No. 347636.

per JSB

(371)

Tuscola Postoffice.

H. R. INGRAHAM, Postmaster.

PENSION OFFICE JUN 18 85

Tuscola Ill June 12 1885

Com Pensions

Sir

in reply to the enclosed I would say that to the best of my recollection (after the lapse of so long time) that Josiah M Ephlin late a private in Co A 85 Ind Vols. was a sufferer from Diarrhoea contracted as I believe while a prisoner of war en route from Spring Hill Tenn to Richmond Va during the month of March 1863 I was personally with the Company and know the exposure and hardships incident to a prisoners life we were marched from Spring Hill via Columbia to Tullahoma Tenn. where by order Genl Bragg we were divested of our Overcoats and Blankets and those who had blankets they were also taken during this march it rained almost constantly had to wade streams sometimes waist deep and at night to stand or lay on the ground in mud and water upon arriving at

Tuscola Postoffice.

H. R. INGRAHAM, Postmaster.

PENSION OFFICE

Tuscola, Ill. 188

Tullahoma Tenn we were put upon Cattle & Box Cars and sent by way of Chattanooga Knoxville & Lynchburgh to Libby at Richmond Va my recollection is that we were seventeen days from date of Capture to Arrival at Richmond there we were separated the privates being in separate rooms from the Officers Ephlins condition was brought to my notice while on the above trip he then had diarrhoea and after Ex. and up to the time I left ~~the Company~~ active duty with the Reg. on or about May 10th 1864 the said Ephlin was still a sufferer more or less from diarrhoea my memory is that he was often on light duty on acct of his physical condition I have not seen Ephlin but few times since his discharge. Mr John R Tenbrook a reliable citizen of Tuscola Ill was I think a mess mate and bunked with Ephlin while in the service until the close of the war

Very Respectfully

H R Ingraham

late Lieut Co A 85 Ind Vols

N B the 85 Ind was in Coburns Brigade Captured by Vandorn Wheeler & Cy at Thompsons Sta Tenn March 5 1863

ACT OF MAY 11, 1912. 3—014.

DECLARATION FOR PENSION.

THE PENSION CERTIFICATE SHOULD NOT BE FORWARDED WITH THE APPLICATION.

State of Indiana, County of Parke, ss:

On this 7th day of June, A. D. one thousand nine hundred and twelve personally appeared before me, a Notary Public within and for the county and State aforesaid, Josiah M. Ephlin who, being duly sworn according to law, declares that he is 72 years of age, and a resident of Bloomingdale, county of Parke, State of Indiana; and that he is the identical person who was ENROLLED at Annapolis Indiana, under the name of Josiah M. Ephlin on the First day of August, 1862 as a Private, in Company "A" 85th Regiment Indiana Infantry Volunteers (Here state rank, and company and regiment in the Army, or vessels if in the Navy.) in the service of the United States, in the Civil (State name of war, Civil or Mexican.) war, and was HONORABLY DISCHARGED at near Washington D.C., on the twelfth day of June 1865.

That he also served (Here give a complete statement of all other services, if any.)

That he was not employed in the military or naval service of the United States otherwise than as stated above. That his personal description at enlistment was as follows: Height, Five feet 5½ inches; complexion, ~~dark~~ light; color of eyes, dark; color of hair, dark; that his occupation was Farmer; that he was born May 4th, 1840, at Annapolis Parke County Indiana.

That his several places of residence since leaving the service have been as follows: near Annapolis Indiana. (Bloomingdale Post Office recently) (State date of each change, as nearly as possible.)

That he is a pensioner under certificate No. 301926. That he has not applied for pension under original No. ... as to execution

That he makes this declaration for the purpose of being placed on the pension roll of the United States under the provisions of the act of May 11, 1912.

That his post-office address is Bloomingdale, county of Parke, State of Indiana.

Attest: (1) A.R. Shoemaker
(2) Charles C. Vickory

Josiah M. Ephlin (Claimant's signature in full.)

SUBSCRIBED and sworn to before me this 7th day of June, A. D. 1912, and I hereby certify that the contents of the above declaration were fully made known and explained to the applicant before swearing, including the words dark, erased, and the words light, added; and that I have no interest, direct or indirect, in the prosecution of this claim.

[L. S.]

Joseph C. Vickory (Signature.)
Notary Public (Official character.)

My Commission Expires Nov 2nd 1915.

IF A PENSIONER, DO NOT FAIL TO GIVE CERTIFICATE NUMBER.

#366,230.

War Department,

ADJUTANT GENERAL'S OFFICE,

Washington, May 27, 1885.

Respectfully returned to the Commissioner of Pensions.

Josiah N. Ephlin, a Private of Company A, 85th Regiment Indiana Volunteers, was enrolled on the 1st day of August, 1862, at Annapolis Ind. for 3 yrs., and is reported: on Rolls to February 28/63. Present. March & April /63. Absent. Captured at Thompson's Station Tenn. March 5/63. (Co. in action at that place and date.) Subsequent Rolls to April 30/64 Present. May & June /64 Absent sick in Hospt. Madison Ind. July & Aug /64 Present. Subsequent Rolls to April 30/65. Absent detached Brigade Provost Guard. Muster out Roll of Company dated Washington D.C. June 12/65, reports him present & mustered out.

Name also borne as Josiah M. Ephlin.

Prisoner of War Records show him captured at Thompsons Sta. Tenn. March 5th 1863, Conf'd at Richmond Va. Mar. 22d 63. Paroled at City Point Va. March 31, 1863. (over)

[3—011.]

DECLARATION FOR THE INCREASE OF AN INVALID PENSION.

State of Indiana }
County of Parke } ss:

On this 9 *day of* November, *A. D. one thousand eight hundred and eighty-*Seven *personally appeared before me, a* Notary Public *within and for the County and State aforesaid,* Josiah M. Ephlin *aged* 48 *years, a resident of the* ___ *of* Annapolis *county of* Parke, *State of* Indiana, *who, being duly sworn according to law, declares that he is a pensioner of the United States, enrolled at the* Indianapolis *Pension Agency at the rate of* Six *dollars per month, by reason of disability from* Chronic diarrhoea and resulting disease (Here name the disability for which pension was granted.) of liver and spleen & rectum

incurred in the Mil (Military or Naval.) *service of the United States while* Private (Here state rank, company and regiment, if in the Army—vessel, if in the Navy.) Co A - 85 Regiment Indiana Vols -

That he believes himself to be entitled to an increase of pension on account of (Here state the reasons for applying for increase. If on account of increase in the disability for which already pensioned, that should be described. If on account of disability for which not pensioned, the location of the wound or injury, the nature of the disease, and the time, place, and circumstances of its origin, and the names of hospitals where treated in the service, should be fully stated. The dates of treatment should be given as nearly as possible.) too low rating for and an increase of the disability Chronic diarrhoea and resulting disease of the liver and Rectum and that the above disability has resulted in disease of the Stomach and spleen. and the disease of the Rectum has resulted in piles and disease of the urinary organs (Enlarged Prostate) -

that he appoints KNEFLER & LOPP, OF INDIANAPOLIS, COUNTY OF MARION, STATE OF INDIANA, *his true and lawful attorneys, to prosecute his claim. That his Post-office address is* Annapolis *County of* Parke, *State of* Indiana

Claimant's signature: Josiah M Ephlin

Attest: David Montgomery

John S McClure

(Two Witnesses to Claimant's Signature.)

3—402.

Certificate No. 301926

Name Josiah M. Ephlin

Department of the Interior,

BUREAU OF PENSIONS.

Washington, D. C., January 15, 1898.

SIR:

In forwarding to the pension agent the executed voucher for your next quarterly payment please favor me by returning this circular to him with replies to the questions enumerated below.

Very respectfully,

H. Clay Evans
Commissioner.

First. Are you married? If so, please state your wife's full name and her maiden name.

Answer. Yes, Anna Jane Ten Brook

Second. When, where, and by whom were you married?

Answer. October 2nd 1867, at Annapolis Ind. By Rev W. P. Cummings

Third. What record of marriage exists?

Answer. Records kept by Clerk of County

Fourth. Were you previously married? If so, please state the name of your former wife and the date and place of her death or divorce.

Answer. ——

Fifth. Have you any children living? If so, please state their names and the dates of their birth.

Answer. Yes, Addie born 1868

William B born 1869

Theodosia B. born 1873

Date of reply, May 4th, 1898

Josiah M. Ephlin (Signature.)

5301b750m1-98

Supplemental Declaration for Additional Pension.

SEE FOOT NOTE.

STATE OF INDIANA. }
COUNTY OF Parke } ss:

Personally appeared Josiah M. Ephlin Age 60 years of Annapolis P. O., County of Parke State of INDIANA, who being duly sworn upon his oath declares as follows:

That he is a Pensioner of Certificate No. 301,926; that his claim is now made to accept a pension under Act approved June 27, 1890. He now draws a pension of $6.00 per month, at Agency of INDIANAPOLIS, INDIANA for the following disability: Chronic diarrhoea and resulting disease of rectum and liver.

In addition to which he suffers with disability as follows: Stomach, heart and debility

Served more than 90 days in War of Rebellion and was honorably discharged from United States Service

The above disability he believes to be permanent, and is not the result of vicious habits.

He hereby appoints HENRY HOLT, of INDIANAPOLIS Ind., his lawful attorney to prosecute this claim to a final issue, the fee to be but $10 in case claim is allowed under Act June 27, 1890. Nothing contained in this application shall in any manner debar or affect claimant's rights under the General Pension Law. He was late a member of Co. "A" of the 85 Reg't of Indiana Vols.

(Must have two persons witness here.)

2 Henry C. Lamb
2 Thomas B. Evans

1 Josiah M. Ephlin
(Signature of Claimant)

Subscribed and sworn to before me, this 29th day of March 1901 189, and I certify that the party whose name appear signed to the foregoing affidavit is the person he represents himself to be, and that the contents of the foregoing affidavit were duly read and fully known to affiant before making oath to the same, and that I have no interest in the matter.

[SEAL] (Official Signature) 3 Joseph C. Vickory
Notary Public

My commission expires Nov. 11th, 1903.

NOTE.—This may be executed before a Clerk or Notary Public.

When complete return to

Cert on file in Pension Bureau Washington DC.

PENSION OFFICE U.S. APR 1 1901

FILED

SUPPLEMENTAL DECLARATION

For Additional Pension.

ACT JUNE 27, 1890.

ORIGINAL CLAIM OF

Josiah M. Ephlin

Co. "A" 85th Reg't. Indiana Inf Vols.

P. O. Annapolis

County Parke

State Indiana.

Claim under Act Approved June 27, 1890.

Draws $ 6.00 per month under general law.

Certificate 301,926

FILED BY HENRY HOLT, Claim Attorney, Indianapolis, Ind.

301,926 57309

W. B.

(b) Robert Tilghman Ephlin, s/o Alexander P.) - b. 14 Mar 1846 - 1887 Parke Co., Ind., buried Linebarger cem - m. Bertha - b. 1853 Ind

i. Dora Ephlin - b. 1872 Parke Co., Ind.
ii. Charles T. Ephlin - b. 1873
iii. Eva L. Ephlin - b. 1876
iv. Edna May Ephlin - b. 1879 Parke Co.

(c) Mary Z. Ephlin - b. 19 Sep 1855 Parke Co - 9 Aug 1882, Linebarger Cem - m. ? McIntire
(d) Rachel Ephlin - b. 1848 Parke Co
(e) Fanny Catherine Ephlin - b. 1848 Parke Co.

(7) Elizabeth Finney, d/o Joseph - b. 9 Mar 1820 Ind - 22 Aug 1900 Prairietown, Vigo Co., Ind - m. 7 Oct 1849 Daniel MATER (Rev) - b. 1 May 1810 Butler Co., Oh. Daniel and his brother John were the co-founders of the Offerbein United Brethren Church, Bellmore, Ind.

(a) George Wesley Scott Mater - b. 1850 - d. 1856
(b) John Winfield Russell Mater - b. 28 July 1852 - 1 May 1927 Danville, Ill. A contractor and Builder - m. 19 Mar 1874 Vermillion Co., Ill Sarah Ann DARR
(c) Daniel Harrison Riley Mater - b. 1854 - 18 Feb 1904 Ottawa, LaSalle Co., Ill. - m. Mary E. BELL
(d) Mary Jane Mater - b. 3 Jan 1857 - 9 Aug 1938 Terre Haute, Ind - m. C. Lee PHILLIPS
(e) Hiram Reasant Moore Mater - b. 4 Feb 1859 - 1921 - m. Mary Eva WATSON

(8) Rachel Finney - b. 27 Mar 1821 Ind - 21 Apr 1860 Wilmington, Will Co., Ill - m. 4 Nov 1838 Nacy Harrison JONES

(a) Joseph Wesley Jones - b. 13 Nov 1841
(b) Oliver Perry Jones - b. 14 May 1840

(9) Wesley Finney - b. 10 May 1823 Lawrence Co., Ind - 3 Oct 1904 Wayside, Montgomery Co., Ks, buried Fawn Creek Cem. Married 29 Aug 1850 Mary Matilda HINSHAW - b. 29 Oct 1829 Ind - 5 Feb 1900, d/o Jesse & Hannah (Moon) Hinshaw

(a) Samantha Jane Finney - b.7 Aug 1851 Parke Co., Ind - 26 Apr 1937 Wayside - m. 27 Feb 1868 Abner H. COPELAND - 28 May 1838 NC - 1 Nov 1909 Wayside, Ks.

i. Samuel Gilbert Copeland - 14 Dec 1868 Parke Co - 3 Jan 1940 - m. 1893 Mary Susan PENCE who d. 12 Feb 1955 - lvd. Chewalah, Wash. in 1936

a. Hugh Copeland - m. Pearl - had dau. Pearl Mary m. John CLARK
b. L. D. Copeland - m. Muriel - had a son
c. Nora Copeland - m. Fred SHIELDS - d. 19 July 1963

1. Betty Lou Shields
2. Robert Shields

ii. Sabina Evaline Copeland - b. 7 Nov 1870 - 10 Sep 1873
iii. John Wesley Copeland - b. 21 Dec 1872 - 13 Sep 1873
iv. Austin Hawkins Copeland - 11 Aug 1874 Ind - 18 Nov 1957 - m. Rhoda Pearl STEWART who d. 17 Dec 1957 - lvd. Independence, Ks 1937

a. John Earl Copeland - b. @ 1920 - 10 Apr 1944 WW II - m. Betty HOPKINS

1. John Earl Copeland - b. @ 1941

b. Ivella Copeland - m. BARNES - lvd.Kansas City 1944
c. Helen Mildred Copeland - m. DAVIS

v. Elbert "Epps" Copeland - 27 Nov 1877 - Apr 1943 - m. Vella WHEELER, who died 31 May 1955, lvd Sela, Wash. 1937

a. Bertha Copeland - m. Harold WEBBER
b. Gladys Copeland - m. Doug STONER

vi. Clarissa Copeland - b. 5 Oct 1879 Parke Co., Ind - 5 Sep 1970, unmarried, lived Harrisonville,Ks. with her mother

vii. Archie Jackson Copeland - 29 Mar 1882 - 27 Nov 1948 Spokane, Wash, unm.
viii. William Quincy Copeland - 23 Sep 1884 Ks - 7 Aug 1955 - m. Agnes Elizabeth McKAY - died 10 Dec 1933, lvd. Jacksonville, Ore. in 1937

a. Donald Copeland
b. Pearl Dewey Copeland
c. Deloss Copeland

Wesley and Mary Matilda (Hinshaw) Finney; James and Emily (Moon) Hinshaw (Mary's brother)

Mary Elizabeth (Finney) Mater (Wesley Finney's sister)

C. G. GLASS,

One door North Southern Hotel.

COFFEYVILLE, KAN.

DEED RECORD, MONTGOMERY COUNTY, KANSAS.

Saml Croft & wife TO Wesley Finney

Warranty Deed.

THIS INDENTURE, Made this 10th day of December in the year of our Lord One Thousand Eight Hundred and Eighty One between Saml Croft and Delia Croft Husband and Wife of Independence Tp in the County of Montgomery and State of Kansas of the first part, and Wesley Finney of in the County of Park in the State of Indiana of the second part.

WITNESSETH, That the said parties of the first part, in consideration of the sum of Four Thousand DOLLARS, to them duly paid, have sold, and by these presents do grant and convey to the said party of the second part, his heirs and assigns all that tract or parcel of land situated in the County of Montgomery and State of Kansas, and described as follows, to wit:

The South half of the South East Quarter 1/4 of Section No Thirty One (31) in Township No Thirty three (33) South and the North 1/2 of the North East 1/4 of Section No Six (6) in Township No Thirty four (34) South all of Range No Fifteen (15) East containing 160 acres more or less according to Government Survey

Wesley Finney land deed

160 acres more or less according to Government Survey

with the appurtenances, and all the estate, title, and interest of the said parties of the first part therein. And the said parties of the first part do hereby covenant and agree that at the delivery hereof they are the lawful owner of the premises above granted, and seized of a good and indefeasible estate of inheritance therein, free and clear of all incumbrances,

and that they will WARRANT AND DEFEND the same in the quiet and peaceable possession of the said party of the second part, his heirs and assigns forever, against all persons lawfully claiming the same

IN WITNESS WHEREOF, The said parties of the first part have hereunto set their hands and seals the day and year above written.

Signed, Sealed, and Delivered in the Presence of

Samuel Croft [SEAL.]

Delia Croft [SEAL.]

STATE OF Kansas, Montgomery COUNTY,—SS.

BE IT REMEMBERED, That on this 10th day of December A. D. 1881, before me, a Notary Public in and for said County, came Samuel Croft and Delia Croft Husband and Wife to me personally known to be the same person who executed the foregoing instrument, and duly acknowledged the execution of the same.

(L.S.) IN TESTIMONY WHEREOF, I have hereunto subscribed my name and affixed my official seal on the day and year last above written.

My notary commission expires the 10th day of December A. D. 1884

A. J. Keifer Notary Public
Montgomery Co. Ks.

Entered in Transfer Record in my office this 24th day of December A. D 1881. No.

Ernest Way County Clerk.

This Instrument was filed for Record on the 24th day of December A. D. 1881, at 3 o'clock P. M.

E. P. Allen Register of Deeds

Home of Mary Matilda (Hinshaw) and Wesley Finney (note on photo says "house in Kansas before he built a room and porch on the west (side)"

From left to right – Clara (Finney) Farlow, unidentified but I believe this is John Wesley Finney, Minnie Rayl, unidentified but I believe this is John Wesley's wife Nannie Brooks, Anson Madison, Mollie Rayl, Louisa (Finney) Madison, Mary Matilda (Hinshaw) Finney, Elwood Rayl, Wesley Finney, Daniel Webster Finney (in buggy), Hiram Rayl near wheelbarrow; baby on ground Mary Madison

From Jan Hinshaw of the Hinshaw Family Association

Mary Matilda Hinshaw was born into a Quaker family. Quakers were known for being very very "liberal" with people of other races – there were many Indians who would trust no white people, except Quakers. Quakers spoke out for Indian rights (as well as abolition) long before it became fashionable.

Yes Quakers did indeed mingle with Indians, opened and ran Indian schools and orphanages, and often adopted Indian children. We know of several Hinshaw families who did exactly these things (although Oklahoma was a more likely place for this to happen rather than Indiana – by the mid 1800s I don't think there were too many Indians left in Indiana).

From Margaret Bisch-Markowitz

The following photo was taken in Indiana (probably in Parke County, IN) about 1906. That is my best guess. The boy in the front row is my grandfather Ralph, who was born in 1892, making him about 13 or 14 then. The three girls on either side of him are his three sisters, Nan (10), May (7) and Margaret (5).

The tall gentleman top (or back) row, farthest left, is my great grandfather, Zachary Taylor Stuart and next to him and slightly behind him is his wife, Margaret. Zachary (or Z.T. as he was called) died in 1913 so the picture must have been taken before then.

The gentleman seated farthest left in the second or middle row is Z.T.'s brother, John Milton Stuart and next to him is his wife, **Anna Hinshaw Stuart (Mary Matilda Hinshaw's niece).** The other two couples in that row are two of my great grandfather's other brothers and their wives.

Stuart family photo – relations of Mary Matilda (Hinshaw) Finney (photo from Margaret Bisch-Markowitz)

Finney family photo – children of Wesley and Mary Matilda (Hinshaw) Finney
T – John Wesley, Daniel Webster, Clara Ellen
B – Samantha, Anna Elizabeth, Mary Catherine

Clara E., Wesley, Matilda & Daniel W. Finney

Wesley and Mary Finney (seated) with children Clara Ellen (Finney) Farlow and Daniel Webster Finney

Abner Copeland – 1861

John Copeland (Abner's brother – Union uniform); Andrew (Andy) and Nancy (Abner's brother and sister)

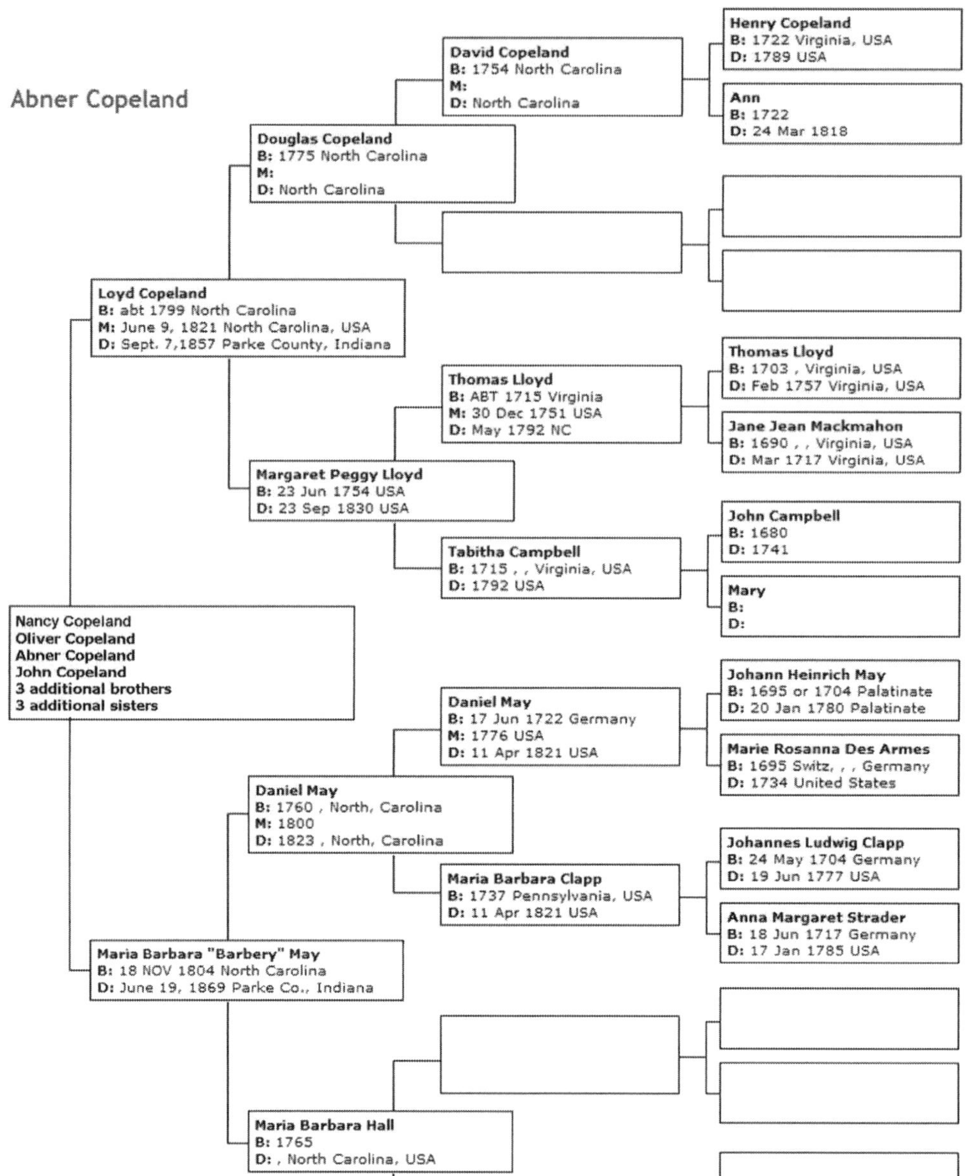
Abner Copeland
Henry Copeland
B: 1722 Virginia, USA
D: 1789 USA
David Copeland
B: 1754 North Carolina
M:
D: North Carolina
Ann
B: 1722
D: 24 Mar 1818
Douglas Copeland
B: 1775 North Carolina
M:
D: North Carolina
Loyd Copeland
B: abt 1799 North Carolina
M: June 9, 1821 North Carolina, USA
D: Sept. 7,1857 Parke County, Indiana
Thomas Lloyd
B: 1703 , Virginia, USA
D: Feb 1757 Virginia, USA
Thomas Lloyd
B: ABT 1715 Virginia
M: 30 Dec 1751 USA
D: May 1792 NC
Jane Jean Mackmahon
B: 1690 , , Virginia, USA
D: Mar 1717 Virginia, USA
Margaret Peggy Lloyd
B: 23 Jun 1754 USA
D: 23 Sep 1830 USA
John Campbell
B: 1680
D: 1741
Tabitha Campbell
B: 1715 , , Virginia, USA
D: 1792 USA
Mary
B:
D:
Nancy Copeland
Oliver Copeland
Abner Copeland
John Copeland
3 additional brothers
3 additional sisters
Johann Heinrich May
B: 1695 or 1704 Palatinate
D: 20 Jan 1780 Palatinate
Daniel May
B: 17 Jun 1722 Germany
M: 1776 USA
D: 11 Apr 1821 USA
Marie Rosanna Des Armes
B: 1695 Switz, , , Germany
D: 1734 United States
Daniel May
B: 1760 , North, Carolina
M: 1800
D: 1823 , North, Carolina
Johannes Ludwig Clapp
B: 24 May 1704 Germany
D: 19 Jun 1777 USA
Maria Barbara Clapp
B: 1737 Pennsylvania, USA
D: 11 Apr 1821 USA
Anna Margaret Strader
B: 18 Jun 1717 Germany
D: 17 Jan 1785 USA
Maria Barbara "Barbery" May
B: 18 NOV 1804 North Carolina
D: June 19, 1869 Parke Co., Indiana
Maria Barbara Hall
B: 1765
D: , North Carolina, USA

Family tree for Samantha Jane (Finney) and Abner Copeland and their children

Descendants of Samantha Jane (Finney) + Abner Copeland

Middle of page 98

(a) Samantha Jane Finney + Abner Copeland

NOTE: Samantha was the FIRST child of Wesley and Mary Matilda (Hinshaw) Finney.

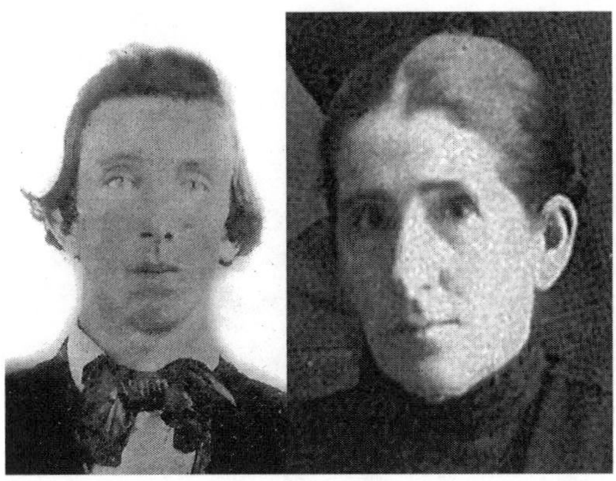

Abner Copeland – b. May 28, 1838 Alamance, KS; d. Nov. 1, 1909 (age 71) Wayside, Montgomery County, KS; m. Feb. 27, 1868 Rockville, Parke County, IN (age 29) to Samantha Jane Finney (age 16)

Samantha Jane Finney – b. Aug. 7, 1851 Clinton, Vermillion, IN; d. Mar. 26, 1937 (age 85) Wayside, Montgomery, KS

Abner and Samantha Jane (Finney) Copeland

Top row – Archibald Jackson, Austin Hawkins, Clarissa, Samuel Gilbert, Elbert Epps; Bottom row – Charles Owen, Abner, Emery Loyd, William Quincy, Pearl, Samantha Jane (Finney), Daniel Ezra Copeland – 1896

1. Samuel Gilbert Copeland – b. Dec. 14, 1868 Annapolis, Parke County, IN; d. Jan. 2, 1941 Spokane, WA (age 62); m Jan. 11, 1893 Tyro, Montgomery, KS (age 23) to Susan Pence (age 20)

Susan Mary Pence – b. Oct. 4, 1872 Cerro Gordo, IA; d. Feb. 12, 1955 (age 82)

4 generations – Samuel, Hugh, Hugh's daughter Pearl Mary, and Samantha

a. Hugh Earl Copeland (married Pearl Leona Jones) b. Jan. 15, 1894 (Tyro, KS); d. Jan. 18, 1958 (age 64); m. Mar. 23, 1914 (age 20) to Pearl Leona Jones (age 30) (she said she was 25 on the marriage certificate)

Pearl Leona Jones – b. Aug. 2, 1883 Blue Springs, MO; d. Nov. 16, 1982 (age 99)

Hugh and Pearl Leona (Jones) Copeland

i. Hugh's only child Pearl Mary Copeland – b. Apr. 8, 1918; d. Sept. 24, 2004 (age 86); married June 22, 1947 (age 29) John Stone Clark (age 28) b. Oct. 22, 1918 New Richmond, WI; d. Feb. 21, 2001 (age 82)

Pearl Mary (Copeland) Clark

aa. Janine Clark – married Clyde Edward Winder; they divorced; their children:

i. Lorene Lee Winder, who married Charles Bridges. Their daughters are Vivian and Charlotte Bridges.

ii. Rebecca Ann Winder married James Casarella, and their children are Lalana and Anthony.

iii. Mollie Beth, who married Trevor Pike. Their children are Lilian Pearl and Jack Stone Pike.

iv. Sally Jean Winder married Quinn Newton. Their child is Jacob Newton.

v. Susan Leona Winder

vi. Jesse Lee Winder married Shannon Hodges

b. Lenora (Nora) Lettie Copeland – b. Dec. 27, 1896 Tyro, KS; d. Mar. 13, 1969 (age 72); m. Feb. 15, 1922 (age 25) married Frederick Scheel (age 34) b. Feb. 4, 1888 Ritzville, WA; d. July 19, 1963 (age 75)

Frederick and Lenora (Copeland) Scheel

i. Betty Lou Scheel – b. 1923; d. June 13, 2000 (age 77); Dec. 2, 1946 (age 23) married Clarence Hubert Marshall (32) b. July 2, 1915 Aberdeen, TX; d. Jan. 12, 1988 (age 72) San Antonio, TX; married Henry Johnston

Clarence Hubert and Betty Lou (Scheel) Marshall

James Herbert Ayers (married to Beccy Marshall); Beccy and Judith Marshall

aa. Judith "Judy" Marshall - (married Clinton Kruiswyk)

i. William "Bill" Kruiswyk (married Diane Miner)

aaa. Nicholas "Nick" Kruiswyk

bbb. Taylor Kruiswyk

ccc. Katelyn Kruiswyk

ii. Thomas "Tom" Kruiswyk (married Shannon Roscamp)

aaa. Carolynne Kruiswyk

bbb. Erica Kruiswyk

bb. Rebecca "Beccy" Marshall (married James Ayers) divorced

i. Megan Ayers

aaa. Chance Ayers

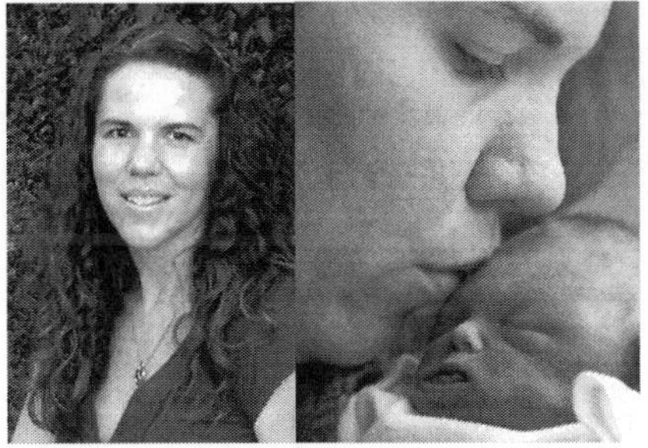

Megan Ayers; Megan and Chance Ayers

ii. Ryan Ayers (married Stephanie Martin) divorced

aaa. Ryan "Frankie" Ayers

bbb. Trace Ayers

i. Robert “Bob” Earl Scheel (married #1 Helen Joyce Olson) (married #2 Mildred Marmont)

Robert Scheel

Barbara, Deborah, David, and Elizabeth Scheel

aa. Barbara “Barb” Scheel (married Richard Bauer, divorced, and then married James Robbins)

i. Scott Royal (Bauer) Robbins, was adopted by Jim Robbins; married Dawna Alvarado;

aaa. Layne Arthur Robbins

bbb. Robert James Robbins

ii. Christopher Allen, married Mia Melinda Gillespie

aaa. Riley Melinda Allen

bb. Deborah Louise Scheel married James Lambert (divorced)

i. Jennifer Ann Lambert married Duane Nathan Little

aaa. Amilee Helen Little

bbb. Joseph Ronald Little

ii. Bonnie Kay Lambert married/divorced Porter Phillips

aaa. Natissa Joyce Phillips

iii. Debbie married Odell Leffall (2nd marriage)

cc. David Frederick Scheel married Bernita Elizabeth Vails

i. Aubrey Michelle Scheel married/divorced Wade Lynn Lafferty *ii.* Nicholas Robert Scheel married Kelly Anne Svoboda

aaa. Hailey Jo Svoboda

bbb. Jackson David Svoboda

dd. Elizabeth Marie Scheel

c. L. D. Abner Copeland (always used initials L.D. – which stood for Loyd Douglas) married to Merle (Muriel was her birth name) Gladys Compton. Lived in WA and settled in Alameda, CA.

L.D. Abner & Merle (Compton) Copeland; Jack Gilbert Copeland with parents

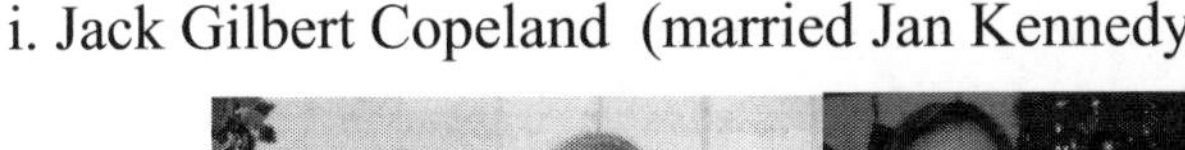

i. Jack Gilbert Copeland (married Jan Kennedy)

Jan and Jack Gilbert Copeland; Linda (Copeland) and Butch Shaw, Carrie (Shaw) and Arturo Limon and their children - Anthony, Emily, Jacob

aa. Linda Gay Copeland (married Butch Shaw)

i. Carrie (married Arturo Limon; they have 2 sons and 1 daughter)

bb. Mark Copeland

i. Ashley

ii. Ryan

2. Sabina Eveline

Born Nov. 7, 1870, lived, and died Sept. 10, 1873 – Annapolis, Parke County, Indiana – almost 2 years old

3. John Wesley Copeland

Born Dec. 21, 1872, lived, and died Sept. 13, 1873 – Annapolis, Parke County, Indiana – 8-1/2 months old - Both children died in infancy, possibly of diphtheria, in Annapolis, Parke County, Indiana.

4. Austin Hawkins Copeland – b. Aug. 11, 1874 in Annapolis, Parke County, IN; d. Nov. 18, 1957 Independence, Montgomery, KS (age 83); m. May 31, 1910 Jackson, MO (age 35) to Carrie May Swisher (age 36); second marriage before 1920 to Rhoda Pearl (Hancock) Stewart (age 33 in 1920)

Rhoda Pearl Hancock – b. 1887 KS; m. Robert W. Stewart about 1905; widowed by Mr. Stewart before 1920; had 3 children with Mr. Stewart that were raised with Austin Copeland; d. Dec. 19, 1957 (age 70)

a. John Earl Copeland – b. 1923 Montgomery, KS; d. Monday, April 10, 1944 New Guinea (age 21) (shot down and killed in New Guinea in WWII); m. Betty or Elizabeth Hopkins from Cherryvale in 1941 or 1942

John Earl (Sr) and Betty (Hopkins) Copeland

i. John Earl Copeland, Jr – b. July 13, 1943; d. Apr. 2, 1965 (age 21) (died in car wreck) m. Linda Louise Maher

John Earl Copeland Jr; Belinda & Taina Copeland

aa. Taina Copeland and daughter

i. Belinda

b. Ivella Stewart - stepdaughter; b. 1908 KS; d. Jan. 12, 1988 Portland, Multnomah, OR (age 80); Ivella married three times. She had one child – Richard Foulk. Her last husband was Ralph Barnes.

c. Mildred Helen Stewart – stepdaughter; b. June 18, 1913 CO; (married 5 times) last marriage. May 9, 1935 (age 21) Jackson, MO to Dewey Brown; d. Nov. 5, 1975 Portland, Multnomah, OR (age 62)

d. Robert Stewart Jr. – stepson; b. 1917 CO; d. 14 January 1935 of diabetes (age 18)

Ivella Stewart holding John Earl Copeland, with Mildred Helen Stewart & Robert Stewart – 4 July 1923; Rhoda with her son John Earl Copeland, son Robert Stewart, and her daughter Helen who is holding Ivella's son Richard Foulk

5. Elbert Epps Copeland – b. Nov. 27, 1877 in Annapolis, Parke County, IN; m. about 1900 (age 21) to Vella M. Wheeler (age 15); d. Apr. 29, 1943 in Yakima, WA (age 65)

Vella M. Wheeler – b. 1885 IL; d. May 30, 1955 (age 70)

Samantha, Epps, Vella, Clarissa, Beulah, Gladys, Bertha

a. Bertha M. Copeland – b. 1902 in Yakima, WA; m. Harold Webber

b. Gladys M. Copeland – b. 1905 in Yakima, WA; m. Doug Stover; d. 1978 (age 72)

i. Vella Lenora Stover–b.1925

c. Beulah A. Copeland – b. 1908 in Yakima, WA; m. John C. Schoonover; d. 1936 (died of influenza, age 28)

Dorothy Schoonover, Aunt Bertha (Copeland) Webber, Vella Lenora Stover

Beulah & John Schoonover Sr; John Jr and Dorothy Schoonover

i. Dorothy May Schoonover; b. 1924; d. June 2011 (87) m. Chuck or Charles Goeppner

Dorothy (Schoonover) and Charles Goeppner

aa. Kevin Goeppner

bb. Tim Goeppner

cc. Chuck Goeppner Jr.

ii. John C. Schoonover Jr. ; m. 1961 22 Apr to Jeanne Elizabeth Buergin (b. 25 Oct 1925; d. 20 Jan 2011)

John Schoonover, Jr; John and Jeanne (Buergin) Schoonover, Jr.

aa. Gary Schoonover

bb. Alan Schoonover

cc. Karen Schoonover; m. William Hosking

i. Christopher Hosking

ii. Twins Melissa and Megan Hosking

6. Clarissa Copeland – b. Oct. 5, 1879 in Penne, Parke, IN; d. Sept. 5, 1960 in Independence, Montgomery, KS (age 90); never married

7. Archibald Jackson Copeland – b. Mar. 29, 1882 in Independence, Montgomery, KS; d. Nov. 28, 1959 in Spokane, WA (age 77); late in life married Elaine; but he was a widower when he died.

8. William Quincy Copeland – b. Sept. 23, 1884 in Tyro, Montgomery, KS; m. June 7, 1910 (age 35) to Agnes Elizabeth McKay (age 27) Independence, Montgomery, KS; d. Aug. 7, 1955 Medford, OR (age 70)

Agnes Elizabeth McKay – b. Jan. 27, 1893 Independence, Montgomery, KS; d. Dec. 10, 1933 (age 40) Medford, Jackson, OR

William and Agnes had 1 daughter and 3 sons.

Agnes holding James Delos Copeland; Agnes and Willie with boys in Upper Applegate, Jackson County, OR shortly before Agnes died

a. Margaret Copeland – born and died on New Year's Day 1922; Montgomery County, KS

Donald William and Pearl Dewey Copeland; James Delos, Donald William, and Pearl Dewey Copeland

b. Donald William Copeland – b. June 12, 1924 Independence, Montgomery, KS; d. Mar. 22, 1968 Medford, Jackson, OR (age 43)

- First marriage: Mar. 26, 1947 (age 22) Medford, OR to Ruby Ilene "Patsy" Hall (age 31) (usually called Pat, she was divorced from Mr. Daugherty, with whom she had 2 daughters – Sharon and Kathlene (Katy). Daughter Katy lived with Pat and Don Copeland until Pat's death. Pat was born Apr. 16, 1915 Minnewauken, Benson, ND; d. Jan. 10, 1956 Medford, Jackson, OR (age 40)

Donald William Copeland and buddy; Donald William Copeland; Ruby Ilene (Hall) Copeland (known as Pat; Don's 1st wife)

i. Donna Elizabeth Copeland – married/divorced David Knight

aa. Daniel Steven Knight – married Kathleen Elizabeth Reinke

i. Lindsey Tenaya Knight

ii. Justyn McKinley Knight

iii. Lauryn Sierra Knight

Don Jr, Donna, and Walter; Donna, Don Jr, and Walter Copeland

Donna Elizabeth (Copeland) Knight; Daniel Steven Knight, wife Kathleen Elizabeth (Reinke), Lindsey (top), Justyn, and Lauryn

ii. Donald William Copeland, Jr. – married/divorced Tania

aa. James (Jimmie) (Tania's son from previous marriage) (married Taunya – has three children)

bb. Donald William III

cc. Sallie

- Second marriage: 1957 (age 33) Medford, OR to Mary Margaret Ricks (age 28) b. Mar. 17, 1929; d. 2 Oct. 2002 (age 73). Margaret was previously married to Joe Lovejoy (had 2 children – Mary Carol and Ricky), and Willie Pratt (1 child – Kelly); after Don Copeland's death, she married Harold Corliss.

Don and Margaret on wedding day

i. Walter Donald Copeland, married to Kimberly

c. Pearl Dewey Copeland - b. 1928, Tyro, Montgomery, KS; d. 17 Sept. 1939 (age 9 or 10) Medford, OR

Pearl Dewey and James Delos Copeland

d. James Delos Copeland – b. June 2, 1929 Medford, Jackson, OR; m. Mar. 3, 1952 (age 22) Osaka, Japan to Shuko Mine; d. Dec. 3, 1972 Mt. View, Santa Clara, CA (age 43)

i. Cousette Copeland

ii. Francis Ann Copeland married/divorced Renee Gardner

aa. Delos Thomas Gardner

iii. Stuart Justin Copeland

James Delos Copeland

Cousette, Shuko (Mine), Stuart Justin, Francis Ann, and James Delos Copeland

Cousette, Fran, Delos Thomas Gardner, Shuko, and Stuart Justin Copeland

Clarissa Copeland with brothers William (left) and Daniel Ezra (right)

Is this Pearl Copeland (Abner's daughter) or Lenora Copeland (Samuel Gilbert's daughter)? Photo wasn't labeled. Compare Pearl's photo on left, Nora's on right.

Samantha, Clarissa, and Pearl Copeland

Descendants of Samantha Jane (Finney) + Abner Copeland (continued)

This section replaces and updates the names from the original page 95, which contained dates for LIVING Copeland descendants.

ix. Daniel Ezra Copeland

9. Daniel Ezra Copeland – b. Oct. 19, 1886 in Independence, Montgomery, KS; m. *Unknown;* divorced soon after; d. Nov. 6, 1966 Independence, Montgomery, KS (age 80)

Worked on farms, following the wheat harvests. Later, he lived with his sister Clarissa in Independence, KS.

10. Emery Loyd Copeland – b. Nov. 19, 1889 in Independence, Montgomery, KS; age 27 m. Mary Clark (age 26); d. Jan. 5, 1964 in Independence, KS (age 74)

Mary Elizabeth Clark – b. Jan. 8, 1891 W. Virginia; d. May 1982 (age 91) Bartlett, Labette, KS

George Clark Copeland

a. George Clark Copeland – married Clara Maxine Kircher

i. Gregory Clark Copeland married Carrie Frank

aa. Holly Amber

bb. James Gregory

ii. Cynthia Ann Copeland - married Col. Kenneth Wayne Devan

aa. Jessica

bb. Megan

iii. Mary Jeanne Copeland – married Keith James

Back row, left to right – Jim Copeland, Keith James, Kenneth Devan; Middle row, Greg Copeland, Megan Devan, Jessica Devan, Jeanne James, Cynthia Devan; Front row, Holly Copeland, George and Maxine Copeland

b. Virginia Jane Copeland – m. June 2, 1965 to Frank Noble (age 51) (b. June 11, 1913; d. April 11th, 1977)

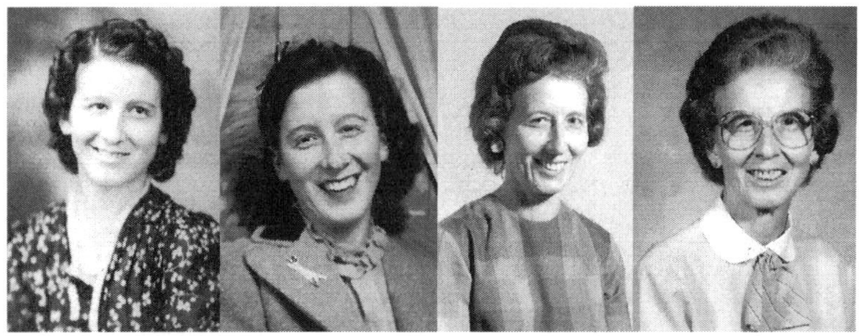

Virginia (Copeland) Noble

George Copeland and Virginia (Copeland) Noble with awards for the Copeland family having the farm in the family for over 100 years!

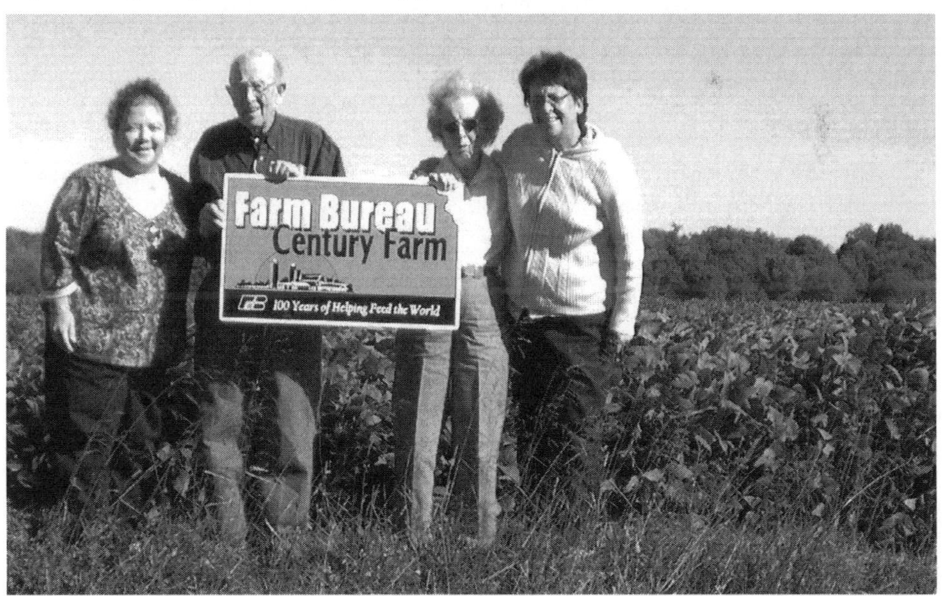

Cousette Copeland, George Copeland, Virginia (Copeland) Noble, and Fran (Copeland) Gardner stand on the land that the Copelands have owned and farmed since the 1890s! It's just down the road from "the old Finney place."

Descendants of Samantha Jane (Finney) + Abner Copeland (continued)

This section replaces and updates the names from the original page 96, which contained dates for LIVING Copeland descendants.

Charles and Stella (Hudson) Copeland; Stella and Charlie Copeland

11. Charles Orien Copeland – b. Mar. 6, 1892 in Bolton, KS; about 1920 (age 28), married Marie Stella Hudson (age 23); d. Aug. 31, 1969 in Wichita, KS (age 77)

Stella Marie or Marie Stella Hudson – b. 13 Dec. 1897; d. 25 Dec.1976 (age 79)

a. Ralph Owen Copeland – b. Nov. 5, 1923 in Independence, Montgomery, KS; d. Aug. 11, 2011 Coffeyville, KS – age 87; May 27, 1953 married Arlene Webb (b. 27 Apr 1923 Coffeyville, Montgomery County, KS; d. 21 June 2010 Coffeyville, Montgomery County, Kansas – age 87)

Ralph Owen and Arlene (Webb) Copeland – on their wedding day May 24, 1953

Ralph and Arlene with Pat and Lorna Patchen, at a birthday celebration for Ralph at local restaurant Mahoney Club House in Independence Nov. 4, 1984

b. Henry Harper Copeland - b. Mar. 5, 1926, in Bolton, Montgomery, KS; married Norma White (b. Sept. 22, 1919 in Caney, KS; d. Nov. 18, 2003 – age 84); d. Aug. 24, 1997 in Wichita, Sedgwick, KS (age 71)

Henry Harper Copeland; Norma and Henry Copeland

12. Pearl Copeland – b. Nov. 9, 1895 in Bolton, Montgomery, KS; (age 25) m. Dec. 22, 1920 to Frank Wilburn Koons (age 28); d. Nov. 26, 1964 in Wynona, OK (age 69)

Frank Wilburn Koons – b. Sept. 16, 1892 in Drywood, Pittsburg County, KS; d. Jan. 7, 1959 (age 66) in Wichita, KS

a. Claude Wilburn Koons - b. July 25, 1924; m. Hester Luvada Justus; d. Mar. 2, 1973 (age 48)

Claude Wilburn Koons

i. Sharon Fay Koons (Child with Hester Luvada Justus)

i. Claudia Pearl Koons (Child with Laural)

b. Melvin Leigh Koons – m. Earlene Fay Wright

Melvin Leigh and Earlene Fay (Wright) Koons

i. Karl Melvin Koons – m. Brenda Ann Garin

ii. Kevin Leigh Koons - married/divorced Brenda Van Duyn

aa. Benjamin Wayne Koons

bb. Jessica Pearl Koons

Jessica and Melvin Koons; Earlene Koons

iii. Kerry Wayne Koons

Karl, Kerry, and Kevin

Kevin's children - Jessica, and Ben Koons

c. Myron Wayne Koons – b. July 7, 1929 in Elgin, Chautauqua, KS; d. Jan. 2, 1987 in Kansas City, Wyandotte, KS (age 57)

Myron Wayne Koons; Robert Leon Koons

d. Robert Leon Koons – b. Nov. 20, 1931 in KS; d. Feb. 18, 2003 in Tulsa, OK (age 71)

Wilburn, Frank, Pearl, Wayne, Melvin, Robert Koons 1949 Xmas Wynona OK

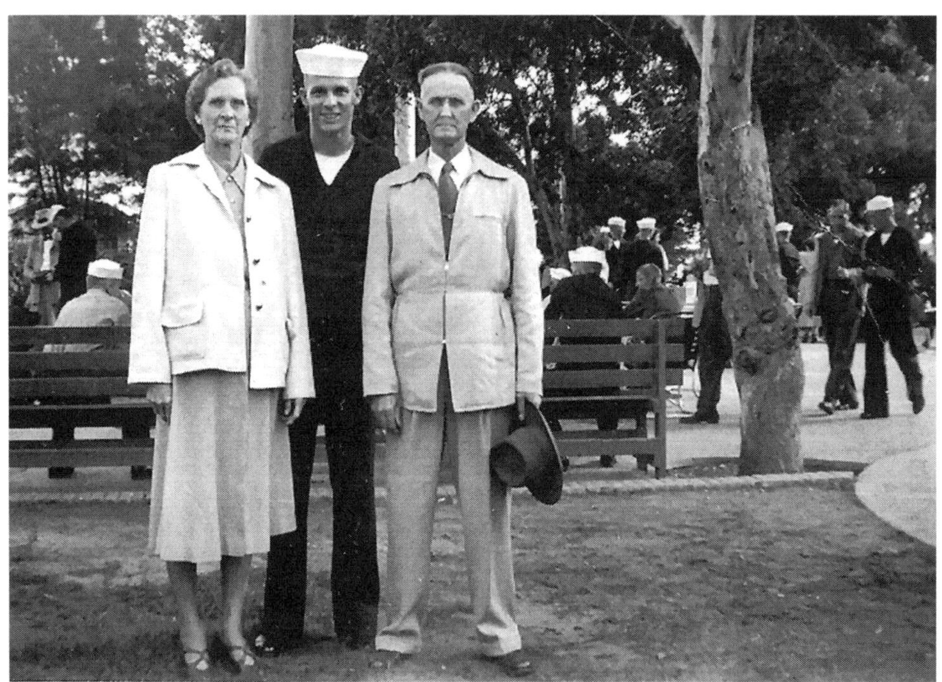

Anna (Allen – granddaughter of Mary Catherine Finney) Koons (Pearl's cousin), Myron Wayne Koons (Frank and Pearl Koons' son), and Vinson Koons

Finney descendancy continues with the Allen family from bottom of page 96.

(b) James Anderson Finney, son of Wesley – b. 10 Jan 1854 – d. 1858

(c) Mary Catherine Finney (b. 9 May 1857 Parke County IN – d. 22 Aug. 1926 – m 5 Sept 1880) + William Henry ALLEN (b. 3 June 1856 NC, son of Herman and Louise (Lamb) Allen – lvd. Montgomery Co KS 1900, later Canyon City CO)

i. Clara Belle Allen (b. 21 June 1882 IN – d. 23 Dec. 1931 – lvd Texas 1926 – m. 13 Aug. 1912) + Herbert NICHOLSON; she signed Daniel Webster Finney's autograph book on 28 Dec. 1897

ii. Nereas Lafayette Allen – b. 21 Feb 1883, d. 17 Dec. 1912 – m. 12 Sept. 1906 Sarah A. MILLER.

Clarissa and Pearl Copeland, and Clara Allen – perhaps 1905

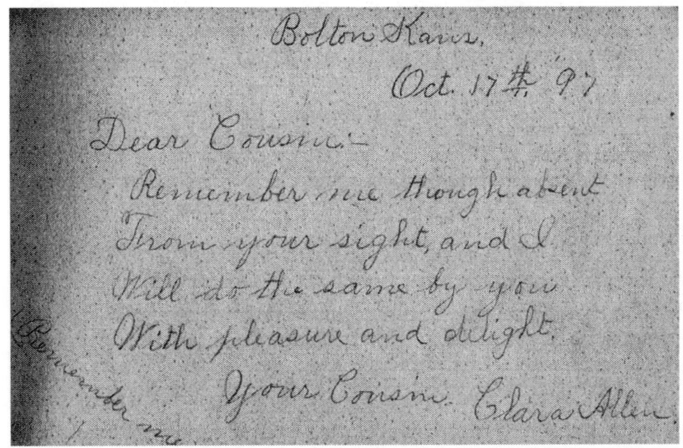

Bolton Kans,
Oct. 17th 97

Dear Cousin:-
Remember me though absent
From your sight, and I
Will do the same by you
With pleasure and delight.
Your Cousin Clara Allen

Remember me

Clara Allen signed Clarissa Copeland's autograph book in 1897

It is interesting to note that William Henry Allen's father (Herman Allen) came from Alamance County, NC, which is where the Copeland family came from. It seems that there was a wave of Quaker families who left NC before the Civil War, joining other abolitionists who were moving to Indiana. From Indiana, the Allens moved to Kansas and then to Colorado.

Also interesting is that William Henry Allen's direct ancestor is John Allen, who was born in 1722 in Chester, PA near where the original Finney family settled! Also, John Allen's grandfather came from Ireland, as did Robert Finney, but much earlier – about 1713.

The original John Allen who arrived in 1713 married Amy Cox in 1719. Amy is supposedly a descendant of Pocohontas and John Rolfe. However, this is not clear in genealogy information that I reviewed.

For those interested in a complete and detailed history of John Allen and his early colonial family, please refer to:

http://family-forest.net/JohnAllen1694Notes.html

Mary Catherine (Finney) Allen and Samantha (Finney) Copeland – sisters

This section replaces and updates the names from the original page 97, which contained dates for LIVING Finney descendants.

iii. Myrtle May Allen (daughter of William Henry Allen and Mary Catherine Finney) - b. 9 Jan 1887 – d. 22 Feb 1961 Tonasket, Wash. – m1. 25 Dec 1906 George Hamilton HENDRICKSON (son of Amariah Hendrickson and Mary Ann Smith) (b. 10 Nov. 1882; d. 20 Nov. 1954); m2. Jan. 1, 1951 Luther Shatto

Myrtle; Myrtle May Allen (age 18); George Hamilton and Myrtle May Hendrickson (wedding photo 1906)

Myrtle holding deer head and rifle; Myrtle and George Hendrickson (1934 or 1935)

Luther Shatto and Myrtle May Allen (wedding photo 1951); Myrtle

a. Mary Inez Hendrickson - b.28 Nov 1907 Wayside, Ks – d. 20 June 1975 Caney, KS - m. 19 Mar 1927 Forest Everett WILLIAMS b. 31 Aug 1904

Inez and Howard Hendrickson; Howard and Inez Hendrickson

1. Wanda May Williams - 20 May 1929 Okla – d 15 Apr 1973 Bartlesville, Ok - m. 11 July 1949 Donald Henry MORGAN

A. Donald Gene Morgan - m. Linda Hauser JEROME

B. John Everett Morgan - m. Joleah HARRIS

C. Robert Roy Morgan

D. Byron Lee Morgan

E. Ralph Eldon Morgan - m. Brigette WACHTERFIEL

2. George Marion Williams - m. Emma Jean VIGIL - d/o Eduardo

A. Jean Camille Williams

B. Forest Edward Williams

C. James Steven Williams

Back row – Laveve, Howard, Alta Marie; Front row – Myrtle, Keith, George, DeWayne, Inez; Front – Zula Mae Hendrickson

Front – Myrtle, Alonzo Keith, George Hendrickson; Rear – Nereas DeWayne and Zula May Hendrickson; Inez with son George Marion Hendrickson

3. Nelson Ernest Williams - m. Mary Ellen KING d/o Austin S.

A. Keith Alan Williams - m. Cathyrn

B. Mark Everett Williams

C. Nelson David Williams - m. Brenda RUSSELL

Left to right – Marion, Forest Dale, Mary Inez, Forest Everett, Wanda May, Nelson Ernest

4. Forest Dale Williams - 14 Aug 1934 Wann, Okla – d. 8 Nov. 2009 Bartlesville, OK. - m. 3 June 1959 Barbara Carol PLUMB - d/o Edward W. & Ila M. (Riley) Plumb; all three children are adopted

A. Kristen Mary William - m. Otis Keith Slocum

(1) Nathan Keith Slocum

(2) Brandon Lee Slocum

(3) Ryan Dale Slocum

(4) Kevin Michael Slocum

(5) Courtney Nicole Slocum

B. Charles Nelson Williams - m. Shelley Kay Kessler; divorced; m. Connie Marie Leggit

Children with Shelley

(1) Megan Marie Williams Norwood

(2) Gillian Kay Williams

(3) Katelyn Kristine Williams

Connie had 1 son and 4 daughters; Connie and Charlie adopted Karen Danielle Williams and Daniel Jason Williams (10 children total for Charlie)

C. Larry Dale Williams

Barbara and Dale Williams with Fran (Copeland) Gardner, Bartlesville OK

b. Infant daughter of George H. Hendrickson – born and died 8 July 1909

c. William Howard Hendrickson - b. 29 June 1910 Havana, Ks – d 23 Apr 1989 Pend Orielle Co. Washington- m. 1 Jan 1928 Gladys KINCAID; divorced

1. Dorothy Hendrickson

2. Norma Hendrickson

3. George Ray Hendrickson - m. Lorraine

d. Alta Marie Hendrickson - 15 May 1912 Havana, Ks – d 14 Apr 1982 Tempe, Maricopa Co, AZ- m. 23 Nov 1929 Harold Eugene FURNAS

1. Beulah May Belle FURNAS - m. 1 Oct 1949 Alonzo HOLMES

A. Mary Holmes - b. 28 May 1950

B. Kathlein Marie Holmes - b. 1 Mar 1952

C. Brody Holmes - b. 9 July 1957

2. Billy Eugene FURNAS - m. Mildred Maxine BROWN d/o Earl Griffen & Ada Belle (Stone) Brown

A. Paulette Maxine FURNAS - m. Paul Dean SUPLEY

B. Jeanette Lee FURNAS - m. James LAWRENCE

C. David Eugene FURNAS - m. Dale Marie SUMMERVILLE

D. Paul Earl FURNAS - m. Christine Jane FARNSWORTH

e. Alma Laveve Hendrickson - b. 13 Aug 1915 Havana, KS – d. 17 Feb 1962 Washington - m. 20 June 1936 Robert ALLEN

NOTE: Forest Dale Williams provided these wonderful photos of the Allen family moving from Kansas to Colorado. Dale's great great grandmother was Mary Catherine Finney who married William Allen, whose daughter Anna Allen was the gal who traveled with Pearl and Clarissa Copeland on their own trip down memory lane on the 1914 trip to Indiana. The photos Dale had were great - people in wagon trains, people on donkeys, and people up a tree!

Another mountain scene - all of us from Kansas but one (Dale's label)

An early 'mobile home!'

A Colorado "Christmas Tree" with the Allens as ornaments!

Who is Marcia Allen? Is she a relation of the Allen family? Did she marry into the Allen family? This is a mystery – can a member of the Allen family help identify her?

Close-up –Marcia Allen, Agnes (McKay) Copeland, Frank Koons, and William Quincy Copeland – circa 1920

Marcia Allen (standing) and Pearl Copeland (seated) 1914 Bloomingdale IN

1920s - Pearl and Samantha Copeland, Elmer Farlow, Nellie and Anna Wood, Dan Finney, Tim Wood, Perry Wood, Ella Farlow, and Clarissa Copeland

Samantha, Anna Finney Wood, Dan Finney, Clara Ellen Finney Farlow

f. Nereas DeWayne Hendrickson - b. 1 Apr 1922 - m (1) Velma, m (2) Edith
g. Zula Mae Hendrickson - b. 16 Sep 1926 - 2 Nov 1968 - m. (1) Harold E. RECORD, m (2) Ed LOWE
h. Alonzo Keith Hendrickson - b. 14 Sep 1928 - 25 June 1958 - m. 4 Apr 1954 Chloe SIMON

iv. Minnie Lou Ella Allen, d/o Wm. Henry - b. 8 Aug 1889 - 11 Feb 1922 - m. 18 Dec 1912 Grant J. ROGERS
v. Anna Matilda Allen - b. 18 Oct 1891 - 15 June 1963 - m. 28 Sep 1916 Grant Vincent KOONS - lvd. Coffeyville, Ks.
vi. Herman Wesley Allen - 23 Oct 1893 - 10 Oct 1936 - m. Sep 1918 Nettie P. HAAG
vii. Elmer Elsworth Allen - 17 Nov 1898 Montgomery Co., Ks - 26 May 1930 - m. 5 Oct 1920 Covetta KRUTZ - lvd. Texas in 1926
viii. Lillian Ester Allen - b. 10 sep 1900 - 24 Feb 1930 - m. 9 Jan 1919 Earl HARRIS

(d) Anna E. Finney, d/o Wesley - b. 24 May 1859 Parke Co., Ind. - d. May 1928 m. 18 Mar 1878 Tilghman WOOD - b. 9 June 1851 Ind - d. 1 May 1927

i. Perry Wood - b. 12 Nov 1886 Montgomery Co., Ks - d. 27 Jan 1962
ii. Nellie Wood - b. 10 Aug 1882 Montgomery Co., Ks - d. May 1929, unm.

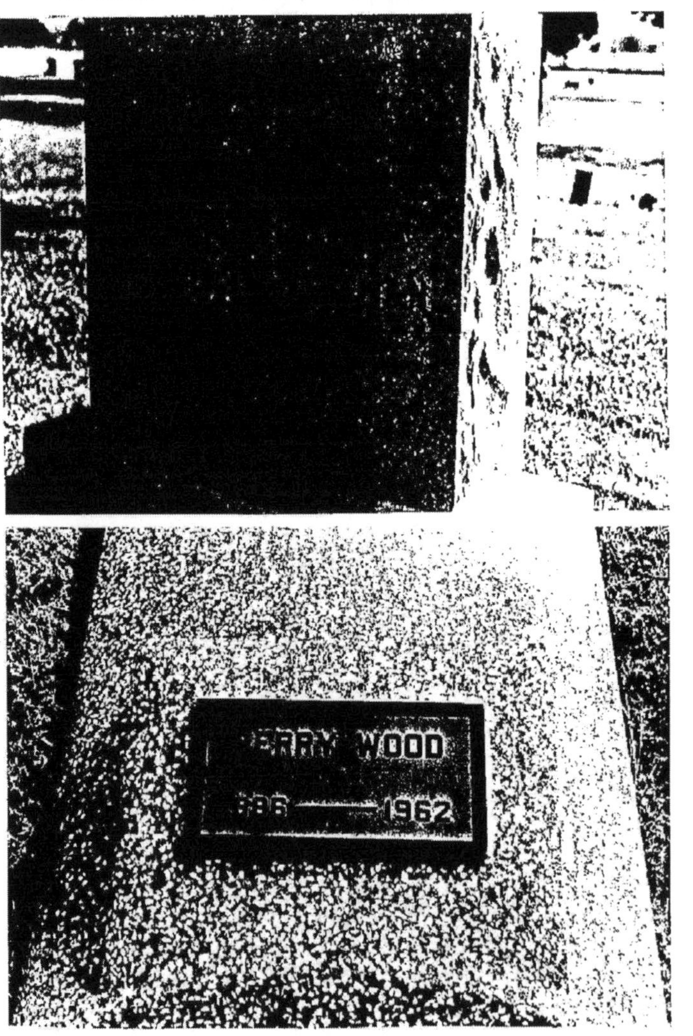

Hendrickson descendancy continues from the top of page 98.

f. Nereas DeWayne Hendrickson - b. 1 Apr 1922 Havana, KS, d. 17 Apr 1985 Washington - m (1) Velma GUSTIN, m (2) Edith

g. Zula Mae Hendrickson - b. 16 sep 1926 Havana, KS - 2 NOV 1968 Washington - m. (1) Harold E. RECORD, m (2) Ed LOWE

h. Alonzo Keith Hendrickson - b. 14 Sep 1928 Havana, KS - 25 June 1958 Washington - m. 4 Apr 1954 Chloe SIMON

Finney descendancy continues with the Allen family from top third of page 98. Living descendants do not have birth information listed.

v. Anna Matilda Allen (b. 28 Oct. 1891 Tyro, Montgomery, KS; d. 15 Jul. 1963 San Diego, CA) + Grant Venson or Grant Vinison or Grant Vincent Koons (b. 28 Feb. 1883 Sullivan, Moultrie, IL; d. 21 Oct. 1960 San Diego, CA); m. 1916 28 Sep Coffeyville, KS.

a. Gerald A. Koons (b. 1 Aug. 1917 OK; d. 23 Nov. 1998 CO)

b. Oren Carl Koons (b. 18 Sept 1919 OK; d. 17 Dec 1988 CO)

c. Mary A. Koons

d. Margaret E. Koons

e. Lily Louise Koons

f. Leona Koons

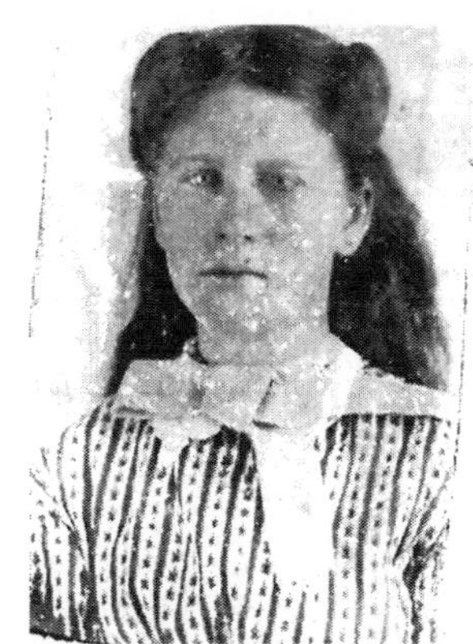

Anna Matilda Allen

Allen family moving by wagon train from Kansas to Colorado

Pearl Copeland (19), Anna Matilda Allen (23), and Clarissa Copeland (35), 1914 Indiana; Pearl, Anna, and Clarissa traveled from Montgomery County, KS to Parke County, IN 1914 to visit relatives.

Family photo – (front row) Emanuel, Arthur, Grant Vinson, (back row) William Hardy and Anna Koons

Anna Matilda Allen married Grant Vinson (or Venson) Koons. The Anna in this photograph is his sister.

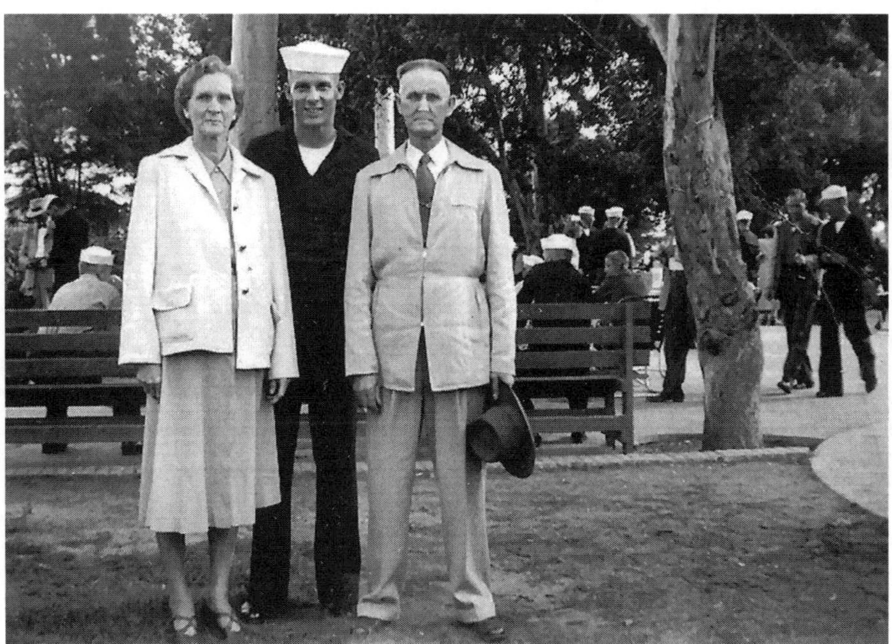

Anna (Allen) Koons (Pearl's cousin), Myron Wayne Koons (Frank and Pearl Koons' son), and Vinson Koons (Frank Koons' brother) where they lived in San Diego, CA; Myron Koons was nephew to Anna and Vinson (Venson) Koons.

These are Anna and Vinson's children (and other nephew) as adults.

Front row: Margaret, Louise, Debbie Caperton (Louise's daughter), and Dr. Jess Koons; Back row: Leona, Patti (Leona's daughter), Eva Lou (Mrs. Jess Koons)

Left to right - Margaret, Louise, Leona Koons– children of Anna Allen and Vinson Koons – and Dr. Jess Koons (son of Arthur and Laura Koons)

(e) Polly Hannah Finney - b. 23 Mar 1864 Ind - 12 Dec 1886 - m. 25 Dec 1885 James CUMMINGS - b. 1858

(f) John Wesley Finney - b. 14 Feb 1862 Parke Co., Ind - d. 6 Oct 1945 - m. 6 Oct 1886 Sedan, Ks to Nancy BROOKS - b. 18 Dec 1886 Sedan, Ks - lvd. Niataze, Chautauqua Co., Ks. 1904 when his father died

i. Nora Ellen Finney - b. 22 July 1887 Niotaze, Ks - d. 22 Jan 1961 - m. 22 Sep 1907 Sapulpa, Ok James Monroe NORRIS - b. 17 Sep 1888 - d. 10 Apr 1957

a. Harold Lenard Morris - b. 3 Aug 1908 - m. Lahuma D. EASLEY - divorced, m (2) 18 Feb 1949 Gainesville, Tex Lillian ARMERUSTER - b. 5 Apr 1913 Burlington, Ok.

1. Donald Wayne Norris - b. 19 Dec 1929 Ponca City, Ok.

b. Lyman Obedith Norris - b. 9 Aug 1910 Ponca City - m. 27 Jan 1936 Thelma Louise SADLER - b. 31 May 1914 - no children

c. Beatrice Lucille Norris - b. 26 Apr 1912 Niotaze, Ks - m. 27 Jan 1936 Benjamin Thomas SIMS - b. 31 Mar 1914

1. Gene Wesley Sims - b. 27 Feb 1932 Okmulgee, Ok. - m. 23 Nov 1951 Wichita, Ks. Mary Belle ST. PETERS - b. 17 Jan 1933

A. Mark Wesley Sims - b. 15 Jan 1954 Wichita, Sedgwick Co., Ks.
B. Lori Sims - b. 12 Jan 1958 Wichita, Ks.
C. Eric Wayne Sims - b. 3 Dec 1962 Ponca City, Ok.

2. James Edgar Sims - b. 1 Aug 1834 Ponca City, Ok - m. 29 July 1954 Marliene Carol MINTON - b. 5 June 1935 Wichita, Ks.

A. Dale Benjamin Sims - b. Apr 1955
B. Linda Kay Sims - b. 26 Oct 1956 Wichita, Ks.
C. Roger Allen Sims - b. 3 Oct 1968 Wichita, Ks.
D. Paul James Sims - b. 23 May 1961 Ft. Worth, Tx.

3. Jerry Lee Sims - b. 28 June 1937
4. Mary Ellen Sims - b. 2 Jan 1940

ii. Frank Finney, s/o John Wesley - b. 27 Nov 1888 - 15 Dec 1954 - m. 23 Nov 1916 Hattie Nichelson COLE - b. 13 Mar 1897

a. Melrena June Finney - b. 6 June 1917 Niotaze, Ks - m (1) 15 Dec 1943 Arnold W. HERTWICK - b. 16 Dec 1912, divorced, m (2) 17 june 1973 Clyde BISHOP - b. 2 Jan 1890 - 15 Aug 1985

b. Gordon Jack Finney - b. 17 Nov 1919 Niotaze, Ks - m. 1945 Ellen Josephine JOHNSON - b. 11 Nov 1932 - divorced

1. Nancy Lee Finney - b. 24 Jan 1947 - m. 28 Apr 1982 Frank Edwin PYLE
2. Gordon Jack Finney, Jr - b. 4 Feb 1948 Coffeyville, Ks. - m. (1)3 June 1967 Janice Elaine BRUNNENBARG - divorced - m (2) 23 Apr 1976 Cindy Lee PIPER b.25 Mar 1952 K. C., Ks. She was formerly married to Larry Robert COOK, deceased

A. Gordon Jack Finney - b. 26 Jan 1968 Coffeyville, Ks.
B. Michele Elaine Finney - b. 22 Mar 1970 Johnson Co., Ks.
C. Cari Denise Cook - 25 Apr 1973 Clay Co., Mo.
D. Aaron Scott Finney - b. 1 June 1980 Clay Co., Mo.

3. Nickie Geniva Finney - b. 31 Oct 1949 - m (1) Clarence GREEN - b. 4 Nov 1941 - married 14 July 1966, divorced, M arried (2) Billie W. CLAYTON - divorced

A. Lee Ann Green - b. 16 Feb 1967 - m. 14 June 1985 Wesley Dale CRANOR

(1) Corleigh Ashton Cranor - b. 23 Sep 1986
(2) Autumn Joy Cranor - b. 21 Sep 1889

B. Billy Lawrence Wayne Clayton, Jr - b. 22 May 1975
C. Birgindi Patrice Clayton - b. 12 Jan 1978

c. George Wesley Finney - b. 23 Feb 1922 - d. 26 Sep 1989 - m. July 1942 Mary Ellen SWANK - b. 11 Dec 1927 - lvd. Independence, Ks.

John Wesley and Nannie Finney

Descendants of John Wesley and Nannie (Brooks) Finney

Top of page 99 - corrections underlined

(f) John Wesley Finney m. to Anna Nancy (Nannie or Nonnie) Brooks

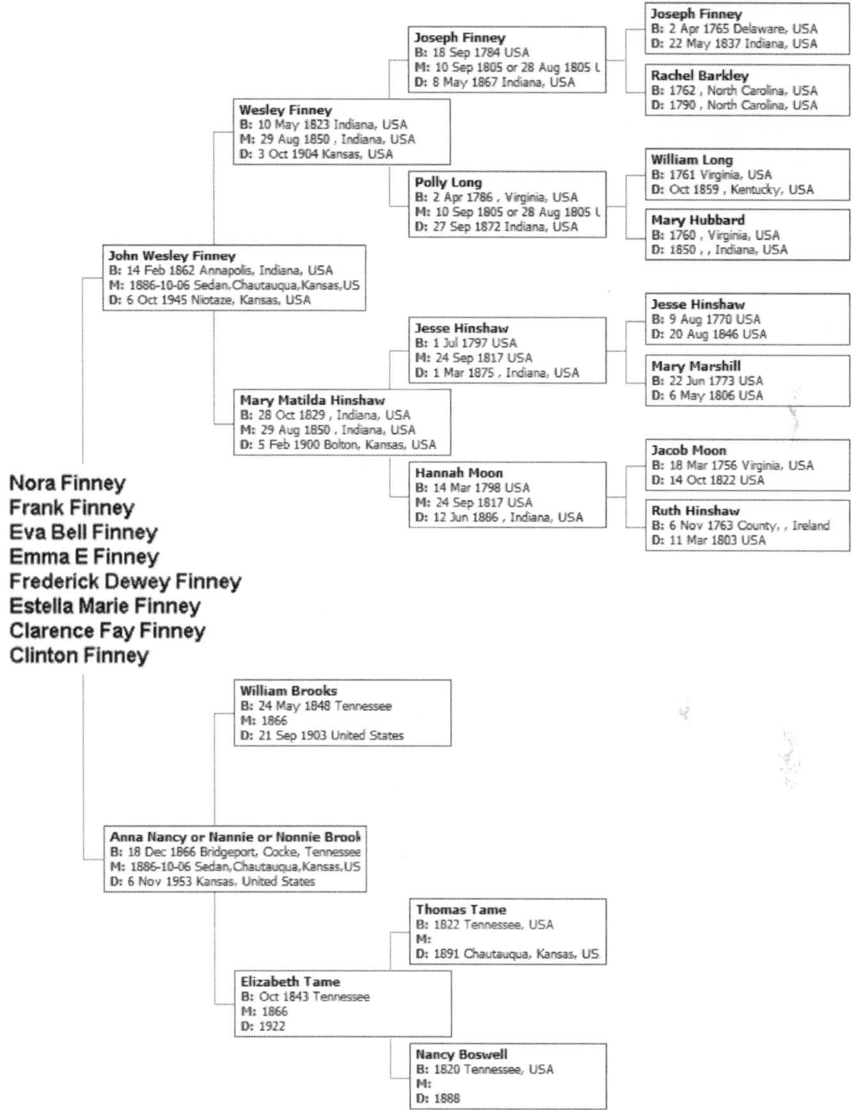

Family tree for John Wesley and Nannie (Brooks) Finney and their children

Until this book, most of the family did not know anything about Nannie Brooks' family. Her given name was actually ANNA NANCY BROOKS – but she was always known as Nannie or Nonnie (Brooks) Finney. Her parents were William and Elizabeth (Tame) Brooks. She had brothers - John David Brooks and Walter Alexander Brooks. She had sisters - Flora B. Brooks and Cora B. Brooks.

DEED RECORD No. 7, MONTGOMERY COUNTY, KANSAS.

Daniel B Snell & wife
TO
John W Finney

WARRANTY DEED.

This Indenture, Made this 1st day of August in the year of our Lord One Thousand Eight Hundred and Eighty four, between Daniel B Snell and Jennette A Snell his wife of in the County of Montgomery and State of Kansas of the first part, and John W Finney of in the County of Montgomery in the State of Kansas of the second part:

WITNESSETH, That the said parties of the first part, in consideration of the sum of Eight hundred and fifty DOLLARS, to them duly paid, ha sold, and by these presents do grant and convey to the said part of the second part, his heirs and assigns, all that tract or parcel of land situated in the County of Montgomery and State of Kansas, and described as follows, to-wit:

The South East quarter (1/4) of the South West quarter (1/4) of Section No thirty five (35) in Township No thirty four (34) and Lot No three (3) in Section No two (2) all in Township No. thirty five (35) South of Range No. Fourteen (14) East

John Wesley Finney land deed

with the appurtenances and all the estate, title and interest of the said parties of the first part therein. And the said parties of the first part do hereby covenant and agree that at the delivery hereof they are the lawful owners of the premises above granted, and seized of a good and indefeasible estate of inheritance therein, free and clear of all incumbrance,

and that they will WARRANT AND DEFEND the same in the quiet and peaceable possession of the said part of the second part, his heirs and assigns forever, against all persons lawfully claiming the same.

IN WITNESS WHEREOF, The said parties of the first part have hereunto set their hands and seals the day and year above written.

Signed, Sealed and Delivered in Presence of

Daniel B. Snell (Seal)
Jennette A Snell (Seal)

State of Kansas, Montgomery County, ss.

BE IT REMEMBERED, That on this 1 day of August A. D. 1884 before me, a Notary Public in and for said County, came Daniel B Snell and Jennette A Snell his wife who are to me personally known to be the same person who executed the foregoing instrument, and duly acknowledged the execution of the same.

(L S)

IN TESTIMONY WHEREOF, I have hereunto subscribed my name and affixed my official seal on the day and year last above written.

Wm C Otis Notary Public.

My Notary Commission expires the 1 day of Nov A. D. 1884

This instrument was filed for Record on the 4 day of August A. D. 1884 at 11 o'clock a M.

Jno F Nolte Register of Deeds.

John Wesley and Nannie Brooks and their children - Top row: Frederick, Emma, Nora, Eva; Bottom row: Clinton, John, Clarence, Nannie, Estella, Frank

John Wesley and Nannie Finney had eight children.

1. Nora Ellen Finney dob: 7/22/1887 - Spouse: James Monroe NORRIS m. Sep 22, 1907 - Supulpa, OK.
2. Frank Finney dob: 11/27/1888 - d. 15 Dec 1954 m. Nov 23 1916 Hattie Nicholson COLE
3. Eva Belle Finney dob: 12/24/1890 - Spouse: Thomas Blodgett McCARTHY
4. Emma Elizabeth Finney dob: 3/25/1894 - d. Sep 1958 m. 22 May 1911 Benjamin G. SHAFER - Sedan, KS.
5. Frederick Dewey Finney dob: 11/27/1898
6. Estella Marie 'Stella' Finney dob: 1/5/1902 - d. 21 Aug 1981 m. 3 June 1922 William Henry HILBERT
7. Clarence Fay Finney dob: 1/18/1904 - d. 6/23/72 m. 7/3/24 Martha Myrtle HANN
8. Clinton 'Red' Finney dob: 9/27/1907 - d. 9/29/86 m. 28 Mar 1929 Georgia Kathryn Irene LEWIS

John Wesley and Nannie (Brooks) Finney with some of their adult children – Nora, Stella, Frank, Clarence, Emma, Fred, and Clinton

John Wesley and Nannie Finney on their 50th wedding anniversary 1936; Mr. and Mrs. Earnest H Hanns (in-laws of Clarence Finney) (left) with John Wesley and Nannie Finney (right)

Underlined indicates corrections or additions:

ii. Frank Finney + Hattie Nicholson Cole (b. 13 Mar. 1899; d. 1 Jan. 1990)

NOTE: Hattie's real name may have been Hadlyne Hattie Nicholson Cole, as indicated in a census record. She was known as Hattie. It is likely that she was named after her aunt Hattie Hazeltine (or Haseltine) Cole.

From Gwendora Avon Finney Johnston

a. Melrena June Finney d. 26 Apr. 2006

1. Nancy Lee Finney d. 24 Apr. 2010; m. Claude Belknap

   a. Zachary Belknap

2. Gordon Jack Finney Jr.–
1 m. Janice Elain Brondenberg – divorced
2 m. Cindy Lee Piper - divorced
3 m. Evelyn

3. Nickie Geneva Finney b. 31 Oct. 1949; d. 18 Jan 2009 - m. Ricardo Simpson

C. George Wesley Finney – m. Mary Ellen Swank b. 11 Dec. 1927, d. Jan. 19th, 2008

Nancy (Finney) Belknap

Nickie (Finney) Simpson

F.A. Dwight, Hattie, and Lottie Cole (mother) (photo was taken in front of the bank in GODDARD, Ks)

Frank Finney in the Niotaze Sunflower Band; Frank is in the 2nd row with his name above his hat. Early 1900's

Hattie's father George Robert Cole, his siblings and mother Ellen Nicholson Cole

The Coles in Kansas City, MO.

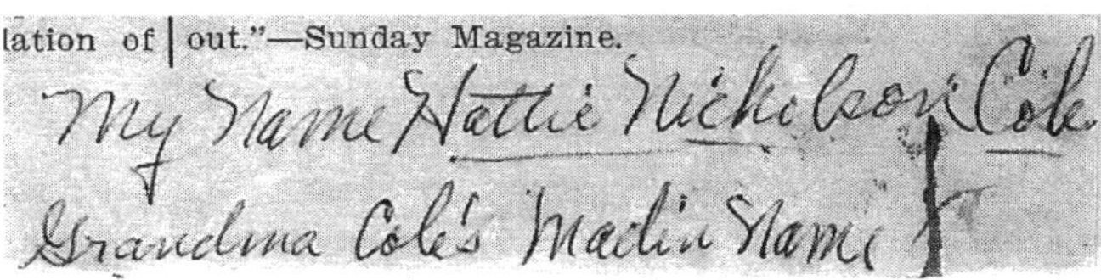

Hattie Nicholson Cole Finney's notes on how to spell her maiden name

Melrena Finney (Frank and Hattie's eldest daughter); Dwight, Gordon, Hadlyn or Hattie, and Mother Lottie Cole

A LETTER TO MA

(By Hattie Finney)

Just plain Ma we called you.

But, O! How dear that name, the sweetest, dearest mother-in-law any girl could claim.

Just six weeks ago today, Ma, God called you home to join Pa, and now I konw you are happy. And I wouldn't be surprised if God hasn't crowned you and dear old Pa, King and Queen up there.

Today, Ma, is your birthday—87 beautiful years you would have spent. I say beautiful, Ma, because that is what you were to me the short 36 years that I spent with you.

You were small and dainty, but a heart so big and strong.

I remember, Ma, when my children were born. It was your loving little hands that tended each one. And now, Ma, you are gone—we all miss you so.

This will be our first Christmas without you, Ma, and it just won't seem right. But God knows what is best for all and He just took you away to brighten up Heaven with your smile—and, I think, too—to teach us a lesson down here: That we cannot be sure of anything—only death; and Ma, I cannot think of you that way because you are not dead. In my heart you still live, so I'll close now, Ma, wishing you a most wonderful birthday with God and Pa—and we'll be seeing you some day. —Your loving, never-forgetting daughter-in-law, Hattie, and son, Frank.

Letter written by Hattie and Frank on Hattie's mother-in-law Nannie's death; Hattie Cole Finney

Hattie; Hattie and Frank Finney; Monica Finney (Frank and Hattie's youngest child)

Hattie, Monica, George, Jack, Melrena, and Frank Finney

George and Mary Ellen (Swank) Finney (son of Frank and Hattie); Mary holding Van, George, Gwendora, and Jerrold Finney

George Finney

The Finneys gathered at the home of Wesley and Mary Matilda (Hinshaw) Finney

1. Gwendora Avon Finney - b. 9 Nov 1950 - m. 25 Nov 1970 John Anthony JOHNSTON - b. 15 Jan 1955

A. Tark Anthony Johnston - b. 28 Aug 1979

2. Jerrod Martin Finney - b. 25 Apr 1952 - m. Pamela Jane PERRON b. 8 Aug 1953

A. Michael Graig Finney - b. 29 Nov 1984

3. Van Wesley Finney - b. 17 Apr 1957 - m. 2 May 1987 Rhonda Sue McSPALDEN

d. Monica Avon Finney - b. 13 Mar 1925 Niotaze, Ks - m. 16 Dec 1959 Virgil KIDWELL - divorced - m (2) Bill WEBB.- b. 21 Sep 1929

1. Pamelia D. Kidwell - b. 10 Jan 1945 - m. 1968 Charles ADAMS

A. Darin C. Adams - b. 21 July 1969
B. Mathew C. Adams - b. 25 Sep 1976

iii. Eva Bell Finney - b. 24 Dec 1890 Niotze, Ks - m. Thomas Blodgett McCARTHY - b. 23 Sep 1891 Uniontown, Ind.

a. Thomas Blair McCarthy - b. 25 Apr 1915 Denver, Colo.
b. Benita Viene McCArthy - b. 1 Dec 1916 Baltimore, Md - m. 22 Dec 1940 Orange, Va.Austin Marcus DRUMM - b. 14 Jan 1915 Uniontown, Mich.

1. David Blair Drumm - b. 30 June 1948 Albemarle, Va.
2. Richard Baldwin Drumm - b. 4 Feb 1950 Salt Lake City, Utah

c. Elsie McCarthy - b. 1 Sep 1920 Denver, Colo - d. 22 July 1975 - m. 21 July 1943 Robert F. SAMSON - b. 31 July 1920

1. Thomas (or John?) McCarthy Samson - b. 16 Mar 1947 Charlottes-ville, Va - m. Christine Ann PETERSON
2. Michael Robert Samson - b. 22 Feb 1949 Utica, N.Y.- m. Michele SAYEN
3. Thomas Kevin Samson - b. 25 July 1953 Urica, NY - m. Sandra DIBBLE
4. Timothy Brian Samson - b. 26 July 1958 Utica, NY

d. John Edward McCarthy - b. 3 Apr 1923 Denver, Colo.

iv. Emma Elizabeth Finney, d/o John Wesley - b. 25 Mar 1894 Ks - d. Sep 1958 - m. 22 May 1911 Sedan, Ks. Benjamin G. SHAFER - b. 22 Oct 1889 Nevada, Mo. - d. 9 June 1962 Bartlesville, Okla.

a. Robert Lowell Shafer - b. 19 Apr 1913 Caney,Ks - m (1) Claire ALCOT, divorced - m (2) Kathleen

1. Ronald Lowell Shafer
2. Douglas Glen Shafer
3. Dallas Ben Shafer
4. Roger Norman Shafer

b. Clifford William Shafer - b. 27 Jan 1916 Niotaze, Ks - d. Apr 1969 - m. 19 Aug 1939 Bartlesville, Ok. Bonnie - b. 30 Apr 1919

1. Carl Leon Shafer - b. 12 Mar 1944

c. Berniece Lorraine Shafer - b. 11 May 1919 Niotaze, Ks - m. 10 July 1937 Norman Luther MAYFIELD - b. 8 June 1918 Portland, Ore.

1. Anita Louise Mayfield - b. 25 May 1939 Coffeyville, Ks - m. 1959 Bob EDMONDS, m (2) 1960 Curtis Shiver, divorced, m (3) 1966 Don BASS

A. Cindy Edmonds - b. 22 Aug 1958 Nashville, Tenn - m. 25 May 1975 Albert GOFORTH, divorced, m (2) 5 Apr 1986 James SMITH, Jr.

(1) John David Goforth - b. 12 May 1976
(2) Christopher Wayne Goforth - b. 30 Oct 1977
(3) Jamie Lynn Goforth - b. 6 July 1983
(4) Jermey Raymond Smith - b. 19 Jan 1987
(5) Jenell Marie Smith - b. 12 Dec 1987

B. Michael Shiver - b. 21 Jan 1961 - m. Jan 1981 Sharon COLLINS

Descendants of John Wesley and Nannie (Brooks) Finney (continued)

Corrections to page 100 – **underlined indicates corrections or additions**

From Gwendora Avon Finney Johnston

1. Gwendora Avon Finney

    A. Todd Alan <u>Trimmell</u>

    B. Tark Anthony Johnston

2. Jerrold Martin Finney

    A. Michael Craig Finney

3. Van Wesley Finney m. Rhonda Sue McSpadden (b. 17 Oct. 1957;<u> d. 13 Aug. 2001</u>)

    A. Kayla Finney

    B.Brandon Finney

    C. Monica Avon Finney

        1. Pamela D. Kidwell

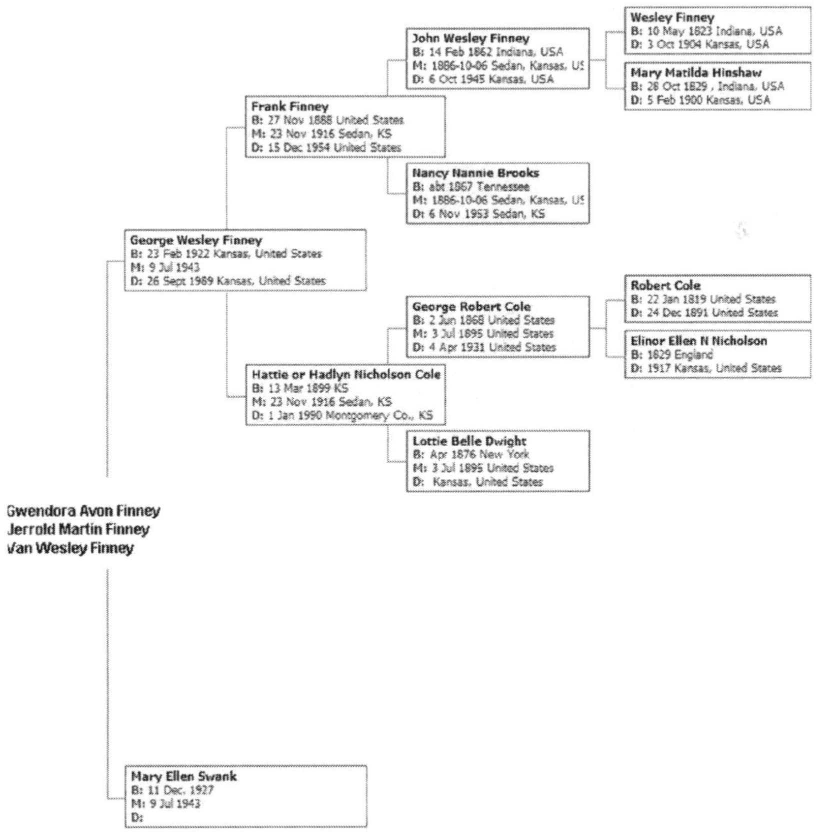

Family tree for George Wesley & Mary Ellen (Swank) Finney and children

Top row: Tark Johnston and Gwendora (daughter of George and Mary Ellen Finney); Bottom row: Leila Blum (Tony's maternal grandmother) and Tony Johnston

Gwendora's son Todd Trimmell, wife Amanda, and children Seth and Haley

Jerrold and grandmother Hattie Finney 1976

Pamela and Jerrold Finney (son of George and Mary Ellen Finney); Michael Craig Finney (son of Jerrold and Pamela Finney)

Wednesday, Jan. 21, 1987

Engagement

Mr. and Mrs. Bert McSpadden of Overland Park, Kans., announce the engagement of their daughter, Rhonda Sue, to Van Wesley Finney. He is the son of Edgar and Mary Ellen Youngberg of Chanute, Kans., and George Finney, Independence. Van is the grandson of Marie Swank and the late Lester Swank and Hattie Finney and the late Frank Finney.

The bride elect is a 1976 graduate of Shawnee Mission West, Shawnee, Kans. She is currently employed with St. Paul Insurance Co. in Overland Park.

Finney is a 1975 graduate of Chanute High School and the Navy Nuclear Power School of Florida. He is currently employed by Electronic Specialist Co. of Olathe.

The couple plan a May 2 wedding at Rolling Hills Presbyterian Church in Overland Park.

Van Wesley and Rhonda (McSpadden) Finney engagement announcement; Rhonda and Van Wesley Finney wedding photo

Van, Brandon, Rhonda, and Kayla Finney; Brandon and Kayla Finney

This is a story for Eva Belle Finney, who appears in the top third of page 100.

iii. Eva Bell Finney - b. 24 Dec 1890 Niotaze, Ks - m. Thomas Blodgett MCCARTHY - b. 23 Sep 1891 Uniontown, IN.

From Richard Drumm

The only Finney story I can remember is told of Bonnie's mother, who was born Eva Bell Finney but married into the McCarthy family. She had decided that she was of Finnish extraction (because of the similarity with her family name) and she thought this was great. She thought Finland was exotic! This was probably when she was young. Later on I suspect she learned that Finney is as Irish a name as you can get! However I have married a lady of part Finnish extraction, so my Grandma's great-granddaughters are part Finnish! She'd have liked that!

a. Thomas Blair McCarthy - b. 25 Apr 1915 Denver, Colo.

b. Benita Viene McCarthy - b. 1 Dec 1916 Baltimore, MD - m. 22 Dec 1940 Orange, Va. Austin Marcus Drumm - b. 14 Jan 1915 Uniontown IN.

1. David Blair Drumm

2. Richard Baldwin Drumm

c. Elsie McCarthy - b. 1 Sep 1920 Denver, Colo - d. 22 July 1975 - m. 21 July 1943 Robert F. SAMSON - b. 31 July 1920

1. Thomas (or John?) McCarthy Samson - Charlottesville, Va - m. Christine Ann –

2. Michael Robert Samson - m. Michele SAYEN

3. Thomas Kevin Samson - m. Sandra DIBBLE

4. Timothy Brian Samson - b. 26 July 1958 Utica, NY

d. John Edward McCarthy - b. 3 Apr 1923 Denver, Colo.

Anna Elizabeth, John Wesley, Polly, and Clara Ellen

Daniel Webster and Mary Catherine

(1) Michael Wayne Shiver - b. 8 Oct 1981
(2) Jennifer Lynn Shiver - b. 12 Mar 1988

C. Jeffrey Scott Shiver - b. 18 July 1962 St. Petersburg, Flor. - m. 5 Oct 1985 Debbie BATCHWELDER

(1) Nickelie Scott Shiver - 14 Feb 1987 Tampa, Flor.
(2) Joshua Shiver - b. 20 Jan 1989 Flint, Mich.

D. Tracy Bass

2. Sherry Ann Mayfield - b. 2 Dec 1941 Newport News, Va. - m. 1961 Gene SMITH, divorced - m (2) 1973 Tony CISSUE, divorced - m (3) Jay CLERENGER, m (4) 1983 Jerry MAYO

A. Timothy Smith - b. 16 Jan 1963 - m. 5 Jan 1985 Tammy
B. Keith Smith - b. 10 Sep 1964 - m. Jan 1988 Pam
C. Hope Smith - b. 8 July 1968

3. Gloria Jean Mayfield - b. 25 Sep 1944 Jacksonville, Flor - m. 1962 Eulos L. BECKNER II

A. Roxann Beckner - b. 13 Oct 1962 - m. Joseph BRYNES
B. Eulos Leon Beckner - b. 1 Oct 1964 - m. 15 Apr 1989 Wendy SAILER

d. Carl George Shafer - b. 10 Mar 1924 Caney, Ks - d. 13 Nov 1942 on board ship - World War II

v. Fred Dewey Finney, s/o John Wesley - b. 27 Feb 1898 Miotaze, Ks - d. 11 Feb 1960 - m. 2 May 1917 Sedan, Ks to Pearl Clairdia NORRIS - b. 9 Feb 1900 Fayetteville, Ark - d. 14 Nov 1970

a. Fern Finney - b. 5 Jan 1919 Towanda, Ks - m. 15 Aug 1936 Verne E. GILLILAND - b. 24 Nov 1916 Tyro, Ks.

1. Shirley Ann Gilliland - b. 15 Jan 1937 Tyro, Ks - m. 21 Mar 1954 Cozad, Nebr. Ernest LaDean SMIDT - b. 20 Apr 1934

A. Steven LaDean Smidt - b. 29 Dec 1955 - m. 25 Oct 1980 Judy Lynn ESSLINGER

(1) Brandy Chantille Esslinger - b. 20 Oct 1983
(2) Justin LaDean Esslinger - b. 22 Nov 1988

B. Michael Alan Smidt - b. 23 Oct 1957 - m. 5 Aug 1978 Terri Jean NIEDAN - b. 25 May 1958 - divorced July 1985

(1) Tiffany Elizabeth Smidt - b. 8 Aug 1980
(2) Melissa Jean Smidt - b. 9 July 1982

C. Shelly Sue Smidt - b. 28 Sep 1960 - m. 6 Jan 1980 Thomas Warren KNOBEL - b. 24 Feb 1956

(1) David Warren Knobel - b. 11 Mar 1980

D. Randy Wes Smidt - b. 12 May 1963 - m. 4 Jan 1986 Barbara Jo POTTER - b. 3 June 1964

(1) Rachel Nicole Smidt - b. 7 July 1989

2. Karen Sue Gilliland - b. 11 July 1941 Tyro, Ks - m. 20 June 1965 Sterling, Colo. Eldon Eugene ANDERSON - b. 25 Mar 1935

A. Scott Derek Anderson - b. 11 May 1970 Steamboat Springs, Colo.
B. Stephanie Lynn Anderson - b. 2 Jan 1973 Rifle, Colo.

3. Larry Dean Gilliland - b. 12 Oct 1965 Sandra Kay MONTAGUE - b. 7 Oct 1946 Sterling, Colo.

A. Jody Lynn Gilliland - b. 12 Oct 1965 Sterling, Colo - m. 27 July 1984 Steve STANLEY - b. 28 Nov 1962

(1) Kara Lanae Stanley - b. 19 Aug 1985
(2) Larissa Ann Stanley - b. 11 Sep 1987

B. Larry Dean Gilliland - b. 21 Feb 1968 Greeley, Colo.
C. Graig Eugene Gilliland - b. 23 Aug 1974 Sterling, Colo.
D. Lynnette Renee Gilliland - b. 7 Apr 1979 Sterling, Colo.

4. Sharon Kay Gilliland - b. 1 June 1945 Caney, Ks - m. 26 Dec 1965 Larry Dean WEBER - b. 7 Mar 1944 Holyoke, Colo.

Fred and Pearl (Norris) Finney

Family photos for the Gilliland Family, which begins at the top third of page 101.

v. Fred Dewey Finney, S/o John Wesley - b. 27 Feb 1898 Niotaze, Ks - d. 11 Feb 1960 - m. 2 May 1917 Sedan, Ks to Pearl Claudia NORRIS - b. 9 Feb 1900 Fayetteville, Ark - d. 14 Nov 1970

Fred Finney; Fred and Pearl Finney

Fred Finney with his sons: left to right: Paul, Glen, Fred, Gerald, Russell, Warren; Jerry (in front)

a. Fern Finney - b. 5 Jan 1919 Towanda. Ks - m. 15 Aug 1936 Verne E. GILLILAND - b. 24 Nov 1916 Tyro, Ks.

Scott, Karen, and Stephanie Gilliland

2. Karen Sue Gilliland - m. Eldon Eugene ANDERSON

A. Scott Derek Anderson

B. Stephanie Lynn Anderson.

For page 102

Shane Bowman (son of Woodson Lee Bowman; grandson of Leatha Finney Bowman) –1989 – top of page 102

BIRTHS

Andrew Dennis Bowman — Shaycee Fawn Bowman, age 4, Havana, announces the birth of her brother, Andrew Dennis Bowman, born at 4:53 p.m., Thursday, Feb. 14, 2002, at Jane Phillips Medical Center, Bartlesville, Okla.

The baby weighed 9 pounds 6 ounces and was 22 inches in length.

Parents are Shane and Kasey Bowman.

Grandparents include DeWayne and Kathy Rose, Caney; Woodson Bowman, Caney; and Don and Donna Armitage, Havana.

Great-grandparents are Billy and Ginger Duncan and Bud and Faye Rose, all of Alva, Okla., Leatha Bowman, Caney, and Stephen Bowman, Caney.

For Warren E. Finney – middle of page 102

A. Marc Dean Weber - b. 5 Apr 1969 Holyoke, Colo.
B. Marla Kay Weber - b. 17 Sep 1970 Holyoke, Colo.
C. Monica Ann Weber - b. 12 Oct 1976 Wray, Colo.

b. Leatha Finney, d/o Fred Dewey - b. 26 Oct 1920 Niotaze, Ks - m. Stephen Woodson BOWMAN - b. 11 Oct 1919

1. Woodson Lee Bowman - b. 4 Nov 1943 Wichita, Ks - m (1) Pauline MONTOYA, divorced - m (2) June 1968 Donna SAYE - b. 15 July 1949, divorced

A. Shawn Lee Bowman - b. 25 June 1966
B. Shane Alan Bowman - b. 19 Mar 1971
C. Gerald Woodson Bowman - b. 4 Sep 1973
D. Sholene Denise Bowman - b. 21 Nov 1975

c. Nancy Aileen Finney - b. 5 May 1922 Niotaze, Ks - m (1) 1 Aug 1946 Arthur Lee JAMES - b. 27 May 1923 Peru, Ks - d. 10 May 1981 auto accident - m (2) 15 Nov 1985 Biesley, Tex. Robert Dale BUSTER - b. 24 Sep 1921 - no children

d. Paul James Finney - b. 4 Dec 1924 Havana, Ks - d. 15 Sep 1962 - m. 31 Dec 1948 Betty June ATKINSON - b. 19 June 1930

1. James Leslie Finney - b. 10 Oct 1949 Wayside, Ks.
2. Wayne Steven Finney - b. 5 Oct 1950 Wayside, Ks - m. 27 Aug 1976 Miami, Okla. Paula Jean NAKAYOMA - b. 1 Oct 1952 Odessa, Texas

A. Laurie Jean Finney - b. 2 Aug 1977 Bartlesville, Okla.
B. Lisa Marie Finney - 7 Apr 1980
C. Jason Paul Finney - b. 13 Dec 1982

3. Michael Dean Finney - b. 19 July 1953 - m. 4 Jan 1984 Las Vegas, Nev. Katherine June COMER - b. Aug 1950

A. Mark A. Comer (step-son) - b. 23 June 1967 Des Moines, Iowa
B. Kimberly L. Comer (step-dau) - b. 14 Jan 1969 Mt. Ayr, Iowa

4. Kurt Allen Finney - b. 2 Mar 1955 - m. 24 Aug 1980 Sharon BURROW - b. 31 Mar 1956

A. Kole Alan Finney - b. 23 May 1982 Bartlesville, Okla.
B. Kyler Arthur Finney - b. 17 Mar 1986

e. Warren Eugene Finney, s/o Fred Dewey - b. 1 Nov 1928 - m (1) 31 Dec 1948 Betty Darlene TOLBERT - b. 26 Nov 1932, divorced - m (2) 4 June 1967 Wydene Mae (Smolherman) OWENS - b. 18 Aug 1937. She has three children - Brandon, Robin and Ryan OWENS.

1. Linda Diane Finney - b. 9 Jan 1951 Coffeyville, Ks - m. 1 Apr 1976 Mike Lee CUMMINGS - b. 11 Apr 1956 - divorced 16 July 1980 - m (2) Apr 1984 Herbert Lynn KROESCHE - b. 18 Dec 1958

A. Cam Lee Cummings - b. 16 June 1977 Amarillo, Texas
B. Dusty Warren Kroesche - b. 3 June 1985 Wharton, Texas
C. Rusty Roland Kroesche - b. 3 June 1985 (twin)

2. Sandra Elaine Finney - b. 27 Aug 1953 Coffeyville, Ks - m. 5 Dec 1970 David Robert PRESLEY - b. 16 Sep 1948

A. Amber Dawn Presley - b. 25 July 1974 Claremore, Okla.
B. Matthew Leland Presley - b. 27 Jan 1979 Dallas
C. Jonathan David Presley - b. 16 Dec 1983 in Houston, Tex - d. 22 Dec 1987

3. Jeffrey Lane Finney - b. 22 Dec 1959 Coffeyville, Ks - m. 23 Nov 1985 Bartlesville, Okla Denise Deann WOODLEY - b. 30 Sep 1965 Ft. Dodge, Iowa

A. Christopher Lane Finney - b. 4 July 1987 Bartlesville, Okla.

Paul J. Finney Dies Saturday; Rites Tuesday

CANEY — Paul James Finney, 37, well known young farmer and stockman of rural Havana, was pronounced dead on arrival at the local hospital Saturday night at 11:25.

Finney, an apparent heart attack victim had been hunting coyotes northeast of Caney when he was stricken ill.

Funeral services will be held Tuesday at 2 p.m. at the Graves Chapel in this city with Rev. Joe Brown presiding. Burial will be in Havana.

The deceased was born Dec. 4, 1924 at Havana the son of Fred D. and Pearl Norris Finney. He had resided in the county all his life. He was a veteran of World War II serving in the U.S. Army. On Dec. 31, 1948 at Caney he was married to Miss Betty Atkinson who survives. The family home is four miles east of Havana.

Mr. Finney was a member of the Independence VFW Post.

Surviving are: The wife and four sons, Jimmy, Wayne, Michael and Kurt, all of the home; his mother, Mrs. Pearl Finney, Caney; four sisters, Mrs. Letha Bowman, Fairview, N.M., Mrs. Nancy James, Caney, Mrs. Fern Gilliland, Sterling, Colo., and Miss Twila Finney, Wichita; four brothers, Warren, rural Caney, Russell, rural Caney and Jerry and Gerald, rural Caney.

4. Robin Paige Finney - adopted - b. 1 Dec 1959 - m. 21 Aug 1977 Charles Allen KAMINSHA - b. 20 July 1959

A. Michael Jerrod Kaminska - b. 17 Oct 1977
B. Craig Allen Kaminska - b. 14 May 1981
C. Chelsi Marie Kaminska - b. 8 Mar 1987

5. Ryan Delen Finney - adopted - b. 30 Jan 1966 Coffeyville, Ks - unmarried
6. MegginR-Nae Finney - b. 16 May 1968 Bartlesville, Ok
7. Reggin L. Rae Finney - b. 16 May 1968 - m. 8 Aug 1987 James R. KEENE - b. 4 Nov 1966 Coffeyville, Ks.

f. Glen Dewayne Finney - b. 19 Aug 1931 Wayside, Ks - d. 11 June 1953 - Korean War - m. 21 Mar 1952 Alene DENNY - no children
g. Gerald Dean Finney - b. 19 May 1936 Wayside, Ks - m. 27 Dec 1957 Dearing, Ks Amelia Ival DYE - b. 10 Dec 1940

1. Ricky Dean Finney - b. 13 Aug 1958 - m. 19 Nov 1983 Judith Sue BURNS - b. 14 Feb 1960

A. Clinton Dean Finney - b. 31 Dec 1985 Wichita, Ks
B. Kayla Maxine Finney - b. 3 Jan 1989 Wichita, Ks
C. Craig Michael Finney - b. 9 May 1989 Wichita, Ks.

2. Bradley Scott Finney - b. 14 July 1960 - m. Nancy DURST MATA. She has two children: Carrie Lynn Mata and Shana Mata.

3. Tracy Lynn Finney - b. 11 Aug 1961 - m. 13 Nov 1981 Caney, Ks Angela Jo GRAYUM - b. 5 Nov 1962

A. Andrew Lynn Finney - b. 27 Sep 1986
B. Mathew Lee Finney - b. 17 Oct 1988

h. Russell Dallas Finney - b. 28 Jan 1939 Wayside, Ks - m. 31 Dec 1958 Georgia Anne GRUVER - b. 29 July 1942 - divorced

1. Dallas Ann Finney - b. 5 Sep 1959 Seattle, Wash.
2. Kandy Kylene Finney - b. 25 Apr 1962 Independence, Ks - m. 14 July 1979 Mitchell Robert DOWELL - b. 21 Mar 1961

A. Justin Mitchell Dowell - b. 22 Jan 1980 Independence, Ks
B.Kyler Hamilton Dowell - b. 26 Mar 1982
C. Matthew Russell Dowell - b. 20 May 1986 Pratt, Ks
D. Adam Samuel Dowell - b. 11 Oct 1988 Pratt, Ks

3. Teresa Dawn Finney - b. 22 June 1965 - d. 29 May 1972
4. Cherie Kaye Finney - b. 1 Nov 1969 Independence, Ks.

i. Twyla Louise Finney - b. 16 Oct 1941 Wayside, Ks - m. David T. SAWDY b. 28 Dec 1937

1. Bruce Allen Sawdy - b. 30 June 1963 - m. 10 Aug 1985 Jennifer Lynne ULRICH - b. 1 Nov 1962

A. Terrance Marie Sawdy - b. 16 Sep 1986 Wichita,Ks
B. Mallory Sawdy - b. 11 Nov 1989

2. Brant Curtis Sawdy - b. 30 Mar 1965 Lawrence, Ks
3. Terri Lynn Sawdy - b. 3 July 1969 Pasadena, Texas

j. Jerry Lee Finney - b. 17 Sep 1943 Wayside, Ks - m. 1 June 1968 Marilyn Kay KELLER - b. 28 June 1944 Wichita. Jerry adopted Mark and Tamara.

1. Mark Allen Finney - b. 17 July 1962 - m. 16 Apr 1987 Renate J. DODSON - b. 15 Jan 1960

A. Amber Lynn Dodson - b. 29 Jan 1981 Independence, Ks
B. Kristie Dawn Dodson - b. 19 May 1983 Coffeyville, Ks
C. Tara LeAnn Finney - b. 2 Dec 1983 Texas

2. Tamara Kay Finney - b. 17 Aug 1964 Independence, Ks
3. Buddy J. Finney - b. 15 Feb 1972
4. Jason Lee Finney - b. 8 Aug 1977 Bartlesville, Okla.

vi. Stella Marie Finney - b. 5 Jan 1902 - d. 21 Aug 1981 - m. 3 June 1922 William Henry HILBERT - b. Nov 1899 Niotaze, Ks

a. Anna Francis Hilbert - b. Oct 1923 - d. 14 Dec 1923
b. Willie Henry Hilbert - b. 9 July 1930 Niotze, Ks - m. 29 Aug 1954 Myrtle Belle MURDIE - b. 15 June 1936 Eskridge, Ks - divorced - m (2) 19 May 1989 Thelma SEYLER - b. 10 Oct 1922 Topeka, Ks

Martha Myrtle (Hann) and Clarence Finney with Alta and Johnny Finney

Top of page 104

1. Robin Annetta Hilbert - m. David Michael Temple
    A. Ian Michael Temple
    B. Kyle Larkin Temple
2. William Todd Hilbert

Family of Clarence and Martha Finney

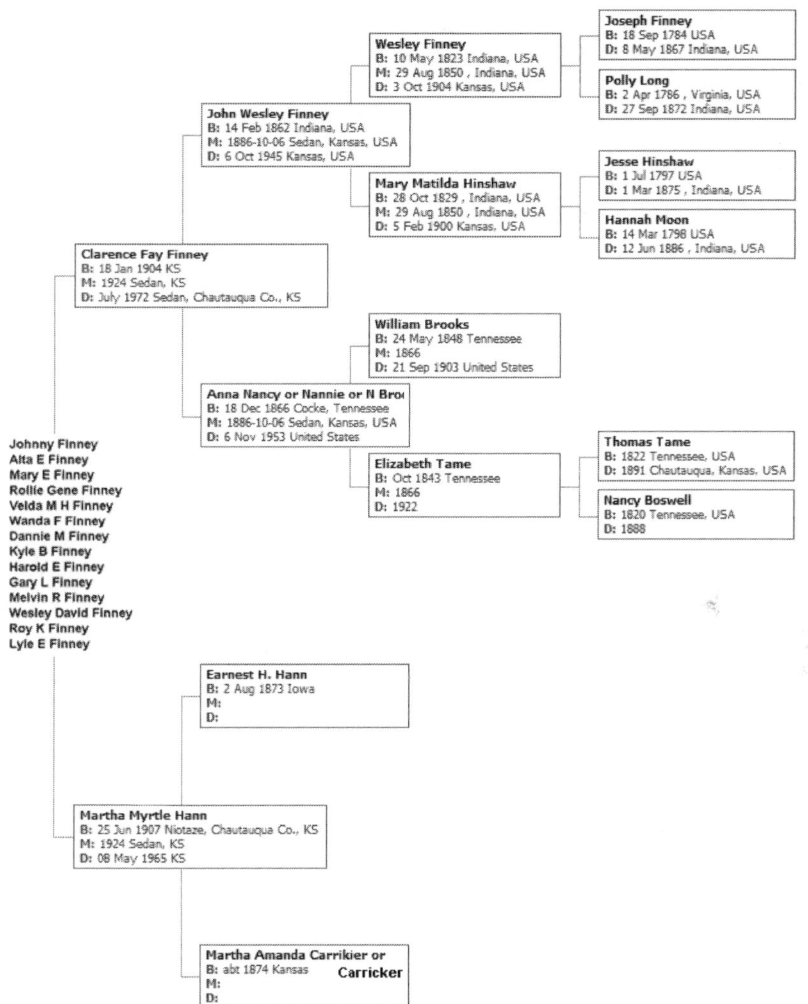

Family tree for Clarence Fay and Martha Myrtle (Hann) Finney and their children

Clarence and Myrtle had 14 children.

1. Johnny Ernest Finney dob: 12/13/1925 Deceased 7/4/2002-buried 7/10/02 in Fairview Cemetery, Niotaze, KS.- m. May 15 1947 - Paula Pearl COURTNEY
2. Alta Elizabeth Finney dob: 1/13/1928 - m. (1) Harold Tubalcain KIRCHNER 1/27/1946 (2) Paul O'Dell FULLER 5/4/1998
3. Mary Evelyn Finney dob: 2/23/1930 - m. (1) Claude Marion DUFOE 7/6/1948 (2) Robert Emil McMURTRY
4. Rollie Gene Finney dob: 1/17/1932-divorced Gloria LOVEGREEN
5. Velda Marie Hilta Finney dob: 8/27/1934 - m. Kenneth Earl GORBY 5/6/1954
6. Danny Merl (or Dannie Merle) Finney dob: 8/4/1937 Deceased 3/4/1937 b: Fairview Cemetery, Niotaze, KS.
7. Wanda Faye Finney dob: 5/16/1938-m. Carl Floyd RILEY 7/9/1955
8. Kyle B Finney dob: 9/4/1942 - m. Joyce Ann BARR 6/6/1964
9. Harold Edward Finney dob: 7/6/1943-m. Bonnie Jean TWITCHELL 11/22/1964
10. Gary Lee Finney dob: 1/25/1945 - m. Cynthia Louise Owens 12/27/1970
11. Melvin Ray Finney dob: 2/18/1947 - m. Mary Lue MALONE 11/20/1970
12. Wesley David Finney dob: 12/16/1949 - m. Janice Sue SCOTT 7/28/1972
13. Roy Keith Finney dob: 1/12/1952 - m. (1) Carroll Sue BAYS died 5/18/1986 (2) Carol Ann Berry HAWKINS 11/6/1986
14. Lyle Eugene Finney dob: 1/4/1954 - m. Suzanne Marie COLE 11/4/1983

Clarence Fay Finney + Martha Myrtle Hann

vii.Clarence Fay Finney_-b. 18 Jan 1904 d. June 21, 1972, Sedan KS, buried 6/23/72, Niaotaze, KS; m 3 July1924 Martha Myrtle HANN - b. 25 June 1907 - d. 8 May 1965 Sedan KS, buried 5/12/65 Fairview Cemetery, Niotaze KS

Martha Hann's parents: Earnest H. Hann b. 2 Aug 1873 Iowa d. 24 Dec.1951 and Martha Amanda Carrikier (or Carricker) b. 1874 or 1873 d. 1966

Martha Myrtle Hann; Mr. and Mrs. Earnest H Hann (left) with John Wesley and Nannie Finney (right)

About Myrtle's family name: William Hand or Hann from 1790 until 1880 was spelled Hand. He was born in 1802. Then Benjamin F. Hand had the name changed to Hann. Benjamin Hann was born July 25, 1819 and died Mar 18 1892. He was 73 years old at the time of his death.

Myrtle and Clarence Finney with Alta and Johnny Finney; Clarence Finney in Wichita, KS

Top left picture: Grandma Hann on porch, back row- Clarence Finney, Johnny, Alta, Martha holding Faye; front row-Mary, Gene, Hilta (left to right)

Mary, Johnny, and Alta; Gene and poodle

Myrtle in 1942

Left to right: Faye, Clarence, Kenneth Gorby behind Clarence, Hilta holding Glenda, Eugene held by Myrtle (with glasses), Pearl (with arms crossed); children left to right and in front: Melvin (striped shirt), David, Roy, Harold (in front of Myrtle), Donna, with Johnny holding Ira and Debbie

a. Johnny Ernest Finney - b. 13 Dec 1925 Ks; d. 4 July 2002 Collinsville, OK, buried 7/10/2002 in Fairview Cemetery, Niotaze KS - m. 15 May 1947 Paula Pearl COURTNEY - b. 4 Apr 1929 Caney, Ks

Johnny Finney lived off and on with his grandparents – John Wesley and Nannie (Brooks) Finney, starting at the age of 8 years old.

Pearl and Johnny with Debbie, Donna, and Ira; Back row – Donna and Ira; Front row – Johnny, Pearl, and Debbie

Johnny and Pearl Finney; Johnny Finney's 70th birthday – Dec. 13, 1995

1. Donna Jean Finney - m. Steve Dean L0FFER

A. Eric Franklin Loffer

(1) McKenzie Kalyn Loffer

(2) Wyatt Dean Loffer

B. Anita Ann Loffer m. Brent Kerri Patterson

(1) Madeline Mae

(2) Jillian Leigh

Donna and Steve Loffer's 25th anniversary 1996

2. Ira Clarence Finney m. Melinda Jean BROOKS divorced

A. Michael DeShawn Finney m. Crystal Griffith

(1) Kellen Michael Finney

B. Rachel Michelle Finney

3. Debra Jane Finney - m (1) James Lloyd LAWRENCE, Jr. who died 16 Apr 1977 Tulsa; m (2) 22 July 1978 Terry Eli PLEASANT, divorced; m (3) Larry Dean MASON

A. Elizabeth Paula Pleasant Mason m. Johnathen Michael Schenk

(1) Gaberiel Matthew Schenk

(2) Regan Marie Schenk

(3) Garrett William Schenk

Baby Garrett (one month), Regan (2 years), Gabe (6 years) picture taken 2010; Picture taken 2009 John, Paula, Gabe (5 years) & Regan (1 year old) Schenk

B. Jonathan Richard Mason

Johnathan and Paula Elizabeth Mason 1997

C. Valerie Nancy Mason, m. Tony HURD

(1) Halo Jane Hurd

Reception to honor the 50th anniversary of Mr. and Mrs. John Finney

Mr. and Mrs. John Finney in 1947 and in 1997.

Friends and relatives of Mr. and Mrs. John Finney, Collinsville, OK, are invited to a reception from 3 to 5 p.m. Saturday, May 24, 1997 at Verdigris Valley Electric Company, Collinsville, to celebrate the couple's 50th wedding anniversary.

Johnny Finney and Pearl Courtney were married May 15, 1947 in Caney, KS.

Mr. Finney served in the U.S. Army during World War II. They moved to Collinsville in 1963. Mr. Finney retired from American Airlines in 1988.

Johnny and Pearl are the parents of three children, Donna Loffer of Collinsville, Debra Mason of Tyro and Ira Finney of Salt Lake City, UT.

Johnny and Pearl are also the proud grandparents of seven grandchildren and one great-granddaughter. They are Eric and Kim Loffer and McKenzie of Collinsville and Anita Loffer, also of Collinsville; Elizabeth, Johnathon and Valerie Mason of Tyro and Mike and Rachel Finney of Salt Lake City.

Johnny and Pearl Finney's 50th Wedding Anniversary 1997

b. Alta Elizabeth Finney - m. Harold Tubalcain KIRCHNER - b. 13 Mar 1912 Sedan, KB d. 1 Apr. 1991; m. Paul O'Dell Fuller

Alta and Paul Fuller1999

1. Harold Ray Kirchner - b. 8 June 1947 Sedan, Ks - m. 13 Aug 1966 d. July 2, 2006 m. Katherine Marie BOHANNAN

A. Scotty Eugene Kirchner - m. Carolyn LITTRELL - annulled; m. Sherry

(1) Silverlyn Dawn Kirchner

(2) Stormy Richard Ray Kirchner

B. Brenda Lynn Kirchner

A. Courtney Nicole Kirchner

C. Teresa Annette Kirchner m. Mr. Lessman

(1) Morgan Waytt Leseman

D. Bobby Darin Kirchner

2. Harry Dean Kirchner

3. Carolyn Ann Kirchner - m. Melvin Edward GRAVES

A. Michael Jon Graves - m. Nicole Diane Stinner

B. Roger Lee Graves - b. 18 Feb 1984 Wichita, KS; d. 7/15/98

4. Larry Wayne Kirchner Sr - m. 29 Nov 1975 Deborah Jean Waller

A. Crystal Ann Kirchner

B. Bradley Allen Kirchner

C. Larry Wayne Kirchner Jr

5. Henry Lee Kirchner - m Sandra Sue CARRA

A. Corey Michael Kirchner m. Marianne Johnson

B. Amy Michelle Kirchner

C. Heidi Marie Kirchner m. Ian Griffith

c. Mary Evelyn Finney - m. Claude Marion Dufoe b. 8/11/1920, d. 11/25/93; m. Robert Emil McMurtry d. 3/6/04

Pearl Finney & Mary (Duefoe) McMurtry; Mary and Bob McMurtry 1999

1. Joyce Marie Dufoe - b. 11 Jan 1948 - m Jimmie Eugene WRIGHT - b. 17 Jan 1949, d. 11/28/75; companion Harold Lee Eytchenson d. Mar 9, 2007; companion Judd Phillip

Harold and Joyce Dufoe Eytchenson 1999

A. William Eugene Wright

B. Grady Dewayne Wright m. Lottie May Ash

(1) Dakota William Wright

(2) Colten James Dewayne Wright

(3) Randi Renea Wright

C. Kimberly Dawn Wright - m. Michael Dean Casady; divorced

(1) Dustyn Michael Casady

(2) Gabriel Lane Casady

(3) Cody James Casady

D. LeeAnn Wright - m. Robert John Smart

(1) Ethen John Smart

(2) Leana Marie Smart

2. Juanita Jo Dufoe - m Johnny HUNT, divorced 1973; m. Walter Loyd Simpson; divorced

A. John Roy Hunt III

B. Juanita (Tina) Christina Hunt - m. Shaun L. Steed

(1) Samuel James Steed

(2) Tamika Rashell Steed

(3) Joseph Frank Hunt

C. Joseph Frank Hunt - m. Andria

(1) Kayden Hunt

(2) Kinley Hunt

3. Judith Claudette Dufoe - m. Billy Wayne WRIGHT b. 27 June 1951 deceased; m. Dan Smith

Left to right Martha Myrtle, Johnny, Clarence Finney; Alta Finney

Johnny Finney; Left to right-Kyle 3, Harold 10 mos 29 days, Faye 6, Hilta 9

Jerry Reding

September 12, 2011

STANLEY — The Custer County Sheriff's Office has identified two Canyon County men who died in a plane crash near Stanley earlier this week.

Pilot Jerry Reding, 55, of Nampa, and his brother-in-law Jamie Sexton, 38, of Caldwell, were flying from Salmon to Caldwell when their Cessna 182 aircraft disappeared before midnight Monday in the eastern foothills of central Idaho's Sawtooth Mountains.

Radar tracking indicated the airplane lost altitude and descended rapidly, according to Angie Reding Thueson, Reding's sister, the family received a text from Sexton before the men left Salmon, indicating that they experienced turbulence on ride over and asking their family to pray for them.

The airplane left Salmon at about 10:30 Monday night and was expected to arrive at the Caldwell airport — a distance of about 175 miles — around midnight. The wreckage of the plane was discovered at 4:30 p.m. Tuesday west of Stanley near the Iron Creek Trailhead.

Reding had been flying for 10-15 years, Thueson said, and his plane had been inspected recently.

"He loved flying," she said of her brother, "It was his passion."

The men came from a family of Idaho wildland fire contractors and were dropping off firefighters at the Salt fire in the Salmon-Challis National Forest shortly before the crash.

"My brother … he would do anything for anybody," Thueson said. "He was the right hand man for the whole family." She described her brother-in-law, Jamie, as a great family man, who was married for 12 years with an 11-year-old son.

A. Mary Claudette Wright - m. Patrick Wade Bottorff

(1) Amber Nicole Bottorff, m. Eric Barney

a. Bodie Stephaun Bottorff

b. Brady Bottorff

4. Jimmy Lee Dufoe - m. Pamela Sue GREIER

A. Cheryl Lee Dufoe - b. July 1975 - d. July 1975

5. Janice Kay Dufoe - m Mike William MURPHY divorced

A. Russell Ray Murphy - m. Melissa Jo Holty

(1) Isaac Allen Murphy

(2) Russell Jacob Murphy

(3) Emily Marie Murphy

B. Benjamin Robert Murphy m. Julia

(1) Meghan Rose Murphy

C. Sarah Elizabeth Murphy

(1) Natasha

D. Rebekah Diane Murphy - m. Chris Burke

(1) Zander Addin

6. Jerry Evelyn Dufoe - m. Curtis Lee HENSLY

A. Samuel Arron Hensly - m. Stacy Lynn Mushlitz

B. Jacob Lee Hensly - m. Andrea Arnae Jones

(1) Jacoby Carl Hensly

(2) Nikole Lee Hensly

C. Matthew Shane Hensly

D. Letisha Eva Hensly

7. Jane Amanda Dufoe m. Jerry Raymond REDING

A. Michelle Erin Reding

B. Brenda Marie Reding

C. Andrew Ryne Reding

D. Lucas Kyle Reding

8. Marion Charles Dufoe - m. Dana Nicole Read

9. Michael Clive Dufoe - m. Cheryl Lynn HIX, divorced

A. Misty Gale Dufoe

(1) Abigail Haley Dufoe

(2) Jasmen Lyn Dufoe

B. Chad Michael Dufoe

10. Claude Ernest Dufoe - m. Sonya Lee MADDUK divorced

A. SaVanna LaVon Dufoe, m. Barry Dixon

(1) Bladen Allan Dixon

(2) Claden Eli Dixon

(3) Anna Marie LaVon Dixon

B. Satanna Lee Dufoe, m. Mr. Layton divorced

(1) Dominique Dean Layton

11. Martha May Dufoe - m. Ronald Lyle Hall

A. Ronald Lyle Hall II

B. Tristan Levi Hall

C. Morgan May

12. Tommy Lyne Dufoe

13. Todd Glenn Dufoe - m. Jennifer Rebecca Brooks

A. Trystn Craig Dufoe

B. Toby Dufoe

C. Jeremy Dufoe (twin)

D. Jerret Dufoe (twin)

d. Rollie Gene Finney (s/o Clarence) - m. Gloria LOVEGREEN divorced

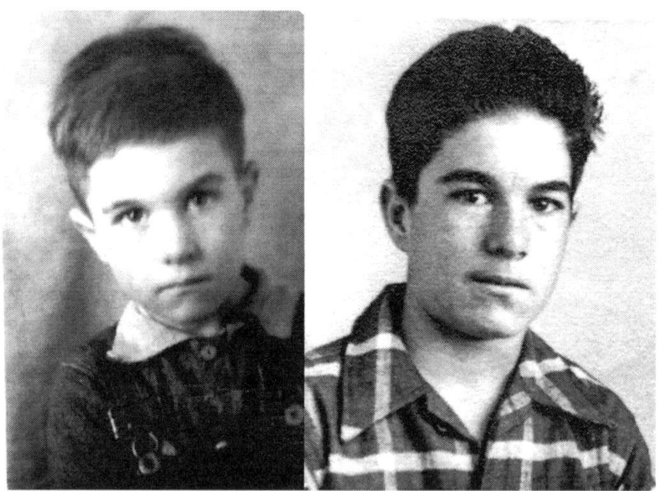

Rollie Gene Finney (known as Gene)

Gene (Rollie) and Harold Finney

e. Velda Marie Hilta Finney - b. 27 Aug 1934 – m. Kenneth Early GORBY - b. 30 Mar 1934 Peru, Ks

Hilta Finney and Kenneth Gorby on the day of their son, Kenneth Jr.'s wedding in 1999

1. Glenda Marie Gorby - m Clifford John MOST; divorced; m. Charles B. Robb

A. Martha Marie Most - m. Tim Harper

(1) Shawn Edward Harper (stepson)

(2) Cassidy Marie Harper

(3) Sarah Elizabeth Harper

B. Rebecca Michelle Most

C. Jonathan Andrew Most

2. Linda Faye Gorby - m Edward Joshua PEAK

A. Joshua Edward Peak - m. Jesse Creekmore

(1) Rhett Morgan Peak

(2) Blair Olivia Peak

(3) Jude London Peak

B. Phillip Ryan Peak, married Jamie Marie York

(1) Parker James Peak

C. Gregory Allen Peak, married Rochelle Dawn Dixon

Back row - Kenneth Jr, Linda, Glenda, and Kevin; Front row - Hilta & Kenneth Gorby taken Jan. 27, 2002

3. Kenneth Earl Gorby Jr - m Diane Michelle Beu

Kenneth and wife Diane; Kenneth and his brother Kevin

A. Ryan James Humphrey (step-son)

B. Jared Tyler Gorby

4. Kevin Merle Gorby - m Sara Cerese ALLEN divorced

f. Wanda Fay Finney - b. 16 May 1938 - m. Carl Floyd RILEY b. 9 May 1933

Wanda Fay and Carl Riley

1. Floyd James Riley - m. Cheryl Ann ROBERTS, divorced; m. Debra Kay Walker (Clark), divorced

A. Alan James Riley - m. Melissa Ann Himber

(1) Nicholas Alan Riley

(2) Brett James Riley

Nicholas and Brett Riley

B. Aaron Shane Riley

C. Carrie Lynn Clark (step-daughter)

D. Cassandra Marie Clark (step-daughter)

2. Dorothy Faye Riley - m. Samuel Ray Talley

g. Dannie Merle or Danny Merl Finney - b. 4 Mar 1937 - d. Apr 1937

Martha Myrtle (Hann), Clarence Finney, and their children

h. Kyle B. Finney - m. Joyce Ann BARR

Kyle Finney high school photo; Kyle and Joyce Finney wedding photo

Kyle & Joyce Finney with Judith and Jeffrey; Joyce and Kyle Finney

Karen & Jeff Finney & son Braden; Judith Finney; Judith & Jerry Davis

1. Jeffrey Ernest Finney - m. Karen Ann Reiss

A. Kyle Braden Finney

B. Landon Brice Finney

Karen and husband Jeff (son of Kyle & Joyce Finney) and sons Kyle Braden and Landon Brice Finney

2. Judith Annette Finney - m. Jerry Michael Davis

Mr. and Mrs. Jerry Davis
(Nee Judith Finney)

Couple exchange wedding promises

Judith Finney and Jerry Davis exchanged wedding vows on Saturday, Dec. 19 in a 2 p.m. double-ring ceremony at the First Church of the Nazarene, Coffeyville, with the Rev. Ford Hall officiating.

The bride is the daughter of Kyle and Joyce Finney, of Niotaze. The bridegroom is the son of Maxine and the late Robert Davis, of Coffeyville.

Escorted by her father, the bride wore a white satin scoop neck A-line gown with lace appliques on the skirt and a beaded bodice and a chapel length train. Her waist length veil had beading and a scalloped edging. Red and white roses adorned the church with silver on the Christmas tree.

Karen Finney, of Olathe, was the maid of honor, and LaDonna Forman, of Coffeyville, was a bridesmaid. They wore red satin floor-length gowns with white fur muffs and shoulder wraps.

Danny Grigg, of Coffeyville, was the best man, with Jeff Finney, of Olathe, as a groomsman.

Shaelea Finney, of South Coffeyville, Okla., was the flower girl, and Landon Finney, of Olathe, was ring bearer. Seating the wedding guests were Harley Forman and Bob Vanderhoof, of Coffeyville. Providing music for the ceremony were Al and Ruth Penner and Dana J. Saliba. McKenzie Loffer, of Collinsville, Okla., and Braden Finney, of Olathe, were candle lighters.

Following the ceremony, a reception was held at the church with Connie Thompson, Rene' Aitkin, Brenda Grigg, and Amber and Sandy Vanderhoof, all of Coffeyville, Tonya Vass, of Caney, and Bethany Bowers, of Niotaze, assisting.

The bride is a graduate of Arvada West High School and Colorado State University. She is a paraeducator for Tri-County Special Education in Coffeyville.

The bridegroom is a graduate of Field Kindley High School, Coffeyville. He is a paint shop leader for Cessna Aircraft Company, Independence.

Following a wedding trip to Shreveport, La. the couple will make their home in Coffeyville.

i. Harold Edward Finney - m. Bonnie Jean TWITCHELL

Harold Finney – graduation photo; Harold Finney – Air Force 1962

Harold and Bonnie (Twitchell) Finney

Bonnie's parents – Floye Annalorene (Proter) and Wincle Twitchell

Bonnie's sisters – Carmelea and Phyllis Twitchell

Harold and Bonnie's children – Marsha, Mike, and Jeanie

1. Jeanie Lorene Finney - m. Benjamin ORTIZ Jr.
   - A. Benjamin Daniel Ortiz
   - B. Danielle Sierre Ortiz
   - C. Robert Edward Isaak Ortiz

Front – Ben & Jeanie Ortiz; Back – Isaak, Daniel, Sierre Ortiz

2. Marsha Ann Finney - m. Daniel Lewis Knight
   - A. Rachel Elizabeth Knight
   - B. Sarah Christine Knight

Marsha, Sarah & Rachel Knight 2002; Dan, Marsha, Rachel & Sarah Knight

Harold & Bonnie's Children and Grandchildren – Top row: Daniel Ortiz, Shaelea Finney, Rachel Knight, Sierre Ortiz; Bottom: Isaak Ortiz, Stephen Finney, and Sarah Knight

3. Michael Edward Finney m. Angela Denise Huff

   A. Stephen Michael Finney

   B. Shaelea Mykiah Finney

Mike, Angela, Stephen & Shaelea Finney 2008; Harold, Stephen and Mike Finney Coffeyville, at Lewark Church of God, KS on Father's Day 2011

j. Gary Lee Finney - m. Cynthia Louise OWENS

Gary Finney; Dec. 1995 Lee Anna, Clayton, Louise, Gary Finney

1. Clayton Owens Finney - m. Jenny Lee Rice
2. Lee Anna Rachelle Finney - m. Ankur Khanphilal Darji

    A. Evan Ankur Darji

Evan Darji

Evan, Gary, Louise, Lee Anna, Ankur, Clayton, Jenny; Evan Darji

k. Melvin Ray Finney - m. Mary Lue MALONE

Melvin Finney

Steve, Mary, Melvin, and Randy Finney

1. Steven Ray Finney - m. Gina LoAnn Dixon
2. Randolph Linn Finney - m. Denise Lynn Richebacher

Gina and Steve Finney; Denise and Randy Finney

Melvin, Denise, Randy, Gina, Steven & Mary Finney May 27, 2001 taken at Finney get-together in Sedan, Kansas

1. Wesley David (David) Finney - m. Janice Sue SCOTT

Wesley David Finney – graduation, ARMY

Back row – Scott, Ronda, and Tonya Finney; Front row – Janice and Wesley David Finney

1. Ronda Lynn Finney - m. Patrick Ryan Bowers

A. Wesley John Bowers

B. Daniel Lee Bowers

C. Bethany Marie Bowers

2. Tonya Sue Finney - m. Jeremy Don Vass

A. Brianna Vass

3. Scott Wesley Finney - m. Tammy Sue Windsor

A. Curtis Lee Brown (step-son)

B. Heath Michael Brown (step-son)

C. Bryson Wesley Finney

David Finney's son, Scott. Scott's wife Tammy and their son Bryson

m. Roy Keith Finney - m. (1) Carroll Sue BAYS d. 18 May 1986; m (2) 6 Nov 1986 Carol Ann Berry HAWKINS

Roy Finney

Roy and Shawn Finney; Amanda Finney

1. Karen Lynn Finney - m. Bryan Keith Fish

    A. Daniel Keith

    B. Allison Renee

2. Shawn Keith Finney - m. Debra Sue Wilson; divorced

    A. Kay Lynn Finney

3. Amanda Marie Finney - m. Shawn Goodlavage

4. Jodie Lynn (step-son) Hawkins m. April

5. Nicole Ann (Nikki) Hawkins m. Kris Bilbrey

6. Heather Lynette (step-daughter) Hawkins m. James Frisbie

7. Ashley Loren (step-son) Hawkins m. Stacy Catherine Waters

n. Lyle Eugene Finney - m. (1) Sherry de Laubenfels; divorced; m. (2) Suzanne (Suzie) Marie Cole (previous married name was Richard)

1. Jeannie May Clark (step-daughter); m. Oron Ray McIntosh

    A. Michael Ray McIntosh

    B. Isaac Brandt Clark

    C. Brenda Marie McIntosh

    D. Joshua Ray McIntosh

2. Michael Dean Richard (step-son); m. Tempe Ann Seckman

    A. Justin Andrew Richard

    B. Abigale LeAnne Richard

3. Melissa Dawn Finney (daughter of Lyle Finney and Sherry de Laubenfels) m. and divorced Mr. Hickenbottom

    A. Kendralyn Ried Finney

    B. Joshua Sean Eugene Terry

Melissa and Derek Finney

4. Derek Dwayne Finney (son of Lyle Finney and Sherry de Laubenfels) - m. Amy Marie Swopes

A. Aaron Matthew Free

B. Adrien Michael Free and Kameri Parmer

(1) Ava Marie Free

C. Kiara Jessie Lynn Finney

5. Kendralyn Ried Finney (Lyle and Suzie adopted their granddaughter)

Suzie, granddaughter Kendralyn, and Lyle Finney

Kendralyn, Suzie, and Lyle Finney

iii. Clinton (Red) Finney, s/o John Wesley Finney - b. 27 Sep 1907 in Niotaze, Ks, d. Sept. 1986 - m. 28 1929 Georgia Kathryn Irene LEWIS - b. 4 Apr 1910,

d. Aug. 27, 1997

a. Thomas Blair Finney

b. Julie Katherine Finney - m. Jack L. PERRY

1. Kevin Lee Perry
2. Jack P. Perry

c. Timothy Ray Finney – b. 27 Feb. 1947; d. 7 June 2006; m. Rosemary Moore

children:

1. Kelly, m. Mr. Sloan; b. Oct. 29, 1965 - d. Dec. 5, 2008
2. Georgia Joann, m. Mr. Dial

step-children

3. Kimberly, m. Mr. Patterson
4. Angela, m. Mr. Schrader
5. Roseanna, m. Mr. Prater; b. 1976 and died Jan. 29, 2010

Timothy Ray Finney

d. Susian Grace Finney (d. before 2006)- m. (1) Johnny Ray Perry divorced; m (2) Steven Lee Galemore

1. Angela Perry
2. Sandra Kay Perry

John Wesley Finney descendants get together1937 or 1938 with 1936 Chevy

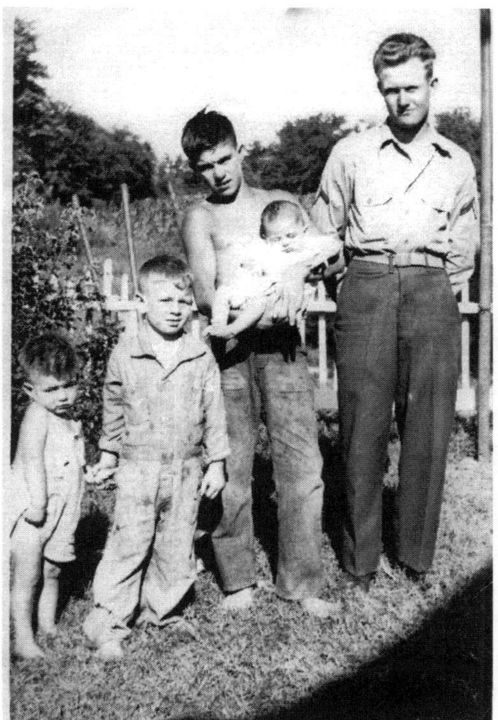

1945-Harold, Kyle B, Gene holding Gary, and Johnny Finney

Back L-R: Harold, Gary, Johnny, Martha, Kyle, Melvin, Gene
Front L-R: Roy, Eugene, David (1963)

Clarence Finney's wife and sons 1963

Finney Get-together taken in Sedan, KS. Gene was home for a visit so everyone was contacted and got together at the 4-H building in Sedan, KS. 1999

Top row - Gene, Roy, Harold, Kyle, David, Gary, Melvin

Bottom row - Hilta (Finney) Gorby, Mary (Finney, Dufoe) McMurtry, Johnny Finney, Alta (Finney, Kirchner) Fuller, Faye (Finney) Riley

At Kyle and Joyce Finney's home after Johnny's funeral: Top row: Lyle Eugene, Melvin, Harold; Middle row - Gene, David, Kyle, Roy, Gary; Bottom row - Alta, Mary, Hilta, Faye

Pearl Finney and some of the Finney children was taken in Collinsville, OK celebrating Pearl's 80th birthday; Gary and Pearl (seated); Hilta (behind Gary); back row, left to right: Harold, Kyle, Melvin, and David Finney

Finney "kids" Niotaze School 2011 - Top row: David, Gary, Wanda Faye, Harold; Middle row: Alta, Gene, Kyle, Melvin, Hilta; Bottom row: Lyle Eugene

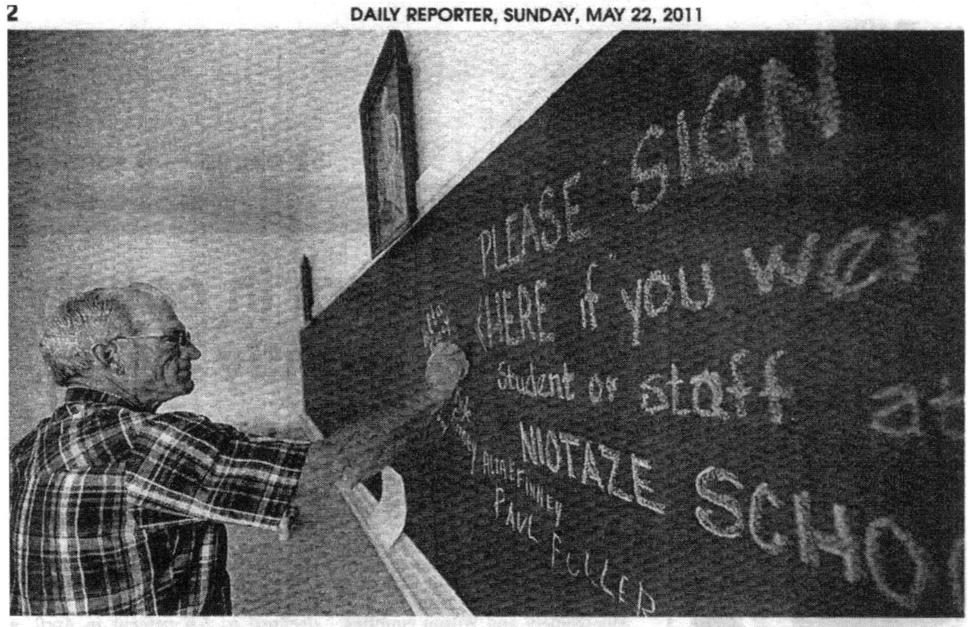

2 DAILY REPORTER, SUNDAY, MAY 22, 2011

BACK TO SCHOOL — Harold Finney, a 1958 graduate of the Niotaze School, signs his name on the chalkboard at the site Saturday afternoon. Finney was attending an event to raise money to help turn the school, which was closed in 1972, into a museum.

(Photo by Rob Morgan)

Harold Finney at the Niotaze School

This section provides updates for page 107.

(g) Louisa May Finney - b. 8 Jan 1867 - d. 6 Jan 1919 - m. 29 Sep 1887 Anson Joseph MADISON - b. May 1866 IN - d. 1924 Dodge City, Ford, KS. To Buffalo, Okla. 1901 with their many children, in a covered wagon. Listed in Montgomery Co., Ks. Census in 1900. To Harper Co., Ks. 1905 - they had 13 children.

i. Calvin Madison - b. July 1889 Montgomery Co., Ks - lived High River, Canada – m. Bessie; had 10 children. Left home for Canada 1917 - did not return home until 1950

ii. Mary J. Madison - b. Jan 1891 - lived Tulsa, Okla; d. 1968 Tulsa OK - m. Will F. SWAN

Anson and Louisa Finney Madison's youngest boys – Henry, Floyd, William, and Stephen Madison (this photo did not have the boys' names on it, but it had their parents' names. Based on the difference in their ages, I have identified the boys.

MRS. MADISON DIES SUDDENLY

Cooking for Harvesters and Became Overheated. Buried Tuesday

The whole community was saddened Sunday morning when the word was passed around that Mrs. Madison had died during the night. She had been cooking for the W. C. Broberg harvesting crew and became overheated. She had lived here for many years, and was well-liked for the many kind words spoken and deeds performed, and her many friends join the Republican in extending sympathy to the bereaved family.

Obituary

Louise May Finney was born in Park County, Indiana, January 8, 1867, married to Joseph A. Madison, September 20, 1887 in Montgomery county, Kansas, and moved to Harper county in [illegible].

To this union thirteen children were born, twelve of whom with the husband and father survive. The children are: Mrs. Mary Sullivan, Merlin, Canada, Mrs. Iola Marley, Ft. Smith, Arkansas; Mrs. Ethel West, Independence, Kansas; Miss Bernice Madison, Wichita, Kansas. Calvin and Dewey Madison of Sedwick, Canada. Misses Nellie and Olga, Henry, Floyd, Willis and Stephen of Buffalo.

Mrs. Madison died Sunday morning, July 6, of a congestive chill.

At the time of her death she was a member of the M. E. Church of Buffalo.

Funeral services were conducted at the M. E. Church Tuesday afternoon by Rev. W. C. Heaton and the Rebekah Lodge.

Interment at Buffalo cemetery.

Early Coffeyville

—World Staff Photo

HAIL, HAIL THE GANG'S ALL HERE!

Twelve brothers and sisters, who had never all been together at one time sat down Tuesday to a dinner in Tulsa. They are, left to right, sisters, Mrs. Iola Marley, Ft. Smith, Ark.; Mrs. Bernice Smith-erman, Wichita, Kans.; Mrs. Olga Reedy, Mrs. Mary Sullivan and Mrs. Nell Ravencroft, all of Tulsa; and Mrs. Ethyl Wiley, Independence, Kans.; standing, Floyd Madison, Bay Town, Tex.; Calvin Madison, High River, Caada; Dewey Madison, Libby, Mont.; and Henry Madison, Houston, Tex.; Stephen Madison, Houston, Tex. and W. A. Madison, San Francisco, Calif.

12 Brothers, Sisters Meet For First Time at Reunion

By YVONNE LITCHFIELD
Of The World Staff

For the first time in their lives, the 12 Madisons, six sons and six daughters, were together Tuesday.

Gathering at the home of Mrs. Will F. Sullivan, 507 S. Xanthus ave., for a family reunion the brothers and sisters talked about childhood days over a fried chicken dinner.

Their parents, Mr. and Mrs. J. A. Madison took their family in a covered wagon from Kansas to a farm near Buffalo, Okla., in 1901. The parents died when some of the children were young. Some of the older daughters had married before the last of the 12 children had arrived.

The separation began when their mother died 31 years ago at the age of 51, leaving six children at home ranging from 6 to 16 years of age. The father died 4 years later.

* * *

Mrs. Sullivan came to Oklahoma and took the four youngest boys to live with her in Texas.

Although, the family hold gatherings over the years they were never able to get the whole gang together at one time.

But, last year someone in the family started a round robin letter and the Tuesday reunion resulted.

There had been no deaths among the children and in the letter each person suggested that he was getting along in years and would like to have the whole gang together just once.

Calvin, the oldest member of the family, who went to Canada in 1917, hadn't been home since and he saw some members of the family for the first time in 40 years.

It took 12 chickens for lunch Tuesday. The afternoon was taken up with the family photograph album and childhood memories and of course the usual family jokes were told on each member.

* * *

Talk about their children filled in the gaps of time, with Calvin holding the record of 10 children. He was the only member to duplicate the large family. Three of the men and three of the women had no children. Counting the 10 children of Calvin, the 12 Madisons had only 26 offspring.

They will all be in Tulsa for two or three days before returning to their homes over the nation.

Members of the family and their ages are: Calvin, High River, Canada, 61; Mrs. Sullivan, 59; Mrs. Iola Marley, Fort Smith, Ark., 57; Mrs. Ethyl Wiley, 54, Independence, Kans., 54; Mrs. Bernice Smitherman, Wichita, Kans., 53; Dewey Madison, Libby, Mont., 51; Mrs. Nell Ravencroft, 1343 S. Florence ave., 50; Mrs. Olga Reedy, 1343 S. Florence ave., 48; Henry, Houston, Tex., 46; Floyd, Bay Town, Tex., 43; Bill M., San Francisco, Calif., 42, and Stephen, Houston, 39.

Information for Louisa May Finney Madison family, which continues on page 109.

iii. Iola Ellen Madison - b. Mar 1893 Montgomery Co., Ks; d. Jan 1977 Van Buren, Crawford, Arkansas, United States of America - m. Frank MARLEY - lvd. Fort Smith, Ark. 1950

a. Richard Marley 1913 –

b. Charolette Marley 1915 –

c. Bernice Marley 1918 –

d. Nada Marley 1922 –

e. Cecil Marley 1927 –

iv. Ethel Edna Madison - b. Sep 1896 - m (11 WEST, m (2) 7 WIILEY, lvd. supply. OK

v. Anna Bernice Madison - b. July 1897; d. 1975 Wichita, Sedgwick, Kansas,- m. SMITHERMAN, lvd. Wichita, Sedgwick Co., Ks 1950

vi. Dewey Delmon Madison - b. Jan 1898 Ks; d. 22 Mar 1978 in Libby, Lincoln, Montana, United States of America - lvd Libby, Montana in 1950; m. Violet COYNE.

a. Bernice Madison 1924 –

b. Morris Madison 1925 –

c. James Madison 1927 –

d. Donald Madison 1928 –

e. Richard Kyle Madison 1930 – 2001

vii. Nellie May Madison - b. Dec 1899; d. 1981 - m. Lot J. RAVENSCROFT, lvd Tulsa, Okla.

ix. Joseph Henry Madison – b. 1903; d. 14 Aug 1975 in , Austin, Texas, USA

x. Olga Forest Madison - b. 1904 - m. REEDY, lvd. Tulsa, Okla.

xi. Floyd Harold Madison - b. 20 Apr 1906 OK; d. May 1982 in Lufkin, Angelina, Texas, lvd. Baytown, Texas

xii. William Anson Madison – b. 1907 OK; d. 1985; lived in San Francisco CA

xiii. Stephen Harrison Madison - b. 1910 Harper, OK; d. 1964, lvd. Houston, Texas

Family photos for the Daniel Webster Finney Family, which begins on page 109.

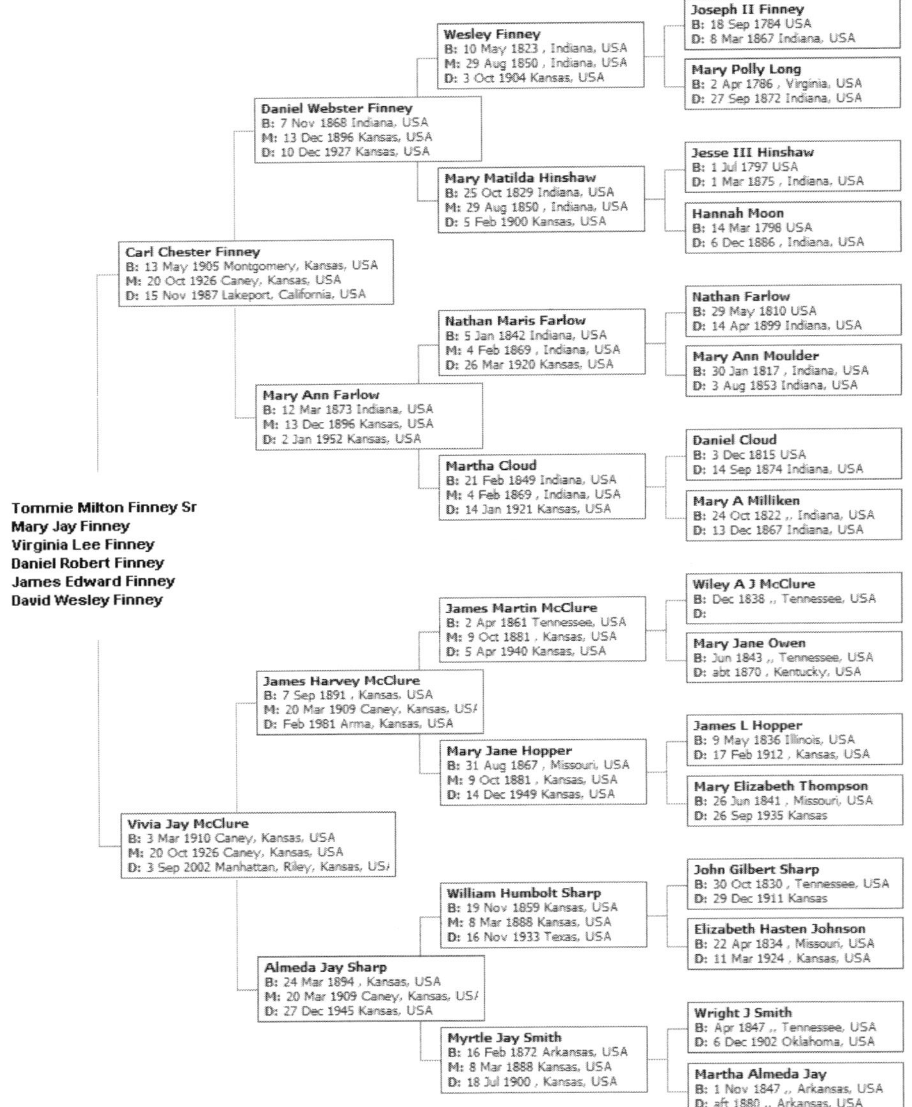

Family tree for Carl Chester and Vivia Jay (McClure) Finney

Top of page 110 – Clara Ellen Finney + Elmer Farlow

Clara Ellen Finney is the youngest child of Wesley and Mary Matilda Finney. In looking at her family photos, she seems to be the "fashionable" lady in nice clothing.

Elmer, Clara Ellen, Merl and Orville Farlow

Valentine Greetings

May St. Valentine bring to you
Much of love and laughter,
Leave pleasant thoughts to cheer your heart
All the days thereafter.

Elmer + Ella Farlow

Clara Ellen (Finney), Merle, Orville, and Elmer Farlow

Elmer Farlow's father Nathan Maris Farlow – b. 5 Jan 1842 Paoli, Orange County, IN; d. 26 Mar 1922 Bolton, Montgomery County, KS

Lower part of page 110 – Mary Belle Farlow married William W. Butts; They had 4 children. Bottom of page 110 – Fanny Finney (child of Joseph and Mary Polly (Long) Finney; younger sister of Wesley Finney) and married to Jabez Rayl.

Fanny Finney (Wesley's sister) was married to Jabez Rayl, whose brothers and wives are shown in the family photo of the Wesley and Mary Matilda (Hinshaw) farm (see page 93a); The Rayl men always wore Black Hats in outdoor photos.

(10) Fanny Finney - Born in Parke, Indiana, USA on 1828 to Joseph Finney and Polly Long. Fanny married Jabez Rayl and had 7 children. She passed away on 18 Dec 1901 in Annapolis, Parke, Indiana, USA.

Jabez Rayl - Born in Cumberland, North Carolina, USA on 18 Nov 1820 to **Nathan Rayl** and **Susanna Thornburgh**. Jabez passed away on 20 Dec 1891 in Parke, Indiana, USA.

(a) Josephine Catherine Rayl - Born in Indianopolis, Parke, Indiana, USA on 26 Jan 1852 to Jabez Rayl and Fanny Finney. Josephine Catherine married Samuel F Smith and had a child. She passed away on 11 Jan 1913 in Junction City, Lane, Oregon, USA.

(b) Alvin Asbury Rayl - Born in Indianapolis, Parke, Indiana, USA on 1853 to Jabez Rayl and Fanny Finney. Alvin Asbury married Anna Elizabeth Roadmark and had 6 children. He passed away on 26 Nov 1935 in Chautauqua, Kansas, USA.

1. Frank Anderson Rayl
2. Harry Levi Rayl
3. Newton Henry Rayl
4. William L. Rayl
5. George Wesley Rayl
6. Anna May Rayl

(c) Hiram Alexander Rayl - Born in Indianapolis, Parke, Indiana, USA on 1 Feb 1856 to Jabez Rayl and Fanny Finney. Hyrum Alexander married Elizabeth Burt. Hyrum Alexander married Ellen Nellie Dunford. He passed away on 27 Jun 1927 in Oregon City, Oregon, USA.

Fannie (Finney) and Jabez Rayl

Jabez Rayl and Hiram Alexander Rayl

Jabez and Fanny (Finney) Rayl

1. Jabez Rayl - b. July 1884
2. John W. Rayl - b. May 1895, s/o Hiram Rayl

(d) Harriet Rayl - b. 1854
(e) Elwood Rayl - b. 1861 Ind
(f) Amanda Rayl - b. 1863
(g) William Ulysses Grant Rayl - b. 23 July 1865 Parke Co., Ind - d. 9 Aug 1944 Youngwood, Pa - m. 25 July 1888 St. Louis to Alice Virginia DUNFORD - b. 14 Dec 1866 St. Louis - 25 Mar 1925 St. Louis, buried Joplin, Missouri

1. Charles Jabez Rayl - b. 17 June 1889 Parke Co., Ind - m. 7 Apr 1912 Ethel WISHLER
2. Lester Willard Rayl - b. 4 Mar 1891 - m. 14 June 1919 Joplin, Mo Edith Ruth CALLENTINE - b. 26 Sep 1901, d/o Bert Earl & Flossie (Jones)

   a. James Willard Rayl - b. 31 June 1920 Joplin, Mo - m. 29 Jan 1947 Vida KENISON
   b. Norma Myrtle Rayl - b. 28 Oct 1923 - m. 1 Jan 1951 Henry William ROCK
   c. Layton Lester Ray - b. 20 Apr 1925 - m. 7 Apr 1948 Vida LuJean PETERSON
   d. Doris Kay Rayl - 2 July 1927 - m. 25 Feb 1946 Clarence J. WICK
   e. Clifford Lamont Rayl - 10 Oct 1930 - m. 11 Oct 1950 Claudia CARTER
   f. Ruth Elizabeth Rayl - 2 Oct 1932 - m. 7 Aug 1950 Ronald BROWN
   g. Ellen Marie Rayl - 14 Nov 1934 - m. 8 Jan 1952 James Cottrell KNIGHTON
   h. Jennie Lee Rayl - b. 31 Dec 1938 Joplin, Mo
   i. Elaine Janet Rayl - b. 21 July 1943 Joplin, Mo

3. Alma Alphonza Rayl - b. 9 Apr 1893 Parke Co., Ind - m. 19 Dec 1911 Bertie PATTERSON
4. Jennie Alice Rayl - b. 9 Jan 1896 Montgomery Co., Ks - m. 4 Aug 1917 Frank Guy BUICK
5. Lillie May Rayl - b. 15 Apr 1898
6. Milly Marie Rayl - b. 15 Apr 1898
7. Arthur Leonard Rayl - b. 8 Jan 1901 Wyandotte Co., Ks - m. 21 Feb 1922 Olive LAIR
8. Mary Orvilla Rayl - b. 11 June 1904 Cherokee Co., Ks - m. 12 May 1924 Arthur W. LINK

Ethel Fannie Jeter and husband Jabez Alexander Rayl

Middle of page 111 – **Rayl family (continued)**

Hyrum or Hiram and Ellen Rayl's children

1. Jabez Rayl – m. Ethel Fannie Jeter

Jabez Alexander Rayl is the son of Hiram Rayl and the grandson of Fanny Finney (child of Joseph and Mary Polly (Long) Finney; younger sister of Wesley Finney) and Jabez Rayl.

Ethel Fannie Jeter and husband Jabez Alexander Rayl; Jabez A Rayl

2. John W Rayl

(d) Harriet S Rayl - Born in Indianapolis, Parke, Indiana, USA on 1857 to Jabez Rayl and Fanny Finney. Harriet S married George Featherstone and had 2 children. She passed away on 26 Feb 1936 in Montezuma, Parke, Indiana, USA.

1. Lydia Featherstone
2. Ida M. Featherstone

George Featherstone with his horses

(e) Cyrenius Elwood Rayl - Born in Indianapolis, Parke, Indiana, USA on 24 Jan 1861 to Jabez Rayl and Fanny Finney. Cyrenius Elwood married Minnie Perkins. He passed away on 8 Jul 1930 in Albion, Edwards, Illinois, USA.

(f) Amanda Jane Rayl - Born in Indianapolis, Parke, Indiana, USA on 19 Jan 1863 to Jabez Rayl and Fanny Finney. Amanda Jane married Patrick Featherstone and had 3 children. She passed away on 16 Jul 1898 in Indianapolis, Parke, Indiana, USA.

1. Luther Featherstone
2. Herman Featherstone
3. Alvin Featherstone

(g) William Ulyssus Rayl - Born in Indianapolis, Parke, Indiana, USA on 23 Jul 1865 to Jabez Rayl and Fanny Finney. William Ulysus married Alice Virginia Dunford and had 8 children. He passed away on 9 Aug 1944 in Youngwood, Westmoreland, Pennsylvania, USA.

William Ulysses Grant Rayl; Lester W. Rayl; Jennie Alice Rayl

1. Charles Jabez Rayl
2. Lester Willard Rayl
3. Alma Alfonso Rayl
4. Jennie Alice Rayl
5. Lillie May Rayl
6. Arthur Leonard Rayl
7. Mary Arvilla Rayl

BOLTON FRIENDS CHURCH

In 1882, the Copeland family helped build this church in Harrisonville. Later it was moved to Bolton.

In 2011, Ralph Copeland passed away. He left his home and the contents to the Bolton Friends Church. He always had fondness for "the little church in the country."

Pastor Grady Miller found and returned many, many family photographs that included the Finneys, Ephlins, Copelands, and more to the family members, thus helping preserve our family history. God Bless the Bolton Friends Church!

Children (Pearl Copeland in white dress by shutter) by the Bolton Church; adults to the left

(11) Catherine Finney, d/o Joseph - b. 1 Jan 1828 Parke Co., Ind - d. after 1911 m. 28 Oct 1849 David BRADFORD - on tax record in Reserve Twp., Parke Co., Ind. in 1851

(12) Mary Ann Finney - b. 22 Jan 1832 Parke Co., Ind. - d. 2 Aug 1908 - m. John Hamilton WEAVER - b. 15 Dec 1824 Ind - d. 28 Jan 1896, s/o John & Margaret [Crecilius] Weaver

(a) Jane Ann Weaver - b. 1861 Parke Co., Ind
(b) Joseph A. Weaver - b. 1861 Parke Co., Ind - d. 1933
(c) Andrew Weaver - b. 1865 Parke Co., Ind.
(d) Mary E. Weaver - b. 1867 Parke Co., Ind
(e) William H. Weaver - b. 1869 Parke Co., Ind

Catherine (Finney) Bradford (Wesley Finney's sister)

Mary Ann (Finney) Weaver (Wesley Finney's sister)

There are un-numbered pages in this section. This section was written separately by another Finney family member and submitted for this book.

Rosamary High Finney included this Direct Line from Robert Finney to her husband's father Carl Chester Finney. There are additional documents that supplement earlier documents in this book.

As for the 'direct line,' don't miss reading "Controversy, Science, and Revelation" later in this book!

DIRECT LINE
ROBERT FINNEY – BORN 1630
TO
CARL CHESTER FINNEY – BORN 1905

*Note – the information gathered by Rosamary High Finney was based on information available in the late 1980s and early 1990s.

FINNEY FAMILY - *This section contains notes transcribed by a Finney family member from Rosamary's original text.

This family was traditionally Scotch-Irish, Presbyterians, and either the father or grandfather of ROBERT FINNEY, b. 1667/8 is believed to have been born in Scotland or England where the Finney's were a very old family which has been traced directly back to Baron John de Fienes (Fenis). He was related to William the Conqueror, who went to England with him. William the Conqueror appointed him Lord Warden of the Cinque Forts, and in 1083 A. D. appointed him Heriditary Constable of Dover Castle, calling him our "kinsman Fenis."

ROBERT FINNEY was born Scotland or England @ 1630 and married Isabell b. @ 1635. Their children are believed to have been Henry b. 30 Nov 1657; James b. 4 July 1659 - d. 10 Aug 1659; William b. 4 May 1664; Mary b. 29 Aug 1666 and Robert b. 1667/8 - d. Mar 1755.

Will filed in Londonderry, Ireland of ROBERT FINNEY was dated August 1692 and named his wife Isabell, but no children. The will indicates he was a man of extensive land interests. The above named children are shown in the parish register of Londonderry cathedral, Parish of Templemore, Diocese of Deny and are presumably those of Robert and Isabell since there are no other records of a Finney family to be found in Londonderry in that period or any period earlier.

Londonderry, a maritime county, 804 square miles in Northern Ireland, in Ulster, is largely a mountainous area with damp, cold climate, and is situated on the Foyle River. It is a major Irish seaport.

COPY OF WILL OF ROBERT FINNEY - Drawn in Diocese of Deny, Ireland and dated in the year of 1692. Wording as follows:

In the name of God, Amen, I Robert Finney, of the City of Londonderry and , being of weak in body but of sound and perfect memory (Praise be to God) do make, ordain and appoint this my last will and testament in manner following -

I bequeath my sould unto Almighty God hoping through the passion and merits of my Savior, Jesus Christ, to receive remission and forgiveness of all my sins and iniquities and as for my body I desire that it may be decently interred -1 give and bequeath unto my well beloved wife, Isabell Finney, all my houses within and without the gates of Londonderry with the rights, members and appurtenances thereunto belonging with all and singular my goods and chattels real and personal, moveable and unmoveable and all my cash debts and worldly substance to be converted by her to her own use or disposal of as she shall see fit. I do hereby nominate and appoint my wife, Isabell Finney, my sole execrutrix of this my last will and testament, desiring that she may honestly discharge my just debts by me and I desire that Henry Ash and Samuel Lesson, Exq., may be assisting to my said wife in the management of my concerns hereby revoking and disannuling all former wills by me heretofore made. As witness my hand and seal this 25th day of August, 1692. - Robert Finney

****

ROBERT FINNEY, son of Robert - b. @ 1667/8 (Londonderry) Ulster Co., Ireland - d. March 1755 (London Grove) Chester Co., New London Township, PA. He is buried in the Finney Cemetery at Thunder Hill Estate. He was married in Ireland @ 1690 to Dorothea FRENCH - b. May 1670 Ireland - d. May 1752 Chester Co. New London, PA.

Tradition states that Robert was one of the defenders of Londonderry, Ireland when the city withstood the siege of James II's forces for 105 days in 1689. (Robert was then about 21 years old.) In 1690 he participtated in the Battle of Boyne, was wounded and left on the battlefield to die. He regained consciousness during the night, and finding a

2 horse grazing nearby, managed to mount it and ride away. It is also said that at the burial of some unknown person many years after Robert's death, his skull was discovered with a hole in it, showing where his wound had been.

Another often repeated tradition is to the effect that before leaving Ireland he dreamed that he had emigrated and purchased land in America, and when he actually came to this country he recognized in the Thunder Hill estate the home of his dreams.

A glimpse of the character of Dorothea, who was forced to endure the suffering accompanying the siege of Deny and her husband's being wounded, is vividly pictured in an episode that must certainly have made an impression on their household. According to family history, Dorothea promptly boxed the ears of one of her daughter-in-laws when she was seen wasting a crust of bread.

Robert Finney and Dorothea came to America as early as 1720 when he was about 52 years old and Dorothea 50, with all of their children. He must have been a person of some means or good credit for he purchased the 900 acres of land called Thunder Hill, one mile southwest of New London, Chester Co., PA. from Michael Harlan in June 1722 for which a patent dated 4 Aug 1733 was afterward granted him. He bought 900 acres for 535 pounds and 54 pounds for the patent, which was about $2,945.00 in our money. Thunder Hill was settled by the noted Joran Kyn, a famous Swedish immigrant, and is situated on the northeast side of Elk River about one mile South of New London. The valley is watered by the Susquehanna River and a road through their farm was often used by traveling stage coaches.

Robert helped to establish the first of the Presbyterian Churches at New London in 1726 and was its first filling elder. Robert and his wife owned and occupied Thunder Hill from 1722 until Robert's death in 1755, and in 1973 the old home was still standing and was occupied. The land estate which was divided between the children at the time of Robert's death, passed out of the family many generations ago. The Finney graveyard is owned by the Finneys now living in Philadelphia who have cared for, cleaned and maintained it on a regular basis. Five generations of the family are buried in this cemetery. The ones who maintain it are descendents of William and Jean (Jane) Stepheson Finney to whom his parents Robert and Dorothea conveyed the property by deed of gift on 2 Feb 1744/5 with their nephew, David, of New Castle, one of the executors of the will.

The family cemetery is located on a corner of the old Thunder Hill farm left by the will of Robert "as a graveyard of my relatives forever." The bodies of Robert and Dorothea are buried there with the following inscriptions:

> Interred the body of Robert Finney, died March A. D. 1755 being the Eighty seven year of age.
>
> Interred the body of Dorothea Finney, died May A. D. 1752 being the Eighty two year of age.

Robert and Dorothea had the following children:

1. Dr. John Finney - b. @ 1690 Londonderry, Ireland - d. Mar 1774 New Castle, DE. - m. Elizabeth FRENCH - b. 1693 New Castle., DE - d. Apr 1740 - m. Sarah RICHARSON
2. Robert Finney - b. - d. @1782, a physician, unmarried (Thunderhill)
3. William Finney - b. 1710 Ireland - d.« 1751 New London, PA., a carpenter, will dated 12 Jan 1749, probated Apr 1751 - m. Jean STEPHENSON - they had 11 children
4. Thomas Finney - b. - d. @ 1767 - m. Mary CHESTER
5. Ann Finney - b. - d. after 1778, buried Thunder Hill - m. John McCLENAHAN - d. after 1778
    a. Elijah McClenahan - b. 3 Nov 1728 - d. 23 Feb 1810 New London, PA. - m. Mary -b. 1737 - d. 30 Apr 1780
        1. Samuel Blair McClenahan - b. 1 May 1775 -11 Sept 1851 - m (1) Amay CHARLTON, m (2) Sarah JOHNSON
6. Letitia Finney -b. -d. 1742 - m. William McKEAN (William's son, Thomas Mckean, was a signer of the Declaration of Independence)
7. **LAZARUS FINNEY** - b. Ireland - d. 1740 Chester Co., PA., buried Thunder Hill - m. Catharine SIMONTON (Symonton) (I found the spelling to be Simmons)

LAZARUS FINNEY was born in Northern Ireland. He was the son of Robert and Dorothea Finney and he died in 1740 in Chester County, Pennsylvania.

Lazarus Finney owned a tavern, opened in 1729, in New London and was the first tavern keeper in the township. He was granted a Warrantee of Land on January 17, 1734/5 for 250 acres. After his death in 1740, his wife Catherine

SYMONTON (Simonton), was left alone to raise her four children. She remarried in 1741 to Colonel John FREW of East Nottingham and New London Twp., and the maintained the tavern until it was sold in 1746. The tavern was still in existence in 1940 and in use as a tavern. Colonel Frew was a merchant. Catherine was finally granted letters of administration on the estate of Lazarus on January 21, 1741 and the estate was settled in 1746. It is unknown what happened to Catherine after that time. A Thomas Frew witnessed the will of Robert Finney in 1824 and the will mentions the old John Frew tract.

The children of Lazarus and Catherine were:

1. Robert Finney dob: 1727 - d. 29 Oct 1822
2. **John** Finney **dob:** 1730-5 July 1783
3. Dorothea Finney
4. Catherine Finney

JOHN FINNEY was born 1730 in Chester County, Pennsylvania and died July 5, 1783 in New Castle County, Delaware. John was the son of Lazarus Finney. John was married January 9, 1758 to Ruth LLOYD (daughter of Johesph LLoyd). They were married in the Old Swedes Holy Trinity Church, Wilmington, Delaware (built 1698), and are buried in that cemetery.

John and Ruth had five children:

1. James Finney dob: 1768
2. Robert Finney dob: 1783 Grayson County, Virginia-d. 10 July 1866
3. John Finney
4. William Finney
5. **Joseph Finney dob: 4/2/1765** - d. 22 Mar 1837

JOSEPH FINNEY was born April 2, 1765 in New Castle County, Delaware. From 1785 to 1826 Joseph lived in Surrey County, North Carolina. In 1790 he was granted land in that county and on February 11,1800 he was granted 60 acres also in Surry County by the state of North Carolina. On April 24, 1804 he sold 80 acres in western Grayson County, Virginia near Rugby on the south fork of Bowers and Mill Creek, branch of the New River. This land bordered on that of Jesse Rector. In the 1810 census he is listed in both Surry County, North Carolina and in Washington county, Virginia. In 1820 and 1825/6 he was in Grayson County, Virginia. On June 15,1822 he and his second wife Ann lived near the town of Seven-Mile-Ford in Western Grayson County, Virginia.

4 In 1826, as of March 6th, he was a teacher at the Laurel Branch School, on the left fork of the Holsten River, in Washington County, Virginia. On October 21, 1825 when he was 60 years old, he transferred land in Smyth County, Virginia to John FINNEY and then on October 12,1826 he purchased 80 acres of United States land in Penn Twp., Parke County, Indiana, recorded at the land office in Crawfordsville, Indiana. He and Ann and son Richard, age 18, and daughter Peggy, age 14, moved to Parke County, Indiana in 1826. NOTE: His location in Grayson County, Virginia was very near the Washington County line and it is probable that he was located in the section now a part of Grayson County.

When he went to Indiana his son Joseph did not accompany him because the son Joseph had moved to Green County, Tennessee and married there. The son Joshua had also moved to Greene County, Tennessee.

Joseph was married first to Rachel Barkley, December 13, 1783, who died in 1795 in Surry County, North Carolina. He then married Ann KESSTER, in the 1800's, who was the daughter of John and Sarah Kesster. Joseph died March 22,

1837 in Parke County, Indiana and is buried in Rawlins Cemetery, east of Annapolis, Indiana.

Joseph and Ann had four children:

1. Joseph Finney **dob:** 9/18/1784 -d. 8 Mar 1867
2. Joshua Finney dob: 1790 -d. after 1850
3. Richard King Finney dob: 3/9/1808 - d. 22 Feb 1875
4. Margaret (Peggy) Rector Finney dob: 6/27/1812 - after 1880

JOSEPH FINNEY was born September 18, 1784 in Orange County, North Carolina. He married Mary (Polly) Long September 10, 1805 in Greene County, Tennessee. Mary was born April 2, 1786 in Virginia. Joseph died March 8,1867 and Mary died September 27, 1872 in Parke County, Indiana. Both are buried in Linebarger Cemetery near West Union.

Between 1795 and 1809, Joseph, who was a farmer lived most of the time in Green County, Tennessee; however, two of his children were born in Surry County, North Carolina—John Long Finney and Nancy Finney. The next child, Hawkins Cook Finney, was born in Tennessee. Joseph served in the War of 1812, 2nd Surry Regiment of North Carolina Militia, also called Capt. James Martin's Company, Infantry, 7th Regiment (Pearson's). He was granted land based on his war service and was also granted a pension later in life.

From Tennessee they went to Lawrence County, Indiana in 1815-17 and settled finally in 1826 in Parke County, Indiana. On September 1831 he purchased United States land in Penn Twp., Parke County, one mile west of Annapolis.

He and Polly had twelve children:

1. Robert Finney dob: 8/23/1806 - d. 9 Mar 1861
2. Joseph Finney dob: 12/19/1808 - d. 4 May 1854
3. John Long Finney dob: 12/16/1810-d. before 1903
4. Nancy Finney dob: 10/16/1812 - d. ?
5. Hawkins Cook Finney dob: 8/28/1815 -d. 1 Jan 1889
6. Polly Finney dob: 1/21/1818 - d. 21 June 1896
7. Elizabeth Finney dob: 3/9/1820 - d. 22 Aug 1900
8. Rachel Finney dob: 3/27/1821 - d. 21 Apr 1860
9. **Wesley Finney dob: 5/10/1823** d. Oct. 3, 1904
10. Fanny Finney dob: 2/16/1825-d. 18 Dec 1891
11. Catherine Finney dob: 1/1/1828 - d. after 1911
12. Mary Ann Finney dob: 22 Jan 1832 - 2 Aug 1908

WESLEY FINNEY was born May 10,1823 in Lawrence County, Indiana. His parents were Joseph Finney and Mary (Polly) Long. Wesley and Mary Matilda Hinshaw were married August 27, 1850 in (Parke Co.) Indiana. Mary Matilda was born October 29, 1829 to Jesse and Hannah (Moon) Hinshaw. Wesley and

Mary Matilda had nine children while living in Indiana.

1. Samantha Jane Finney dob: 8/7/1851-26 Apr 1937
2. James Anderson Finney dob: 1854 - d. 1858 in Indiana
3. Mary Catherine Finney dob: 5/9/1857-22 Aug 1926
4. Anna E.Finney dob: 3/24/1859-March 1928
5. **John Wesley Finney dob: 2/14/62** - 6 Oct 1945
6. Polly Hannah Finney dob: 3/23/1864-d. 12 Dec 1886
7. Louisa May Finney dob: 1/8/1867 - d. 6 Jan 1919
8. Daniel Webster Finney dob: 11/7/1868-d. 10 Dec 1927
9. Clara Ellen Finney dob: 5/27/1872-d. 12 Dec 1945

JOHN WESLEY FINNEY was born February 14, 1862 in (South Beford Co. seat) Lawrence Co., (Marion) Indianapolis, IN to Wesley and Mary Matilda (Hinshaw) Finney.

John's parents and eight siblings moved to Montgomery County, KS about 1882, settling on a farm 2 miles south of Bolton. They moved their belongings and their livestock in railroad boxcars on a freight train. In 1900, after John's mother died, his father, Wesley lived with Elmer and Clara Ellen Farlow, Clara Ellen being his youngest child. However, Wesley, died at the residence of his son, John Wesley, near Niotaze, KS. on Monday, October 3, 1904.

Wesley was a member of the U. B. church and in former years did ministerial work for that church. Funeral services were held at the U. B. church which was conducted by his old friend, Elder J. I. Robinson, after which his remains were taken to the cemetery in Fawn Creek township and deposited beside his wife, Mary Matilda, who had preceded him to the tomb February 5, 1900.

John Wesley Finney was married to Nannie (Brooks) in Bridgeport, Cooke Co., TN. on October 6, 1886. Nannie Brooks was born on December 18, 1866 in Bridgeport, Cooke Co., TN.

John Wesley Finney bought a small orchard, one and some odd acres in Bolton. Later he bought 280 acres in Niotaze, Kansas. Part of the land was River Bottom, in which, John's cousin, Asbury Rale (Rayl?), helped to turn over the land by bringing mules from Indiana.

When the old Methodist Church in Niotaze was built, John W. Finney hauled the stone with a team of horses. The stone came from over the hill from a quarry that is located behind the Methodist Church in Niotaze, Kansas.

John and Nannie Finney had eight children.

1. Nora Ellen Finney dob: 7/22/1887 - Spouse: James Monroe NORRIS m. Sep 22, 1907 - Supulpa, OK.
2. Frank Finney dob: 11/27/1888 - d. 15 Dec 1954 m. Nov 23 1916 Hattie Nichelson COLE
3. Eva Belle Finney dob: 12/24/1890 - Spouse: Thomas Blodgett McCARTHY
4. Emma Elizabeth Finney dob: 3/25/1894 - d. Sep 1958 m. 22 May 1911 Benjamin G. SHAFER - Sedan, KS.

5. Frederick Dewey Finney dob: 11/27/1898
6. Estella Marie 'Stella' Finney dob: 1/5/1902 - d. 21 Aug 1981 m. 3 June 1922 William Henry HILBERT
7. Clarence Fay Finney dob: 1/18/1904 - d. 6/23/72 m. 7/3/24 Martha Myrtle HANN
8. Clinton 'Red' Finney dob: 9/27/1907 - d. 9/ 29/ 1986 m. 28 Mar 1929 Georgia Kathryn Irene LEWIS

CLARENCE FAY FINNEY was born January 18,1904 in Niotaze, KS. He died in Sedan, KS. June 21, 1972 and was buried in Fairview Cemetery located in Niotaze, KS. Clarence married to Martha Myrtle Harm July 3, 1924. They were said to have met at a square dance where Clarence played the violin. First home was said to be the Chrisman's Place or (Minor's Place) which was located on the Montgomery-Chautauqua County Line. Then they moved to Monet for a short time and then back to the Finney Farm into the old Weaning House.

Clarence and his dad, John W., went together and farmed the river bottom growing Alfalfa. Clarence also had a team of mares and mules. The young team consisted of Bird and Bell. The older mules were Tim & Pete, Jack & Bill. The team of mares and mules were used for road grading. These teams 'drugged' all the roads in that area and Clarence was paid by the county for this job. (This information was told to Harold E. Finney before his brother, Johnny, passed away.

Clarence and Myrtle had 14 children.

1. Johnny Ernest Finney dob: 12/13/1925 Deceased 7/4/2002-buried 7/10/02 in Fairview Cemetery, Niotaze, KS.- m. May 15 1947 - Paula Pearl COURTNEY
2. Alta Elizabeth Finney dob: 1/13/1928 - m. (1) Harold Tubalcain KJRCHNER 1/27/1946 (2) Paul O'Dell FULLER 5/4/1998
3. Mary Evelyn Finney dob: 2/23/1930 - m. (1) Claude Marrion DUFOE 7/6/1948 (2) Robert Emil McMURTRY
4. Rollie Gene Finney dob: 1/17/1932-divorced Gloria LOVEGREEN
5. Velda Marie Hilta Finney dob: 8/27/1934 - m. Kenneth Earl GORBY 5/6/1954
6. Danny Merle Finney dob: 8/4/1937 Deceased 3/4/1937 b: Fairview Cemetery, Niotaze, KS.
7. Wanda Faye Finney dob: 5/16/1938-m. Carl Floyd RILEY 7/9/1955
8. Kyle B Finney dob: 9/4/1942 - m. Joyce Ann BARR 6/6/1964
9. Harold Edward Finney dob: 7/6/1943-m. Bonnie Jean TWITCHELL 11/22/1964
10. Gary Lee Finney dob: 1/25/1945 - m. Cynthia Louise Owens 12/27/1970
11. Melvin Ray Finney dob: 2/18/1947 - m. Mary Lue MALONE 11/20/1970
12. Wesley David Finney dob: 12/16/1949 - m. Janice Sue SCOTT 7/28/1972
13. Roy Keith Finney dob: 1/12/1952 - m. (1) CarroU Sue BAYS died 5/18/1986 (2) Carol Ann Berry HAWKINS 11/6/1986
14. Lyle Eugene Finney dob: 1/4/1954 - m. Suzanne Marie COLE 11/4/1983

Most of the information came from History of Finney Family 1692 -1990 by Rosamary (High) Finney Heart of America Genealogical Society & Library Inc., 311 East 12th Street, Kansas City, Missouri.

The oldest child, Johnny Finney, lived oft and on with his Grandparents, John and Nannie Finney, starting at the age of eight years old.

FINNEY FAMILY

This family was traditionally Scotch-Irish, Presbyterians, and either the father or grandfather of ROBERT FINNEY, b. 1667/8 is believed to have been born in Scotland or England where the Finneys were a very old family which has been traced directly back to Baron John de Fienes [Fenis]. He was related to William the Conqueror, who went to England with him, William the Conqueror appointed him Lord Warden of the Cinque Forts, and in 1083 A. D. appointed him Heriditary Constable of Dover Castle, calling him our "kinsman Fenis."

ROBERT FINNEY was born Scotland or England @ 1630 and married Isabell b. @ 1635 Their children are believed to have been Henry b. 30 Nov 1657; James b. 4 July 1659 - d. 10 Aug 1659; William b. 4 May 1664; Mary b. 29 Aug 1666 and Robert b. 1667/8.

Will filed in Londonderry, Ireland of ROBERT FINNEY was dated August 1692 and named his wife Isabell, but no children. The will indicates he was a man of extensive land interests. The above named children are shown in the parish register of Londonderry cathedral, Parish of Templemore, Diocese of Derry and are presumably those of Robert and Isabell since there are no other records of a Finney family to be found in Londonderry in that period or any period earlier.

Londonderry, a maritime county, 804 square miles in Northern Ireland, in Ulster, is Largely a mountainous area with damp, cold climate, and is situated on the Foyle River. It is a major Irish seaport.

COPY OF WILL OF ROBERT FINNEY - Drawn in Diocese of Derry, Ireland and dated in the year of 1692. Wording as follows:

In the name of God, Amen, I Robert Finney, of the City of Londonderry and , being weak in body but of sound and perfect memory [Praise be to God] do make, ordain and appoint this my last will and testament in manner following -

I bequeath my soul unto Almighty God hoping through the passion and merits of my Saviour, Jesus Christ, to receive remission and forgiveness of all my sins and iniquities and as for my body I desire that it may be decently interred - I give and bequeath unto my well beloved wife, Isabell Finney, all my houses within and without the gates of Londonderry with the rights, members and appurtenances thereunto belonging with all and singular my goods and chattels real and personal, moveable and unmoveable and all my cash debts and worldly substance to be converted by her to her own use or disposal of as she shall see fit. I do hereby nominate and appoint my wife, Isabell Finney, my sole execrutrix of this my last will and testament, desiring that she may honestly discharge my just debts by me and I desire that Henry Ash and Samuel Lesson, Esq., may be assisting to my said wife in the management of my concerns hereby revoking and disannuling all former wills by me heretofore made. As witness my hand and seal this 25th day of August, 1692.

Robert Finney

Witnesses:

Hugh Thompson
John Patersone

* * * * * *

ROBERT FINNEY, s/o Robert - b. @ 1667/8 Ulster Co., Ireland - d. Mar 1755 Chester Co., New London Twp., Pa. He is buried in the Finney Cemetery at Thunder Hill Estate. He was married in Ireland @ 1690 to Dorothea FRENCH - b. @ 1670 Ireland - d. May 1752 Chester Co.

Tradition states that Robert was one of the defenders of Londonderry, Ireland when the city withstood the siege of James II's forces for 105 days in 1689. [Robert was then about 21 years old.] In 1690 he participated in the Battle of Boyne, was wounded and left on the battlefield to die. He regained consciousness during the night, and finding a horse grazing nearby, managed to mount it and ride away. It is also said that at the burial of some unknown person many years after Robert's death, his skull was discovered with a hole in it, showing where his wound had been. Another often repeated tradition is to the effect that before leaving Ireland he dreamed that he had emigrated and purchased land in America, and when he actually came to this country he recognized in the Thunder Hill estate the home of his dreams.

A glimpse of the character of Dorothea, who was forced to endure the suffering accompanying the siege of Derry and her husband's being wounded, is vividly pictured in an episode that must certainly have made an impression on their household. According to family history, Dorothea promptly boxed the ears of one of her daughter-in-laws when she was seen wasting a crust of bread.

Robert and Dorothea came to America as early as 1720 when he was about 52 years old and Dorothea 50, with all of their children. He must have been a person of some means or good credit for he purchased the 900 acres of land called Thunder Hill, one mile southwest of New London, Chester Co., Pa. from Michael Harlan in June 1722 for which a patent dated 4 Aug 1733 was afterward granted him. He bought the 900 acres for 535 pounds and 54 pounds for the patent, which was about $2,945.00 in our money. Thunder Hill was settled by the noted Joran Kyn, a famous Swedish immigrant, and is situated on the northeast side of Elk River about one mile south of New London. The valley is watered by the Susquehanna River and a road through their farm was often used by traveling stage coaches.

Robert helped to establish the first of the Presbyterian Churches at New London in 1726 and was its first ruling elder. Robert and his wife owned and occupied Thunder Hill from 1722 until Robert's death in 1755, and in 1973 the old home was still standing and was occupied. The land estate which was divided between the children at the time of Robert's death, passed out of the family many generations ago. The Finney graveyard is owned by the Finneys now living in Philadelphia who have cared for, cleaned and maintained it on a regular basis. Five generations of the family are buried in this cemetery. The ones who maintain it are descendents of William and Jean [Jane] Stephenson Finney to whom his parents Robert and Dorothea conveyed the property by deed of gift on 2 Feb 1744/5 with their nephew, David, of New Castle, one of the executors of the will.

The family cemetery is located on a corner of the old Thunder Hill farm left by the will of Robert "as a graveyard of my relatives forever." The bodies of Robert and Dorothea are buried there with the following inscriptions:

> Interred the body of Robert Finney,
> died March A. D. 1755 being the Eighty seven year of age.
> Interred the body of Dorothea Finney,
> died May A. D. 1752 being the Eighty 2 year of age.

Robert and Dorothea had the following children:

- i. Dr. John French Finney - b. @ 1690 - d. Mar 1774
- ii. Robert Finney - b. - d. @ 1782, a physician, unmarried
- iii. William Finney - b. @ 1700 - d. 1750
- iv. Thomas Finney - b. - d. @ 1767
- v. Ann Finney - b. - d. after 1778
- vi. James Finney - b. - d. 1774
- vii. Letitia Finney - b. - d. 1742
- viii. LAZARUS FINNEY - b. - d. 1740

LAZARUS FINNEY - b. Northern Ireland - d. 1740 Chester Co., Pa. [s/o Robert & Dorothea] - he is buried at Thunder Hill - m. Catherine SYMONTON [Simonton]

Lazarus owned a tavern, opened in 1729, in New London and was the first tavern keeper in the township. He was granted a Warrantee of Land on 17 Jan 1734/5 for 250 acres. After his death in 1740 Catherine was left alone to raise her four children. She remarried in 1741 to Colonel John FREW of East Nottingham and New London Twp., and they maintained the tavern until it was sold in 1746. The tavern was still in existance in 1940 and in use as a tavern. Colonel Frew was a merchant. Catherine was finally granted letters of administration on the estate of Lazarus on 21 January 1741 and the estate was settled in 1746. It is unknown what happened to catherine after that time. A Thomas Frew witnessed the c will of Robert Finney in 1824 and the will mentions the old John Frew tract.

The children of Lazarus and Catherine were:

- i. Robert Finney - b. 1727 - d. 29 Oct 1822
- ii. JOHN FINNEY - b. 1730 - d. 5 July 1783
- iii. Dorothea Finney
- iv. Catherine Finney

Know all men by these presents that wee Katherine Finney Robt. Finney
& Nathan Worley all of the County of Chester & Province of Pensylvania Yeoman are
held and firmly Bound unto Peter Evans Regr. Generall for the probate of
Wills & Granting Letters of Admon in and for the Province afsd. in the Sum
of Twelve hundred pounds lawfull money of the sd. province to be paid
to the sd. Regr. Generall his Exrs. Admrs. or Assigns to which Payment well
and truly to be made Wee bind our selves our Heirs Exrs. and Admrs. & every of
them in the whole and for the whole Joyntly & severally firmly by these pts.
Sealed with our Seals Dated the twenty first Day of January Anno Dom 1740/41
The Condition of this Obligation is Such That if the above bounden
Katherine Finney Admx. of all and Singular the Goods Chattles & Credits of Lazarus Finney
Decd. do make or Cause to be made a true & perfect Inventory of all & singular
the Goods Chattles and Credits of the said Decd. which have or shall Come to the
hands Possession or Knowledge of her the sd. Katherine Finney or into the hands & Possession or knowledge of any other person or Persons for her and the same
so made Exhibit or Cause to be Exhibited into the Regrs. Office for the sd. County
on or before the first Day of March next Ensuing and the same Goods
and Chattles Credits of the sd. Decd. at the time of his Death or which at
any time after Shall Come to the hands or Possession of any Other Person or
for her do well and truly Administer according to Law and further do make
or Cause to be made a True and Just acct. of her Admon when Legally thereunto Required & all the Rest and Residue of the sd. Chattles and Credits which shall
be found Remaining upon the sd. Administratrix acct. the same being first Examined & allowed of by the Orphans Court of the County of Chester Shall Deliver
& pay to such Person & Persons Respectively as the sd. Court by their Decree or
Sentence pursuant to Law shall Limit and appoint And if it shall hereafter appear
that any Last Will and Testament was made by the Decd. & the Exr. or Exrs. therein
named do Exhibit into the Regrs. Office for the said County making Request to
have the same Allowed and Approved of Accordingly if the sd. Katherine Finney being
thereunto Required do Render & Deliver up the sd. Letters of Admon Appro-
=bation of Such Testament being first had and made at the sd. office then
this Obligation to be Void Otherwise to be and Remain in full force &
Virtue

Sealed and Delivered in the presence of
Thos. Cummings
Jo Parker

Catharine Finney

Robt. Finney

Nathan Worley

A true inventory of all & singular Ye Goods, Chattels & credits of Laz: Finney deceased, priced for new London Township in Ye County of Chester, on Ye 25th Day of year 1740/41: by mr. Fra: Johnston and mr. Willm Finney, as followeth — — —

		£	S	D
Imprimis,	His Cash, apparall, saddle & Books	33	05	0
Items	houshold goods & liquor	9.0	13	0
	The ladds time besides freedom	10	00	
	The girls time	02	10	
	Wheat 44 Bushels	07	03	
	Chattels	32	00	
	Wallnut boards	03	00	
	Cartes, plows, irons & collors	03	08	
		187	19	0
	Book debts	£418	15	6
	Bonds & notes	87	06	2
		688	00	8

The above apriasment was taken by us — — —

William Finney
Ffrancis Johnston

(These were little slips pasted on yellowed pages - alphabetically and chronologically.) "CHESTER CO., PA. TAX LISTS - D-G, 1693 - 1740." from Collections of the Genealogical Society of Pennsylvania, Gilbert Cope collection.

Newgarden 1720 Tax L 3s d	Robert Finney
Newgarden 1721 Tax L 2s6d	Robert Finney
Newgarden 1722 Tax L 8s9d	Robert Finney
New London 1726 Tax L 6s6d	Robert Finney
New London 1729 Tax L 2s6d	William Finney
New London 1729 Tax L 1s d	Thomas Finney
New London 1729 Tax L 6s6d	Robert Finney
New London 1729 Tax L 3s d	Lazarus Finney
New London 1730 Tax L 2s6d	Thomas Finney
New London 1730 Tax L 2s6d	William Finney
New London 1730 Tax L 2s6d	Lazarus Finney
New London 1730 Tax L 6s6d	Robert Finney
New London 1732 Tax L 5s d	Robert Finney
New London 1732 Tax L 1s6d	John Finney
New London 1732 Tax L 1s6d	William Finney
New London 1732 Tax L. 3s d	Thomas Finney
New London 1732 Tax L 3s d	Lazarus Finney
New London 1734 Tax L 2s6d	Thomas Finney
New London 1734 Tax L 1s3d	William Finney
New London 1734 Tax L 3s d	Lazarus Finney
New London 1734 Tax L 4s d	Robert Finney
New London 1735 Tax L 4s6d	Robert Finney
New London 1735 Tax L 2s6d	Thomas Finney
New London 1735 Tax L. 2s d	William Finney
New London 1735 Tax L 4s d	Lazarus Finney
New London 1737 Tax L 1s9d	William Finney
New London 1737 Tax L 5s d	Robert Finney
New London 1737 Tax L 4s d	Lazarus Finney
New London 1737 Tax L 2s6d	Thomas Finney
New London 1739 Tax L 4s6d	Laures Finney
New London 1739 Tax L 4s d	Robert ffiney
New London 1739 Tax L 2s10d	Thomas Ffiney
New London 1740 Tax L 2s3d	Thomas Finey
New London 1740 Tax L 3s6d	Robert Finey
New London 1740 Tax L 2s3d	William Finey
New London 1740 Tax L 4s6d	Lazarus Finney

JOHN FINNEY - b. 1730 Chester Co., Pa. - d. 5 July 1783 New Castle Co., Del., [s/o Lazarus] m. 9 Jan 1758 Ruth LLOYD [d/o Joseph Lloyd]. They were married in the Old Swedes Holy Trinity Church, Wilmington, Delaware [built 1698], and are buried in that cemetery.

The children of John and Ruth were:

i. James Finney - b. 1768
ii. Robert Finney - b. 1783 Grayson Co., Va - d. 10 July 1866
iii. John Finney
iv. William Finney
v. JOSEPH FINNEY - b. 2 Apr 1765 - d. 22 Mar 1837

JOSEPH FINNEY - b. 2 Apr 1765 New Castle Co., Del. - d. 22 Mar 1837 Parke Co., IND. - buried Rawlins Cemetery, east of Annapolis, Indiana - m [1] 13 Dec 1783 Orange Co., NC to Rachel BARKLEY who died in 1795 in Surry Co., N.C. - m [2] @ 1800 Ann KESSTER - b. 9 Jan 1774 NC - d. 15 Mar 1853 Parke Co., Ind., d/o John & Sarah Kesster

From 1785 to 1826 Joseph lived in Surry Co., North Carolina. In 1790 he was granted land in that county and on 11 Feb 1800 he was granted 60 acres also in Surry Co. by the state of NOrth Carolina. On 24 Apr 1804 he sold 80 acres in western Grayson Co., Virginia near Rugby on the south fork of Bowers and Mill Creek, branch of the New River. This land bordered on that of Jesse RECTOR. In the 1810 census he is listed in both Surry Co., NC and in Washington Co., Va. In 1820 and 1825/6 he was in Grayson Co., Va. On 15 June 1822 he and his second wife Ann lived near the town of Seven-Mile-Ford in Western Grayson Co., Va. In 1826, as of March 6th, he was a teacher at the Laurel Branch School, on the left fork of the Holsten River, in Washington Co., Va. On 21 Oct 1825 when he was 60 years old, he transferred land in Smyth Co., Va. to John FINNEY and then on 12 October 1826 he purchased 80 acres of U. S. land in Penn Twp., Parke Co., Indiana, recorded at the land office in Crawfordsville, Indiana. He and Ann and son Richard, age 18, and daughter Peggy, age 14, moved to Parke Co., Ind. in 1826. NOTE: His locations in Grayson Co., Va. were very near the Washington County line and it is probable that he was located in the section now a part of Grayson County.

When he went to Indiana his son Joseph did not accompany him because the son Joseph had moved to Greene Co., Tenn. and married there. The son Joshua had also moved to Greene Co., Tenn.

Children of Joseph were:

i. JOSEPH FINNEY - b. 18 Sep 1784 - d. 8 Mar 1867
ii. Joshua Finney - b. 1790 - d. after 1850
iii. Richard King Finney - b. 9 Mar 1808 - d. 22 Feb 1875
iv. Margaret [Peggy] Rector Finney - 27 June 1812 - d. after 1880

JOSEPH FINNEY - b. 18 Sep 1784 Orange Co., NC - d. 8 Mar 1867 Parke Co., Ind. [s/o Joseph] - m. 10 Sep 1805 Greene Co., Tenn. to Mary [Polly] LONG - b. 2 Apr 1786 Va - d. 27 Sep 1872 Parke Co., Ind. Joseph's name appears on the Tax Records of Reserve Twp., Parke Co., Ind. 1851.

Between 1795 and 1809, Joseph, who was a farmer lived most of the time in Greene Co., Tenn; however, two of his children were born in Surry Co., NC - John Long Finney born 1810 and Nancy 1812, both in Surry Co. The next child was born in Tennessee. Joseph served in the War of 1812, 2nd Surry Regiment of North Carolina Militia, also called Capt. James Martin's Company, Infantry, 7th Regiment [Pearson's]. He was granted land based on his war service and was also granted a pension later in life.

From Tennessee they went to Lawrence Co., Ind. 1815-17 and settled finally in 1826 in Parke Co., Ind. On 19 Sep 1831 he purchased U.S. land in Penn Twp., Parke Co. one mile west of Annapolis. He and Polly are both buried Linebarger Cemetery near West Union.

i. Robert Finney - b. 23 Aug 1806 - d. 9 Mar 1861
ii. Joseph Finney - b. 19 Dec 1808 - d. 4 May 1854
iii. John Long Finney - b. 16 Dec 1810 - d. before 1903
iv. Nancy Finney - b. 16 Oct 1812 - d. ?
v. Hawkins Cook Finney - b. 28 Aug 1815 - d. 1 Jan 1889
vi. Polly Finney - b. 21 Jan 1818 - d. 21 June 1896
vii. Elizabeth Finney - b. 9 Mar 1820 - d. 22 Aug 1900

Know all men by these present that we Joseph Finney and Daniel Small of the County of Greene and State of Tennessee our Heirs Executors and Administrators, are held and firmly bound unto John Sevier, Governor of the State of Tennessee for the time being, and to his Successor in office, in the Sum of Twelve Hundred and fifty Dollars, to be Void on Condition there be no Legal Cause to obstruct the Marriage of the Said Joseph Finney, to Mary Lang Given under our hands and Seal this 28th day of August 1805.

Test
V. Sevier,

Joseph Finney (Seal)
Daniel Small (Seal)

Endorsed Joseph Finney to Mary Lang, Taken 28th August 1805.

State of Tennessee } I, V. S. Mcalaney Clerk of the County Court
Greene County } of Said County do certify that the foregoing File in my office,

Given under my hand and Seal of office at office in Greeneville the 7th day of February 1872.

V. S. Mcalaney Clerk

I also certify that the Laws of Tennessee did not require Marriage License to be returned to office, until the Year 1815. and that the License in the above case was never returned to office,

Given under my hand and Seal of office at office in Greeneville the 7th day of February 1872,

V. S. Mcalaney Clerk

F | 7 (Pearson's) | N. C. Militia.

Joseph Finney

Pri | Capt. James Martin's Co. of Inf., belonging to a Reg't North Carolina Militia, commanded by Col. Jesse A. Pearson.

(War of 1812.)

Appears on

Company Muster Roll

for to Mar 28, 1814.

Roll dated Fort Hawkins

Mar 28, 1814.

Commencement of service, Feb 1, 1814.

For what time engaged, 6 mon

Present or absent, Present

Remarks:

E W Moore

(609) Copyist.

F | 7 (Pearson's) | N. C. Militia.

Joseph Finny

Pri | Capt. James Martin's Company of Inf., 7 Reg't North Carolina State Troops.

(War of 1812.)

Appears on

Company Muster Roll

for Mar 28 to May 11, 1814.

Roll dated Camp Jackson near Coosa

May 11, 1814.

Commencement of service, Feb 1, 1814.

For what time engaged, Six months

Present or absent, Present

Remarks: Drawd one pair of shoes

E W Moore

(609) Copyist.

F | 7 (Pearson's) | N. C. Militia.

Joseph Finny

Pri | Capt. James Martin's Company of Inf., 7 Reg't North Carolina State Troops.

(War of 1812.)

Appears on

Company Muster Roll

for May 11 to Aug 17, 1814.

Roll dated Camp Pike

Aug 17, 1814.

Commencement of service, Feb 1, 1814.

For what time engaged, Six months

Present or absent, Present

Remarks: one pair of shoes

E W Moore

(609) Copyist.

F | 7 (Pearson's) | N. C. Militia.

Joseph Finney

Pri | Capt. James Martin's Company of Infantry, 7 Reg't North Carolina Detached Militia.

(War of 1812.)

Appears on

Company Pay Roll

for Feb 1 to Sept 4, 1814.

Roll dated Not dated, 181

Commencement of service, Feb 1, 1814.

Expiration of service or date of discharge, Sept 4, 1814.

Term of service charged, 7 months, 4 days.

Pay per month, 8 dollars.

Amount of pay, 57 dollars, 06 cents.

Traveling allowance from home to rendezvous and from place discharge home:

No. miles traveling, 120

No. days allowed for traveling, 6

Subsistence for traveling, ... dollars, 72 cents.

Pay for traveling, 1 dollars, 30 cents.

Amount for mileage, 2 dollars, 22 cents.

Aggregate amount due, 59 dollars, 28 cents.

Remarks: deduct 125 cts for 1 pair shoes

E W Moore

(672) Copyist.

F | 7 (Pearson's) | N. C. Militia.

Joseph Finny

Appears with the rank of Pri on a

Supplemental Muster Roll

of Capt. James Martin's Company of Infantry, 7 Reg't North Carolina State Troops,

(War of 1812.)

for Aug 17 to Sept 4, 1814, when discharged.

Roll dated Salisbury

Sept 14, 1814.

Commencement of service, Feb 1, 1814.

Date of discharge, Sept 4, 1814.

Present or absent, Present

Distance for mileage, 120

Remarks: Residence Surry county

E W Moore

(609) Copyist.

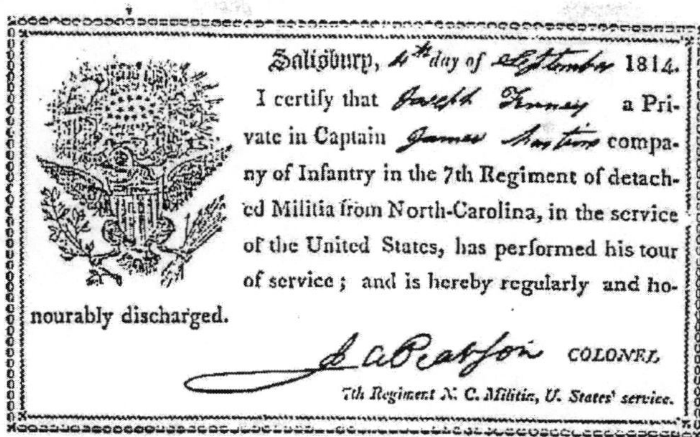

Salisbury, 4th day of September 1814.

I certify that Joseph Finney a Private in Captain James Austin's company of Infantry in the 7th Regiment of detached Militia from North-Carolina, in the service of the United States, has performed his tour of service; and is hereby regularly and honourably discharged.

J. A. Pearson COLONEL

7th Regiment N. C. Militia, U. States' service.

Bloomingdale Indiana Sept. 19th 1927

Dept. Interior, Bureau of Pensions

Washington D. C.

Hon. Commissioner: Can you give me some information concerning Joseph Finney, born April 2-1765, (a record his pocket book states he was born in Washington County Virginia Laurel Branch School House left fork Holston (River) which entry was made March 6-1826)

Joseph Finney may have removed to North Carolina about this time as his son Johna Finney remained there.

In 1826 his son Joseph Finney came to Indiana probably from North Carolina. Joseph Finney (Born Apr 2-1765) was a soldier in the war of 1812, entering the service in his 48 year. I think he must have seen service in the Revolutionary War or he would not have enlisted in the War of 1812: unless he was an officer in the war of 1812.

This man died in this community and is burried in the Kings Cemetery, date not known grave unmarked.

Was this man Joseph Finney born Apr 2-1765 in the Revolutionary War?

This man was a school "master" and much of his records were made in his own hand-writing.

He is my great grandfather on my mother's side.

I am anxious to get his complete record. and will appreciate any information you may give

Respectfully

J. A. Weaver.

128846
44439 May

Joseph Finney
1 pvt

Capt Ja. Martin
Col M H Pearson N C Mil

War 1812

reg Wart 80
14197 G.

80 acres
January 1. 1856
Ja. Sheidel

Saml A. Fisher
Rockville Ind

44439 Dec 30/50
128344
Joseph Finney Pri
Capt Jas Martin
7th Reg N. C. Mil
Ent 1814
Dis 1814 War 1812

3 Audit off Aug 29/51
Joseph Fisher Serg
from 1 Feb 1814
to 4 Sep 1814

M Gafleaker
for 3 Aud
Adm 80 acres

80 acre Warrant
No. 14197
Iss Sep 2/51
Jos B Connet
Vol 4 Rockville
Page 152 Ind.

JOSEPH FINNEY

MARY "POLLY" LONG FINNEY

State of Indiana,
Parke County ss. } On this 20th day of December A.D. Eighteen hundred and fifty, personally appeared before me the undersigned P. S. Cornelius a Notary Public in and for the County and State aforesaid, Joseph Finney aged sixty six years a resident of Parke County State of Indiana, who being duly sworn according to law, declares that he is the identical "Joseph Finney" who was a private in the Company Commanded by Captain James Martin in the 7th Regiment of detached Militia from North Carolina, Commanded by Colonel Jeh. Pearson in the war with Great Britain declared by the United States on the 18th day of June 1812: that he volunteered in the fall of the year 1813 and rendezvoused at Salisbury North Carolina on or about the 1st day of February A.D. 1814 for the term of six months and Continued in actual service in said war for the term of seven months, and was honorably discharged at Salisbury North Carolina on the 4th day of September A.D. 1814 as will appear by his original certificate of discharge herewith presented.

Joseph Finney Home - Annapolis, Indiana

He makes this declaration for the purpose of obtaining the bounty land to which he may be entitled under the "act granting bounty land to certain officers and soldiers who have been engaged in the military service of the United States."

Joseph Finney

Subscribed and sworn to before me on the day and year first above written. and I do hereby certify that I believe the said Joseph Finney to be the identical man who served as aforesaid. and that he is of the age above stated.

Witness my hand and Notarial Seal at Rockville, Indiana, on this 20th day of December A.D. 1850.

P. S. Cornelius
Notary Public
Parke Co. Ind.

State of Indiana County of Parke

On this 5th day of April A. D. one thousand eight hundred and fifty five personally appeared before me a Justice of the peace within and for the County and State aforesaid Joseph Finney aged Sixty years a resident of Parke County in the State of Indiana who being duly sworn according to law declares that he is the identical Joseph Finney who was a volunteer in the Company Commanded by Captain Jos Martin in the 7th Regiment of Detached Militia commanded by Col J. A. [illegible] in the war with Great Britain declared by the United States on the 18th day of June, 1812 for the term of 6 months and continued in actual service in said war for fourteen days; that he has heretofore made application for bounty land under the act of September 28, 1850 and received a land Warrant No for Eighty acres, which he has since legally disposed of and cannot now return nor can he remember the No of said Warrant He makes this declaration for the purpose of obtaining the additional bounty land to which he may be entitled under the act approved the 3rd day of March 1855. He also declares, that he has never applied for nor received, under this or any other act of Congress, any bounty land Warrant except the one above mentioned

Joseph Finney

We W G Coffin and John W Welch residents of Parke County in the State of Indiana, upon our oaths, declare that the foregoing declaration was signed and acknowledged by Joseph

State of Indiana
County of Parke ss

On this 14th day of April 1871, before me John D Hunt, Clerk of the Circuit Court in and for said County personally appeared Polly Finney aged 85 years, a resident of Penn Tp. in County and State aforesaid, who being duly sworn according to law declares, that she is the widow of Joseph Finney That her maiden name was Polly Long: that she was married to said Joseph on the 10th day of Septem 1805 in Green County, Tennessee, by a Justice of the Peace whose name she does not now remember. That her husband the said Joseph Finney served the full period of Sixty days in the military service of the United States in the war of 1812: That he was the identical Joseph Finney who enlisted in Captain James Martin company Col. Adkinson's Regiment Brigade Division, at Surrey County North Carolina on or about day of ; and was honorably discharged at Salisbury North Carolina, on the day of 18 ; that said Soldier served at Fort Jackson in the State of

As a private

That the said Joseph Finney died on the 8th day of Mar 1867. in Parke County Indiana: that he, or this applicant at no time during the late Rebellion against the authority of the

United States, adhered to the cause of the enemies of the Government; giving them aid or comfort, or exercised the functions of any office whatever under any authority, or pretended authority, in hos to the United States; That neither she nor her said husband is or was in receipt of a Pension under any previous act; that she makes this declaration of the United States under the provisions of the act approved February 14th 1871, and she hereby constitutes and appoints, with full power of substitution and revocation, Wm H Nye of Rockville Indn her true and lawful Attorney, to prosecute her claim, and obtain the Pension Certificate that may be issued: that her Post office add is Annapolis, Parke County, Indiana.

That her domicile or place of abode is on the place of Wesley Finney - one and a half mile west of Annapolis Parke County Indiana.

Attest Wesley Finney Polly her X mark Finney Applicant

Wesley Finney

Mary M. Finney

Also personally appeared Wesley Finney and Mary M Finney residing in Penn Twp. Parke County Ind persons well known to me and whom I certify to be respectable and entitled to credit; and who being by me duly sworn, say: they were present and saw Polly Finney make her mark to the foregoing declaration; that they have lived near neighbors and known said Applicant for thirty years last past, and Know her to be the identical person she represents herself & that they knew said soldier for many years in his life time; that to our certain knowledge, being present at the time, he died March 8th 1867. and that at no time during the late Rebellion against the authority of the United States, did either said soldier or his widow the above named applicant; adhere to the cause of the enemies of the government; giving them aid or comfort; and that they have no interest in the prosecution of this claim; that their residence is as above stated and their Post office address is Annapolis, Parke County, Indiana.

Wesley Finney
Mary M. Finney

Sworn to and subscribed before me this 14th day of April A.D 1871, and I hereby Certify that the Contents of the above declaration, and Statements were fully made known and explained to the applicant and Witnesses before swearing, including the words, "or this applic[ant]" interlined in line marked "A" above; And that I have no interest direct or indirect, in the prosecution of this Claim

John D. Hunt, Clerk
Parke Circuit Court

Department of the Interior.
PENSION OFFICE.

Washington, D.C. June 12" 1872

Sir,

In the claim of Polly Finney No 8245. for a widows pension under the act of Feb. 14" 1871 proof of continued widowhood of the claimant since death of the soldier. by affidavit of two persons acquainted with the fact. is required

Please return this letter with the evidence,

Very respectfully,
C. W. Seaton
Acting Commissioner,

Wm. H. Nye,
Rockville,
Park Co,
Ind.

N. F. L.

The State of Indiana } ss.
County of Parke }

On this 21st day of June 1872, personally appeared before me a Notary Public in and for the County above named Samuel T. Ensey and William C Woody, residents of said County who upon oath say that they are well acquainted with Polly Finney, widow of Joseph Finney, who is an applicant for a pension as surviv of War 1812, and that she has not remarried since the death of her said husband, but has continued in widowhood to the present time -

That their Post Office address is Annapolis, County of Parke, State of Indiana, and that they have no interest direct or indirect in the claim of said Polly Finney for pension -

Samuel T. Ensey
William C Woody

Affirmed and subscribed before me the date above named
[...]ly certify that the contents of the above affida[vit were]
[...]fully made known to the affiants before ~~swearing~~ affirming,
[...] I have no interest direct or indirect in the
[...] of said claim

James W Connelly
Notary Public

COUNTY OF Parke }
STATE OF Indiana } ss:

Personally appeared before me, a Notary Public in and for the county above named, Polly Finney who, upon oath, says: That neither I nor my said husband at no time during the late rebellion against the authority of the United States, adhered to the cause of the enemies of the Government, giving them aid or comfort, or exercised the functions of any office, under any authority or pretended authority, in hostility to the United States, and that I will support the Constitution of the United States.

her mark
Polly X Finney
mark

Affirmed ~~Sworn~~ to and subscribed before me this 22nd day of June, A. D. 1872; and I hereby certify that the contents of the above affidavit were fully made known to the affiant before swearing, including the words — added; and that I have no interest, direct or indirect, in the prosecution of this claim.

James H. Connelly
Notary Public

NOTE.—If a widow, insert "neither" before "I," and "nor my said husband," after it.

WAR OF 1812. 5245 Ind 3415

ACT OF FEBRUARY 14, 1871.

BRIEF OF CLAIM FOR A WIDOW'S PENSION

In the case of Polly Finney widow of Joseph Finney, a of Captain James Martin's Company, Colonel Reg't, N.C. Mil.

Residence, Parke Co. Ind.

Post Office address, Annapolis. Parke Co. Ind.

Soldier enlisted February 1st, 1814, Discharged September 4th, 1814.

Served afterward from , 18 , to , 18

in Captain Company, Colonel Reg't,

Declaration and Identification in due form, filed March 2d, 1872.

SERVICE FOR SIXTY DAYS SHOWN AS FOLLOWS:

3ty. L. Div. report shows service in Capt. Jas Martin's Co. N. C. Mil from Feb. 1st to Sept. 4th 1814.

Total service 216 days.

Soldier died March 8th, 1867, date and fact established by testimony of Wesley Finney and Mary M. Finney.

Continued widowhood since his death established by testimony of Samuel S. Encey, and William C. Woody.

Marriage to soldier prior to February 17, 1815, established by a certified copy of the marriage Bond from the records of Greene Co. Penn. bearing date of August 28th 1805. Maiden name of claimant "Polly Long" who gives date of marriage Sept. 10th 1805.

Oath to support the Constitution of the United States subscribed. Non-receipt of pension declared. Loyalty established by affidavits of Wesley Finney and Mary M. Finney. Their credibility certified by

Admitted July 28th, 1872, to a pension of eight dollars per month, from February 14, 1871.

A. F. Lingeley Examiner.

Approved:

No. 3415

WAR OF 1812.

WIDOWS' PENSION.

Indiana

Polly Finney

widow of

Joseph Finney

Rank

Company Capt J. Martin

Regiment

N. C. Mil

Indianapolis Agency.

Rate per month— Eight dollars.

Commencing February 14, 1871.

Certificate dated July 27" 1872

and sent to Pension Agent.

Act 14th February, 1871.

Vol. Ind'd Page 26

A. M. Kavanaugh Clerk.

18825-80-55

1927 Dec 5- Hist. to Hon. ... J. Johnson for J. A. ...

1934 Dec. 12- Hist. to Lester Dillard Payl — MLB

1937 July 27- Hist. to Mr. Charles W. Finney MLB

1939- Sept. 15: Chas. W. Finney only Joseph Finney - claim for pension etc

No.

ACT OF FEBRUARY 14, 1871.

WAR OF 1812.

Polly Finney
Penn Parke Co. Ind.
widow of
Joseph Finney
Cap. Jas. Martin's Co. N.C. Mil.
Died Mar. 8. 1867.

widowhood & oath to clnt

Received Mar 2, 1872
William H. Nye
Rockville Parke Co.
Ind.
Attorney.

Apr. 4, 1872, B.B.O.
for Service, &c.
W.W.

June 12/72, widowhood
& oath to clnt: [illegible]

June 27/72. Oath to clnt
A.F.

Admitted July 25th 1872
A.F.

July 31. Certif. O.P.F.C.A.

B. Joshua Finney [s/o Joseph b. 1765] - b. 1790 Surry Co., NC - d. after 1850 in Surry or Yadkin Co., NC - m. Juriah COLLINS - b. 1796 NC - d. after 1850. He served in War of 1812 from Green Co., Tenn. Militia, also 2nd Surry Regiment NC. Their old home on the Boone Trail, 10 miles southwest of Yadkinville, NC. They lived 1820-1850 Surry Co. (now Yadkin) - a farmer and a teacher

C. Richard King Finney - b. 8 Mar 1808 Va - d. 22 Feb 1875 Parke Co., Ind. On Tax Record in Reserve Twp. 1851 - m. 25 Apr 1847 Rebecca DAVIES - b. 11 Sep 1809 Berks Co., Pa. - d. 29 Sep 1891 - buried Rush Creek Cem., Parke Co., d/o Joseph & Lydia (Kennedy) Davies. Joseph & Lydia Davies were both born Pennsylvania, married in Chester Co. and both died enroute to Indiana. Their five children, including Rebecca, age 18, continued the trip, reaching Parke Co., Ind. 1827.

Richard was a farmer, purchasing U. S. land, Penn. Twp., in Parke Co. on 13 Jan 1836, later bought land and moved to northern part of Parke Co. on Rush Creek where he lived when he died. They had two children.

(1) Joseph Davies Finney - b. 13 Apr 1848 Parke Co - 15 Mar 1928 Kingman, Ind - buried Fraternal Cemetery - m (1) 16 Apr 1868 Elminda E. MILLIKAN - b. 14 Sep 1847 Parke Co., d/o Jonathan & Elizabeth [Brown] Millikan - m (2) 5 June 1886 in Harveysburg, Ind. Mrs. Sarah M. FISHER who died 15 May 1920

(a) William Arvel Finney - b. 17 Sep 1869 Parke Co - 22 Nov 1934 Monrovia, Calif. - m. 22 Nov 1889 in Colorado Claudia BAILEY - lvd. Oroville, Calif. in 1940 w/daughter Edna

i. Edna May Finney - b. 22 Nov 1899 - m (1) Walter ROBINSON, m (2) Sydney TYSON

(b) Asa Albert Finney - b. 24 Nov 1872 Parke Co - 11 June 1909 Parke Co., buried West Union, Ind - m (1) 11 Oct 1896 Anna WILLIAMSON - b. 16 Nov 1877 - d. 25 Dec 1958, m (2) A. K. ARNOLD
(c) Charles L. Finney - b. 3 May 1875 - 4 May 1875 Rush Creek Cem.
(d) Richard Harrison Finney - b. 11 May 1877 Parke Co - lvd. on farm of his grand-father Richard King Finney - m. 30 June 1926 Etta Lucille NEWMAN - b. 7 Dec 1898 Fountain Co., Ind. , d/o Embert & Nancy Effie [Atkinson] Newman

i. Charles Lee Finney - b. 21 Oct 1929 Kingman, Ind.
ii. Marcia Helen Finney - b. 20 Feb 1932 Kingman, Ind.

(2) Lydia Ann Finney - b. 7 Nov 1849 Parke Co - 2 Jan 1930 Parke Co - m. William R. PATTON - b. 1850 - 15 Apr 1929 Kingman, Ind - no children

D. Margaret [Peggy] Rector Finney, d/o Joseph - b. 27 June 1812 Grayson Co., Va - d. after 1880 Parke Co., Ind., buried Rush Creek Cemetery. Never married. In 1860 with brother Richard King Finney and his family. In 1880 she lived with her nephew Wesleyand his wife.

c. Dorothea Finney, d/o Lazarus & catharine - m. John OCHILTREE - lvd Wilmington, Del.

d. Catherine Finney - b. New London, Pa - m. 25 July 1758 Old Swedes Holy Trinity Church, New Castle, Del. to James LOUGHEAD, s/o Robert of Chester Co., Pa. James went to Philadelphia where he was a merchant. On 11 Aug 1778 he submitted a petition to be appointed Vendue-Master for the City of Philadelphia.

1. James Loughead - b. 1765 - lvd. Danville, Pa. 1833, was postmaster. Danville was in Columbia Co., Pa. This James wrote a letter concerning Lazarus Finney's pension claim.

* * * * * * *

PENNSYLVANIA RECORDS ON A SAMUEL FINNEY

This Samuel Finney's connection with the other Finney's is unknown and is included for the sake of information, since he located in the Philadelphia area.

Jno. Tyzack, by Ind'res of L. and Real., dated 4 and 5 days of Fbr. 1697, Mortgaged to Ann Moore, of Stepney, in the County of Middlesex, Widow, all that Brick Messuage or Tenem't, and also that tract of land situated at the mouth of Tacconinek Creek, in the County of Philadelphia, being the 2 aforesaid Tracts, for 615, 18s, 9d, which not being paid, Wm. Reed, with his wife, Ann, Elizab., Rachael, Naomi Moore, all daughters and coheiresses of the said Ann Moore, joyntly with John Tyzack, by L. and Real., dated 6 and 7th February, 1700, Gave, Granted, Released and Confirmed all the said Messuage and Tenem't to SAMUEL FINNEY, of Cheatam Hill, in the County of Lancaster, Merchant, now of this Province, who requests a Patent for the same according to the Present Bounds and Contests, having been tried by David Powell and found to be rather difficient in quantity than abound. - Minute Book G.

Ordered that a Patent be forthwith passed to Capt. Finney for his land bought of John Tyzack for 150 acres, found upon a resurvey to contain 187 acres, it being found that the 100 acres he purchased from the property encroached upon the T. Lloyd's lands which he has since bought and upon a resurvey was found deficient in quantity by that Means.

Captain Samuel FINNEY haveing frequently solicited for a vacant lott where it may be found, to build a stable on for accomodateing his horses when he comes to town, and haveing made inquiry where Any lotts may be found vacant, pitches upon a lott next above the lott now in the possession of Gabriel Wilkinson, in the 3d Str. between Sassafras and Vine Str., on the consideration of his many services at half a Crown Sterling p'r annum, and a Warrant and Patent for it, Warrant dat. this day.

Captain Samuel FINNEY arrived in Pennsylvania from England about 1701. As stated his relationship is unknown.

viii. Rachel Finney, d/o Joseph & Polly - b. 27 Mar 1821 - 21 Apr 1860
ix. WESLEY FINNEY - b. 10 May 1823 - 3 Oct 1904
x. Fanny Finney - b. 16 Feb 1825 - 18 Dec 1891
xi. Catherine Finney - b. 1 Jan 1828 - d.after 1911
xii. Mary Ann Finney - b. 22 Jan 1832 - 2 Aug 1908

WESLEY FINNEY - b. 10 May 1823 Lawrence Co., Ind - d. 3 Oct 1904 Wayside, Montgomery Co., KS. Married 29 Aug 1850 Mary Matilda HINSHAW - b. 29 Oct 1829 Ind - d. 5 Feb 1900 Montgomery Co., Ks. Both are buried in Fawn Creek Cemetery. Mary Matilda was daughter of Jesse and Hannah [Moon] Hinshaw. Wesley and Mary M. had nine children, all born in Indiana, and family is shown on 1880 census of Parke Co., Ind. About 1882 Wesley and Mary moved to Montgomery Co., Ks, settling on a farm 2 miles south of Bolton. They moved their belongings and their livestock in railroad boxcars on a freight train. In 1900 after his wife died Wesley lived with Elmer and Clara Ellen FARLOW, Clara Ellen being his youngest child.

Wesley & Mary Matilda [Hinshaw] Finney

James Hinshaw, and wife, bro. of Mary Matilda Finney

Wesley Finney died on Monday, Oct. 3, at the residence of his son, John Finney, near Niotaze, Kansas, aged 81 years, being born in Indiana in 1823. His home was near Bolton where he had lived many years a highly respected citizen. He was a member of the U. B. church and in former years did ministerial work for that church. Funeral services were held at the U. B. church here conducted by his old friend, Elder J. I. Robinson, after which his remains were taken to the cemetery in Fawn Creek township and deposited beside his wife who had preceded him to the tomb nearly four years ago.

CHILDREN OF WESLEY AND MARY MATILDA [Hinshaw] FINNEY WERE:

i. Samantha Jane Finney - b. 7 Aug 1851 - 26 Apr 1937
ii. James Anderson Finney - b. 1854 - d. 1858 in Indiana
iii. Mary Catherine Finney - b. 9 May 1857 - 22 Aug 1926
iv. Anna E. Finney - b. 24 May 1859 - Mar. 1928
v. Polly Hannah Finney - b. 23 Mar 1864 - 12 Dec 1886
vi. John Wesley Finney - b. 14 Feb 1862 - 6 Oct 1945
vii. Louisa May Finney - b. 8 Jan 1867 - 6 Jan 1919
viii. DANIEL WEBSTER FINNEY _ B. 7 Nov 1868 - 10 Dec 1927
ix. Clara Ellen Finney - b. 27 May 1872 - 12 Dec 1945

John W., Daniel W., Clara Ellen
Samantha J., Anne E., and Mary C. Finney

Clara E., Wesley, Matilda & Daniel W. Finney

Wesley Finney Born May 10th 1823
Died Oct 3 1904

Mary Matilda Finney his wife Born Oct 28-1829
Died Feb 5 -1900

Sons and daughters of Wesley & Matilda Finney

Smantha Jane Born Aug 7 -1851 deceased april -1937
married to Abner Copeland Feb 27-1858

James Anderson Born 1854 Died 1858

Mary C. Born May 8-1857 Died Aug 22-1926
maried to Wm H allen Sept 5-1880

Anna E. Born May 24- 1859 Died Mar 1925
married to Tilgman Wood Mar 14-1878

Polly H. Born Mar 23 -1864 Died Dec 12-1885
married to James Cummings Dec 25-1885

John W. Born Feb 14-1862 died Oct 6 1945
married to Nancy Brooks Oct 6-1886

Louisa May, Born Jan 8- 1867 Died 19
married to Anson Madison Sept 20-1889

Daniel Webster Born Nov 7-1868 Died Dec 10 1927
married to Mary A Farlow Dec 13-1896 Jan 2-1952

Clara Ellen Born May 27-1872 Died Dec 12 1945
married to Elmer Farlow Feb 13-1896

FARLOW - FINNEY - CLOUD BIBLE

The Holy Bible
Philadelphia
John E. Potter and Company
No. 617 Samson Street

This is to certify that Mr. Nathan M. Farlow and Martha Cloud were solemnly united by me in Holy Matrimony at Daniel Cloud's, Paoli, Indiana on the 4th fourth day of February in the year of our LORD, One Thousand Eight Hundred and Sixty-nine, Conformably to the Ordinance of GOD and the Laws of the State. In presence of

Daniel Cloud — Solomon Lindley
Nancy Cox — Mary Lindley

Lawrence Jones, Pastor

MARRIAGES:

Harry Farlow & Carrie Metzger Sep 1st 1893 by Isaac Lindley, Bolton, Kansas
Elmer Farlow & Ella C. Finney Feb 13, 1895 by C. E. Jones, Bolton, Kansas
Mary A. Farlow & Daniel W. Finney Dec 13th 1896 by C. E. Jones, Bolton, Kansas
William C. Farlow & Blanche Brownlee Aug 27, 1902 by C. E. Jones, Bolton, Kansas
Harry FArlow & Carrie M. Metzger Sept 1, 1893
Carl C. Finney & Vivia Jay McClure Oct 20th, 1926 Caney, Kansas

BIRTHS:

Nathan M. Farlow born (blank) Mo. 5th 1842
Martha Farlow born Second Month 21st 1849
Elmer Farlow born 11th Mo 12th 1869
Harry Farlow born 11th Mo 29th 1870
Mary Ann Farlow born 3rd Mo 12th 1872 - Jan 2, 1952
Willie C. Farlow born October 10th, 1879
Tommie Milton Finney born Oct 2, 1927, son of Carl C. & Vivia Jay Finney
Mary Jay Finney born Mar 2nd 1930
Denzel M. Farlow born Jan 8th 1895
Virginia Lee Finney born Nov 1931 - Sept 17, 1971
Daniel W. Finney, son of Wesley Finney born Nov 7th 1868 Deceased Dec 10th 1927
Mabel Estella Finney born July 9th 1899, Deceased Feb 13, 1903
Carl Chester Finney, born May 13th 1905, son of Daniel W. & Mary A. Finney
Daniel Robert Finney son of Carl C. & Vivia Finney born Nov 13, 1935 deceased
James Edward Finney son of Carl C. & Vivia Finney born June 22nd 1937
David Wesley Finney born July 22 1949 Los Angeles, Calif son of Carl C. & Vivia Finney

DEATHS:

Nathan M. Farlow deceased Mar 26th 1920, Bolton, Kansas
Martha Farlow deceased Jan 14th 1921, Wayside, Kansas R. R.
Elmer deceased Sept 18th 1941
C. Ella Farlow deceased Dec 12, 1945
Cary M. Farlow deceased Mar 4, 1949
Harry Farlow deceased (no date)
Susan Blanche Farlow July 23, 1959 - Deceased
Mabel Estella Finney deceased Feb 13th 1903, Bolton, Kansas
Daniel W. Finney deceased Dec 10th, 1927, Independence, Kansas
Daniel Cloud Died Sep 14, 1874, aged 59 yrs, 9 mo, 10 days, born Jan 1st, 1815
Mary Ann Cloud Died Dec 13, 1867, aged 44 yrs, 11 mo & 19 days
Jonathan Farlow born July 18, 1807, Died Sept 14, 1873
Ann Cloud Jones Died October 8, 1862, aged 17 yrs, 11 mo & 25 days
Ruth Farlow Maris born July 18, 1814, died 12, 1843
Nathan Farlow born May 10, 1810, died April 14, 1890, 80 years, 4 days
Ruth Farlow born Sep 9, 1856, died Sep 7, 1875

This Bible record was copied exactly as written. The handwriting was in several different hands and the entries are not in proper order. This Bible is in the possession of Vivia (McClure) Finney, living in Kelseyville, California in 1988.

* * * * * * * * * * * * *

FINNEY BIBLE

No information on the publisher.

MARRIAGES:

John Long Finney, son of Joseph Finney & Polly Long Finney was married to Elizabeth Camel the 13th of November 1832
Robert Finney & Malinda Finney was married May 10th 1835
Joseph Finney & Polly Long was married Sept 10 1805
Thomas B. Wade & Nancy Finney were married Sep 27th, 1838
Harrison Jones and Rachel Finney were married Nov 4th, 1838
Hawkins C. Finney, son of J. Finney & Polly was married to Martha Counts on the 16th Nov 1837
Wesley Finney and Mary Matilda Hinshaw was married August the 29th 1850
Daniel Mater and Elizabeth Finney were married October the 7th 1849
David Bradford and Catherine Finney were married Oct the 28th 1849
Jabel Rayle and Fanney Finney were married August the 18th 1850

BIRTHS:

Robert Finney son of Joseph Finney & Polly his wife was born the 23rd of August 1806
Joseph Finney son of Joseph Finney & Polly was born December the 19th 1808
John Finney son of Joseph Finney & Polly was born December the 16th 1810
Nancy Finney daughter of Joseph Finney & Polly was born January the 21st 1818
Elizabeth Finney daughter of Joseph Finney & Polly was born March the 7th 1820
Rachel Finney daughter of Joseph Finney & Polly was born March the 27th 1821
Wesley Finney son of Joseph Finney & Polly was born May the 10th 1823
Fanny Finney daughter of Joseph Finney & Polly was born February the 16th 1825
Katherine Finney daughter of Joseph Finney & Polly was born January the 1st 1828
Mary Ann Finney was born January 22nd 1832
Mary Jane the daughter of John Finney and Elizabeth his wife was born Jan 29, 1834
Elizabeth daughter of John Finney and Elizabeth was born August the 29th 1836
Joseph Wesley Jones, son of Harrison Jones & Rachel his wife was born Nov 13th 1841
Elijah Finney was born the 4 day of Apr in the year of our Lord 1836, son of Robert Finney and Melinda Finney
Elijah Cook, son of Robert Finney and Melinda his wife was born April the 4th 1836
George Picket, son of Thomas Wade and Nancy his wife was born July the 12th 1839
Oliver Perry Jones son of Harrison Jones & Rachel his wife was born May 14th, 1840

DEATHS:

Elizabeth Finney, the consort of John Finney, deceased this life on the 6th of Nov, 1836
Elizabeth Finney the daughter of John Finney & Elizabeth his wife, deceased this life Dec 1st 1837
Joseph Finney, Junr. deceased this life May the 5th 1854
Joseph Finney Sen. son of Joseph & Rachel Finney was born Sept 18, 1784 and departed this life March the 8th 1867 and interred in the Linebarger Graveyard
Presley Finney born May 10, 1823, deceased Oct 3rd 1904
Mary Matilda Finney born Oct 28 - 1829, deceased Feb 5th, 1900

The above Bible pages were copied exactly as written and show various handwritings. This Bible is in the possession of Vivia (McClure) Finney, Kelseyville, California in 1988.

DANIEL WEBSTER FINNEY

DANIEL WEBSTER FINNEY

Daniel Webster Finney - b. 7 Nov 1868 in Annapolis, Parke Co., Ind - d. 10 Dec 1927 Independence, Montgomery Co., Ks. Married 13 Dec 1896 Mary Ann FARLOW. Mary Ann was born 12 Mar 1873 Paoli, Orange Co., Indiana, the daughter of Nathan & Martha [Cloud] Farlow, who came to Montgomery Co.,Ks. in 1887 and lived Rutland Twp. After their marriage Daniel and Mary Ann built a large, white frame farm house, two stories, with seven rooms in the Wayside area. It is situated 16 miles southwest of the city of Independence, Kansas, county seat of Montgomery Co. In 1988 this house still stands, but a new home has been built behind it. On the same road, a mile's distance, is the location of "Little House on the Prairie", the setting for the book written in 1935 by Laura Ingalls Wilder. This land is owned by William & Wilma Kurtis and is now part of a 1,000 acre cattle ranch. The present owners are restoring the "Little House" site. The old Ingalls well is still on the property and two suitable buildings have been found - one is the Sunnyside School, built in 1872, and used as a school until 1947, and a log cabin. Dr. George Tann, "Dr. Tan" in the book, is buried in Mt. Hope Cemetery in Independence. Mary Ann Farlow Finney was a student at the Sunnyside School as a child.

This notation of events was found in
Mary Ann Farlow Finney's Bible

Carl sick April 1934
" made sale May "
" went Calif June 27 "
Culps moved in 509 Feb 1 - 1934
Traman " " " " 1 - 1933 out Jan 1934
Copeland moved on Farm May 1934
I went to Calif Jan 10 - 1928 back in June &
back to Calif in July 1928 sick in Nov
came back to Kan Mar 1929 Carls came too
went back West in May 1929 & came back
to Ks Dec 1929 Mary Jay born Mar 1930
Virginia Lee " Nov 1931
Carls moved to Farm Mar 1 1931
" lived here 1930
" " on farm 3½ yrs
D. W. Finney deceased Dec 10 - 1927
made first sale Nov 7 - 1927
Barn burned 1923 — Mar 11
Ira Towell deceased April 1934
Ed Farlow in Ks Nov 1934
Had Wen took off head May 30 - 1934
Dr DeMott Deceased 1934
Carl was married Oct - 1926
Com Bank Closed 1920 $
Paid 1st Dividend 1934 70.
Security Paid
Put shingles of Farm
Bought Jollars property Sept 14 - 1926 $5250.

MARRIAGE OF DANIEL WEBSTER FINNEY & MARY ANN FARLOW

BE IT REMEMBERED, That on 11th day of December A. D., 1896 there was issued from the office of said Probate Court a Marriage License, of which the following is a true copy:

STATE OF KANSAS
THE KANSAS STATE BOARD OF HEALTH
DIVISION OF VITAL STATISTICS

No. --
P. J. No. --

MARRIAGE LICENSE

IN THE PROBATE COURT OF MONTGOMERY COUNTY December 11th 1896

To Any Person Authorized by Law to Perform the Marriage Ceremony, Greeting:

YOU ARE HEREBY AUTHORIZED TO JOIN IN MARRIAGE

Daniel W. Finney (Groom), of Bolton, age 28, and
Mary A. Farlow (Bride), of ", age 23, and

with the consent of

And of this license, duly endorsed, you will make return to my office at Independence, Kansas, within ten days after performing the ceremony.

(SEAL)

N.E. Bouton
Probate Judge

And which said Marriage License was afterward, to-wit, on the 15th day of Dec. A. D., 1896 returned to said Probate Court with the following certificate endorsed thereon, to-wit:

ENDORSEMENT

TO WHOM IT MAY CONCERN:

I hereby certify that I performed the ceremony joining in marriage the above named couple on the 13th day of December, 1896 at Bolton

(SEAL)

Signed C.W. Jones
Title M.G.
Address --

Recorded in Book H, Page 300, Marriage Records of Montgomery County, Kansas.

Daniel Webster and Mary Ann Finney had two children - a daughter, Mabel Estella Finney - born 9 July 1899 - died at age 3 years, 7 months on 13 February 1903 of pneumonia. They also had a son Carl Chester Finney - b. 13 May 1905 - d. 15 November 1987 California.

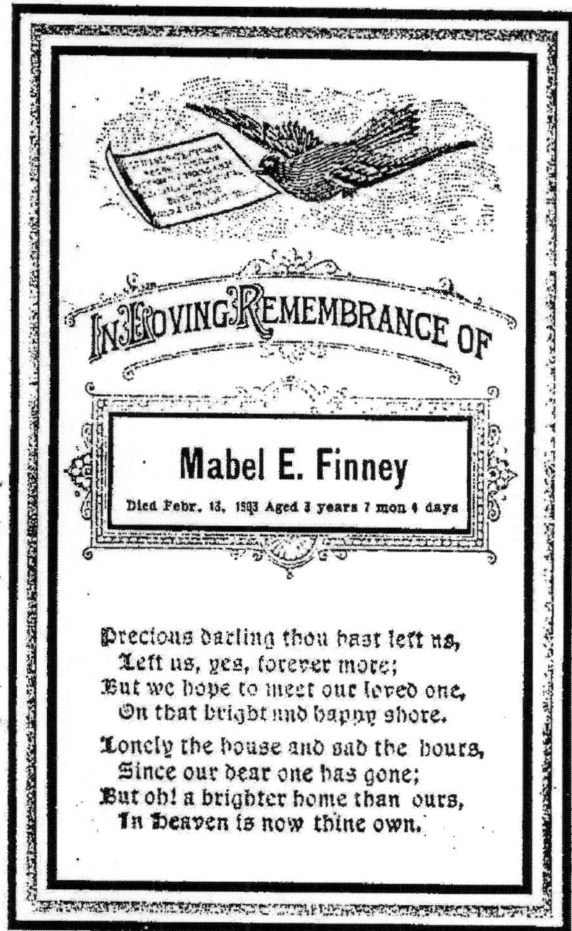

In Loving Remembrance of

Mabel E. Finney

Died Febr. 13, 1903 Aged 3 years 7 mon 4 days

Precious darling thou hast left us,
Left us, yes, forever more;
But we hope to meet our loved one,
On that bright and happy shore.

Lonely the house and sad the hours,
Since our dear one has gone;
But oh! a brighter home than ours,
In Heaven is now thine own.

Obituary.

Death ever busy reaping his harvest has entered the home of Mr. and Mrs. D. W. Finney and taken the joy and pride of their home, their baby, their only child--Mabel, and left in her place sorrowing hearts and sad memories of her childish prattle and pleasant ways. She was a bright, laughing, pleasant little girl, almost worshipped by papa and mamma, and loved by all who knew her. Little Mabel was born July 9th 1899, died Feb. 13th, 1903. She was a veritable ray of sunshine in the hearts of parents and friends, and the hold she had on the hearts and affections of friends and neighbors was shown by their constant attendance during her illness.

The last two days of her life were those of intense suffering from pneumonia, and death came as a relief.

and gas.....Mabel, aged 3-years and 7 months, daughter of D. W. and Mary E. Finney, died February 13. She was sick only a few days. The funeral was held February 15 and interment made in Harrisonville cemetery.

On the following pages are copies of pages from an old autograph book which was dated 1891 and belonged to Daniel Webster Finney. It is now in the possession of his daughter-in-law Vivia Finney (in 1988).

To my friends

My album opens come and see
What? Wont you waste a line on me
Write just a thought a word or two
That memory may revert to you.

Daniel W. Tinney

March 15-1891 Bolton Kansas

Bolton Kansas
March 16-91.

Tis friendship that connects these lines
And love that holds them dear.
May memory often bring to mind:
The hand that traced them here.

Your Sister
Ella.

March 18th 1891

Fall from the ocean to the deck
Fall down stairs and break your neck
Fall from some high place above
But never never fall in love.

Your Friend.

Wayside Kansas.
Eva Knotts.

Cerro Gordo Ind
Oct 2 1894

Friend Dannie.
When you are sitting all alone
Reflecting on the past;
Remember that we have a friend
That will forever last.
Compliments of
J. M. Wachman.

Fawn Kansas
March 23rd 51

Uncle Dan
When far away and Friends are few
Remember that this one is just & true
Samuel Copeland.

Tyro Kan
Brother Dan, Jan 23. 1897.

When you get old and ugly
As people sometimes do,
Remember you have a sister
Who is old and ugly too.
Your Sister
Anne.

With Kind Regards of
your Cousin E C Finney
Tuscola Ill

Uncle Dani- Dec 28, 1897

When you fall down and hurt your knee
jump up and think of me

Safie Allen.

Daniel Webster Finney earned a substantial living from the farm, raising corn, oats, wheat, alfalfa and livestock. In March 1920 their barn, two-thirs full of hay and standing just east of the house, was struck by lightning. The flames, fed by the wood and hay, consumed the barn and left a pile of charred embers. They lost one mule, dazed by the lightning and impossible to get out safely, and also lost their chickens and some of their pigs. When Daniel's health failed and just prior to his death on 10 December 1927, they held an auction on 7 November 1927 and moved from the farm to Independence where they had purchased a large home. It had an entry hall, living room, a large kitchen and pantry, and one bedroom downstairs, with four bedrooms and a bath upstairs. After Daniel's death, Mary Ann rented the bedrooms upstairs to students who stayed in town to attend school. She only rented to girls. She was able to live quite comfortably with money earned on the farm which was rented. The farm was eventually left to Carl, her only surviving child.

Carl, Daniel W. & Mary Ann (Farlow) Finney

1908

BOLTON BUZZINGS.

Dan Finney and family were shopping in Bolton Saturday.

Quite a number are in attendance at the Quaker church this morning.

Mrs. Delbert Brooks went to Coffeyville Saturday evening.

Ed. Collett and family of Independence are visiting relatives in Bolton today.

Lyda Bloomer and Scatsy Barker were in Bolton Saturday evening.

Mrs. Meal was shopping in town this morning.

Mrs. S. Mills and daughter are trading with Bolton merchants today.

Ed. Tucker was among the callers in Bolton Friday night.

Miss Alice Huffman was in Bolton Friday.

B. H. Lindley was a business caller yesterday.

Mr. and Mrs. B. S. Adam and family visited their daughter, Mrs. James Adam yesterday.

Miss Condfra, school mam at Bolton, went to her home Friday evening to spenl Sunday with home folks.

Mr. and Mrs. Isaac Lindley and wife preached at the Quaker church Sunday morning.

1908

Mr. and Mrs. Erhart spent Sunday afternoon with relatives in Bolton.

A pretty wedding occurred at the home of Mr. and Mrs. Wm. Baker, Sunday Sept. 20, at twelve o'clock. When thier daughter, Miss Mae, was united in holy wedlock to Mr. John Moon. The ceremony was performed by Rev. and Mrs. Isaac Lindley of Independence. Miss Mae was one of the most popular young ladies o fthis community and was a favorite among her many friends. Mr. Moon has grown to manhood in this vicinity, and was a prosperous young man. Immediately after the ceremony a most sumptuous three-course dinner was served. None but the close relatives attended the wedding but nevertheless Mr. and Mrs. Moon have the heartiest congratulations of the entire community.

Rev. Haffner, of Havana, preached at the U. B. church Sunday night with quitea number in attendance.

Mr. Goodwin and Mr. West of Jefferson attended church at Bolton Sunday night.

Mr. O. J. Smith spent Sunday with Mrs. L. Sewell.

Mary Ann & Daniel Finney and their new car

March 1920

BARN STRUCK BY LIGHTNING

The large barn of D. W. Finney, located three miles east of Wayside was struck by lightning yesterday at 11 o'clock and totally destroyed. The loss is partly covered by insurance. In the barn at the time were several horses and mules. All were saved with the exception of one mule. The barn was two-tthirds full of hay which was burned up. Two sets of harness were also destroyed.

Orville Farlow and Carl Finney

Mary Ann had an upright piano and liked to "mother" her renters by always having sugar cookies on hand for them to eat. The house is well kept today in 1989 and looks extremely nice. A carport and patio has been added to the back. When Mary Ann lived there she enjoyed electricty and the indoor plumbing for the first time, a blessed change from farm life. Heat was provided by gas room heaters in each room. At the back door was a cistern to catch rainwater. She had an electric washing machine with wringer attachment to do laundry; it was kept on the back porch. Her grandson, Tom, recalls her being a good cook - chicken and dumplings, GOOD biscuits and many berry and particularly rhubarb pies. She gardened each year, tended her flowers, attended the Friends Church close to her home. She did some canning. Mary Ann carried herself very erect and was a good money manager. However, she lost some money when the bank failed during the Depression in the 1930's. She died 2 Jan., 1952 in Independence, Ks., age 79 years. She and Daniel are buried Mt. Hope Cemetery.

divinity Candy
2 cp sugar
1 " nuts
2 egg whites beaten stiff
1/2 cp corn sirup
1/2 " boiling water
1/2 ts vanila
1/8 ts salt
sugar water syrup salt
Cook to soft ball 248°F
Pour slowly beat over egg white
Beat until mixture holds shape
dropped from spoon add nuts
flavor pour in oil pan

Mary Ann's Recipe

Mary Ann 1950 and friend

HOME OF DANIEL WEBSTER FINNEY

OBITUARY

Daniel Webster Finney.

Daniel Webster Finney, son of Wesley and Matilda Finney was born Nov. 7, 1868 near Anapolis, Park county, Indiana. His parents moved to Montgomery county, Kas., in 1882, locating on a farm two miles south of Bolton.

In 1896 Mr. Finney was united in marriage to Mary Farlow and to this union two children were born: Mabel Estella who passed away at the age of three years, and Carl Chester. Besides the wife and son, Carl Chester of Independence, he leaves one brother, John W. Finney of Niotaze and three sisters: Mrs. Anna Woods of Tyro, Mrs. Samantha Copeland of Wayside, and Mrs. Ella Farlow of Wayside. Besides these there are a number of nieces and nephews, a grandson and a great number of friends.

Mr. Finney had lived in Montgomery county for years, having lived on the home place east of Wayside for twenty years and had proven himself a good neighbor and Christian gentleman.

His father was a United Brethren minister for years and Mr. Finney, due to the influence of the home, became a Christian, and united with the church at an early age. He held his membership in the United Brethren church at Bolton and was a trustee of that church for some time. He showed by his life he had faith in God and a love for his fellowmen. When told that he had only a brief time to live he told those about him that he was ready to go.

He passed away at Mercy hospital, Independence, December 10, 1927 at the age of 59 years, 1 month, and 3 days after a long illness.

His funeral was conducted Monday, December 12 at 2 o'clock at the Friends church in Independence, by Rev. Donovan Smith of the United Brethren church, assisted by Rev. Jones of Bolton, and Rev. Earl Cox of the Friends church of Independence. Burial was in Mount Hope cemetery.

Mary Ann Farlow Finney

Mary Ann Farlow, a daughter of Nathan and Martha Farlow, was born March 12, 1873, near Paoli, in Orange County, Indiana. She passed away January 2, 1952.

In 1887, she came to Kansas with her parents and lived in the Rutland Township where she attended school at Sunnyside.

She was united in marriage to Daniel W. Finney in 1896 and lived in Harrisonville District on a farm until December 1927, when her husband passed away. She moved to 400 North 12th and shared her home with roomers.

She was the mother of two children: Mable Estella who passed away at the age of 3½ and Carl Chester who lives in South Gate, California. There are five grandchildren and one great-grandchild. She had three brothers: Harry Farlow of Coffeyville, Kansas; Will Farlow of rural Independence; and Elmer Farlow, deceased.

Since the age of 14 she has been a member of the Friends Church.

Funeral services were held Saturday morning and interment was made in Mt. Hope cemetery.

Card of Thanks

We wish to thank our many friends and neighbors for their acts of kindness and expressions of sympathy during our recent bereavement. Mr. and Mrs. Carl Finney and family, Mr. and Mrs. T. M. Finney and family and Mr. and Mrs. C. L. Plum. Adv. XX

Finney Rites

Funeral services were conducted in the Webb chapel at 11 a. m. today for Mrs. Mary A. Finney who passed away Wednesday morning in Mercy hospital. The Rev. Blaine Stands, pastor of the Friends church presided and burial was in Mt. Hope cemetery.

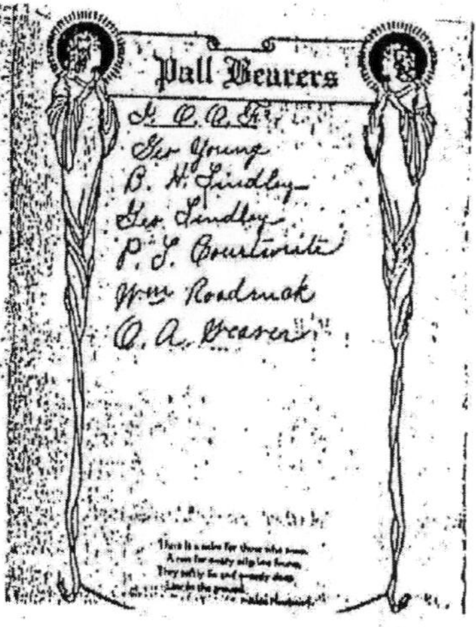

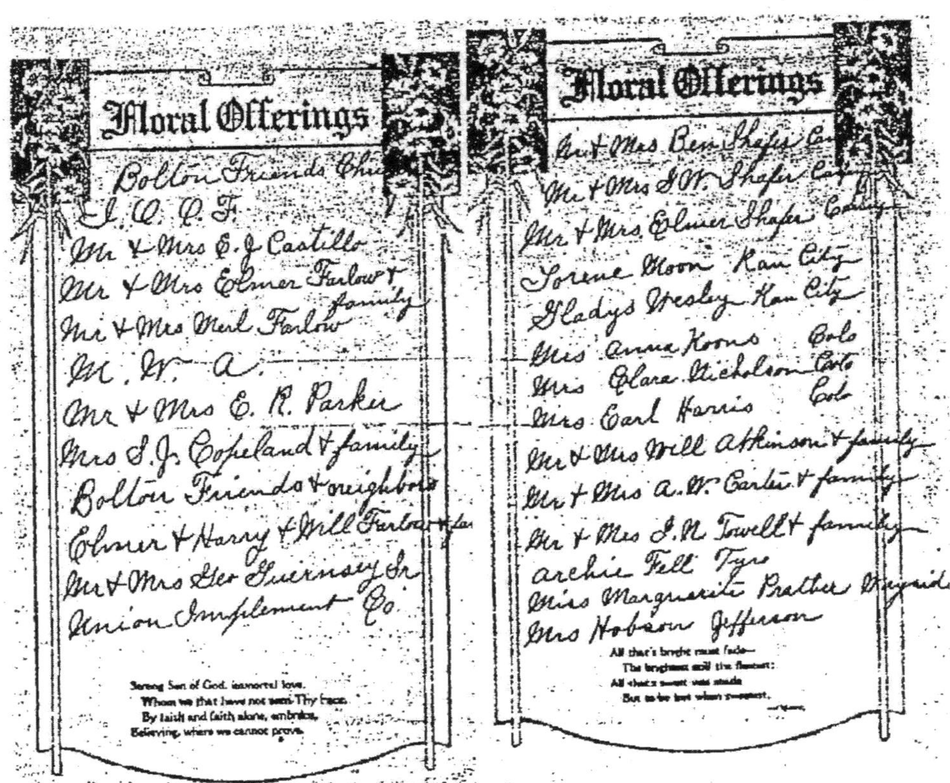

Floral Offerings

Bolton Friends Chu

I. O. O. F.

Mr & Mrs E. J. Castillo

Mr & Mrs Elmer Farlow & family

Mr & Mrs Merl Farlow

M. W. A.

Mr & Mrs E. R. Parker

Mrs S. J. Copeland & family

Bolton Friends & neighbors

Elmer & Harry & Will Farlow & fa

Mr & Mrs Geo Guernsey Sr

Union Implement Co.

Strong Son of God, immortal love,
Whom we that have not seen Thy face,
By faith and faith alone, embrace,
Believing, where we cannot prove.

Floral Offerings

Mr & Mrs Ben Shafer Co

Mr & Mrs J. W. Shafer Co

Mr & Mrs Elmer Shafer Co

Lorene Moon Kan City

Gladys Wesley Kan City

Mrs Anna Koons Colo

Mrs Clara Nicholson Colo

Mrs Earl Harris Colo

Mr & Mrs Will Atkinson & family

Mr & Mrs A. W. Carter & family

Mr & Mrs J. N. Towell & family

Archie Fell Tyro

Miss Marguerite Prather

Mrs Hobson Jefferson

All that's bright must fade—
The brightest still the fleetest;
All that's sweet was made
But to be lost when sweetest.

DANIEL WEBSTER FINNEY

This Indenture, Made this 14 day of July A. D. 1896, between P V Hockett single of Montgomery County, in the State of Kansas of the first part and Milton Hockett of Montgomery County, in the State of Kansas of the second part.

Witnesseth, That said party of the first part, in consideration of the sum of Seventy two hundred & no/100 and DOLLARS, the receipt whereof is hereby acknowledged, do by these presents grant, bargain, sell and convey unto said part of the second part his heirs and assigns, all the following described Real Estate, situated in the County of Montgomery and State of Kansas to wit:

The South West Quarter (S W ¼) of Section thirty one (31) Township thirty three (33) South of Range Fifteen (15) East and the North half of the North West Quarter (N ½ NW ¼) of Section Six (6) Township thirty four (34) Range Fifteen (15) East Sixth p. m. and containing 240 acres more or less

Ex A. RRR.

DEED.

GENERAL WARRANTY.

FROM P V Hockett

TO Milton Hockett

Entered in Transfer Record in my office this 12 day of March, 1897

J H Glass
By H H [illegible]

State of Kansas, County, ss.

This instrument was filed for Record on the 12 day of March 1897, at 3 o'clock P. M., and duly recorded in Book 36, page 592.

Fee, $

J T Stewart
Register of Deeds

To Have and to Hold the Same, Together with all and singular the tenements, hereditaments and appurtenances thereunto belonging or in anywise appertaining, forever:

And said P V Hockett for his heirs, executors or administrators, do hereby covenant, promise and agree, to and with said party of the second part, that at the delivery of these presents he is lawfully seized in his own right, of an absolute and indefeasible estate of inheritance, in fee simple, of and in all and singular the above granted and described premises, with the appurtenances; that the same are free, clear, discharged and unincumbered of and from all former and other grants, titles, charges, estates, judgments, taxes, assessments and incumbrances, of what nature or kind soever;

and that he will warrant and forever defend, the same unto said party of the second part, his heirs and assigns, against said party of the first part, his heirs, and all and every person or persons whomsoever, lawfully claiming or to claim the same.

In Witness Whereof, The said part of the first part ha hereunto set his hand the day and year first above written.

P V Hockett

State of Kansas, Montgomery County, ss.

Be it Remembered, That on this Fourteenth day of July A. D. 1896 before me, the undersigned, a Notary Public in and for the County and State aforesaid, came P. V. Hockett a widower who is personally known to me to be the same person who executed the within instrument of writing, and such person duly acknowledged the execution of the same.

In Testimony Whereof, I have hereunto set my hand and affixed my official seal, the day and year last above written.

Geo T Gurney
Notary Public, term expires July 21/96

UNITED STATES OF AMERICA

REAL ESTATE MORTGAGE

Coupon Bond

SECURED BY FIRST MORTGAGE

PER CENT SEMI ANNUALLY

Negotiated by COMMERCIAL BANK MORTGAGE COMPANY, Independence, Kansas.

Five ~~Seven~~ Years after date for value received We promise to pay
to the order of James H. Tallman, at the Mechanics Savings Bank, Hartford, Conn:
Two Thousand - Dollars Lawful money of the United
States with interest thereon at the rate of 7 per cent per annum payable semi annually on the
first days of April and October in each year, according to the tenor and effect of the Interest
Notes of even date herewith and hereto attached, both principal and interest payable with New York
Exchange.
This Note is to draw interest from date at the rate of Ten per cent per annum if either principal or interest remain unpaid ten days after due. At the option of the legal holder, after any of said Interest Notes
remain due and unpaid ten days the whole of the principal and interest may be declared immediately due
and payable. This Note is given for an actual Loan of the above amount and is secured by a Mortgage of even
date herewith which is a first Lien on the property therein described. Dated at Independence, Kansas
October 18 1897

Witnesses:

J W Fairleigh

Milton Hackett

Emma Hackett

Real Estate Mortgage Coupon

BOND

$ 2000

Milton Hockett

& wife

TO

JAMES H. TALLMAN

Payable at Mechanics Savings Bank

Hartford, Conn.

Dated October ~~First~~ 18th 1897

Due October First 1902

Negotiated by

COMMERCIAL BANK

MORTGAGE COMPANY

500.00 Paid on Principal apl 1/901

700.00 Paid on Principal apl 1/902

$800. Paid on Princl Oct 6 1902

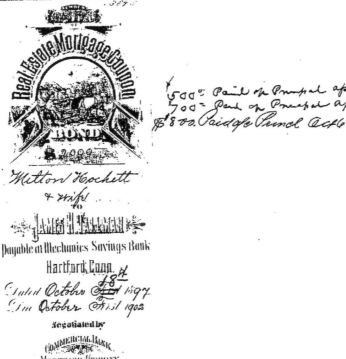

Provided, Always, And this instrument is made, executed and delivered upon the following express conditions, to-wit:

First. Said party of the first part is justly indebted unto the said party of the second part in the principal sum of Two Thousand DOLLARS, lawful money of the United States of America, being for a loan thereof, made by the said party of the second part to the said party of the first part, and payable according to the tenor and effect of a certain *First Mortgage Real Estate Note*, executed and delivered by the said party of the first part to said party of the second part, and payable to the order of the said party of the second part on the first day of October A. D., 1902 after date, at the office of *Mechanic's Savings Bank, Hartford, Connecticut*, with interest thereon, at the rate of Seven per cent. per annum, payable semi-annually on the first days of April and October in each year, and 10 per cent. per annum after maturity, the installments of interest being further evidenced by Ten coupons attached to said principal note, and of even date therewith, and payable to the order of said party of the second part, at the same place.

Second. Said party of the first part hereby agrees to pay all taxes and assessments levied upon said premises, and insurance premiums for the amount of insurance hereinafter specified, when the same are due; and if not so paid, the party of the second part, or the legal holder of this mortgage, may, without notice, declare the whole sum of money herein secured due and payable at once; or may elect to pay such taxes, assessments and insurance premiums; and the amount so paid shall be a lien on the premises aforesaid, and be secured by this mortgage, and collected in the same manner as the principal debt hereby secured, with interest thereon at the rate of 10 per cent. per annum. But whether the legal holder of this mortgage elect to pay such taxes, assessments or insurance premiums or not, it is distinctly understood that the legal holder hereof may declare the debt hereby secured due, and immediately cause this mortgage to be foreclosed.

Third. Said party of the first part hereby promises and agrees that all buildings, fences and other improvements upon said premises shall be kept in as good repair and condition as the same are in at this date, and that no waste shall be committed on said premises until the debt hereby secured is fully paid.

Fourth. Said party of the first part hereby agrees to procure and maintain policies of insurance on the buildings which now are or may hereafter be erected upon the above described premises, in some responsible insurance company, to the satisfaction of the legal holder of this mortgage to the amount of Six Hundred Dollars; loss, if any, payable to the mortgagee herein or assigns. And it is further agreed, that every such policy of insurance shall [illegible] legal holder hereof as collateral and additional security for the payment of the debt hereby secured; and the person or persons so holding such policy or policies of insurance shall have the right to collect and receive any and all moneys which may at any time become payable and receivable thereon, and apply the same, when received, to the payment of the costs and expenses incurred in collecting said insurance, and the residue to the payment of the debt hereby secured; or may elect to have the buildings repaired, or new buildings erected on the aforesaid mortgaged premises. Said party of the second part, or the legal holder hereof, may deliver said policy to said party of the first part, and require the collection of the same, and application and payment made of the proceeds as above mentioned.

Fifth. Said party of the first part hereby agrees that in default of the payment of any sum hereby secured, within ten days after the same becomes due, or in default of the specific performance of any covenant herein contained, said party of the second part, or the legal holder hereof, shall be entitled to have and recover of and from the makers of the note hereby secured, interest at the rate of 10 per cent. per annum, computed annually, on said principal note, from the date thereof to the time when the same shall be actually paid in full, first deducting from the amount of said interest such sums as may have been previously paid on account of interest, so that the total amount of interest from date of note to date of payment shall not be in excess of 10 per cent. per annum.

Sixth. Said party of the first part hereby agrees that if he shall fail to pay, or cause to be paid, any part of said money, either principal or interest, according to the tenor and effect of said note and coupons, within ten days after the same becomes due, or to conform or comply with any of the foregoing conditions or agreements, the said party of the second part, or the legal holder hereof, shall have immediate possession of the premises hereinbefore described, and all the rents, profits and emblements thereof, and the whole sum of money hereby secured shall become due and payable and once, without notice.

And the said party of the first part, for said consideration, hereby expressly waive an appraisement of said real estate and all benefit of the Homestead Exemption and Stay Laws of the State of Kansas.

The foregoing conditions being performed, this conveyance to be void, otherwise of full force and virtue.

In Testimony Whereof, The said parties of the first part have hereunto subscribed their names and affixed their seals, on the 18th day of October A. D. 1897.

Milton Hockett (L. S.)

Executed and Delivered in presence of

Emma Hockett (L. S.)

(L. S.)

(L. S.)

OFFICE OF

GEORGE W. MOORE & CO.,

NEGOTIATORS OF

WESTERN AND SOUTHERN FARM LOANS,

HARTFORD, CONN.

ASSIGNMENT OF MORTGAGE.

Know all Men by these Presents, THAT I, **James H. Tallman,** of the City and County of Hartford, and State of Connecticut, the Mortgagee named in a certain Mortgage bearing date the 8th day of October A. D. 1897, made and executed by Milton Hockett and Emma L Hockett Husband & wife

of the County of Montgomery and State of Kansas, to secure the payment of $ 2000, which said Mortgage is recorded in the County of Montgomery in the State of Kansas in Vol. 38 of Mortgages on page 155 for and in consideration of the sum of Two Thousand and no/100 Dollars, to me in hand paid, the receipt whereof is acknowledged, do hereby sell, assign, transfer and convey all my right, title and interest in and to said Mortgage and the debt secured thereby to Phoenix Mutual Life Insurance Company of Hartford, Conn.

IN WITNESS WHEREOF, I have hereunto set my hand and seal at Hartford, Conn., this 19th day of February A. D. 1898.

Jas H Tallman [L.S.]

State of Connecticut, }
COUNTY OF HARTFORD, } ss.

On this 19th day of February A. D. 1898, before me, the subscriber, a Notary Public, personally appeared JAMES H. TALLMAN, to me known to be the identical person described in and who executed the foregoing instrument as assignor, and duly acknowledged the said instrument to be his voluntary act and deed.

WITNESS my hand and Notarial Seal, at HARTFORD, in said County, the day and year last above written.

Harry R Knox *Notary Public.*

My Commission Expires Feb. 1st, 1900

13845

27863 No. 1587

Mortgage.

Milton Hockett & wife

TO

JAMES H. TALLMAN.

$2000⁻ Due Oct 1st 1902

State of Kansas, Montgomery County, ss:

I, the undersigned, Register of Deeds within and for said County, do hereby certify that this instrument was filed for record in my office on the 21 day of Oct A. D. 1897 at 3 o'clock P M., and duly recorded in Vol. 38, of Mtgs at Page 561

Witness my hand and official seal, on the day and year above written.

J T Stewart
Register of Deeds.

By .... Deputy.

Fees, $..........

NEGOTIATED BY
Independence Savings Bank & Security Co.,
INDEPENDENCE, KANSAS.

MORTGAGE.

Know all Men by these Presents, That Milton Hockett and Emma L Hockett Husband and wife

of the County of Montgomery and the State of Kansas, party of the first part, and ~~JAMES H. TALLMAN, of Hartford, Connecticut, party of the second part.~~

Witnesseth, That the said party of the first part, for and in consideration of the sum of Two Thousand Dollars, to them in hand paid by the said party of the second part, the receipt whereof is hereby acknowledged, has *granted, bargained and sold*, and by these presents does *grant, bargain, sell, convey and confirm* unto the said party of the second part, his heirs or assigns, *forever*, all of the following described tract s piece s or parcel s of land lying and situate in the County of Montgomery, and State of Kansas, to-wit:

The Southwest Quarter of Section Thirtyone (31) Township Thirty three (33) South of Range Fifteen (15) East of 6th P.M.
Also The North half of the Northwest Quarter of Section Six (6) Township Thirtyfour (34) South of Range Fifteen (15) East

Of the sixth principal meridian; containing in all 240 acres, more or less, according to government survey.

To Have and to Hold the Same, with all and singular the emblements, hereditaments and appurtenances thereto belonging, or in anywise appertaining, and all rights of homestead exemption, unto the said party of the second part, and to his heirs or assigns, *forever:* And the said party of the first part does hereby covenant and agree, that at the delivery hereof they are the lawful owner s of the premises above granted, and seized of a good and indefeasible estate of inheritance therein, free and clear of all incumbrances, and that they will *warrant and defend* the same in quiet and peaceable possession of said party of the second part, his heirs or assigns *forever*, against the lawful claims of all persons whomsoever.

Recorded on margin of Page 558 in Book 38 October 13 1902
attest T. F. Burke
Register of Deeds

SATISFACTION OF MORTGAGE ... Montgomery ... October ... 1902 ... J M Coleman

—1736— Saml Dodsworth Book Co., Legal Blank Publishers, Leavenworth, Kan

DEED. General Warranty.

This Indenture, Made this 31st day of January A. D. 1900 between Milton Hockett and Emma L. Hockett

of Chautauqua County, in the State of Kansas of the first part, and Dannie Webster Finney

of Montgomery County, in the State of Kansas of the second part:

Witnesseth, That said parties of the first part, in consideration of the sum of Thirty six hundred and no/100 **Dollars,** the receipt whereof is hereby acknowledged, do by these presents, GRANT, BARGAIN, SELL and CONVEY unto said party of the second part his heirs and assigns, all the following described REAL ESTATE, situated in the County of Montgomery and State of Kansas to wit: The South West quarter (S.W.¼) of Section Thirty One (31) Township Thirty three (33) South of Range Fifteen (15) East, and the North half of the North West quarter (N½ NW¼) of Section Six (6) Township Thirty four (34) Range Fifteen (15) East Sixth P.M. and containing two hundred forty acres more or less. The same incumbered by a mortgage of Two thousand dollars in favor of James H. Tallman which the party of the second part agrees to pay.

To Have and to Hold the Same, Together with all and singular the tenements, hereditaments and appurtenances thereunto belonging, or in anywise appertaining, forever.

And said Milton Hockett and Emma L. Hockett for themselves and their heirs, executors or administrators, do hereby covenant, promise and agree to and with said party of the second part, that at the delivery of these presents, that they are lawfully seized in their own right, of an absolute and indefeasible estate of inheritance, in fee simple, of and in all and singular the above granted and described premises, with the appurtenances; that the same are free, clear, discharged and unincumbered of and from all former and other grants, titles, charges, estates, judgments, taxes, assessments and incumbrances of what nature or kind soever Except above mentioned mortgages

and that they will WARRANT AND FOREVER DEFEND the same unto said party of the second part, his heirs and assigns, against said parties of the first part their heirs, and all and every person or persons whomsoever, lawfully claiming or to claim the same.

In Witness Whereof, The said parties of the first part have hereunto set their hand the day and year first above written.

Milton Hockett
Emma L. Hockett

1736

DEED
GENERAL WARRANTY.

FROM

Milton Hockett and Emma L. Hockett

TO

D. W. Finney

Entered in Transfer Record in my office, this 6 day of March A. D. 1900

D. S. James
By Floyd James Dept. County Clerk

STATE OF KANSAS, Montgomery COUNTY, ss.

This instrument was filed for Record on the 6th day of March A. D. 1900 at 11 65 o'clock A. M., and duly recorded in Book 49 on page 292

Fee, $

T. F. Burke
Register of Deeds

Saml Dodsworth Book Co., Leavenworth, Kansas No. 1736

HARRIS TRUST BUILDING

Harris Trust and Savings Bank

Organized as N.W.Harris & Co.1882. Incorporated 1907

Capital, Surplus and Undivided Profits over $5,000,000

Chicago

Bond Sales Department

January 31, 1917.

BANK INVESTMENT

Mr. D. W. Finney, President,

Wayside State Bank,

Wayside, Kansas.

Dear Sir:-

If you are experiencing difficulty in employing your funds, as are many bankers, we would be pleased to submit offerings of some standard bonds that we believe would prove very satisfactory investments for you. We have numerous issues of carefully selected bonds that we can especially recommend for bank investment.

Will you please wire us, collect, if you would like to receive details of these issues.

Yours very truly,

H. H. Jones

HHJ

Manager.

Number 2373

ONE (1) Preferred Shares

Associated Mill and Elevator Company

PREFERRED BENEFICIAL INTEREST SHARES
PAR VALUE $100.00
FULLY PAID AND NON-ASSESSABLE

THIS CERTIFIES That D. W. FINNEY is the owner
of ONE (1) Preferred Beneficial Interest Shares in the
Associated Mill and Elevator Company, hereinafter called the Company, a Trust Estate, which he holds subject to a Declaration of Trust, dated April 2, 1919, hereby referred to and made part hereof. The owner, by accepting this Certificate, con-
sents to and becomes bound by the provisions thereof.

The shares represented by this Certificate, are transferable by the holder in person, or by attorney, upon the books of the Company,
but not otherwise, and no transfer hereof will be effective as regards the Company, until this Certificate has been surrendered, properly endorsed, and the transfer recorded upon the books of the Company. Thereupon, a new Certificate shall be issued to the transferee, who thereupon becomes the Beneficiary in place of the transferor. The owner hereof, appearing as such upon such books, is entitled to participate in
all dividends made to the owners of Preferred Beneficial Interest Shares under said Declaration of Trust, in the proportion that the number
of Preferred Beneficial Interest Shares evidenced by this Certificate bears to the total number of such Preferred Beneficial Interest Shares
outstanding on the date of declaration of such dividends, and to all the rights vested in the owners of Preferred Beneficial Interest Shares
in the Company, as defined by the Declaration of Trust.

The dividends on the Preferred Beneficial Interest Shares shall be cumulative from January 1, 1920, annually, at Eight (8) per cent per
annum, and dividends on the Preferred Beneficial Interest Shares shall be preferred as to the assets and dividends of the Trust Estate in
the manner and on the conditions provided in said Declaration of Trust.

This Certificate is not made by the undersigned as individuals, but as Trustees under said Declaration of Trust, and is enforceable only
against, and payable only out of the Trust Property held thereunder, and any and all personal liability of the Trustees and Beneficiaries
thereunder is, by the acceptance of, and as consideration for the issue and execution hereof, expressly waived.

IN WITNESS WHEREOF, the Trustees under said Declaration of Trust, designated as the Associated
Mill and Elevator Company, have caused their Common Seal to be hereunto affixed, and this Certificate
to be executed in their name and behalf, by the undersigned officers, thereunto duly authorized.

ASSOCIATED MILL AND ELEVATOR COMPANY,

[illegible signature] President.

ATTEST Paul Noble Secretary.

Warranty Deed

FROM

Carl C. Finney

Independence, Kansas

TO

Daniel Webster Finney

Independence, Kansas.

Entered in Transfer Record in my office this 2 day of Sept 1926

Lee Kelly County Clerk.

Mattie [illegible] Dep

STATE OF KANSAS, ss.

Montgomery County,

This instrument was filed for record on the 2 day of Sept 1926 at 1½ o'clock P. M., and duly recorded in book 152 of [illegible] on page 204

Mary McKittrick Register of Deeds.

Deputy.

Fee $ 1.00 pd.

Call

F. J. Boyles, Publisher of Legal Blanks, Lawrence, Kansas

WARRANTY DEED—Standard Form (No. 50A) F. J. Boyles, Publisher of Legal Blanks, Lawrence, Kansas

This Indenture, Made this 2nd day of September in the year of our Lord nineteen hundred and Twenty-six between Carl C. Finney, a single man of legal age

of Independence in the County of Montgomery and State of Kansas of the first part, and Daniel Webster Finney

of Independence in the County of Montgomery and State of Kansas of the second part.

Witnesseth, That the said part y of the first part, in consideration of the sum of One Dollar and other valuable consideration DOLLARS, to him duly paid, the receipt of which is hereby acknowledged, has sold and by these presents does grant and convey unto the said part y of the second part, his heirs and assigns, all that tract or parcel of land situated in the County of Montgomery and State of Kansas, described as follows, to-wit: The North Half ($N\frac{1}{2}$) of the Northwest Quarter ($NW\frac{1}{4}$) of Section Six (6), Township Thirty-four (34), Range Fifteen (15)

With all the appurtenances, and all the estate, title and interest of the said part y of the first part therein. And the said Carl C. Finney does hereby covenant and agree that at the delivery hereof he is the lawful owner of the premises above granted, and seized of a good and indefeasible estate of inheritance therein, free and clear of all incumbrances

and that he will WARRANT AND DEFEND the same in the quiet and peaceable possession of the said party of the second part, his heirs and assigns, forever, against all persons lawfully claiming the same

IN WITNESS WHEREOF, The said part y of the first part has hereunto set his hand and seal the day and year above written.

Signed, sealed and delivered in presence of

Carl C. Finney (BEAL)

(SEAL)

(SEAL)

(SEAL)

STATE OF KANSAS, Montgomery County, } SS.

Be it Remembered, That on this day of September A. D. 19 26 before me, Kitty Todd, a Notary Public in and for said County and State, came Carl C. Finney a single man of legal age to me personally known to be the same person who executed the foregoing instrument of writing, and duly acknowledged the execution of the same.

IN WITNESS WHEREOF, I have hereunto subscribed my name and affixed my official seal on the day and year last above written.

My Commission Expires October 5th, 1929

Kitty Todd
Notary Public.

PUBLIC SALE!

On account of ill health, I will sell at Public Auction at my farm 12 and three-quarter miles Southwest of Independence, on the Independence-Caney highway, 3¼ miles East of Wayside, 6 miles North and ¼ mile East of Tyro, on

Monday, Nov. 7th

1927, commencing at 10:00 a. m., the following property:

37 Head of Livestock

6 HEAD OF HORSES

1 Gray Mare, weight 1200.
1 Black Mare, weight 1400.
1 Span Black Mares, weight 2800.
1 Span Bay Horses, weight 3000.

17 HEAD OF HOGS

2 Brood Sows, will farrow in December.
15 Head of Shoats, averaging 100 lbs.

14 HEAD OF CATTLE

1 Holstein Cow, fresh.
2 Jersey Cows, giving milk.
2 Grade Jersey Cows, giving milk.
2 Shorthorn Cows, giving milk.
2 Shorthorn Heifers, coming 2 years.
5 Head of Calves.

GRAIN AND HAY—175 bushels Oats, more or less; 400 bushels yellow corn, more or less; 6 or 7 ton loose hay and some kaffir.

FARM MACHINERY AND SUPPLIES

One Farm Wagon, wide tire, with grain bed; One Iron wheel Wagon with hay rack; One Spring Wagon; One seven-ft. McComrick Grain Binder with trucks and Tractor hitch; One 5-ft. McCormick Mower; One 12-ft. Acme Hay Rake; One Sweep Rake; One 12-disc Superior Grain Drill; One Fordson Tractor and plows complete, 12-in bottom, in good running condition; One Disc Gang plow; One P & O, 16-in Sulky plow; One 12-in walking plow Two 4-shovel Cultivators; One Garden Cultivator; One P. & O., 14-disc Harrow; One 12-ft. Harrow, nearly new; One Canton Corn Planter; One 1-horse Corn Drill; One Manure Spreader; One Fanning Mill; One Corn Sheller; One Wheel-barrow; One Grind-stone; Two sets of Harness; 6 Collars; 4 Stands of Bees.

HOUSEHOLD GOODS

One Majestic wood and coal cook Stove; One Coal Heater; One Winsor Automatic Oil Stove, almost new; One Kitchen Cabinet; One Safe; One 11-ft. Dining Table and Chairs; Dishes and Cooking utensils; One Dresser; Two Mattresses; One new Feather Bed; One Spring Cot; One Chiffonier; Three Rugs; Two small Rugs; One Book Case; Two Stand Tables; One Coleman Gasoline Lamp; One Alladin Kerosene Lamp.

MISCELLANEOUS—Cream Separator; Ice Cream Freezer; Canned Fruit, all sizes Lard jars, Fruit jars, some Lard; Sweet and Irish Potatoes; 5 gallon Cream can; 30 gallon Iron Kettle; 3 Oil Drums; One water Tank; 3 or 4 cords of hedge stove wood and many article too numerous to mention.

TERMS—All sums of $10 and under, cash. All sums over $10 a credit of 6 months will be given with bankable note to draw 8 per cent interest from date. 2 per cent off for cash. Nothing to be removed until terms of sale have been complied with.

D. W. FINNEY, Owner

COL. A. C. COLE, Cherryvale
Auctioneer

COMMERCIAL BANK, Clerk
INDEPENDENCE, KANSAS

LUNCH SERVED BY LADIES' AID OF BOLTON

ii. Carl Chester Finney - b. 13 May 1905 Montgomery Co., Ks - d. 15 Nov 1987 Lakeport, Calif, buried Mt. Hope Cemetery, Independence, Ks. - m. 20 Oct 1926 Vivia Jay McCLURE - b. 3 May 1910, d/o James Harvey McCLURE. Carl farmed in Kansas was a machinist in California for 28 years with North American Rockwell Company.

a. Tommie Milton Finney - b. 2 Oct 1927 Montgomery Co., Ks - m (1) 10 Aug 1946 Loris Jane GRISWOLD - b. 30 Sep 1927 - d. 4 Jan 1962 Wichita, Ks - m (2) 27 Jan 1963 to Rosamary Ann (High) AMERINE - b. 15 Nov 1922

1. Tommie Milton Finney, Jr. - b. 5 July 1947 - d. 1 May 1987 Wichita, Ks, buried White Chapel Cemetery - m. 15 July 1967 Marcia OWEN - b.21 May 1949

2. Karen Deanne Finney - b. 16 Nov 1954 Wichita, Ks - adopted - m. 15 Oct 1983 Samuel Joseph OWEN - divorced

3. Christopher Walker (Amerine) Finney - b. 30 June 1952 Riley Co., Ks, adopted by Tom Finney and name legally changed to Finney - m. 22 May 1983 Sandra Jeanne STONE - b. 7 Nov 1960

4. Rebecca Lee (Amerine) Finney - b. 19 Apr 1955 Wichita, Ks - m. 14 Oct 1978 John Edgar BAUGH - divorced

b. Mary Jay Finney - b. 2 Mar 1930 - m. 11 Feb 1949 Charles Leroy PLUM - b. 16 June 1927 - divorced Feb 1966

1. Robert Michael Plum - b. 5 May 1952 - m. 29 Oct 1973 Patricia Ann MONTGOMERY - b. 6 Sep 1952 - divorced Jan 1979

A. Jeffry Michael Plum - b. 22 Apr 1975

2. Judith Ann Plum - b. 22 May 1954 - m. 6 Aug 1977 Steve PIERCE - b. 13 Jan 1953 - divorced Apr 1989

A. Brian Joseph Pierce - b. 1 Oct 1978
B. Mathew Steven Pierce - b. 5 July 1980

3. Dorothy Jean Plum - b. 27 Sep 1955 - m. 16 Aug 1975 Theodore ADAMS - b. 12 Jan 1953

A. Jennifer Renee Adams - b. 18 Oct 1980
B. Scott Ryan Adams - b. 15 May 1982
C. Alex Andrew Adams - b. 9 May 1987

4. Susan Lynn Plum - b. 10 Dec 1960 - m. 10 Feb 1981 Ernie DIAMOND - b. 26 Nov 1951, divorced Apr 1989

A. Sarah Jeanette Diamond - b. 6 Jan 1982
B. Jessie Ernest Diamond - b. 31 Aug 1983

c. Virginia Lee Finney - b. 2 Nov 1931 - d. 17 Sep 1971 South Gate, Calif - buried Mt. Hope Cem., Montgomery Co., Ks - she was an invalid her entire life

d. Daniel Robert Finney - b. 13 Nov 1935 - d. 14 Nov 1935 - bur. Mt. Hope Cemetery
e. James Edward Finney - b. 22 June 1937 - lives Greeley, Ks 1989 - m (1) 22 Aug 1959 Carol SHELLEY - b. 22 May 1941, divorced 12 June 1981 - m (2) 13 June 1981 to Jacqueline (Irish) RUTHERFORD b. 3 Dec 1939

1. Shelley Diane Finney - b. 5 Dec 1963
2. Daniel Edward Finney - b. 12 July 1967 - m. Deborah WARE - b. 25 Nov 1969

A. Amanda Christine Finney - b. 24 Apr 1989

f. David Wesley Finney - b. 22 July 1949 Calif - m (1) 20 Dec 1972 Rebecca BURCH who died 9 Apr 1975 of leukemia - m (2) 16 June 1976 Rhonda Lee Rae BOWEN - b. 21 May 1950

1. Jeremy Scott Finney - b. 4 Nov 1973
2. Stacey Michelle Bowen - b. 4 Dec 1969
3. Brett Matthew Bowen - b. 10 Oct 1971
4. Jonathan David Finney - b. 11 Mar 1977
5. Aaron James Finney - b. 14 Oct 1978 - d. 24 July 1983 in motor home fire

****

In Apr 1926 Carl, through a friend, met Vivia Jay McCLURE on the corner of 3rd & Spring Streets in Caney, Ks, during a very late snowstorm. He, age 21, worked for Prairie Oil Co. as auditor in their main office. Vivia was still in high school and on her way home from rehearsal for her Senior Play, in which she was a French maid. She says that after that meeting Carl always seemed to be coming home from work every afternoon at the right time, in his Ford coupe. Vivia got him a date with her friend Martha, and Martha and

Independence, Kansas, Nov. 3 1927

Mrs Vivia Finney

313 E F . st - City

TO MERCY HOSPITAL DR.

~~BALANCE DUE~~

To R. N C.	54.00
" Anaesth	2.00
" Bach fl.	.85
Opr R for babe	5.00
Aneath " "	5.00
	66.85

Pd in full By Carl B Finney

11-3-27 M. A. Kyne

Tommie M. Finney, Sr.

This Certifies
that
Carl C. Finney
of Independence Ks.
and
Vivia Jay McClure
of Caney, Ks.
were by me united in
Holy Matrimony
at Caney Kansas
According to the Ordinance of God
and the laws of Kansas
on the 20 day of October
in the Year of Our Lord 1926

Alfred C Neal
Minister

Mrs. Roy S. Carr
Mr. Roy S. Carr

Carl Chester Finney

Vivia Jay McClure

By this time Daniel Webster had been a patient in the hospital in Kansas City and diagnosed as having cancer. He returned to the Independence Hospital and Vivia visited with him and he saw his grandson - one time.

After he died on 10 Dec 1927 Mary Ann sold the farm equipment and leased the farm. Daniel had purchased a new Chrysler automobile and they had planned to go to California, and Carl and his mother did go to california in the new car - to live. There was some correspondence at this time, with him urging her to come out to California also. Vivia told him when he had a job she would come, even if they had to live in a tent; he sent money for her fare in September. When she arrived on the west coast they lived on Malabar St. in Huntington Park, in a small one-bedroom house on back of the landlord's property. Mary Ann went to live with her third cousin, Dessie TAYLOR, in Maywood, Calif. Carl was employed at $25 a week delivering laundry so they moved to a newer place, an apartment on a court, rent $35 a month, but it was on Maywood Avenue, same location as his mother. They had no car so, of course, when Mary Ann wanted to go for a drive the Chrysler was used. By April of 1928 Mary Ann wanted to return to Kansas, so Carl quit his job and they drove her back to Kansas. By the 1st of May Carl and Vivia were back in Maywood and it was necessary for him to find employment, this time with the Cloverdale Creamery delivering milk. They lived on 45th Street. While there they all had the mumps and Vivia was expecting her 2nd child. When Carl recovered he began work in the Santa Fe oil field in Inglewood, but that company soon shut down, so by January 30th the little family was on their way back to ka Kansas, but not together. Vivia and Tom went on the train and carl drove a Model A Ford. Vivia and Tom arrived in Independence in a bad snow storm, necessitating her spending Tom's $25 savings for some warm clothes. Meanwhile Carl drove from Pecos, Texas in the same storm. From Bartlesville, Okla. the snow was piled up on each side of the road higher than the car. Naturally the car froze up and required almost two weeks before it was useable again.

Mary Jay, their second child, was born 2 Mar 1930. While in the hospital their bad luck continued. The banks all closed and they were unable to get their money - when the banks reopened they received all of theirs. Mary Ann got her money, a sizeable amount, a little at a time. Carl and Vivia lived in town with Mary Ann until the 30th of October when they once more returned to the farm. Their daughter Virginia Lee was born 2 Nov 1931.

Vivia had to learn to use kerosene lamps and a gasoline fueled cookstove. The house was heated with wood and coal, had no running water. There was a bathtub but water had to be heated on the stove in winter and outdoors in the summer. They eventually got a gasoline washing machine but then she had to do the laundry on the porch even in the winter. She learned to cook, to bake bread, cakes and pies, and how to cut fat from a hog. She says today she didn't have time not to cope - and she was also waiting for the arrival of the daughter Virginia, called Ginger. Carl was not well at this point and the children got whooping cough. A lady who taught school was a friend of Vivia's and she came on week-ends during this time to help out; also, there was a hired hand to fix lunch for. Carl was sick in bed for six weeks; about this time an eventful thing happened - Bonnie and Clyde, notorious outlaws, stopped at their house to use the telephone, calling someone in Tyro, Ks. They were easily recognized since their pictures were in the paper quite frequently. They were later killed in Louisiana.

Needless to say Vivia did not like the farm and it was extremely hard work for her and for Carl - there were chickens, pigs and cows to care for and she had no time to help out-side. It was all work and even then they couldn't make it financially. After Carl's six-week illness he consulted a specialist in Tulsa, thinking at first he had tuberculosis. After extensive x-rays he was diagnosed as having ethmoidal sinus and told he should do no inside work and to be cautious of dust. So they sold the farm equipment and headed west. They had a box of potatoes and canned vegetables and fruit in a sort of trunk on the back of their 1930 Chevrolet.

In New Mexico they stopped at a housekeeping motel and Vivia began getting things prepared for their meal. Carl took Tom, Mary Jay and Ginger down the street to a little carnival so the children could stretch their legs. When they returned they ate, got the children to bed and Carl got very ill, having a bad coughing spell and having difficulty breath-ing - however, he soon recovered and they drove to Santa Fe the next day. They next stopped in Arizona where Tom went to school in a tent of the school grounds. The school had been extensively damaged in a 1933 eathquake and the only useable building remaining was the cafeteria. After that Carl went to work at Lavelle Camps Ranch, 20 acres of walnut grove, in Moreno, California, gathering English walnuts and running them through a dryer and huller; this only lasted about a month, until Hallowe'en to be exact. Later the family moved to a small one-bedroom house on the ranch and Tom finished the first grade there. Vivia was pregnant again and their money had just about been depleted. They made the decision to go back to Kansas in May.

Living in a rented house on 13th St., Carl leased a DX service station on N. Main and they moved to Penn Avenue, so Tom and Mary Jay could attend washington School. This latest child only lived fourteen hours, born 13 Nov 1935. Vivia did not recover quickly from this and the service station was not affording them a decent living, so they once more moved in with Mary Ann, who enjoyed looking after her grandchildren. At this time Vivia's parents took her with them on a two-week vacation, to Arkansas to visit relatives, and the trip helped perk her up. When she returned it was to find Carl was working at

Firestone for $15.00 a month and they rented a house which had to be scrubbed and painted, but they enjoyed doing the work together. However, Vivia got pregnant again and their son James Edward was born 22 June 1937. Ginger was now old enough to begin attending kindergarten and for the first time the family became aware she had a learning disability, and this child required constant care all of her life, living at home until Nov. 1967. She died in a nursing home in September 1971, at age 40 years.

The farm had been leased and the present tenant's lease was running out so in March 1938 Carl and Vivia returned once more. Carl built a 10½ footcabinet, upper and lower, with a maple counter top and a sink for the kitchen and they had 32 volt electricity so they had electric lights and Vivia had a sweeper and an electric motor on her sewing machine. Still, no indoor plumbing. The children were Tom, age 10; Mary Jay, age 8; Ginger, age 7; Jim, age 6 months. They raised chickens, a few hogs, cattle, later sheep. Carl had wheat crops in and grew special feed oats and had experimental plots for several varities of hybrid seed corn of the Kalb Feed Company. Vivia had a pressure cooker to do the canning - 92 quarts of pears, over 100 quarts of corn and green beans, also pork and chicken. Grandma (Mary Ann) Finney always came out to help with the canning. (She killed and helped the children clean the chickens. Vivia never learned to milk a cow or kill a chicken.) They belonged to the Farm Bureau and Mary Jay and Tom were active in 4-H. Carl was on the County Supervisor's board as well as the School Board.

Yet each year they paid off the last year's loan and borrowed to put in the next year's crop, and Carl really did not like farming. By 1941 it became clear the U. S. was going to be involved in the second World War and the Government began setting up training classes for jobs which would need to be filled. Carl went to a machinist and blue printing class and received his certificate for completion of the course. When Pearl Harbor was bombed he put in application at Kansas City, Tulsa and Wichita. He was called to Wichita in March 1942. Vivia and the children remained on the farm while Carl stayed in a Wichita hotel room, later a sleeping room, looking for a residence for his family. Housing was very scarce. They finally located a house with three bedrooms and Mary Jay enrolled in Jr. High School, Tom going to North High School. Soon Vivia decided to also work, taking a training course at Boeing Aircraft, learning to rivet, read blueprints, and went to work on the 4:00 p.m. to midnight shift; Carl was on the "graveyard" shift. When the plant began to be unionized, Vivia went to one of the union meetings and spoke up about women's rights. By doing so she was nominated and elected to serve on the negotiating committee. Four or five days a week she worked with the union, Boeing paying her wages, working with the heads of the company and a General Knudson of Procurement. They eventually got a contract signed, and Vivia found herself Treasurer of the Union. Then she went back to work, ten hours a day. Carl was still on the night shift and Vivia now worked the day shift.

Carl came from work, fixed her breakfast and packed her lunch and walked her to the bus stop. He drove and had five riders every night. May Jay and Tom did the laundry and most of the cooking. In 1943 Tom was working at a flour mill and Mary Jay at a local movie theater. In 1944 Vivia made the decision to give up her job. They had paid off their bills and saved quite a few Government Savings Bonds. Carl received permission to transfer to California. So with gasoline permits, a necessity during the war, for their car and Tom's, they sold most of their furniture and the items remaining at the farm, and were on their way west. Tom was too young to work and enlisted in the Navy, with his parent's signature, entering book camp in San Diego. Carl and Vivia purchased a home at 8127 San Vincente, South Gate, Calif., moving in 3 Mar 1945, their first home of their own. Vivia went to work at Ryan Aircraft and Carl employed at North American Aircraft, remaining at that job until his retirement in February 1972. Thye lived in South Gate for 28 years. Vivia had other sources of income - once at a sewing contract shop, then sewing at home for a designer making samples for his salesmen.

On 22 July 1949 their son David Wesley was born. Mary Jay had married Charles Leroy PLUM in February 1949; Tom returned from the Navy and moved back to Wichita where he married Loris GRISWOLD and had a son, Tommie Milton Finney, Jr in 1947; Jim married Carol SHELLEY in 1958. In 1967 David entered the Army and served in Viet Nam. He returned in 1972 and married Rebecca BURCH on 20 Dec 1972. After her death he married Rhonda BOWEN on 16 June 1976.

Carl and Vivea took a long trip in February 1969, to American and Western Samoa, New Zealand and Australia, and spent four days in Hawaii. He retired in 1972 and they bought a building site in Lake Co., Calif. Virginia died in Sept. 1971 and they sold their house and moved to Lakeport, Calif. on 29 Oct 1973 where they lived while their new home was being built near Kelseyville, Calif. They moved in on 10 July 1974 doing lots of the finish work themselves, finishing by May 1976 and at that time they celebrated their 50th anniversary. All of their children, three daughters-in-law, Vivia's father, step mother and brother were there. Since that time Vivia has lost her husband, father, her step-mother, brother and two grandchildren, but has acquired 15 grand children and 9 great-grand childre. She lives in their home in Kelseyville and has reached her 80th year. She is a member of the Presbyterian Church and an ordained Deacon, and, as she says, "I do as I please now - and I'm still not old."

PROGRAM

Processional. "Salut A. Pesth," Henri Kowalski ....Iva Lee Bolerjack
Independence

Invocation ....Rev. James L. Mitchell
Grace M. E. Church, Independence

Salutatory..Burton Lloyd
Bates, District 48

Mexican Band, "Three Numbers".............West Coffeyville, Dist. 62
M. O. Lancaster, Director

Valedictory ....Clara Morrison
Round Mound, Dist. 93

Address, "The Open Road"..................Rev. Geo. B. Dalrymple
First Christian Church, Independence

Presentation of Diplomas........................M. D. Smith

Benediction..Rev. James L. Mitchell

Recessional, "Salut A. Pesth" Henri Kowalski........Iva Lee Bolerjack

Class Colors—Purple and Gold

Class Flower—Yellow Rose Bud

Class Motto: *"Character is not a happen so; it is like strength and skill*
And is acquired only by regular daily drill."

Commencement Exercises

of the

Montgomery County Rural Schools

1941

ROLL OF HONOR

Name	Dist. No.
Adamson, Lucille	10
Agosto, Virginia	93
Augustine, Billy	49
Baker, Earl Dean	62
Beisly, Jewell	99
Bell, Hazel	23
Benning, Mary Katherine	97
Bishop, Kenneth	54
Black, Elmer	6
Blakely, Beulah	53
Blakslee, Clarence	61
Blevens, Helen	51
Bohannon, Beatrice	10
Bowers, Imogene	106
Boring, Herbert	45
Boring, Wanetta	45
Bowen, Elene	10
Brant, Jack	49
Brew, Laurence	48
Brinkman, Wanda	98
Britton, Patricia	85
Bronnenberg, Dale	66
Brown, Helen	73
Brownlee, Norma Jeanne	39
Bryant, Donald	46
Bryant, Una Bell	45
Burns, Lucille	113
Burton, Connie Sue	22
Canaday, Marjorie	46
Callahan, Clair	4
Carter, Dorothy	40
Childress, Dee	69
Clark, Bobby	66
Clayton, Wilma	46
Cole, Bobby	10
Corner, Melvin	62
Cottle, Bobby	35
Cook, Claude	6
Cox, Neal	46
Crattie, Lyle	62
Crawford, Howard	68
Crossland, Juanita	46
Daves, L. A.	59
Deen, Walter	35
Dickens, Lois	51
Edwards, Lucille	38
Ellison, Reba	65
Evans, Shirley	62
Featherngill, Dean	113
Ferguson, Freddie	23
Finney, Tommie	73
Fletcher, Lillian	25
Foster, Mary Lou	12
Freeman, Wayne	71
Fritz, Betty	40
Frye, Elbert	77
Garling, Lyman	37
Garner, Jack	113
Gillman, Mary Ella	45
Gillman, Eugene	48
Godsey, Gerald	103
Haberly, Marshall	41
Hastings, Jimmie	68
Heape, Robert	47
Hedges, Jean	82
Hensley, Lilbern	62
Hinson, Orene	46
Hodges, Wilma Lea	75
Holbert, Frank, Jr.	88
Holbert, Wayne	68
Holloway, Marvin	56
Houck, Warren	92
Hudiberg, Jo Anne	46
Huff, Clyde	36
John, Billy Jim	72
Kaufman, Genevieve	64
Kettle, Vera Ruth	58
King, Kenneth	33
Lefever, Georgia	44
Leffingwell, Jacqueline	24
Lindsay, Iva	102
Lybarger, Bobby Lee	12
Main, Phyllis	27
Martin, Ruth	35
Mavers, Arthur	48
McCarty, Edith	70
McDowell, Edward Lee	10
McGinnis, Betty	32
McGuire, Bonita	18
McMurray, Rozalie	25
McNeal, Pauline	50
Miller, Bobby	61
Miner, Gerald	28
Mishler, Charles	61
Moline, Rose Anna	16
Morse, Johnnie F.	12
Muir, Bettie Ruth	62

Musgrove, Virgil
Navarre, Sarah Anne
Norris, Paul
O'Brien, Leotis May
Osborn, Edna
Padley, Marcella
Pendleton, Floyd
Pitts, Elmer
Pitts, Rex
Pomeroy, Hubert
Powers, Mary Dean
Pruett, Roy
Quigley, Hazel
Ratzlaff, Betty Jean
Reynolds, Robert
Richardson, Veda
Riggs, Dean
Robison, Clara
Robnett, Gerald
Ross, Clifford
Rutherford, Maxine
Sack, Billy
Schenk, Loren
Schiler, Robert
Sherwin, Jackie
Shockey, Freda
Skinner, John
Smith, Beth
Smith, Billy
Smith, Alvin
Springer, Lee
Starts, Robert
Startz, Elmer
Stewart, Ruth
Stewart, Lorene
Sturgeon, Evelyn
Swaley, Marlin
Tindle, Tom
Thompson, Louise
Todd, Ruby
Vickers, Cora
White, Ben
White, Bobby
Wiley, James
Wilson, Dean
Wilson, Norman
Wilson, Viola
Wise, Maxine
Wright, Wesley

DEPARTMENT OF COMMERCE
THE NATIONAL INVENTORS COUNCIL
WASHINGTON

January 22, 1942

Mr. Carl C. Finney
Wayside, Kansas

In reply refer to: 36555

Dear Mr. Finney:

Your suggestion relative to a radio controlled bomb has been received and has been carefully considered by our engineering staff.

This examination discloses that the suggestion is not of such a character as may be employed in the war effort at the present time.

Reason for this cannot always be disclosed, for to do so might also disclose information of a secret nature.

Please accept our thanks for the patriotic spirit shown in forwarding the material for examination. You may be sure that our technical staff will be glad to examine any and all future ideas which you may care to submit.

Yours very truly,

Thomas R. Taylor
Director of Staff

By: M. S. Steinmetz
M. S. Steinmetz

MSS: bcc

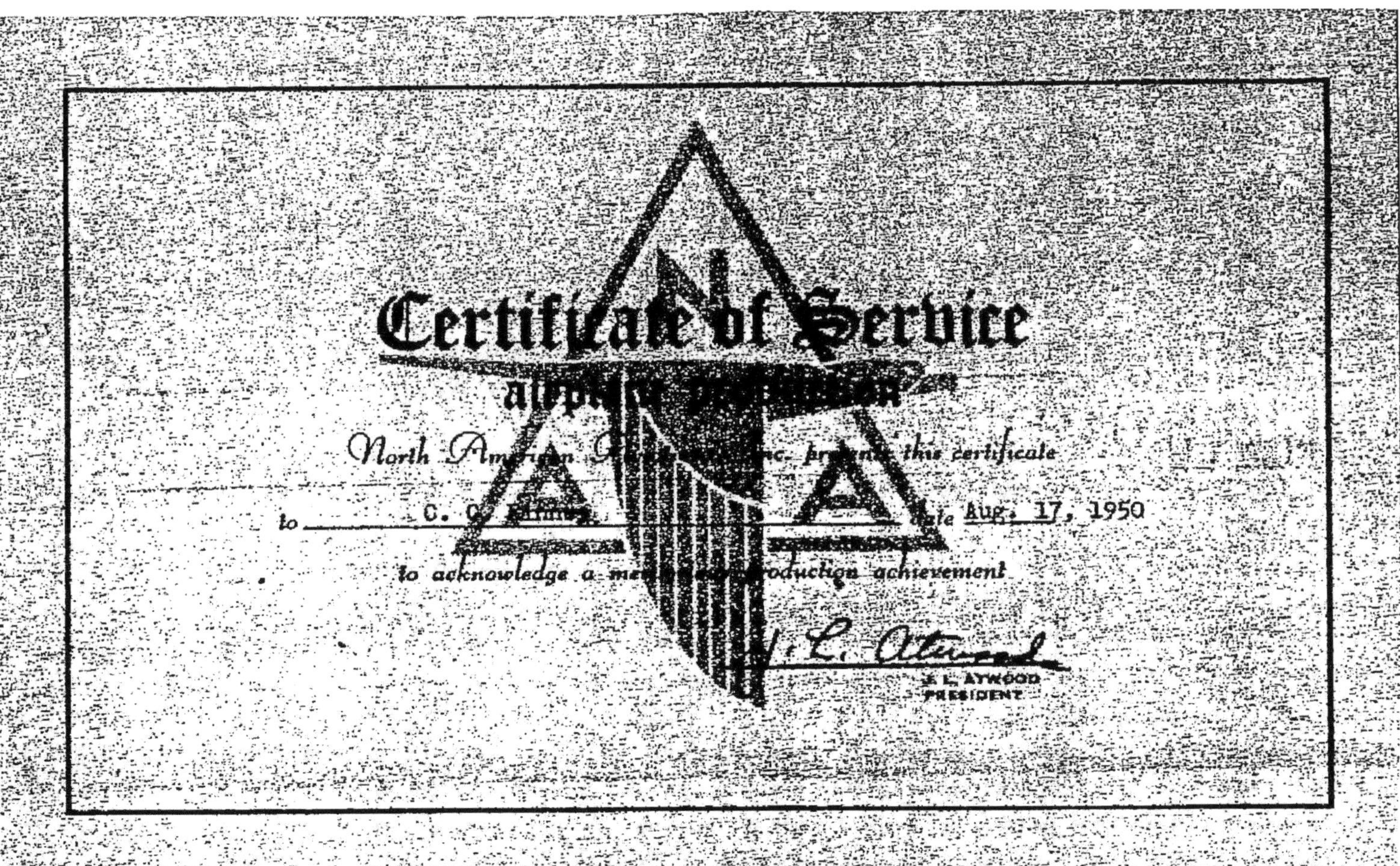
Certificate of Service
North American ... Inc. presents this certificate
to C. C. ... date Aug. 17, 1950
to acknowledge a meritorious production achievement
J. L. ATWOOD
PRESIDENT

THE WICHITA & SANTA FE SHORTLINE RR
OFFICERS AND DIRECTORS

E. L. ATHERTON, Chairman of the Board
LYLE E. ABBOTT, President

NEWTON G. BRETH, Vice President — ROBERT SCHENEWERK, Vice President
★ T. M. Finney, Vice President — A. L. WIDENER, Vice President
JACK K. LASHLEY, Vice President — H. E. MILLER, Secretary-Treasurer
KEITH SANBORN, Vice President — BARNEY MURRAY, Director

FRED HADLEY, Director

THE SPONSORING CLUBS OF WICHITA

THE EXCHANGE CLUB
THE JUNIOR CHAMBER OF COMMERCE
NATIONAL RAILWAY HISTORICAL SOCIETY
OPTIMIST CLUB OF EAST WICHITA

OUR APPRECIATION TO THE FIRMS LISTED FOR THE
ASSISTANCE IN GETTING 3768 TO ITS BASE

SANTA FE RAILWAY
THE EAGLE PRESS
MARTIN EBY CONSTRUCTION CO.
COLORADO FUEL & IRON CO.
WHITE STAR MACHINERY CO.
CRANE COMPANY
WICHITA BEACON
SAM MOBLEY, Architect
CESSNA AIRCRAFT
W. B. CARTER CONSTRUCTION CO.
WICHITA PARK BOARD
WESTERN SIGN CO.
SOUTHWEST PAPER CO.
RAY CHAIR RENTAL
MISSOURI PACIFIC RAILWAY
WICHITA EAGLE PUBLISHING CO.
SHERWOOD CONSTRUCTION CO.
RITCHIE BROS. CONSTRUCTION CO.
PARK LANE CENTER
SERVICE BRASS & ALUMINUM
CHUCK MORAN, Advertising
HAHNER & FOREMAN
ACME PRINTING
WICHITA POLICE DEPARTMENT
BELGER CARTAGE SERVICE
PAGE SIGNS
WESTERN FENCE CO.
KANSAS GAS & ELECTRIC

KAKE KANS KFBI KFH KWBB KAKE-TV
KARD-TV KTVH-TV

AND
TO ALL THOSE CITIZENS OF WICHITA AND ELSEWHERE
WHO BOUGHT STOCK TO HELP GET 3768 PLACED
WE THANK YOU

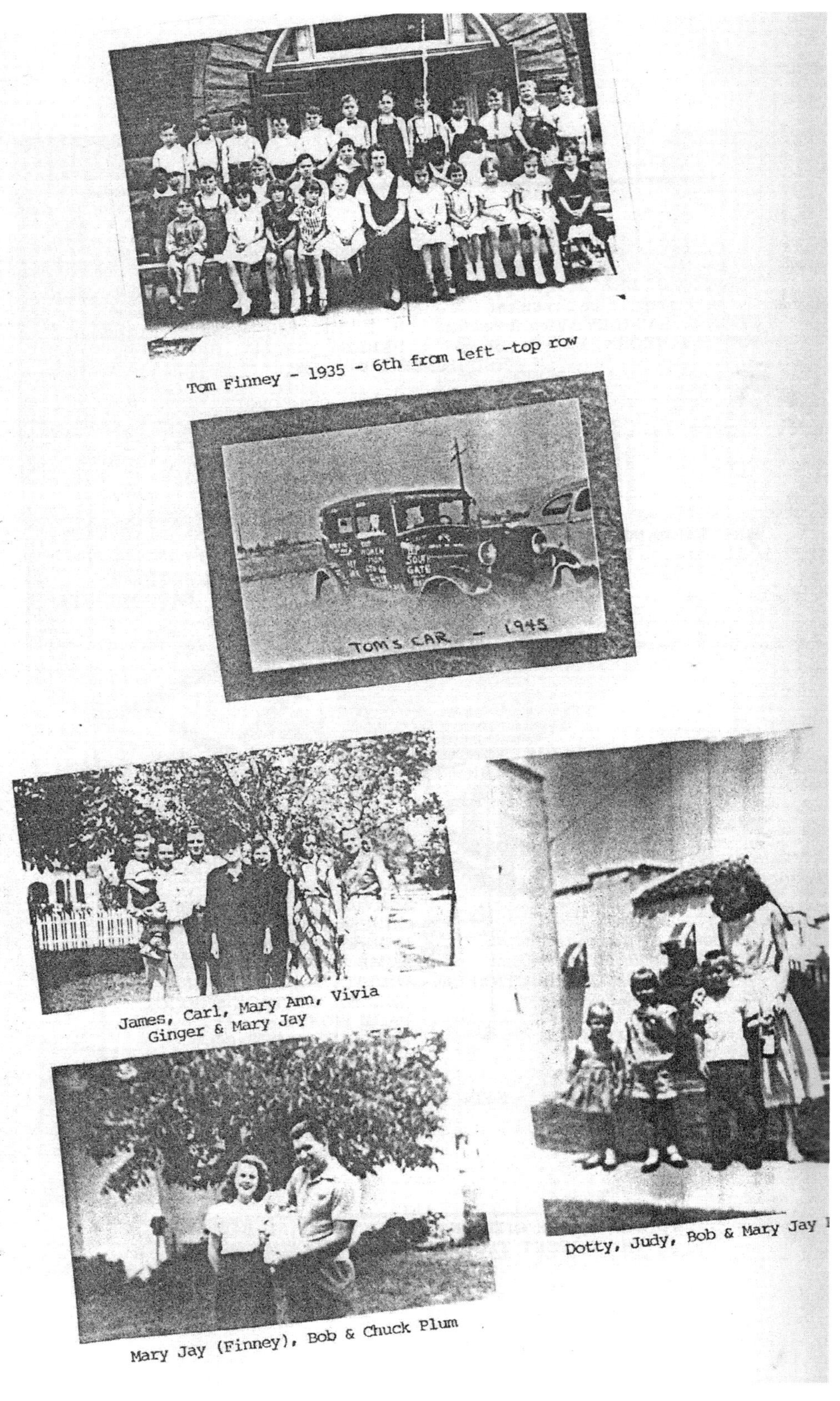

Tom Finney - 1935 - 6th from left -top row

James, Carl, Mary Ann, Vivia
Ginger & Mary Jay

Dotty, Judy, Bob & Mary Jay

Mary Jay (Finney), Bob & Chuck Plum

David, Vivia & Carl Finney

Susan Plum

Vivia & Carl Finney - 1976

Tommie Milton Finney, Jr. 1969

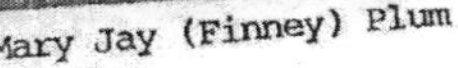

Mary Jay (Finney) Plum

Judy Plum

James Finney

Virginia Finney, Former Local Resident, Dies

9-19-71

Miss Virginia Lee Finney, 39, former local resident, died Friday morning at South Gate, Calif.

The body is to arrive in Independence Monday night. Graveside funeral services will be held Wednesday at 10 a.m. with burial under the direction of the Webb Funeral Home.

Miss Virginia Lee Finney was born Nov. 2, 1931, at Independence, the daughter of Carl and Vivia Finney. The family moved to California 26 years ago.

Survivors include the parents of the home in South Gate, Calif.; one sister, Mrs. Mary J. Plum, Linwood, Calif.; three brothers, Jim and David Finney, South Gate, Calif., and Tommie Finney of Kansas; and a grandfather, J. H. McClure.

9-20-71

Funerals

VIRGINIA LEE FINNEY

Graveside funeral services for Miss Virginia Lee Finney, 39, will be held Wednesday at 10 a.m. in Mount Hope Cemetery with the Rev. Donald Burt, pastor of the First United Presbyterian Church, officiating. Burial will be under the direction of the Webb Funeral Home.

VIRGINIA LEE
DAU. OF CARL & VIVIA
NOV. 2, 1931
SEPT. 17, 1971

KANSAS MOTOR VEHICLE CHAUFFEUR'S LICENSE

No. 57180

NAME Tommie M. Finney,

ST. OR R. F. D. 1125 Lewellen,

CITY Wichita, STATE Kansas

RESIDENT OF Sedgwick, COUNTY

DATE OF BIRTH (MO. DAY YR.)	WEIGHT	HEIGHT	COLOR HAIR	COLOR EYES	SEX	RACE
10 2 27	130	5-11½	Brown	Brown	M	W

SIGNATURE X *Tommie M. Finney*

DIRECTOR STATE HIGHWAY COMMISSION

THIS LICENSE EFFECTIVE FOR TWO YEAR PERIOD July 1, 1943 to July 1, 1945

SUPERINTENDENT MOTOR VEHICLE DEPARTMENT

Tom Finney, Sr. 1975

Rosamary (High) Finney 1975

Tom Finney, Sr. (with glasses) 1985

CARL C.
MAY 13, 1905
NOV. 15, 1987
VIVIA J.
MAR. 3, 1910

Carl C. Finney

Carl C. Finney, 82, Kelleysville, Calif., formerly of this area, died Sunday in a Lakeport, Calif., hospital.

Graveside services will be held at 10 a.m. Monday at Mount Hope Cemetery under the direction of the Webb & Rodrick Funeral Home.

The family will receive friends from 4 p.m. to 7 p.m. Sunday at the funeral home.

Carl C. Finney was born May 13, 1905, at Wayside. He was a machinist for 28 years with North American Rockwell.

He married Vivia Joe McClure. She survives at the home.

Memberships included AFL-CIO, Architectural Board of Riviera Heights in Kelleysville, and the Presbyterian church.

Other survivors include three sons, T.M. Finney of Kansas, James E. Finney, Saugus, Calif., and David W. Finney, Paronan, Utah; and 13 grandchildren and eight great-grandchildren.

One son and one daughter are deceased.

et cetera

Correction — Among the survivors of Carl C. Finney, who died last Sunday in Lakeport, Calif., was a daughter, Mary J. Plum of Upland, Calif. This information was not supplied to the Reporter for the obituary which was published Thursday.

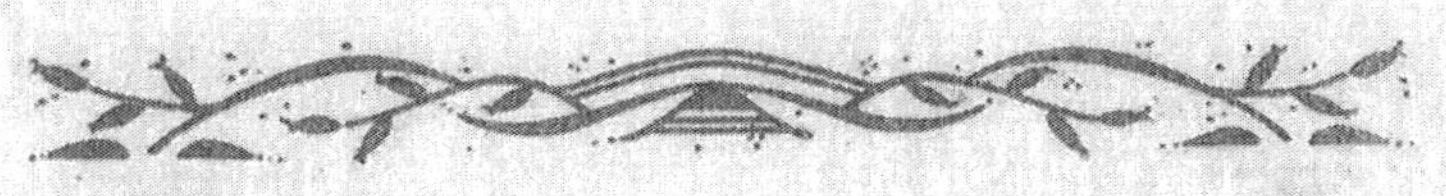

MAY the Memories that enfold the mystic shrine of Life be cherished as precious Treasures of Peace, Comfort and Hope through all the years to come.

I AM the resurrection and the life, saith the Lord; he that believeth in me, though he were dead, yet shall he live, and whosoever liveth and believeth in me, shall never die.
John 11:25

Part Two

CONTROVERSY, SCIENCE, AND REVELATION

Controversy, Science, and Revelation!

This book has the honor to introduce a **controversy** regarding Finney ancestry, the **science** of DNA, and concludes with an important **revelation** that contradicts previously published and accepted Finney genealogies!

Don't skip through this section – it is of importance and a lesson to all genealogists that there is always something new to discover!

Controversy

On the ancestry genealogy message boards, there has been an electric discussion between Lynn Finney Stuter and Gerald Finney, regarding one branch of Finneys and whether or not this branch was directly descended from Robert Finney – the "original" Finney in most published Finney genealogies.

From Lynn Finney Stuter - Background

The ancestry of our first Joseph Finney has been the subject of much research and speculation.

Is our Joseph of the family of Robert and Dorothea of Thunder Hill?

Published genealogies claim our Joseph is actually the John Finney who married Ruth Lloyd at Old Swedes Holy Trinity Church, Wilmington, New Castle County, Delaware on January 28, 1758; Ruth being the name of Joseph Finney's wife.

It is possible that the marriage record at Old Swedes Holy Trinity Church is that of Joseph Finney and Ruth Lloid/Lloyd; the reason being that the records of Old Swedes Holy Trinity Church were originally written in Swedish, transcribed by Horace Burr and originally published in 1890.[1] A photocopy of the transcribed record, from a 1919 *Catalogue* of the names appearing in the 1890 edition, is shown at the top of the next page.

As the record produced by Old Swedes Holy Trinity Church is transcribed, it is possible that …

1. the handwritten record is actually Joseph but has been transcribed as John;

[1] Burr, Horace; The Records of Holy Trinity (Old Swedes) Church, Historical Society of Delaware; 1890; title page. In the Prefatory Remarks, Horace Burr had this to say about the translation of names during those years when the records were written in Swedish:

> "In transcribing the names of persons I have followed the spelling of the recorder, except where there was an evident mistake or slip of the pen.
>
> It will be seen that the names of person not Swedes have been spelt as they would sound to the Swedish ear, and many of them very differently from their proper English orthography."

FILE,	John	to Elizabeth Burgass	727
	*Robert	to Ruth Cling	731
FILLPOT,	see Philpot		
FILSON,	Davison	to Elinor Clark	691
FINLEY,	*Samuel	to Sarah Witterton	398
FINNEY,	John.	to Ruth Lloid	706
FINNIS,	Daniel	to Elinor Dougherty	689
FIRTH,	James	to Jane Peet	716
	James	to Phoebe Thomson	738
	*William	to Jean Olls	729
FISHER,	John	to Margret Gubbens	688

2. the handwritten record should have been Joseph but was recorded and transcribed as John (which means the actual record could never be disproven); or
3. the handwritten record is correct, the man's name was John and was recorded as John (which means this marriage record could not be that of Joseph Finney and Ruth, his wife).

Credence is given to the entry being that of the marriage of Joseph Finney and Ruth Lloid/Lloyd as …

1. the marriage at Old Swedes Holy Trinity Church is in the date range for it to have been the marriage of Joseph and Ruth. Family legend says that Ruth's maiden name was Lloyd. That, however, is family legend and remains unproven.
2. Joseph and Ruth's son, Joseph, was born at Wilmington, New Castle County, Delaware in 1765. Joseph is believed to be their second child which would mean that their first child, Ann, was also born in Delaware. It is probable that Ruth was also born there.
3. There is no known issue of John Finney and Ruth Lloid/Lloyd; nor any further evidence of them found in the records kept in that time in Pennsylvania, Delaware, or Virginia.
4. According to the book, <u>Finney-Phinney Families in America</u>, John Finney died in 1783 and was buried in the cemetery at Old Swedes Holy Trinity Church. Correspondence with Old Swedes, however, indicates that while that is possible, there is no John Finney buried there.

It is of interest to note that neither John Finney nor Ruth Lloid/Lloyd were members of Old Swedes Holy Trinity Church at the time of their marriage; they were also married without a license.

Published genealogies, most notably the previously mentioned <u>Finney-Phinney Families in America</u> by Howard Finney, have surmised that our Joseph Finney was actually John Finney, and was the "lost son" of Lazarus and Catherine (Simonton) Finney; Lazarus the son of Robert and Dorothea (French) Finney of

Thunder Hill acclaim in Pennsylvania. This John Finney was said to have "gone south" and never returned.[2]

These same published genealogies state that Robert Finney is the son of Joseph and Ruth Finney. This is our first clue that the information presented is *not accurate.* Robert Finney was the son of Ann Finney, daughter of Joseph and Ruth Finney. This is clearly stated in Joseph's will, dated 1799, Surry County, North Carolina.

Robert Finney of Thunder Hill was left for dead at the Battle of Boyne, fighting under the standard of William of Orange, in 1690.

Also fighting, at the Battle of Boyne, under the standard of William of Orange, was Henry Patton, father of James Patton who is found at Forks of James River[3], Virginia, circa 1740 along with Michael, James, Joseph[4], Christopher and David Finney[5] and Jane (Finney) Arnold, known to be the sibling of Michael Finney. Both Robert Finney and James Patton came to America from Northern Ireland, Robert Finney before 1720 and James Patton circa 1736.

James Patton captained the ship, the Walpole, built by his father, under lease from its owner. By some accounts, Patton made numerous voyages from America to Europe, carrying tobacco, furs and other goods to those countries, then sailing on to Northern Ireland (Londonderry) where he took on passengers to the colonies, mostly passengers who agreed to settle in Beverly Manor in the Valley of Virginia (Forks of James area).

The Walpole anchored at Hobbs Hole on the Rappahannock River in Virginia. The passenger lists for these voyages have not been found; nor has the entry point for James and Ann (Arnold) Finney, Michael, Joseph and Christopher

---

[2] Edna (Bray) Reece, a direct-line descendant of Joseph Finney via Joshua Finney (the "southern" branch) contacted Howard Finney, author of *Finney-Phinney Families in America*, concerning this claim. Howard Finney responded to her that this book was compiled by his father, published after his father's death, and that the book was all there was; that there was no supporting documentation. Edna (Bray) Reece is the author and compiler of the genealogy titled *Rachel Barkley's Children*. While copies of the first edition of this book do exist, and do claim descendancy from Robert and Dorothea (French) Finney, in the second edition (1978), Edna (Bray) Reece discounted this descendancy, as did Charles Wesley Finney, compiler of the a genealogy dated 19 January 1944 the mainly covers the descendants of Joseph Finney that moved north into Indiana and Ohio.

[3] Also called Forks of James or Forks of the James. This area included the "natural bridge" on the James River found along the James River west of Glasgow, Virginia.

[4] The only mention of Joseph, in the Forks of James area, is on the muster roll of Captain John McDowell. As shown on the next page, this "Joseph" is probably James Finney who died with Capt McDowell December 14, 1742 at Balcony Falls near Glasgow, Virginia. It is believed that, if Joseph is of this family, that he was significantly younger than his siblings.

[5] The entries in Augusta County records referring to David Finney reference legal matters giving rise to the probability that this David Finney was the son of John Finney, grandson of Robert and Dorothea Finney, a lawyer by training, handling legal matters between plaintiffs in Pennsylvania/Delaware and defendants that had removed from the Pennsylvania/Delaware area to Forks of the James, Virginia.

Finney, and Jane (Finney) Arnold. The last known voyage by Patton on the Walpole was 1737/38.

Damping the claim that Joseph Finney is the son of Lazarus and Catherine (Simonton) Finney is the fact that Robert Finney was a staunch Presbyterian, a religious denomination that held no great affection for the Quakers; the very people with whom Joseph Finney lived, associated and moved.

In the summer of 2011, a direct-line male descendant of Joseph Finney submitted a DNA sample for analysis. The DNA submitted did not match that of known descendants of Robert Finney of Thunder Hill.[6]

The descendant referenced above, supplying the DNA for analysis, is of the following lineage:

1. Joseph Finney (md Ruth ?)[7]
    2. Joseph Finney (md Rachel Barkley)
        1. Joseph Finney (md Mary "Polly" Long)
            9. Wesley Finney (md Mary Matilda Hinshaw)

Is our Joseph of the family of Captain Samuel Finney?

Appearing at the Forks of the James River, holding land on the south side of the James River, between land held by the Hadley's (Quakers) and land held by Stephen Arnold (married to Jane Finney), was one John Buchanan who married the daughter of James Patton.

John Buchanan was related to Silas Hart and to Colonel Thomas Thompson whose wife was Ann Finney, daughter of Joseph Finney (not our Joseph), and granddaughter of Capt Samuel Finney; friend and associate of William Penn, Quaker.

The Buchanan's, Hart's and Thompson's are found in Augusta County, Virginia, at the same time as Michael, James, Christopher, and Jane (Finney) Arnold, later appearing in Orange County, North Carolina where they held land in the Greensboro area not far distant from Cane Creek where our Joseph Finney held land near the Quaker settlement.

It is possible that our Joseph is related to Captain Samuel Finney but researchers of that lineage have found no connection, at least not in America.

Is our Joseph of the Finney's found at Forks of James River, Virginia?

Appearing on the muster roll of the militia of Capt John McDowell of Augusta County, Virginia, in 1742, is Michael Finney and James or Joseph Finney.

[6] The results of this DNA analysis can be found at **Family Tree DNA – Finney**.

[7] The leading number is the order of birth of the child.

Captain McDowell held land adjoining that of Michael Finney. (See maps at end of this section.)

The snapshot below is the actual handwritten entry on the muster roll supplied by the Wisconsin Historical Society from the Preston Papers contained in the Draper Manuscripts. The name below that of Michael finey is James Hardiman.

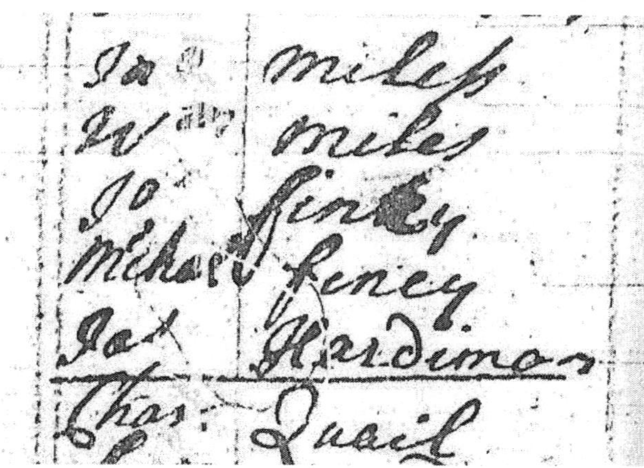
Jas miles
Wm miles
Jo finley
Michael finey
Jas Hardiman
Chas: Quail

Comparison of the name above and below that of Michael finey indicate they both have the same first name – James.

Note how the last name—finey—is not capitalized. This was not an uncommon practice among the Irish. Joseph signed his name this way on several documents known to exist. This suggests Joseph was born in Ireland. Early descendants of Joseph believed this to be the case.

In early 1743, Michael Finney and James Patton were appointed administrators in the estate of James Finney in Augusta County, Virginia. In the margin of the "account against s^{d} Estate of James Finney, dec'd" is written the date December 20, 1742.

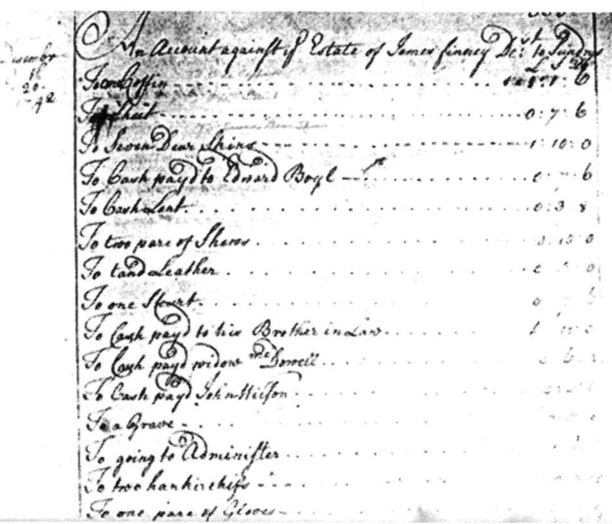
An Account against sd Estate of James finney Dec'd
To one Coffin
To a Shirt ... 0:7:6
To Seven Dear Skins ... 1:10:0
To Cash payd to Edward Boyl
To Cash Lent
To two pare of Shoes
To tand Leather
To one Shirt
To Cash payd to his Brother in Law
To Cash payd widow McDowell
To Cash payd John Wilson
To a Grave
To going to Administer
To two hankirchifs
To one pare of Gloves

Will of James Finney

The following is the inventory of the estate of James Finney, died 14 Dec 1742.

This inventory reads:

And inventory of the effects of James Finney dec'd —

To 1 Black Goldon (gelding?)

To 1 Saddle and bridle

To 1 ax, mall, Rings and weges

To 1 Jaket

To 1 hat

To two pare of ould Stok and Garters

To three Shirts

To five Busshels & three pecks of wheet & Rey

Due by note or bills three pound fifteen Shillings pennsilvania Money. This Given under our hands this 17th Day of September – 1743

Joseph Lapesly

Peter Wallace

At a Court held for Orange County on Thursday the 28th Day of February 1743

This appraisment of the Estate of James Finey Dece'd being Ret into Court by Mich. Finey the same is admitted to Record

Test. Jonath Gibson

On December 14, 1742, Captain John McDowell and seven of his men were killed in a skirmish with a renegade band of Delaware Indians at Balcony Falls near present-day Glasgow, Virginia. The bodies of the slain men were returned to the property of Captain John McDowell, where they were buried[8]. The only headstone erected was for Capt. McDowell; the other graves simply marked by a stone. This ground became part of the McDowell Cemetery and remains on the old McDowell property near Fairfield, Virginia on Timber Ridge (see maps at end of this section).

The "account against said Estate of James Finney, dec'd" of December 20, 1742, lists sundry expenses including a coffin and grave, and mentions cash paid to "his brother-in-law", to Edward Boyl, to John Wilsson and to "widow" McDowell (see actual document at end of this section.)

Edward Boyl held land adjoining that of Michael Finney; John Wilsson held land in proximity to Michael Finney; and, of course, Captain McDowell's land

[8] Waddell, Joseph A.; *Annals of Augusta County, Virginia, from 1726 to 1821*; Clearfield Co, Inc; Baltimore, MD; 1992; page 46-47.

adjoined that of Michael Finney. Indications are that the Finney on Captain John McDowell's muster roll, besides Michael Finney, is James Finney, not Joseph Finney.

In this same vein, those mustered ranged in age from 16 years on. Joseph had, at the least, one daughter and a son by 1765. If he is the son of James Finney and Ann Arnold, he had to have been born before 1742 when James died. If he is the sibling of Michael Finney and Jane (Finney) Arnold, he would, presumably, be within their age range, albeit younger, which means he might or might not have been old enough to be mustered in 1742. More on clues to his probable age a bit later.

Published genealogy records state the parents of Jane (Finney) Arnold to be James Finney and Ann Arnold. This appears to be the accepted lineage. However, as with Joseph Finney, there has been no proof presented that this is the case.

We know, from the fact that Michael Finney was named administrator in the estate of James Finney, that they were related. The meager inventory of the estate of James Finney, after his death, presents the possibility that James Finney was the brother of Michael Finney and Jane (Finney) Arnold who were siblings. This would also suggest that Stephen Arnold, husband of Jane Finney, and Ann Arnold, wife of James Finney, were siblings; and that the "brother-in-law" referenced in the account against the estate of James Finney was, in fact, Stephen Arnold. What became of Ann (Arnold) Finney, after the death of her husband, seems to be a mystery. As James Finney died intestate, who his children were is not known.

Was our Joseph Finney at Forks of James River, Virginia?

Chief among the Quakers with whom Joseph Finney associated were the descendants of Simon Hadley, a Quaker immigrant to America from Ireland whose land holdings straddled the Pennsylvania/Delaware border (see maps following this section) not far distant from Wilmington, New Castle County, Delaware where John Finney married Ruth Lloid/Lloyd on January 28, 1758 at Old Swedes Holy Trinity Church.

Joshua Hadley was the son of the above noted Simon Hadley. Joshua and family are found at Forks of James River, Virginia, circa 1740 at the same time as James Patton and Michael Finney and in the same area.

Simon, the son of Joshua Hadley of Forks of James River, and grandson of Simon Hadley of the Pennsylvania/Delaware area, married Bridget Foote at Old Swedes Holy Trinity Church, Wilmington, New Castle County, Delaware, on March 18, 1756; just short of two years before John Finney married Ruth Lloid/Lloyd at that same church. Simon was disowned for a time by the Quakers for this marriage as it was not sanctioned by the Quaker assembly, Bridget Foote was not Quaker, and the marriage took place in a non-Quaker church.

Simon Hadley was born in 1737, in Pennsylvania. Joseph Finney's life-long association with Simon Hadley suggests that Joseph's birth date is close in range to that of Simon, circa 1737. This would have made Joseph too young to muster in 1742 but in the right date range to be married in 1758 when the entry appears on the registry of Old Swedes Holy Trinity Church for John Finney and Ruth Lloid/Lloyd. Joseph is possibly the younger brother of James Finney or his son. Given the birth dates of the known children of Michael Finney, it is doubtful that Joseph is the son of Michael.

At this time, the Church of England did not recognize many churches[9] so young couples had to either go great distances to be married or send for a minister. This situation existed in Virginia which is probably why Simon Hadley traveled all the way to Delaware to be married (Bridget Foote was born in 1732, Mill Creek Hundred, New Castle County, Delaware). It is very possible, even probable, that our Joseph Finney also traveled from Virginia to Delaware to marry. It is also possible, even probable, that our Joseph Finney and Simon Hadley undertook this journey together.

Simon and Bridget (Foote) Hadley removed from New Garden Monthly Meeting, Pennsylvania to Cane Creek, Chatham County, North Carolina sometime between 1762 (when certificate[10] was granted) and 1763 when Simon and Bridget were "received on certificate" at Cane Creek Monthly Meeting.

It is here, in 1772, that we find Joseph Finney as witness to a transfer of land between Benjamin Landrum and Joshua Hadley in Chatham County, North Carolina. This Joshua Hadley is not the same Joshua Hadley of Forks of James River, Virginia, but his son, brother of Simon Hadley (md Bridget Foote).

Simon Hadley died in Surry County, North Carolina, in 1803, three years after Joseph Finney died. The two men were life-long friends and associates, making their last move to Surry County at about the same time.

Thomas Hadley, son of Simon and Bridget (Foote) Hadley, born in 1756, was the executor of Joseph Finney's will in Surry County, North Carolina in 1800. All of the witnesses to Joseph Finney's will—William Hinshaw, Edward Bass, and Joseph Hinshaw—were Quakers as was Thomas Hadley.

Edward Bass was born 1760 in Dobbs County (now Johnson County), North Carolina. He married Hannah Moon, daughter of James and Ann (Mendenhall) Moon. Hannah's brother, Peter Moon, married Rachel Adams. Jean Adams, sister of Rachel, married Thomas Brown. Jonathan Adams, brother of both Rachel (md Peter Moon) and Jean (md Thomas Brown), married Ann Brown, sister of Thomas Brown. Thomas Brown and Jonathan Adams were witness to

---

[9] Waddell, Jos. A; Annals of Augusta County, Virginia; from 1726 to 1871; Clearfield Company; Second Edition, 1902; page 35.

[10] When Quakers moved from one Monthly Meeting to another, they had to request and receive permission from the Monthly Meeting to do so. This was called a "certificate."

the sale, in 1810, of the property devised to Robert Finney by Joseph Finney in his will, 1799. All of these people were Quakers in good standing with the Society of Friends.

Down through the generations of descendants of Joseph and Ruth Finney are marriages between Finney descendants and Quakers or United Brethren. The community of Woodland in the northern tip of Idaho County, Idaho, where Frank Abraham Finney, his brother and sister, homesteaded in the late 1800's, has one church—the Woodland Friends Church. Frank, his sister and brother, are direct line descendants of Joseph Finney; Frank is my grandfather. The community, in the early days, was home to many Quakers who followed the same migration routes as did the Finney's. My father's paternal grandmother was United Brethren; his paternal grandfather Quaker.

Malinda Hunt, wife of Robert Finney was Quaker (my g-g-grandparents), as was Mary Matilda Hinshaw, wife of Wesley Finney; Robert and Wesley Finney being brothers and the sons of Joseph and Mary "Polly" (Long) Finney (my g-g-g-grandparents). Joseph's step-mother, Ann (Kester) Finney, second wife of his father Joseph (my g-g-g-g-grandfather), was also Quaker. There are many other marriages in this Finney lineage with Quakers and United Brethren.

The wife of Michael Finney of Augusta County, Virginia, was Catherine Armstrong, daughter of Robert and Martha Alice (Calhoun) Armstrong, late of Pennsylvania and Quakers; undoubtedly acquainted with the Hadley's; both undoubtedly attended the same Monthly Meeting[11]. The Arnolds were also Quaker, making it likely that James Finney or at least his wife, Ann (Arnold) Finney, and Stephen Arnold, husband of Jane (Finney) Arnold, were also Quaker.

Joseph's association with the Quakers, particularly the Hadley's and Simon Hadley especially, suggests he grew up in the Forks of James area of Virginia where the Finney's were also married to Quakers.

Is our Joseph Finney related to the other Finney's found in Virginia circa 1740?

The Finney's found in Virginia at this time are many. In going through the records of Amelia, Augusta, Botetourt, Culpepper, Fauquier, Greenbrier, Orange, Rockbridge and Spotsylvania counties, 1700 to 1800, with attention given to names found in land records, wills and probate records, court records and minutes, road building crews, church records, etc, it is more than apparent that the majority of these Finney's were related. How is the question.

[11] The minutes of the Hopewell Monthly Meeting, 1735 to 1759, for this part of Virginia were lost in a fire at the house of the Clerk, William Jolliffe, Jr. (William Wade Hinshaw; *Encyclopedia of American Quaker Genealogy*; Volume VI, Virginia; Genealogical Publishing Co, Inc.; Baltimore, MD; 1993; page 359)

The families of Buchanan, Campbell, Lewis, Lynn, Patton and Preston were all related, spread out over the various counties listed.

Ann (Lynn) Dent, daughter of Dr William Lynn, founder of Fredericksburg, then in Spotsylvania County, married James Finnie of Culpepper County, while Dr Lynn's relative, James Patton, then of Augusta County, was a co-administrator along with Michael Finney, also of Augusta County, in the estate of James Finney of Orange County; James Finney of Orange County and James Finnie of Culpepper County having the same name but not being the same men.

A codicil to the will of Dr William Lynn who died in 1756 was witnessed by a William Finnie.

In Culpepper County, at the same time as the James Finnie who married Ann (Lynn) Dent, were James and Elizabeth (Turner) Finney. At the time of his will, dated 1764, James and Elizabeth Finney's children were listed as James, John, William (a minor), Mary and Elizabeth. James, the son of James and Elizabeth (Turner) Finney, married Elizabeth Gibbs, the daughter of John Gibbs. This John Gibbs was a friend of William Finnie of Amelia County, Virginia, swearing before the probate court of Amelia County that he was at the home of William Finnie shortly before his death and heard William Finnie acknowledge the document that was his last will and testament.

On May 20, 1735, James Finney and Zachary Lewis (related to both William Lynn and James Patton) purchased 400 acres in the "fork of the Robinson River," Culpepper County, Virginia. In 1755 a Zachary Lewis surveyed for Michael Finney 650 acres on the north side of the James River. While the two year dates are twenty years apart, it is possible that this is the same Zachary Lewis.

Holding land in the Northern Neck Proprietary with James Finney (which one is not known) was Thomas Chew who was the judge granting letters of administration to Michael Finney and James Patton of Augusta County in the estate of James Finney of Orange County who died on December 14, 1742 with Captain John McDowell.

In 1795 a Michael Finney appeared as a bondsman on the marriage bond of John Mason and Sarah Todd in Surry County, North Carolina. While Michael Finney of the Forks of James River, later of Laurens County, South Carolina, died intestate in 1787, making it impossible that this Michael Finney and he were one and the same, this could be his son. It is noted that one of the debtors of the estate of Michael Finney was a Patrick Todd. It is also possible this Michael Finney is an unnamed son of Joseph Finney.

In August 12, 1782, William McCulloch of Rockbridge County, Virginia, took bond on his "shortly intended" marriage to Mary Finney. On December 13, 1783, John Hughbanks Jr and Joseph Finney (Sr) were bondsman for the marriage of Joseph Finney (Jr) and Rachel Barkley in Orange County, North Carolina. On January 19, 1784, John Hughbanks Jr and William McCulloch were bondsman on a marriage bond for William Hudson (intended unnamed), also in Orange County, North Carolina. Is Mary Finney related to Joseph Finney?

All these Finney's seemed to know/associate with the same people. What relationship exists between them, however, remains a mystery.

Other Finney's in Virginia, circa 1740-1760, include:

1. John Finney in Fauquier County, Virginia; will probated November 27, 1760, Fauquier County; his wife Ann James, his daughter Hannah.
2. John Finney in Amelia County, Virginia; born circa 1745; died 1790; his wife Margaret, his daughter Ruth.
3. Thomas Finney in Halifax County, Virginia, 1737-8 when he witnessed the land transfers of one John Stuart.
4. John Finney who purchased 100 acres of land in Orange County, Virginia on March 16, 1735.

Who are the parents and siblings of Joseph Finney?

The search for the origins of Joseph Finney has largely been an exercise in learning history, customs, and researching those with whom Joseph was known to associate.

Joseph's association and movement with the Quakers led to finding him at Cane Creek, Chatham County, North Carolina, in 1772. Tracking Joseph's movements has been largely an exercise in tracking the Quakers with whom he associated, particularly the Hadley's who were at Forks of James, Virginia with James and Ann (Arnold) Finney, Michael and Catherine (Armstrong) Finney, and Stephen and Jane (Finney) Arnold. The Armstrong's were Quakers; the Arnolds quite likely Quaker.

We know from family records that Joseph's son, Joseph, was born in Wilmington, New Castle County, Delaware, in 1765. Those same family records list Joseph's wife as Ruth.

In 1756 Simon Hadley married Bridge Foote at the same church—Old Swedes Holy Trinity Church, Wilmington, New Castle County Delaware—where John Finney married Ruth Lloyd on January 28, 1758. It is probable that Joseph is the "John Finney" listed on the marriage register for reasons listed previously.

The known children[12] of Joseph and Ruth Finney were Ann, Joseph and Ruth. Joseph was obviously named for his father, Ruth for her mother. Was Ann named for Ann (Arnold) Finney, wife of James Finney who died in 1742 with Captain John McDowell at Balcony Falls, Virginia?

[12] It was not unusual, at this time in history, for children to receive their inheritance when they left home or married. In this case, these children might or might not be mentioned in the will.

It is my belief that Joseph Finney is related to or descended from the Finney's found at the Forks of the James area of Virginia; that he is either the son of James and Ann (Arnold) Finney, sibling of Michael Finney and Jane (Finney) Arnold or he is the younger brother of James, Michael and Jane Finney.

But that has not been proven.

As such, the hunt for the origins of Joseph Finney continues and the genealogy of this Finney family, as compiled by Charles Wesley Finney, begins with Joseph and Ruth Finney.

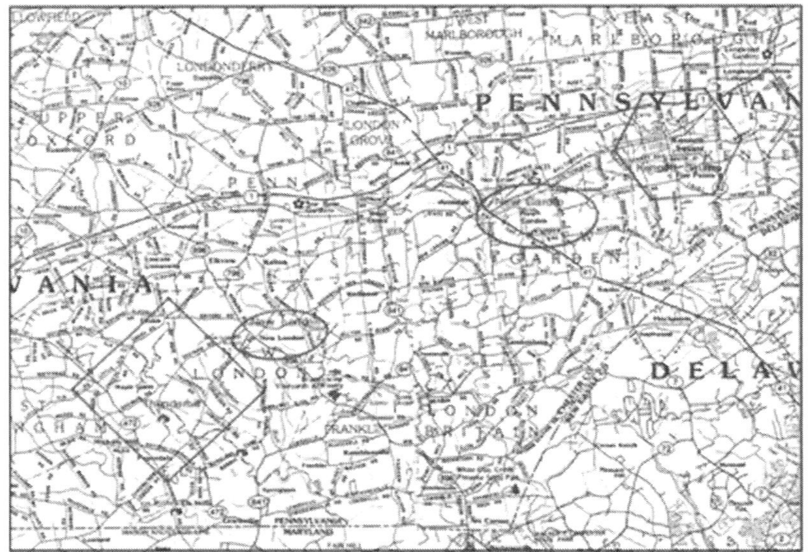

Map showing the position of Thunder Hill (Robert and Dorothea Finney); New Garden, New London, and Kennett Square Meetings (Quaker)

Source: Kegley's Virginia Frontier; Kegley; S W Virginia Historical Society; 1938

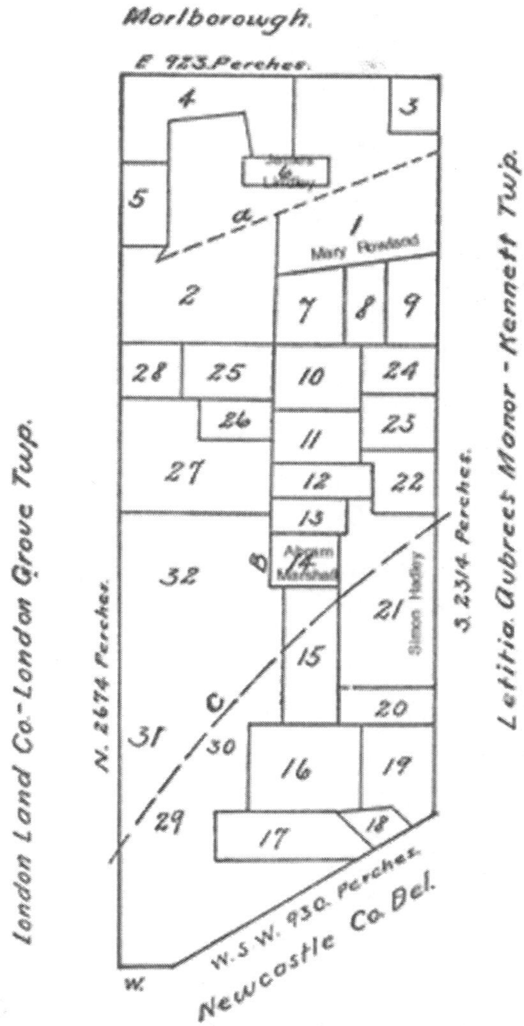

Quaker land holdings on Pennsylvania/Delaware Border

Source: Immigration of the Irish Quakers into Pennsylvania, 1682-1750; Myers; Genealogical Publishing Co; 1994.

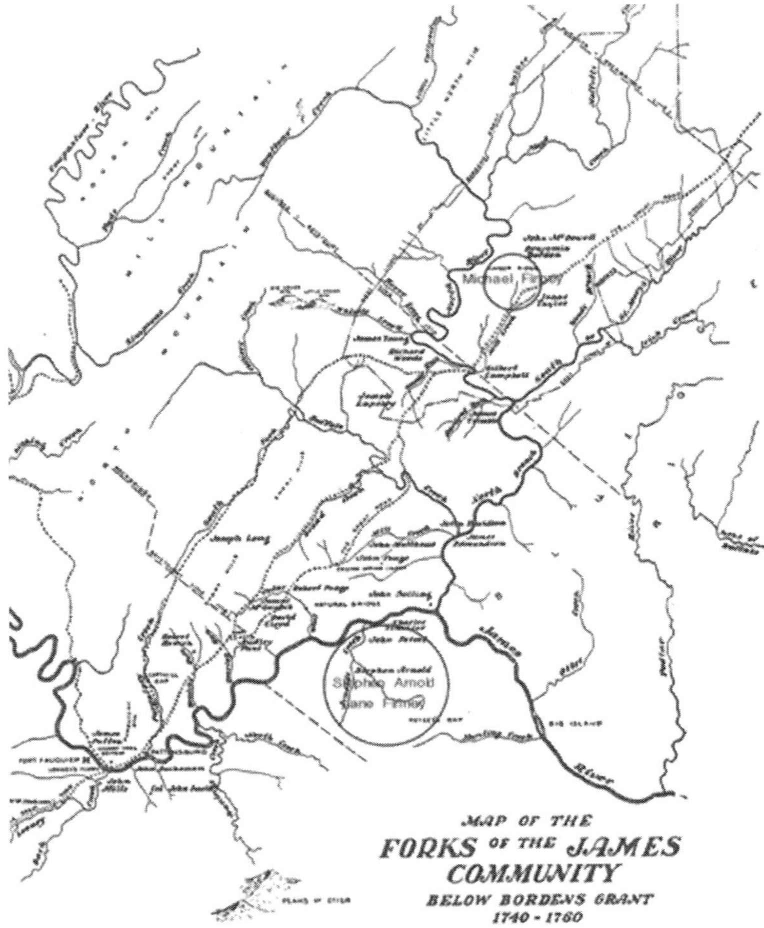

Forks of the James Community; 1740-1760

Source: Kegley's Virginia Frontier; Kegley; S W Virginia Historical Society; 1938

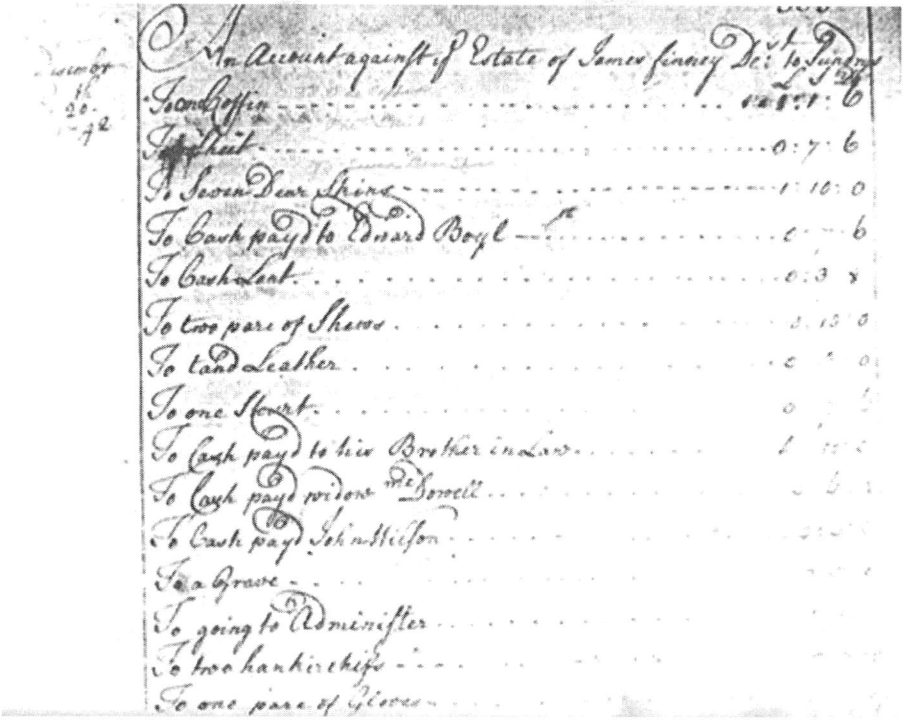
An Account against sd Estate of James finney Dcd to Sundrys
To one Coffin
To one Sheet ... 0:7:6
To Seven Dear Skins ... 1:10:0
To Cash payd to Edward Boyl
To Cash Lent ... 0:3:8
To two pare of Shews
To tand Leather
To one Shirt
To Cash payd to his Brother in Law
To Cash payd widow McDowell
To Cash payd John Wilsson
To a Grave
To going to Administer
To two hankirchefs
To one pare of Gloves

Will dated December 20, 1742

An Account against s^{d} Estate of James finney De^{cd} to Sundrys

To one Coffin

To one Sheet

To Seven Dear Skins

To Cash payd to Edward Boyl

To Cash Lent

To two pare of Shews

To tand Leather

To one Shirt

To Cash payd to his Brother in Law

To Cash payd widow McDowell

To Cash payd John Wilsson

To a Grave

To going to Administer

To two hankerchefs

To one pare of Gloves

Lynn Finney Stuter's lineage

1. Joseph (md Ruth)
    2. Joseph (md Rachel Barkley)
        1. Joseph (md Mary "Polly" Long)
            1. Robert (md Melinda Hunt)
                5. Zimri Dix (md Rachel Stewart)
                    2. Frank Abraham (md Mabel Lily George)
                        7. Charles E Finney (md Nadine Thomsen)
                            5. Lynn M Finney (md B C Stuter)

The leading number is the child order in the family. In other words, Robert is the first child of the first child while Zimri is the fifth child of the first child; I'm the fifth child of the seventh child.

Science

Gerald Finney administrates the Finney DNA Project. This section contains his project information and then the results of Harold Finney (descendant of Wesley and Mary Matilda Hinshaw Finney). It concludes with a surprise!

From Gerald Finney

I am also in the process about writing a book about Robert Finney's family. I have been researching numerous Finney lineages in America for about 16 or 17 years now and I have accumulated a lot of information on various Finney families. I have a brick wall Finney ancestor who lived in Ohio from 1831 to 1874 and I could not document back any further than 1860. A couple years ago I turned to DNA as a tool for my genealogy research and matched with two other Finney's who had documentation back to Robert Finney. I am now in the process of researching the lineage down from Robert to see where my ancestor Isaac Finney of Tuscarawas County Ohio fits in to the family while at the same time writing a book about Robert Finney and his descendents.

From Gerald Finney

The Finney DNA Project

The Finney DNA Project Needs Your Help!

Some DNA surname projects have thirty, forty, fifty, sixty members and more! The Finney Surname only has 18! We need your Help! We need to build a larger database of Finney DNA (male) to assist researchers and to help in the determination of the origin of the Finney surname.

Are you descended from Timothy Finney Botetourt Virginia 1668 - 1755?

The Finney DNA Project has obtained an Y-DNA sample from a descendent of Pleasant Rose Finney. Pleasant Rose Finney was born 1777 in Botetourt, Virginia and married Susanna Manspile. Pleasant Rose Finney also lived in Franklin County, Tennessee and Williamson County, Illinois. We have 37 marker Y-DNA results from one participant and seek another participant to confirm a lineage. Pleasant R Finney is thought to be a son of Timothy Finney of Virginia, born in Ireland. Results are available online.

We also have the DNA results from one of Pleasant R Finney's children's line as well. Pleasant R Finney's daughter Rachel is thought to have married a Native American Indian. All of Rachel Finney's children carried on the Finney surname. The results from this test revealed this family belonged to Haplogroup I1 and sample was taken from descendent of John B. Finney of Tennessee. We also have the results of another person descended from this Rachel Finney and their Haplogroup is R1bR1b2. This means if the paper documentation is correct for those providing the sample, that Rachel Finney had more than one spouse or mate. The results are available online now.

Are you descended from Robert Finney of Chester Co PA 1668 - 1755?

The Finney DNA Project currently has three participants who have participated in the Y-DNA testing process and results have confirmed DNA matches between these three individuals as a subgroup within the project. Rock solid documentation traces the participants to Robert Finney 1668-1775. The project is now seeking other descendents of Robert Finney for the purpose of ancestral origins research. For many years it has been debated on where this family originated.

Researchers have speculated the Finney family of Londonderry, Ireland, was descended through the direct male line of John, Baron Finis, blood relative of William the Conqueror in the place above mentioned in the year of 1066 and more over Hereditary Governor of the Forts of Dover in the county of Kent, and Custodian And Guardian of the Five Ports In the year of 1083. This information on the ancient Finney name is found on the "Fynney Brass" located in St. Edward the Confessor Cheddleton Church, Leek, Staffordshire, England.

No conclusive evidence of such a claim has ever been presented by a Finney researcher connecting the Irish or Scot lineages of Finney to the English Finney lineages. As I stated above these were the conclusions drawn by researchers in the hopes of explaining a single origin of the Finney surname. Researchers of the past such as Minnehaha Finney, Charles Wesley Finney, and Claire Duane Finney may have come to different conclusions had DNA research been available to them in their lifetime.

DNA results provided by various Finney participants indicates there are no distant or ancestral connections between the Finney's of England and the Finney's of Ireland and Scotland. The Finney DNA project has three participants who have documentation on their lineages back to Jeffery Finney 1542 England. The branch of this family who came to America is known as the "Mother Finney" lineage which was very well documented by Howard Finney.

Comparison of the DNA results between the English Finney lineage and the lineage of Robert Finney shows a 0.00% chance of a common ancestor in the last 24 generations. If we use 25 years as an average for generations would mean there is no match between the two Finney lineages in the last 600 years. If we take the year 2011 and subtract 600 years we end up with the year 1411. We now have scientific data showing no connections between the two lineages. So we are now faced with new questions. Where did Robert Finney 1668-1775 come from? Historic documents (will and church records) tell us that his father was another Robert Finney (ca. 1630-1692) who owned a ship and a warehouse in Londonderry. The small existing sample of DNA evidence hints that he was one of the Scots who moved to Londonderry in the early to mid 1600s. Is that so? And if so, from where? We need a larger DNA database of descendents of Robert Finney as well as historical documentation to reach this goal.

We need your help to answer this question. Please consider purchasing a 37 marker Y-DNA test for male Finney descendents in your lineage from Family Tree DNA and participate in the Finney DNA Project. There is a book written in 1996 on this family called "Finney 1720" and it is based on the research of Minnehaha Finney and Charles Wesley Finney. Contributions were made to the book by Fred Austin Finney, Claire Duane Finney, and Maurine Struthers. Fred Austin Finney is one of the participants in the project and as he stated in an email to me "Sure enjoyed the increase in family information in 2010 and am hoping 2011 brings even more". Fred provided me with an Adobe PDF format digital copy of the book "Finney 1720" and I will provide a copy to every participant who purchases a kit and matches with the Robert Finney 1668-1775 sub-group.

Are you descended from Jeffrey Finney England 1500's or Mother Finney's lineage of Plymouth MA?

We have four participants who are descended from this line of Finney's in England and America. This is one of the oldest lines of Finney's in America arriving in the 1600's. We would like to build a greater database of Finney's or Phinney's who are part of this lineage.

Other Finney DNA Results Available

The Finney DNA project also has participants who have not matched enough Y-DNA markers with other participants to create a lineage. These folks are patiently waiting for other Finney's from their lineage to purchase a test kit.

- William Finney Born 1696 Glasgow Scotland
- Fielding Finney Born 1800 in Indiana
- Andrew J. Finney Born 1820 Illinois
- Louis C. H. Finney Born 1822 Virginia
- Nigel Finney

Finney DNA Most Wanted List

The Finney DNA project would like to include the DNA from the following lineages to our Finney DNA Database:

- **Richard Finney** who arrived in Accomack County Virginia in the 1600's. Descendents moved into Amelia and Henry Counties in Virginia
- **Capt James Finney** of Botetourt County Virginia. Scot Irish line of Finney's who settled in Virginia.
- **Capt. Samuel Finney** who arrived in Pennsylvania with William Penn in the 1700's
- **Fielding Best Finney** – Famous Surgeon in England.
- **Col William Finney** of Talbot County Maryland
- **Rev. Thomas Finney** arrived in Virginia around 1660
- **Rev Alexander Finney** arrived in York Co. Virginia in 1660.
- **Michael Finney** arrived in PA in 1734
- **Samuel Greenway Finney** born in England in 1843. Descendents in Tennessee and Louisiana
- **Greenville Penn Finney** born in 1820 in Illinois
- **Alexander Finney** born in Cork Ireland in 1775. Died in Alabama.

Administrators in the DNA projects make no profit and all proceeds goes to and money processing done by Family Tree DNA. Please visit:

http://www.familytreedna.com/public/Finney/default.aspx

Gerald Finney, Finney DNA Project Administrator

From Gerald Finney to Bonnie and Harold Finney

Greetings Bonnie & Harold Finney,

Please allow me to introduce myself. My name is Gerald Leland Finney and I have been researching various Finney lineages found in America for over sixteen years. After many years of research I could not find any documentation listing the names of the parents of my Civil War ancestor Isaac B. Finney and two years ago I turned to DNA to solve the mystery of my Finney family. I am now the administrator of the Finney DNA Project hosted by familytreedna.com.(FTDNA) I am also assisted by Billy Ray Watkins who is descended from a lineage of Finney's from Virginia. I do not make any profit from DNA kits sold and all of my time working the project is donated and I receive no compensation from FTDNA.

I decided to give DNA a try and I purchased a test kit, submitted my sample, and in a few weeks found my DNA matched with two other Finney participants.

Both gentlemen I matched with had solid documentation proving they were both descended from a Robert Finney who arrived in America from Ireland in 1720. One of them is descended through the son William Finney and the other is descended from the son John French Finney. I am currently looking for documentation on how my ancestor fits into this family. DNA has allowed me to narrow the focus of my research, as we all know, the DNA does not lie.

The situation which has presented itself for the descendents of Joseph Finney is a little different It came to my attention last week a researcher has claimed the research done by Finney researchers of the past such as Minnehaha Finney, Maurine Struthers, Charles Wesley Finney, and the Rosemary Finney from your lineage to be incorrect. I do not agree with this researcher but she has produced a will from 1799 in North Carolina which contradicts the research of those previously mentioned. Your Finney DNA will hold the answer to this question. I would like to thank you for taking agreeing to the DNA test to assist with this issue.

I am currently writing a book on Robert Finney's family which will be a comprehensive work of my research as well as the Finney researchers who came before me. I have been researching not just the Finney family but the Scot Irish of North Ireland, also known as the Ulster Scots, as well as the Scot Irish of the Appalachians. I want to include as much information about our Scot Irish history and culture as possible as much has been forgotten by many in this family. I id not even know this was my culture until I did the DNA test! I think it is very important family history is preserved and passed down for future generations. It is of extreme importance we pass on the correct information to our children and grandchildren.

When the kit arrives, it will include instructions on how to obtain the sample. Please follow the instructions carefully to insure a good sample is obtained and the sample must be obtained from a male Finney. When the kit is mailed to FTDNA When the kit is received, FTDNA will provide with a personal web site which will display your results when the come back from the lab. The DNA processing for FTDNA is done by University of Arizona so you can feel safe your DNA is in a trusted and controlled environment. I will also include a link to the Finney project as well as my personal web page.

It was my pleasure to make your acquaintance and I thank you for all of your efforts as they are greatly appreciated. If you have any questions, please do not hesitate to contact me.

Gerald Finney

www.geraldfinney.com

http://www.familytreedna.com/public/Finney/default.aspx

Harold Finney – great grandson of Wesley Finney submits his DNA to the Finney DNA Project – surprising results!

In July 2011, Gerald Finney wrote this about Harold Finney's results and David Finney's interest in participating in the Finney DNA Project.

***

Greetings to All,

I am not sure where to begin because there is much to discuss. I think it would be best to begin by advising DNA does not always give us the answer we want in our genealogical research and we cannot deny the results due to the truth of DNA. **DNA is based on scientific fact and the results cannot be disputed**. DNA does not lie. YDNA is passed down from father to son generation after generation and YDNA is the DNA we test for in genealogy to determine connections between lineages.

Harold Finney's 37 marker YDNA test did not provide enough marker matches with the known descendents of Robert Finney of Chester County PA for Harold Finney to be considered a descendent of Robert Finney. Here are the calculations for the comparison of Harold's YDNA and my YDNA. Below those calculations I will provide the calculations for the other two known descendents of Robert Finney, who I do match with, compared with Harold's DNA:

Gerald Finney:

8 generations is 0.00%.

...12 generations is 0.04%.

...16 generations is 0.46%.

...20 generations is 2.30%.

...24 generations is 7.13%.

Match 1of known Robert Finney descendent

...8 generations is 0.01%.

...12 generations is 0.15%.

...16 generations is 1.27%.

...20 generations is 5.14%.

...24 generations is 13.42%.

Match 2 of known Robert Finney descendent

8 generations is 0.00%.

...12 generations is 0.04%.

...16 generations is 0.41%.

...20 generations is 2.09%.

...24 generations is 6.57%.

As you can see in the calculations there is no chance of a solid connection in the last 24 generations between Harold and the descendents of Robert Finney. Last night another known documented descendent of Robert Finney joined the Finney DNA Project and in a few weeks his YDNA will be available for comparison with Harold's. I will now show how I match with the other two known descendents of Robert Finney who participate in the project. The same ones used to compare with Harold's DNA above, to show the differences in our results.

Match 1

...8 generations is 20.62%.

...12 generations is 50.71%.

...16 generations is 74.69%.

...20 generations is 88.66%.

...24 generations is 95.40%

Match 2

8 generations is 56.43%.

...12 generations is 85.10%.

...16 generations is 95.54%.

...20 generations is 98.78%.

...24 generations is 99.68%.

You can see the differences to the numbers. The three known descendents of Robert Finney all have strong matches. Harold did have a very strong match with someone with the surname of Coleman.

Here are the compared results for **Harold Finney and Kenneth Myer Coleman**.

...8 generations is 57.01%.

...12 generations is 85.52%.

...16 generations is 95.74%.

...20 generations is 98.85%.

...24 generations is 99.71%.

So what did we learn with Harold's YDNA test?

We learned **Harold's lineage is not from Robert Finney of Chester County, PA**. The only way Harold's Finney's could still be related to Robert would be if there was an adoption in the family or an affair no one in the family was aware of. I do not mean to offend anyone in anyway and these are possibilities which could occur and would explain a DNA mismatch. We know Harold was not adopted and the family is well documented by Rosamary High Finney (her 1992 book *"History of Finney Family: 1962 – 1990"*) and Cousette Copeland in this book, and there were no affairs, so I am certain Harold carries the YDNA of his Finney ancestor Joseph Finney.

We learned there was a Finney in the line who had a child with Lucy Coleman and someone from Harold Finney's lineage was living in Virginia in 1871.

The Controversy Continues!

This does not mean Lynn Finney Stutter is correct with all of her assumptions but based on the documentation of Harold's lineage and we know Harold was not adopted so I am of the opinion Harold's Finney lineage is a separate and distinct Irish Finney lineage. On Harold's ancestral origins page, his matches with other surnames indicates his family was in Ireland at one time and has connections to the clans of the Lowlands of Scotland. **I am of the opinion this Finney lineage could be descended from the James Finney who lived in Virginia on the James River**.

Testing of another documented relative of Harold's is very highly recommended and Harold's cousin David Finney's desire to be tested could not have come at a better time. I think testing of another descendent if critical to confirming what I explained above. I do not make any profit from those who join the project. I donate my time for free administrating the project and assisting participants with their research.

Why are we not related to Robert Finney?

I think Lynn was correct when she stated Charles Wesley Finney changed his mind late in his research and determined he was not of Robert's lineage but was indeed descended from James Finney of Virginia. This information was never shared with Minnehaha Finney who passed on Charles earlier research to other Finney researchers and this has been taken as gospel over the years as Minnehaha's research has proven to be quite accurate.

I believe the error was made with the Joseph Finney of North Carolina who was thought to be a son of John/Joseph Finney and Ruth Lloyd. I believe it was a John Finney who married Ruth Lloyd but their children did not move to North Carolina and they did not have a son named Joseph. I believe the Joseph and Joshua Finney who were brothers were not descended from Robert Finney as previously thought but were in fact sons of a Joseph Finney, and I have read his will which states his two sons' names (Joseph and Joshua) and this Joseph Finney is suggested to be the son of a James Finney of Virginia. Further research of documentation and DNA testing is highly suggested.

I am sorry if the information DNA has provided is not what you wanted to learn but as I stated earlier we cannot dispute the results and more testing is needed to confirm a separate Finney lineage exists. If anyone has any questions please do not hesitate to contact me. Comments, critiques and criticisms are always welcomed.

Gerald L. Finney, Finney DNA Project

Gerald Finney's lineage

My Finney family research is mostly in Ohio but one of my great great uncles moved to Indiana in the 1880's and got married twice. Once in Martin and once in Posey county. His name was Ozias Finney and he married a Hester Mitchell the first time and Beatrice Murphy the second time. I did find it interesting that Beatrice Murphy's mothers maiden name was Finney as well.

Revelation

Harold Finney has documented proof that he is a descendant of Joseph Finney and Mary Polly Long. Harold participated in the Finney DNA Project. The results were unexpected, startling, and definitive proof that Lynn Finney Stuter's claims that this branch of the Finney family does NOT descend from Robert Finney.

From Cousette Copeland

What have we learned here? Don't rely what is in published genealogies! Don't always rely on everything that is on Ancestry.com or other genealogy web sites! Unless you check every single fact by going to the source, you cannot guarantee what is in your genealogy research. Even then, a lot of "fact" comes from oral histories, published books, and from those who have had information handed to them second- and third-hand.

Understand that there are still mysteries and truths to be uncovered in modern genealogical research. The old-fashioned way, that is checking sources and doing research, can uncover mysteries that previous researchers and genealogy authors did not.

Understand that modern methods, such as contacting researchers via the internet and the message boards, can lead to debates that will result in new leads and research.

Understand that the ultimate proof is in blood – in DNA!

Thank you to both Lynn Finney Stuter and Gerald L. Finney for their approaches and their generosity in sharing research and science, as well as a special thank you to Harold E. Finney who submitted his DNA – all of which has resulted in the first ever published facts about the descendants of John and Rachel Barkley/Barclay Finney – we are NOT descended from Robert Finney. That makes us not less a Finney, just a different branch of the Finneys!

Last Words

Is this the "last word" on the origins of the Joseph Finney family? Let's restate Lynn Finney Stuter's conclusion:

"It is my belief that Joseph Finney is related to or descended from the Finney's found at the Forks of the James area of Virginia; that he is either the son of James and Ann (Arnold) Finney, sibling of Michael Finney and Jane (Finney) Arnold or he is the younger brother of James, Michael and Jane Finney.

But that has not been proven."

As such, the hunt for the origins of Joseph Finney continues and the genealogy of this Finney family, as compiled by Charles Wesley Finney, begins with Joseph and Ruth Finney."

Let's also restate Gerald L. Finney's conclusion:

"I am of the opinion this Finney lineage could be descended from the James Finney who lived in Virginia on the James River."

My own conclusion is that there is always something new and exciting to discover while researching our genealogy!

ELEVENTH HOUR REVELATION!

Just when I thought that there was nothing left to discover, Gerald Finney sent a surprising email. Harold Finney gave him permission to share additional DNA details. Here are the astonishing details!

HAROLD FINNEY'S DNA IS A NIALL OF THE NINE HOSTAGES MATCH!

A recent study was conducted at Trinity College Dublin, Ireland, which found that a striking % of men in Ireland (and quite a few in Scotland) share the same Y chromosome, suggesting that the 5th-century warlord known as "Niall of the Nine Hostages" may be the ancestor of one in 12 Irishmen. Niall established a dynasty of powerful chieftains that dominated the island for six centuries.

Harold Finney's Y chromosome matches this profile!

In the study scientists found an area in northwest Ireland where they claim 21.5% carry Niall's genetic fingerprint, says Brian McEvoy, one of the team at Trinity. The same area of Ireland has previously been the subject of Anthropological writings…and has shown a strikingly high % of men from Haplogroup R1b (98%) versus 90% in S.E. Ireland. According to McVoy this area was the main powerbase of the Ui Neills, which literally translated means "descendants of Niall".

McEvoy says the Y chromosome appeared to trace back to one person. Following the genealogists trail, McVoy comments: “There are certain surnames that seem to have come from Ui Neill. We studied if there was any association between those surnames and the genetic profile. It is his (Niall’s) family.”

Of note to Family Tree DNA customers, this signature is found in .6 of 1% of the entire Family Tree DNA database. It is characterized by the following Markers when our 12 marker test is applied:

393	390	19	391	385a	385b	426	388	439	389-1	392	389-2
13	25	14	11	11	13	12	12	12	13	14	29

A more detailed signature appears when we apply the Y-DNA 25 marker test and compare to the apparent signature of the Ui Neills. A listing of those values appears in the table below.

393	390	19	391	385a	385b	426	388	439	389-1	392	389-2	458	459a	459b	455	454	447	437	448	449	464a	464b	464c	464d
13	25	14	11	11	13	12	12	12	13	14	29	17	9	10	11	11	25	15	18	30	15	16	16	17

While the signature is typical for R1b European males in general it’s characterized by an 11,13 at DYS 385a/b and a 14 at DYS 392. Within our second panel of markers the most distinctive results from this apparent Modal is the 15,16,16,17 at DYS 464.

McVoy states: “As in other polygynous societies, the siring of offspring was related to power and prestige.” The study mentions that just one of the O’Neill dynasty chieftains who died in 1423 had 18 sons with nearly a dozen women and claimed 59 grandsons.

Niall of the Nine Hostages received his name from the taking of hostages as a strategy for playing mental havoc upon his opponent chieftains. He is known in folklore as a raider of the British and French coasts. **Supposedly slain in the English Channel or in Scotland, his descendants were the most powerful rulers of Ireland until the 11th century.**

Modern surnames tracing their ancestry to Niall include (O’)Neill, (O’)Gallagher, (O’)Boyle, (O’)Doherty, O’Donnell, Connor, Cannon, Bradley, O’Reilly, Flynn, (Mc)Kee, Campbell, Devlin, Donnelly, Egan, Gormley, Hynes, McCaul, McGovern, McLoughlin, McManus, McMenamin, Molloy, O’Kane, O’Rourke and Quinn. **And now – Finney!**

Journal reference: American Journal of Human Genetics (February issue)

A more complete signature of Ui Naill can be found at **www.ysearch.org**

37 Marker - Genetic Distance - 1 3 Match(es)

Mason

Fanning

Fanning (Y67) (Family Finder)

37 Marker - Genetic Distance - 2 19 Match(es)

Fanning

Burris (Family Finder)

Robertson

Fannin

Mays (Y67)

Fanning

Fannin (Y67)

Fannin (Y67)

Fanning

Fanning

Fannon (Y67)

Fannon Sr. (Y67)

Turner

Fannin (Y67)

Fanning (Y67)

Prosser III (Y67)

Fannon (Y67)

Wallace (Y67) (Family Finder)

Bingham

37 Marker - Genetic Distance - 3 21 Match(es)

Burris **

Mullican

O'Neal

Fannon (Y67)

King(Y67)

Williams

Coleman (Y67)

Gilmore(Y67)

McDonald (Y67)

Fannin (Y67)

Hart (Y67)

Conwell (Y67)

Meason

Fanning (Y67)

Byrne

O' Byrne (Y67)

Ward

Manning

Gibbs

O'Shaughnessy (Y111)

McGovern

37 Marker - Genetic Distance - 4 63 Match(es)

Murphy
(Family Finder)

Ferguson
(Y111)

Cunningham
(Y67)

Carroll (Y111)

Hatley (Y67)

Gallagher

McGovern

Pierce (Y67)

Bissett

Sean Byrne

Virgin

Schaber (Y67)

Fanning

King

Fanning

Allison (Y67)

Patterson (Y67)

Macpherson (Y67)

Bartley (Y67)

Donnelly

McKenzie (Y67)

Ford (Y67)

Gray (Y67) (Family Finder)

Brooks (Y67)

Riley

	Y-DNA12	Y-DNA25	Y-DNA37	Y-DNA67	Y-DNA111	Interpretation
Very Tightly Related	N/A	N/A	0	0	0	Your exact match means your relatedness is extremely close. Few people achieve this close level of a match. All confidence levels are well within the time frame that surnames were adopted in Western Europe.
Tightly Related	N/A	N/A	1	1-2	1-2	Few people achieve this close level of a match. All confidence levels are well within the time frame that surnames were adopted in Western Europe.
Related	0	0-1	2-3	3-4	3-5	Your degree of matching is within the range of most well-established surname

						lineages in Western Europe. If you have tested with the Y-DNA12 or Y-DNA25 test, you should consider upgrading to additional STR markers. Doing so will improve your time to common ancestor calculations.
Probably Related	1	2	4	5 - 6	6 - 7	Without additional evidence, it is unlikely that you share a common ancestor in recent genealogical times (1 to 6 generations). You may have a connection in more distant genealogical times (less than 15 generations). If you have traditional genealogy records that indicate a relationship, then by testing additional individuals you will either prove or disprove the connection.
Only Possibly Related	2	3	5	7	8 - 10	It is unlikely that you share a common ancestor in genealogical times (1 to 15 generations). Should you have traditional genealogy records that indicate a relationship, then by testing additional individuals you will either prove or disprove the connection. A careful review of your genealogical records is also recommended.
Not Related	3	4	6	> 7	> 10	You are not related on your Y-chromosome lineage within recent or distant genealogical times (1 to 15 generations).

"The "Niall" chromosome has also been found in 16.7% of men in western and central Scotland and has turned up in multiple North American population samples, including 2% of European-American New Yorkers. "Given historically high rates of Irish emigration to North America and other parts of the world, it seems likely that the number of descendants worldwide runs to perhaps two to three million males," said the study."[13]

A SECOND DNA TEST CONFIRMS THE FIRST TEST

Joseph Finney and Rachel Barkley of North Carolina had two sons named Joseph and Joshua. It has long been recorded that this family was descended from a Lazarus Finney, son of Robert Finney who lived in Chester County, Pennsylvania. Joseph Finney married Mary Polly Long and Joshua Finney married Juriah Collins.

A descendent from Joseph's lineage and a descendent from Joshua's lineage both joined the Finney DNA Project hosted by Family Tree DNA and purchased 37 marker DNA tests. The full results from Joseph's lineage have been returned from the lab and the first 12 markers of Joshua's lineage have been returned.

The first 12 markers from Joshua's lineage are a perfect 12/12 match with the descendent of Joseph's lineage. I am certain the remaining 25 markers will show a strong match. I will post a follow up message when all of the results are returned.

I do feel we have enough information to confirm the claims made by Lynn Finney Stutter. Previously, I was defending the published materials on this family. However, DNA has proved that all of the written and published documentation on this family is discrepant and requires correction.

There was no DNA match between the descendents of Joseph Finney and Rachel Barkley and the known documented descendents of Robert Finney of Chester County, PA. DNA does not lie and removes all human assumptions as documents can be interpreted incorrectly.

If you have the book "Finney 1720" pages 48-67 are no longer applicable to the lineage of the Finney's of Chester County, Pennsylvania. 45 pages of the Robert Finney tree found in the book "Finney 1720" have been pruned by DNA.

Are you certain of your Finney lineage? I think this situation proves YDNA testing is a great tool for genealogy and should not be ignored.

IN CONCLUSION

This branch of the Finney family is not descended from Robert Finney, but instead this branch of the Finney family is descended from the greatest Kings of Ireland!

[13] http://floridairishheritagecenter.wordpress.com/

Who is Niall of the Nine Hostages?

Up to three million men around the world could be descended from a prolific medieval Irish king, according to a new genetic study.

It suggests that the 5th-century warlord known as "Niall of the Nine Hostages" may be the ancestor of about one in 12 Irishmen, say researchers at Trinity College Dublin, Ireland. Niall established a dynasty of powerful chieftains that dominated the island for six centuries.

Niall of the Nine Hostages, who became high king of Ireland, got his name from using the taking of hostages (including St. Patrick) as a strategy for subjugating his opponent chieftains. He is known in folklore as a raider of the British and French coasts. Supposedly slain in the English Channel or in Scotland, his descendants were the most powerful rulers of Ireland until the 11th century.[1]

---

[1] http://www.newscientist.com/article/dn8600-medieval-irish-warlord-boasts-three-million-descendants.html

Part Three

FINNEY REUNIONS AND GATHERINGS

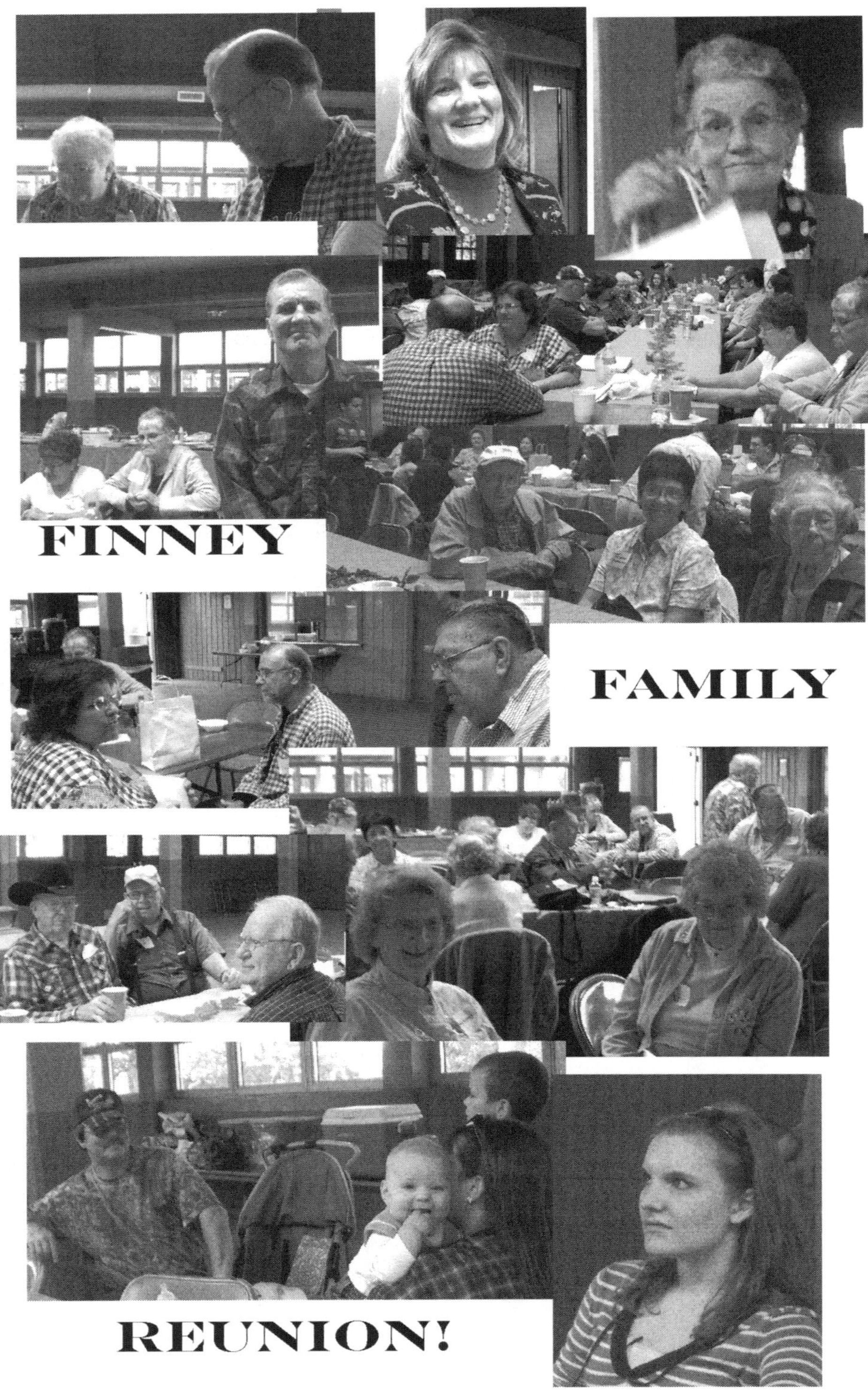
FINNEY
FAMILY
REUNION!

Finney Reunions and Gatherings

When Wesley and Mary Matilda (Hinshaw) Finney came to Kansas in 1882, they had Finney relations who had been in Kansas since 1870. The first Finney reunions were photographed, showing a large gathering of the families. Once a year, they could see each other, exchange stories, and reinforce their family bonds.

Finney reunion about 1900

Seated row, seated man on left with pointed beard is probably Abner Copeland (several others are Finneys); perhaps the man next to him is Wesley Finney;

The men with the black hats (back row) are Rayls.

Finney reunion 1920

Finney reunion 1920 –Left side enlargement

Finney reunion 1920 –Middle enlargement

Samantha Finney Copeland is lady seated in the middle, with both hands on her pocketbook.

The middle (slightly right) lady is Mary Mater Phillips, a daughter of Elizabeth Finney Mater. So she would have been Wesley Finney's niece.

Finney reunion 1920 –Right side enlargement

Cousette holding a 1920 Finney reunion photo – a gift from Melvin Koons

Finney reunion about 1929

Close-up Samantha seated, right (1909);

Close-up showing Clarissa standing on left, Wilburn Koons seated in lower middle, and Samantha seated in lower right (1929)

Finney reunion 1929 –Left side enlargement; bottom row – left to right, 2nd man is Daniel Ezra Copeland, little boy is Forest Dale Williams with mother Mary Inez (Hendrickson) Williams (granddaughter of Mary Catherine Finney and William Allen)

Finney reunion 1929 –Middle enlargement; bottom row, middle, Claude Wilburn Koons and Samantha Jane (Finney) Copeland; top row, first woman on the left is Clarissa Copeland

Finney reunion 1929 –Right side enlargement; bottom row, left to right are John Wesley and Nannie Finney.

At some point in the 1930s, the Finney clan no longer gathered. In 1937, the eldest Finney "child" of Wesley and Mary Matilda Finney – Samantha Jane (Finney) Copeland died. In the late 1930s, the descendants of John Wesley Finney began their own Reunions.

1937 or 1938

John Wesley Finney descendants get together1937 or 1938 with 1936 Chevy

Finney Reunion 1996

The Caney Chronicle, Wednesday, Jan. 31, 1996-Page

Finney family holds reunion

The deceased Clarence and Myrtle Finney, Niotaze, were parents of 13 children, nine boys and four girls. Eight of the sons served in the military from World War II to Desert Storm, and the family has 44 grandchildren.

For the first time in 31 years, all 13 children held a family reunion which began at the Johnny Finney farm, Niotaze, on Jan. 11. On Jan. 14, a reunion dinner was held at the Sedan 4-H Building with 80 in attendance.

Brothers, sisters, children, grandchildren and friends of the family attending were:

Johnny and Pearl Finney, daughter Donna Loffer, all of Collinsville, Okla., daughter, Debra and husband, Larry Mason and children, Paula, Jonathan and Valerie, Tyro; Alta Kirchner and son, Harry, Sedan; Mary Dufoe and sons, Tommy Dufoe, Havana, Chuck Dufoe, Caney, daughter, Joyce Eytcheson and husband Harold with daughter and son-in-law Teresa and Robert Smart, Independence; Janice and Mike Murphy and daughters Sarah and Rebekah, Elk City; Martha, Ron and Ronnil Hall, Wichita; Juanita and Walt Simpson, two sons and one grandson, all of Niotaze; Gene Finney, Melba, Idaho; Hilta and Kenneth Gorby, Nowata, Okla., sons Kenny Gorby, Collinsville, Okla., Kevin Gorby, Buckner, Mo., daughter Glenda Most and son Johnathan, Claremore, Okla.

Also Wanda and Carl Riley and son Floyd, Sedan; Kyle and Joyce Finney, Arvada, Colo.; Harold and Bonnie Finney, Coffeyville, daughter Jeanie and husband Ben and three children, Daniel, Sierra and Isaak, Kansas City, Mo.; Gary Finney, Fort Smith, Ark.; Melvin and Mary Finney, Independence; David and Janice Finney, son Scott and daughter Ronda with husband Ryan Bowser and sons Wesley and Daniel, all of Niotaze; Roy and Carol Finney, Manhattan, and son Shawn with wife Debbie and daughter Kaylynn, daughter Karen with husband Brian Fish and son Daniel, all o Lenapah, Okla.; Lyle and Suzie Finne College Place, Wash.

Friends of the family included:

Paul Fuller, Collinsville, Okla.; Paul and Iris Cox, Copan, Okla.; Paul Mason's friend, Dale Brody, Caney; Elee Thorn and two children, Sedan; Icky an Eileen Farner, Niotaze; and Winon Farner of Christopher Manor, Caney.

Finney Reunion – January 14, 1996

***NOTE**: There were a lot of photos from Finney events/reunions. I chose to include group shots and omitted the ones where people were eating and drinking.*

Back row, left to right: Wanda Faye Riley, Kyle B, Harold, Gary, Melvin, David, Roy, Lyle Eugene Finney; Front row, l to r: Johnny Finney, Alta Kirchner, Mary Dufoe, Gene Finney, Hilta Gorby

Brothers only - Back row, left to right: Gary, Melvin, David, Roy, Lyle Eugene; Front row, l to r: Johnny, Gene, Kyle, Harold Finney

Sisters only - left to right: Alta, Mary, Hilta, Faye Finney

Johnny Finney's family

Mary Finney Dufoe McMurty's family

Roy Finney family and Carol

Hilta and Kenneth Gorby family

Joyce and Kyle Finney

Melvin and Mary Finney

David and Janice Finney and family (David and Janice Finney family - Ronda, Ryan, Wesley, Daniel)

Ben and Jeannie Ortiz with Harold and Bonnie Finney, and the Ortiz children – Isaak, Sierre, and Daniel

Finney Reunion 1998

Mike, Angela, and Stephen Finney 1997

Finney Reunion 1999

Finney reunion meets for 70th annual reunion

The annual Finney reunion was held at the concession house in Riverside Park at Independence, Ks. This was the 70th reunion and the first one was held in September 1928.

The distinction of being the oldest present went to Vivia J. Finney of Manhattan and the youngest was Stephen Finney of So. Coffeyville, Ok. Harold R. Kirchner of Nebraska traveled the farthest. Mr. and Mrs. Larry Mason of Tyro had the largest family present.

The officers for 1999 are Donna Loffer, president; Harold Finney, vice president and Nancy Buster, secretary and treasurer.

A covered dish dinner, games and a day of visiting was enjoyed by all.

There were 53 family members and friends attending this year.

Attending were: Melvin and Mary Finney and Harold and Joyce Eytcheson, Independence; Steve Bowman, Caney; Wydene Finney, Buddy Finney, Erin Cotfelter and Larry, Debra, Jon, Paula and Valerie Mason, Tyro; Shawn Bowman, Pittsburg; Jeffery, Karon and Braden Finney, Olathe; Harold and Bonnie Finney, Coffeyville; Kyle, Joyce and Judith Finney, Niotaze; Reggin and Dakota Kastler, Sabrena Massey and Mike, Angela and Stephen Finney, So. Coffeyville.

Kenneth and Hilta Gorby, Nowata; Glenda and Jonathan Most and Robert Wellert, Claremore, Ok; Paul and Alta Fuller, Donna Loffer, Brent Patterson, Anita Loffer, Michelle Mayer, Shawn Getz and Johnny and Pearl Finney, Collinsville, Ok.

Donald Morgan, Tulsa; Verne Gilliland, Skiatook; Dale and Barbara Williams, Bartlesville, Orval De Lozier, Wann; Nancy Buster, Dewey and Harold R. Kirchner, Nebraska.

The 1999 Finney reunion will be held on Sunday, Sept. 5 at the concession house at Riverside Park in Independence.

70th Reunion – Sept. 5, 1999

Finney Get-together taken in Sedan, KS. Gene was home for a visit so everyone was contacted and got together at the 4-H building in Sedan, KS. 1999

Top row - Gene, Roy, Harold, Kyle, David, Gary, Melvin; Bottom row - Hilta (Finney) Gorby, Mary (Finney, Dufoe) McMurtry, Johnny Finney, Alta (Finney, Kirchner) Fuller, Faye (Finney) Riley

Johnny Finney's family 1999

Mary McMurtry's family 1999

Hilta and Kenneth Gorby's family 1999

David Finney's family 1999

Finney Reunion 2000

Finney "kids" 1999 – top row, left to right: Roy, Harold, Gary, Melvin, Kyle; Bottom row: Alta, Hilta, Mary, Faye, and Johnny Finney

Finney Reunion 2009

Bonnie Finney and I had been e-mail pals for some time. She invited my sister Fran and I to attend. In 2009, we went out and met the Finneys!

Harold and Bonnie Finney at the Finney family reunion 2009

Yes, we Copelands are Finney descendants. Our great grandmother (Fran and mine) and grandmother (the other Copelands) was Samantha Jane (Finney) Copeland – Wesley and Mary Matilda (Hinshaw) Finney's eldest child. With the exception of Ralph and Arlene, the other Copelands hadn't attended a Finney reunion since before WWII. For Fran and Cousette, it was our first reunion!

Left to right – Ralph and Arlene Copeland, Maxine (Kirchner) Copeland, Virginia (Copeland) Noble, Francis (Copeland) Gardner, Cousette Copeland, and George Copeland – 2009

Part Four

THE LITTLE CHURCH AT NIOTAZE

Church of the United Brethren in Christ to the United Methodist Church

The Church of the United Brethren in Christ is an evangelical Christian denomination based in Huntington, Indiana. It is a Protestant denomination of Episcopal structure, Armenian theology, with roots in the Mennonite and German Reformed communities of 18th century Pennsylvania, as well as close ties to Methodism. It was organized in 1800 by Martin Boehm and Philip William Otterbein and is the first American denomination that was not transplanted from Europe.

Though not organized until 1800, the roots of the church reach back to 1767. In May of that year, a *Great Meeting* (part of the interdenominational revival movement known as the "Great Awakening") was held at a barn belonging to Isaac Long in Lancaster, Pennsylvania. Martin Boehm (1725–1812), a Mennonite preacher, spoke of his becoming a Christian through crying out to God while plowing in the field. Philip William Otterbein (1726–1813), a Reformed pastor at York, Pennsylvania, left his seat, embraced Boehm and said to him, "Wir sind Brüder (we are brethren)."

The United Brethren took a strong stand against slavery, beginning around 1820. After 1837, slave owners were no longer allowed to remain as members of the United Brethren Church. Expansion occurred into the western United States, but the church's stance against slavery limited expansion to the south.

In 1889, a controversy over membership in secret societies such as the Freemasons, the proper way to modify the church's constitution, and other issues split the United Brethren into majority liberal and minority conservative blocs, the latter of which was led by Bishop Milton Wright (father of the Wright Brothers). Both groups continued to use the name *Church of the United Brethren in Christ*. The majority faction, known as the Church of the United Brethren in Christ (New Constitution), merged with the Evangelical Church in 1946 to form a new denomination known as the Evangelical United Brethren Church (EUB). This in turn merged in 1968 with The Methodist Church to form the United Methodist Church (UMC).

The *Church of the United Brethren in Christ* is a conservative Trinitarian body of Christians that hold the deity, humanity, and atonement of Jesus; that the Bible, in both the Old and New Testaments, is the inspired Word of God; and that salvation is through faith, repentance and following after Christ. The church holds two ordinances: baptism and the Lord's supper. The church takes a neutral position on the observance of feet washing, stating, "the example of washing feet is left to the judgment of every one to practice or not...".[1]

[1] http://en.wikipedia.org/wiki/Church_of_the_United_Brethren_in_Christ

The Little Church at Niotaze

All good things come to an end. As this book concludes, I offer images from the last day at the Little Church at Niotaze, where John Wesley Finney hauled the stone with a team of horses, and that stone was used to build this church.

Niotaze United Methodist Church

1895 - 2003

Closing Service Of Worship

June 29, 2003

8:45 a.m.

Niotaze Methodist Episcopal Church
1895 - 1939

Niotaze Methodist Church
1939 - 1968

Niotaze United Methodist Church
1968 - 2003

In the second quarterly conference of the Peru circuit, 1889, Niotaze was listed as one of the churches on the circuit. At that time, services were held in the Walnut Grove school.

In 1895 the Methodists decided to erect a church building. The building was dedicated November 24, 1895, by Dr. Murlin, president of Baker University.

The Ladies Aid Society purchased the church bell in 1898. An organ was purchased in 1899.

Over the years Niotaze was on a circuit with other churches. The circuit groupings did change from time to time. Niotaze has shared their pastor with these churches at one time or another: Chautauqua, Elgin, Hewins, Jonesburg, Peru, Monette, Wauneta, Elk City, Sycamore Valley, Lafontaine, Havana, Tyro, and Caney.

The Caney Group Parish was organized in 1974. This cooperative ministry served Caney, Havana, Tyro, and Niotaze.

In 2001 the Caney Group Parish was dissolved. Caney became a single church charge, and Havana, Niotaze, and Tyro formed the HNT Group Parish.

The Niotaze church building and furnishings will be preserved. Niotaze Church In The Vale, Inc. has been established as a subsidiary of Chautauqua County Historical and Genealogical Society, Inc. to maintain the building.

The HNT Group Parish will continue its cooperative ministry at Havana and Tyro.

The Little Church at Niotaze

It was just a little country Church
On the edge of a little town,
Nestling against the woods
Where tangled trees looked down.

It was built of native stone
Weather beaten and gray -
With large rock steps in front
Where children loved to play.

It had a vestibule and a little steeple,
And a bell that sweetly rang,
It had stained glass windows
An organ and a choir that sang.

Back of the Church was the hitching rack
Where the horses and buggies stood -
Dozing in the shade trees,
And the sweet smell of the wood.

There the people came to worship,
The young, the middle aged and the old -
In the happy summer time
Or in winter bleak and cold.

There our family went together,
From the farm, plainly dressed.
There we sat among our neighbors
On the day of rest.

Just a group of humble people
Seeking God and his love -
Knowing that life on this earth
Must be guided from above.

Knowing that the soul cannot live
Without the Heavenly bread -
And so they came each Sunday
To God's table spread.

Just a group of humble people
Lifting their hearts in prayer,
Thanking him for all their blessings,
And finding courage and guidance there.

And today I thank God for the blessing
Of that little country Church,
That stands among the oak trees,
The blackjack and the Birch!

Mattie Miller

JayHawk to Niotaze

By Ivan Pfalser, Caney Valley Historical Society

G

Besides the Methodist Church in Niotaze, there was also a Christian Church, known as the "post card" church because it was featured on early real photo postcards of the community. The wooden church was constructed in 1898. During the next 15 years there was a steady growth. It was closed for a period during the early 1940s but was reorganized with a small congregation. It was closed and torn down in 2001.

A Pentecostal Holiness Church was started in a brush arbor in 1924. It held services in area homes and the Methodist Church for a few years and then disbanded.

Now! When did this all start? In 1871 H. N. Jones (another reference suggests William H. Jones), the owner of a small trading post new to the ford on the Little Caney River a couple miles northeast of the present town site submitted a request to U.S. Post Office Department for a post office. The name proposed was "Matanzus". Supposedly the application was so poorly written that the authorities in Washington, D.C. couldn't decipher the poor handwriting. They contacted the nearest post office, Peru, to solve the mystery. Since the two communities were not on the best of terms and a good joke was in the making, the postmaster replied that they were a community of JayHawkers and that was the name. Consequently, the post office permit was issued under that name. The joke wasn't well taken and a new request was submitted five months later and W. D. Nance was appointed to the new office of Matanzas. Thus it stayed until the spring of 1887 when it was moved to the present town location next to the new Denver, Memphis and Atlantic Railroad (later the Missouri Pacific) that was completed earlier. Someone finally realized that Matanzus was a Spanish word meaning "massacre" or "slaughter" (Matunzus Bay Florida where the Spanish massacred the first Huguenot colony in Florida).

It was then proposed to change the name to Niota but this was too similar to Niola, Kansas located in Labette County. So "Newport" was proposed. After three years the Post Office was having a problem with mail misdirected to Newport, Ky. The postmaster solved the problem by simply adding "ze" to Niota for a unique name without meaning.

The Santa Fe Railroad also built a branch line through the town. By 1904 with the construction of the "Sunflower Refinery" (concrete foundation stone can still be seen in the northeast part of the town) the population expanded to over 500. (It was closed in 1916). If I am not mistaken, this refinery was originally planned to be operated by state prison inmates but the state legislature voted it down as being illegal to use prisoners for such work.

The surrounding land was very rich and productive and to the south there was enough cotton raised for a gin to be built and operated for a few years.

During this period there were three grocery stores, a meat market, ice house, drug store, dentists and doctor's offices, greenhouse, photographer, barber shop, livery stable, pool hall, bank, two depots, a grain elevator and two stockyards.

Jerry (Wilson) Jay has given me a pretty good description of the community as it existed in the 1930s. The Wilson family were very prominent members of the community. Something like nine or 10 brothers and sisters (Jerry's aunts and uncles) were raised and lived in the area.

The present post office building was originally a grocery store operated by Leigh and Pearl Mathers. The post office had been moved into the corner of the store some years before. A photograph I have seen shows an adjacent building to the east, but no one knows what it was. Across the street to the west is the still existing Niotaze National Bank building. When it closed Charles Scott and Pearl Wilson made the transition to the Caney Valley National Bank. Directly to the west of this building was Greer's Grocery Store which was later sold to the Moon family. They also sold gas from a pump in front of the store.

Across the street north was (Uncle) Ben Wilson's general merchandise store which is long gone. Uncle Ben used tokens to make change and advertise his store. These are highly collectible today. Across the street to the east (north of the post office) was a residence which still stands today. It originally had a long porch on the west and south sides. A block to the north is the old rock two story hotel, still being used as a residence today. On the west corner of the block of Uncle Ben's Store was a filling station operated by Jim Williams. Across the street to the west was a large metal building where he sold feed and grain. To the south was another filling station which was owned by Greers before they started their grocery store.

The first school was the Walnut Valley School which was replaced by a large two story wooden building. The ground floor was divided into two rooms. The first through fourth grades used one room and the fifth through eighth grades used the other. The second floor was the gymnasium and later a kitchen for hot lunches was located there. A new school was built in the late 1930s. Some years later when the school closed, the Cooksen Hills Christian School was located in it.

If you would like to see a little scenic beauty I would suggest that you drive north from the post office and around to the north side of what looks like a big hill. There are some phenomenal rock outcroppings on the north side.

Sitting in the pew that their grandfather John Wesley Finney sat in – Kyle and Harold Finney – taken after the Last Service for the Little Church in Niotaze June 29, 2003

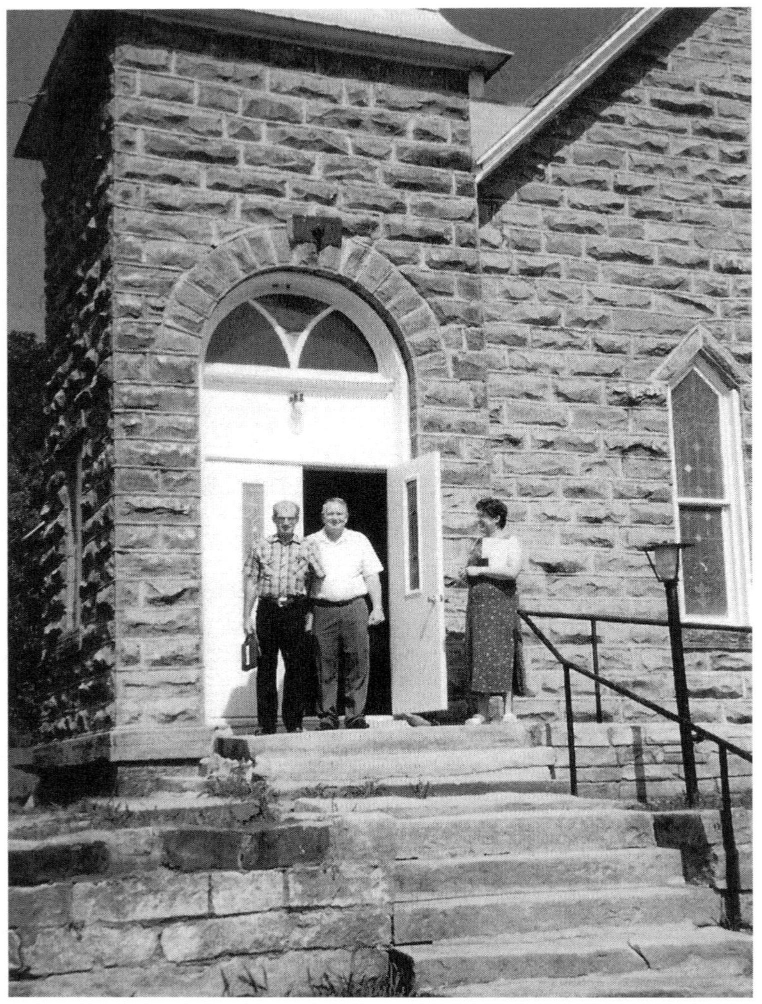

Leaving the Little Church at the Niotaze for the Last Time – Harold and Kyle Finney, and Judith (Finney) Davis

Took these notes before Johnny passed away

Guitar & Banjo- blonged to Johnny
Guitar & Banjo - repaired by son-in-law Steve Loffer
Bought from Sears - Guitar

John Wesley Finney - Bought land in Bolton- small orchard Mont. Co.
Orchard 1 & some odd acres in Bolton
Niotaze 280 acres - Farmed
River Bottom - cousin Asbury Rabe came back with Indiana mules to turn over land.
The old Methodist church in Niotaze - J W Finney hauled the stone with a team of horses to be use to build the Methodist Church. The stone came from behind the church where there is a quarry.
Johnny lived off & on with Grandparents starting at age 8. First home - Mont & Chaut county line
Chrismans Place (Minor Place) before going to Monet then old Weaning House
Then Claronence & Grandpa hooked up & farmed river bottom. Grew ~~Alphalpa~~ Alfalfa
Clarenced - farmed
road ~~sode~~ grading job
team of mares, mules, young team of mules (Bird & Bell). Paid by County.
Drugged all road in that area.
Older mules - Jim Pete - Bird & Bell Jack, Bill
Fawn Creek Cemetery - Wayside

Picture 1937 or 38 Grandpa Finney - J. W. get-together
36 - Chevy
Jack & George 4-sedan

Notes from Johnny Finney before he died

1937 or 1938 John Wesley Finney get-together
Vehicle - 1936 Chevy 4-dr sedan

The photo referred to in Johnny Finney's notes.

Part Five

OBITUARIES

Obituaries – in the Newspaper and Online

Obituaries and Headstones

The oldest obituary – for the matriarch of the Finney family

DIED.—At the residence of Wesley Finney, near Annapolis, on Friday, the 27th ult., Mrs. Polly Finney; aged 87 years, 5 months and 25 days.

Mary Polly (Long) Finney obituary – died 27 Sept. 1872

Headstone of Mary Matilda (Hinshaw) and Wesley Finney

Mary Matilda (Hinshaw) Finney died 5 Feb. 1900 and Wesley Finney died 3 Oct. 1904

Wesley Finney died, on Monday, Oct. 3, at the residence of his son, John Finney, near Niotaze, Kansas, aged 81 years, being born in Indiana in 1823. His home was near Bolton where he had lived many years a highly respected citizen. He was a member of the U. B. church and in former years did ministerial work for that church. Funeral services were held at the U. B. church here conducted by his old friend, Elder I. I. Robinson, after which his remains were taken to the cemetery in Fawn Creek township and deposited beside his wife who had preceded him to the tomb nearly four years ago.

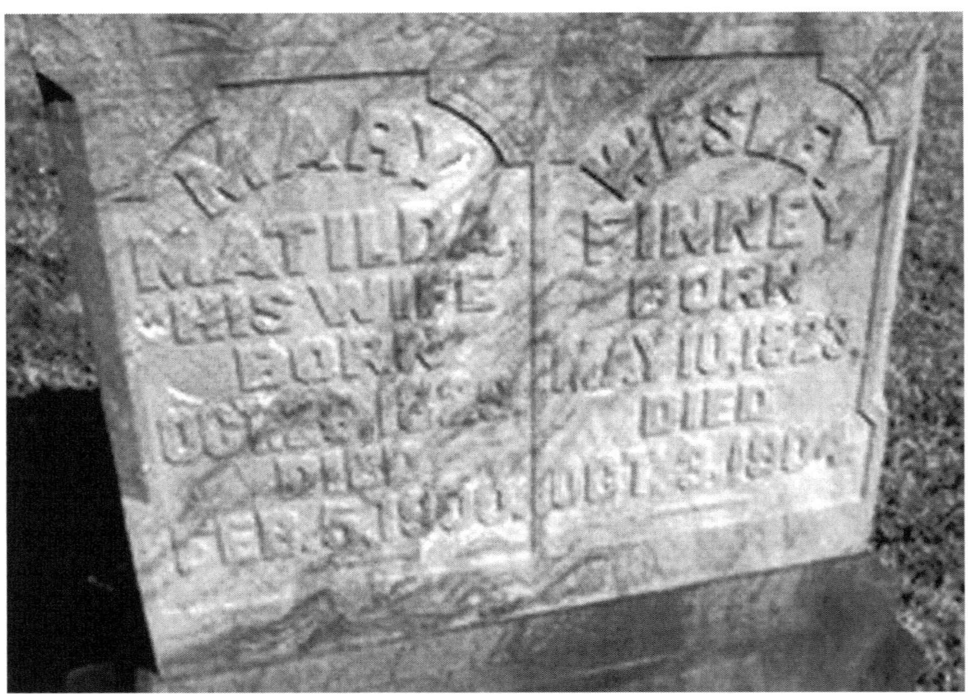

Wesley and Mary Matilda (Hinshaw) Finney headstone

DEATH RETURN.

1. *Name of deceased* Mabel Finney
2. *Age* .... 3. *Sex* Female 4. *Color* white
5. *Residence* Bolton Kansas
6. *Single*—~~*Married Widow Widower*~~. [Cross out words not required.]
7. *Cause of death* Pneumonia
8. *Occupation* ....
9. *Nationality* American
10. *Place of death* Bolton Kansas
11. *Date of death* Feb 13" 1903
12. *Father's name and address* D. W. Finney Bolton Kan
13. *Mother's maiden name and address* Mamie Farlow
14. *Date of return* March 1 - 1903 ~~189~~
15. *Reported by* C. C. Paxson *M. D.*
16. *Post office* Bolton Kansas

Mabel Estella Finney (daughter of Daniel Webster and Mary Ellen (Mamie) (Farlow) Finney) obituary – died of pneumonia 13 Feb. 1903

This section begins with the eldest child of Wesley and Mary Matilda Finney – **Samantha Jane Finney Copeland** – and her family and descendants.

These photos and obituaries were taken from "An American Genealogy: The Copeland Family of Montgomery County Kansas."

Abner Copeland's funeral wreaths - 1909

OLD SETTLER TO THE BEYOND

ABNER COPELAND OF HARRISONVILLE, DIED LAST EVENING ABOUT SIX O'CLOCK.

Abner Copeland, Aged 72 years, died last night at his home near Harrisonville. The funeral will take place tomorrow from the family residence, at 2 o'clock with burial in the Harrisonville cemetery. The deceased was members of the Knights of Pythias and the members of the local order will go down tomorrow to take part in the funeral services.

Abner Copeland leaves a wife and ten children to mourn the passing of a good husband and father. The children are: Samuel, in Spokane, Washington; Austin, of Independence, Effs, of Spokane; Miss Clarissa, residing at home; Arch and Ezra, in Western Kansas; William in Iowa; Emery, Charles and Pearl, at home.

The deceased was born in North Carolina. From there he went to Indiana, and 27 years ago he came to Kansas, purchasing a farm near Harrisonville. Forty-one years ago he was united in marriage to Samantha J. Finney, and together they have made the journey of life to a ripe old age.

Abner Copeland – age 72, d. Nov. 1, 1909; Harrisonville Cemetery, Kansas

DEATH TAKES EARLY SETTLER

Funeral Here Sunday for Samantha Copeland

Samantha Jane Copeland, 85, widow of Abner Copeland, one of the pioneers of this community, died at 12:45 p. m. yesterday at her home south of Bolton, near the Harrisonville schoolhouse, where she had lived for the past 47 years.

Samantha Jane Finney, daughter of Mr. and Mrs. Wesley Finney, was born August 7, 1851 at Park county, Indiana. In 1868 she was united in marriage to Abner Copeland in Rockville, Indiana, and in 1882 the family moved to this vicinity and settled near Tyro. In 1890 they moved to the farm where Mrs. Copeland died. Mr. Copeland passed away in 1909. Mrs. Copeland's father, Rev. Wesley Finney, was a pastor of the United Brethren church and was very well known here among the pioneer residents.

Surviving are 10 children, Clarisa and Ezra of the home; Mrs. Pearl Kontz of Elgin; Charles and Emory of Wayside; William of Jacksonville, Oregon; Arch of Seattle, Washington; Sam of Chewalah, Washington; Epps of Sela, Washington; and Austin H. Copeland of Independence. A sister, Mrs. Elmer Farlow of rural Independence, and a brother, John Finney of Niotaze, 17 grandchildren and six great grandchildren, also survive. A son and daughter preceded their mother in death.

Funeral services will be held Sunday afternoon at 2:30 from the Potts Funeral chapel with Rev. Sadie Pickett in charge. Burial will be in the Harrisonville cemetery.

DEATHS

Samantha Jane Copeland, 85, widow of Abner Copeland, one of the pioneers of this community, died Friday night at her home south of Bolton where she has lived for the past forty-seven years.

Samantha Jane Finney was born in 1851 in Park county, Ind. In 1868 she was united in marriage to Mr. Copeland in Rockville, Ind. In 1882 the family moved to Montgomery county, settling near Tyro. Mr. Copeland passed away in 1909.

Surviving are ten children, Clarisa and Ezra of the home; Mrs. Pearl Kontz of Elgin; Charles and Emory of Wayside; William of Jacksonville, Ore.; Arch of Seattle, Wash.; Sam of Chewalah, Wash.; Epps of Sela, Wash.; and Austin of Independence.

Funeral services were held Sunday afternoon from the Potts chapel with the Rev. Sadie Pickett in charge. Pallbearers were all nephews of the deceased.

SAMANTHA COPELAND DEAD

Funeral Services Tomorrow at Independence for Longtime Resident of Harrisonville Area.

(By a Journal Correspondent)

Independence, March 27.—Mrs. Samantha Jane Copeland, 85, widow of Abner Copeland and for forty-five years a resident of the Harrisonville district, southwest of here, died at her home, south of Bolton, at 12:45 o'clock yesterday afternoon.

She was born in Park county, Ind., Aug. 7, 1851, and was married to Abner Copeland in 1868. They came to Kansas in 1882.

Funeral services will be held at the Potts funeral home here at 2:30 o'clock tomorrow afternoon, with Mrs. Sadie Pickett of the Friends church in charge. Burial will be in Harrisonville cemetery.

Surviving relatives include eight sons and two daughters, Clarisa and Ezra Copeland of the home, Mrs. Pearl Knotz of Elgin, Charles and Emory Copeland of Wayside, William Copeland of Jacksonville, Ore., Arch Copeland of Seattle, Wash., Sam Copeland of Chewelah, Wash., Eps Copeland of Selah, Wash., and Austin H. Copeland of Independence. She also is survived by seventeen grandchildren and six great-grandchildren.

Samantha Copeland – age 85, d. Mar. 26, 1937; Harrisonville Cemetery, KS

COPELAND, Samuel G.—His home was at W2030 Dean. Husband of Susan Copeland, at the home; father of Mrs. Fred Scheel, Spokane; L. D. Copeland, Spokane; Hugh Copeland, Pasco, Wn.; grandfather of Pearl Mary Copeland, a student at W. S. C., whose home is at Pasco, Wn.; Betty Lou, and Robert Scheel, and Jack Copeland, all of Spokane; brother of Clarissa, Pearl, Austin, Emery, Ezra, and Charles Copeland, all of Wayside, Kan.; Willie Copeland of Ore.; Epps Copeland, Selah, Wn.; Arch Copeland, Seattle, Wn. He was a member of the Christian church and the I. O. O. F. Funeral Sat., Jan. 4, at 2:30 p. m., from the ALWIN CHAPEL at the HAZEN & JAEGER FUNERAL HOME, N1306 Monroe st. Dr. H. A. Van Winkle will officiate. Interment Riverside Park.

S. G. Copeland, 72, of Spokane, Washington, has been taken by death. He is a former resident of Tyro.

Samuel G. Copeland died January 2, at 3:30 at his home in Spokane, Wash. Mr. Copeland and family moved to Spokane in 1899 and he was employed there by a Dry Goods store, but was retired at the time of his death.

He was a member of the I. O. O. F. lodge and of the Christian church. Funeral services were held last Saturday afternoon.

He is survived by his wife and two sons, L. D. and Hugh, and one daughter, Mrs. Fred Scheel; four grandchildren; seven brothers, Epps, Arch, Wm., Ezra, Austin, Emery and Charles Copeland; two sisters, Clarissa Copeland and Mrs. Frank Koons.

Samuel Gilbert Copeland – d. Jan. 2, 1941; Riverside Park Cemetery, WA

COPELAND, Susan Mary—Her home, W2030 Dean. Mother of Mrs. Leonora Scheel, Spokane, 2 sons, Hugh Copeland, Pasco, Wash., L. D. Copeland, Alameda, Calif.; 4 grandchildren; 6 great-grandchildren; sister of Mrs. Laura Schrock of Spokane. Funeral, Tues., Feb. 15, 11 a. m. in the ALWIN CHAPEL of the HAZEN & JAEGER FUNERAL HOME, N1306 MONROE ST.

Susan (Pence) Copeland – d. Feb. 12, 1955; Riverside Park Cemetery, WA

Samuel and Susan Copeland's headstones in Riverside Memorial Park, Spokane WA

Lenora and Frederick Scheel headstones – Riverside Memorial Park, Spokane WA

A. H. Copeland Dies in Grocery Store Here Today

Austin H. Copeland, 81, who resided at 301 S. 23rd, died unexpectedly at Darby's IGA grocery this morning about 9 o'clock. He had gone there to purchase some supplies. Mr. Copeland had been in ill health the past few years. He was a retired farmer.

The body is at the Potts Funeral Home. Funeral arrangements are pending.

Mr. and Mrs. Copeland moved to Independence about six years ago from the Harrisonville community. Mrs. Copeland has been ill the past several months and is being cared for at the home of her sister, Dr. Ivy Hancock.

Surviving with the wife are two step daughters, Mrs. Ivella Stewart of this city and Mrs. Helen Dewey of Portland, Ore. Four brothers, Emery and Ezra Copeland of rural Independence, Arch Copeland of Washington and Charles Copeland of Wichita, and two sisters, Miss Clarissa Copeland of rural Independence and Mrs. Pearl Koons of Wynona, OK, also survive. A son, Earl Copeland, was killed in New Guinea in World War II. A stepson, Robert F. Stewart, also preceded Mr. Copeland in death.

County Coroner M. K. Borklund pronounced death was due to a heart attack.

SET COPELAND SERVICES

Services for Austin H. Copeland will be held at 2 o'clock Wednesday afternoon at the Potts Funeral Home with Rev. Joe Brown of Dearing officiating. Interment will be in Mt. Hope cemetery. Graveside services will be conducted by the I. O. O. F. members. Mr. Copeland died unexpectedly Monday morning.

Austin and Rhoda Copeland headstones; photos courtesy of Tami Woldum of the Penwell-Gabel Funeral Home & Crematory, Webb & Rodrick Chapel, Independence, KS

Austin Hawkins Copeland – age 81, d. Nov. 18, 1957; Mt. Hope Cemetery, KS

John Copeland Declared Dead

Had Been Reported Missing in Action

In a message received yesterday from the War Department, Dr. Ivy Hancock of East Beech learned her nephew Sgt. John Earl Copeland had been declared dead. He was reported missing in action on April 10, 1944. He had received his promotion to the rank of sergeant that morning shortly before he left on a mission for Wewak, New Guinea. Sgt. Copeland was a gunner on a B-24 and was with the "Jolly Rogers" group. He had been trained as a gunner on a B-12 before he left for overseas duty in August 1943 and was later sent to Australia for training on a B-24.

A native of rural Independence, Sgt. Copeland was the son of Mr. and Mrs. A.H. Copeland of Dearing. His wife and 2-1/2 year old son John Earl Copeland Jr have been making their home in Cherryvale. Two sisters, Mrs. Ivella Barnes of Kansas City and Mrs. Helen Mildred Davis of Portland also survive.

While attending school in this city, Sgt. Copeland made his home with his aunt Dr. Hancock. He was later employed by the McKirtrick Glass Company and became an employee at the Independence Army Air field prior to entering service in the armed forces in 1942.

JOHN COPELAND DECLARED DEAD

Had Been Reported Missing in Action

John Earl Copeland Sr's obituary

Memorial cross for John Earl Copeland, who died April 10, 1944

John Earl Copeland, Jr. headstone –Fairview Cemetery in Cherryvale, KS

John Earl Copeland Sr's widow Betty Jean Hopkins remarried. She and her husband Laurence Gross had 5 children. They are buried next to each other. – Fairview Cemetery in Cherryvale, KS

Miss Copeland, 90, Dies Here Late Saturday

Miss Clarissa Copeland, 90, a resident of Glenwood Estate the past two years, died Saturday night at 6 o'clock. Her home here was at 507 N. 5th.

Miss Copeland was born Oct. 5, 1879 in Park County, Ind. the daughter of Abner and Samantha Jane Finney Copeland. At an early age she moved to this county and for many years was a resident of the Bolton community. Ten years ago she moved to Independence. She was a member of the Bolton Friends Church.

Miss Copeland was the last of a family of 12 children and she is survived by several nieces and nephews.

Funeral services will be held Tuesday at 2:30 p.m. at the Webb Funeral Home with Rev. Joe Brown of the Wayside Christian Church presiding. Burial will be in Harrisonville Cemetery under the direction of the Webb Funeral Home.

Clarissa Copeland – age 90, d. Sept. 5, 1970; at 90 years old, she was the oldest member of the original Copeland family at her passing; Harrisonville Cemetery, KS

COPELAND, Arch J.—His home, W1129 First Ave. Brother of Miss Claraissa Copeland, Independence, Kans.; Mrs. Pearl Koons, Oklahoma; Ezra Copeland, Emery Copeland, both of Independence, Kans.; Charles Copeland, Wichita, Kan.; uncle of Mrs. Lenora Scheel, Spokane; numerous nieces and nephews. A resident of Spokane 15 years. Funeral services, Wednesday, December 2 at 10 a. m. in the GOTHIC CHAPEL of the HAZEN & JAEGER FUNERAL HOME, N1306 MONROE ST. Rev. Rowan A. O'Brien officiating. Burial Riverside Park cemetery.

Archibald Jackson Copeland – d. Nov. 28, 1959; Riverside Park Cemetery, WA

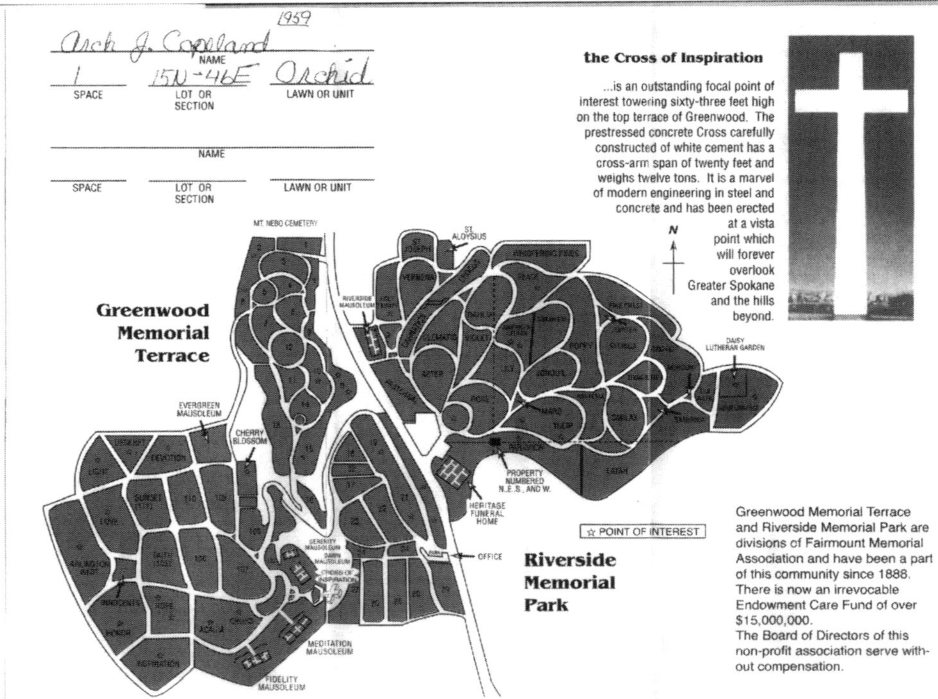

Cemetery map showing Arch's grave location

Obituaries

WILLIAM COPELAND

Funeral services for William Q. Copeland, 70, who died at his home, 1292 Dixie lane, Sunday, will be held at Perl funeral home Thursday at 2:30 p.m. with the Rev. G. H. Hillerman of Zion Lutheran church officiating. Graveside services at Jacksonville cemetery will be conducted by the Masonic lodge.

The deceased was born at Tyro, Kan., on Sept. 23, 1884, and had been a resident of Medford for the past 27 years. He was a member of the Masonic lodge at Independence, Kan.

Survivors include two sons, Donald, Medford,, and Sgt. James, Ft. Lewis, Wash.; three brothers, A. H. and Ezra, both of Independence, and A. J., Spokane, Wash.; two sisters, Miss Clarissa Copeland, Independence, and Mrs. Frank Koons, Wynona, Ola., and five grandchildren.

Agnes Elizabeth (McKay) Copeland – age 40, d. Dec. 10, 1933; Jacksonville Cemetery, OR ; William Quincy Copeland – age 70, died Aug. 7, 1955; Jacksonville Cemetery, OR

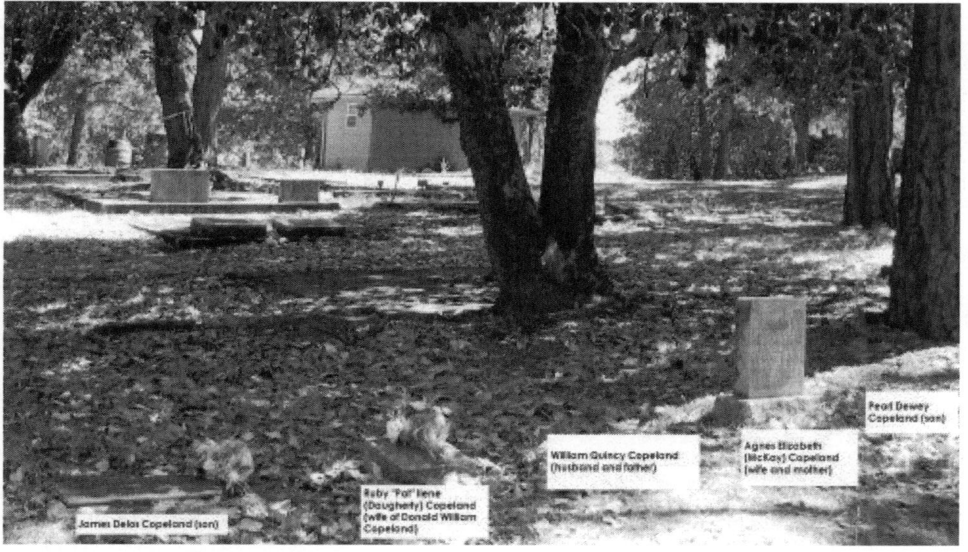

Jacksonville Cemetery with grave locations identified; William and Pearl Dewey Copeland do not have headstones

DONALD W. COPELAND

Funeral services for Donald W. Copeland, 43, of 467 Chestnut St., Ashland, who died Friday, will be conducted at 1 p.m. Tuesday at the Zion Lutheran Church, Medford. The Rev. Charles P. Smith, of the Zion Lutheran Church, Medford, will officiate. Private interment will follow at the Sterling Cemetery, Sterling Creek, Ore.

Mr. Copeland was born June 12, 1924 at Independence, Kan. On Sept. 4, 1955, at Carson City, Nev., he was married to Margaret Ricks, who survives.

He was a veteran of World War II, having served with the U.S. Army in the South Philippine and North Solomon Islands as a private first class with the 164th Infantry Regiment, Americal Division, from Feb. 23, 1943, until Nov. 28, 1945.

He had been a resident of Oregon, and of this community, for the past 38 years, and for the past two years had been associated with the Big Four Markets Corporation.

He was a member of the Zion Lutheran Church.

Survivors besides his wife include three sons, Rick Copeland, U.S. Army in Vietnam, Donald W. Copeland Jr., Ashland, and Walter W. Copeland, Ashland; four daughters, Mrs. Kathleen Corbett, Stockton, Calif., Miss Donna Copeland, Stockton, Calif., Mrs. Mary Carol Sharp, Medford, and Miss Kelly Jean Copeland, Ashland; one brother, James D. Copeland, Santa Clara, Calif., and one grandchild. One brother and one sister preceded him in death.

Honorary pallbearers will include Paul McQuat, Dan Kadin, Joe Foss, Francis McBride, Ray Miller, and Archie Krebs.

Friends who wish may make a donation to the American Cancer Society, Leverette Building, Medford.

Funeral arrangements are entrusted to Siskiyou Funeral Service, directors of Chapel in the Trees Mortuary.

Donald William Copeland – age 43, d. Mar. 22, 1968; Sterlingville Cemetery, OR

Patsy "Pat" Ruby Ilene (Hall) (Daugherty) Copeland (first wife of Donald William Copeland) – age 40, d. Jan 10, 1956; Jacksonville Cemetery, OR

PEARL COPELAND PASSES, AGED 10

Pearl Dewey Copeland, age 10, passed away early Sunday morning in a local hospital. His death came unexpectedly.

He is survived by his father, Wm. Copeland, and two brothers, Donald and DeLos, all of Jacksonville, and his grandfather, B. F. McKay of Kansas. His mother passed away several years ago.

The remains are at the Conger funeral parlors pending funeral arrangements.

Pearl Dewey Copeland – age 9 (almost 10), died 1937; Jacksonville Cemetery, OR

James Delos Copeland – age 43, d. Dec. 3, 1972; Jacksonville Cemetery, OR

Ezra D. Copeland Dies on Sunday; Rites Wednesday

Ezra Daniel Copeland, 80, of 507 N. 5th, died at 11 p.m. Sunday in Mercy Hospital. He had entered the hospital Nov. 2.

Funeral services will be held Wednesday at 2 p.m. in the Rodrick Memorial Chapel with Rev. Fred B. Cain, pastor of the Bolton Friends Church, officiating. Burial will be in the Harrisonville Cemetery.

Ezra Daniel Copeland was born Oct. 19, 1886, at Tyro, the son of Abner and Samantha Copeland. He moved with his family to the Bolton Community while still a small child. The family settled on a farm there and Mr. Copeland was a farmer all his life until 1960. At that time he sold his farm and moved to Independence.

Survivors include one sister, Miss Clarissa Copeland, of the home, and one brother, Charles, of Wichita.

He was preceded in death by his parents, six brothers, and one sister.

RODRICK
FUNERAL HOME

In Memory
of
Ezra Daniel Copeland

BORN
October 19, 1886
Tyro, Kansas

ENTERED INTO REST
11:00 p.m., Nov. 6, 1966
Independence, Kansas

SERVICES
2:00 p.m. Wednesday, Nov. 9, 1966
Rodrick Memorial Chapel

CLERGYMAN
Rev. Fred B. Cain

INTERMENT
Harrisonville Cemetery
Bolton, Kansas

CASKETBEARERS
Frank Noble
Henry Copeland
George Copeland
Ralph Copeland
Dewey Madison
Russell Hudson
Merl Farlow

Daniel Ezra Copeland – died Nov. 6, 1966; Harrisonville Cemetery, KS

E. L. Copeland Of Wayside Dies; Rites Wednesday

Emery Lloyd Copeland, 74, retired farmer residing in the Wayside community, was dead on arrival at Mercy Hospital Sunday morning. He became ill while enroute to Independence with his wife and daughter, Miss Virginia Copeland of Coffeyville.

Funeral services are to be at 10 a.m. Wednesday at the Potts Funeral Home with the Rev. Joe Brown of Dearing officiating. Interment will be in Mt. Hope Cemetery.

Mr. Copeland, son of Abner and Samantha (Finney) Copeland, was born near Tyro on November 19, 1889. His marriage to Mary E. Clark took place in Oswego on September 26, 1917.

Surviving with the widow, Mary, of the home are a son, George E. Copeland, Joplin, and a daughter, Miss Virginia Copeland of Coffeyville. Two grandchildren, two brothers, Ezra Copeland, Independence, and Charles Copeland, Wichita, and two sisters. Miss Clarissa Copeland, Independence, and Mrs. Pearl Koons, Wynona, Okla., are additional survivors.

Mr. Copeland was member of the Havana range and of the Montgomery County Farm Bureau.

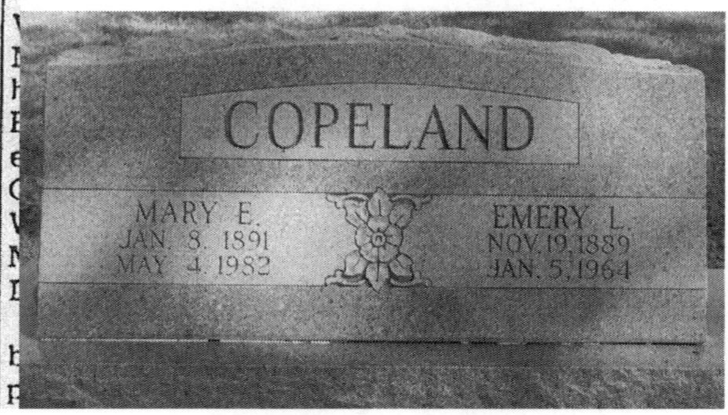

Emery Loyd Copeland – age 74, died Jan. 5, 1964; Mt. Hope Cemetery, KS

CHARLES O. COPELAND

Services for Charles O. Copeland, 77, of 355 N. Hydraulic, a retired farmer who died Sunday, will be at 2:30 p.m. Wednesday at Webb Funeral Home, Independence, Kan. Burial is in Harrisonville Cemetery, near Independence.

Born near Independence, Copeland came to Wichita in 1952.

Survivors include his widow, Marie; two sons, Ralph, Coffeyville, Kan., and Henry, Wichita; and a sister, Miss Clarissa Copeland, Independence.

CHARLES O. COPELAND

INDEPENDENCE (JNS)—Funeral services for Charles O. Copeland, 77, of Wichita, formerly of Coffeyville, who died at 7 p.m. Sunday in St. Francis Hospital at Wichita, will be conducted at 2:30 p.m. Wednesday in the Webb Funeral Home at Independence.

Burial will be in the Harrisonville Cemetery, near Bolton, Kan., southwest of Independence.

Mr. Copeland was born March 6, 1892 at Bolton. He and Marie Hudson, who survives at the home in Wichita, were married at Independence Nov. 30, 1920.

He farmed southwest of Independence until 1942, when he moved to Coffeyville, remaining there until 1952, when he went to Wichita to be employed in a flour mill until retirement some time ago.

Other survivors include two sons, Ralph of 915 W. Ninth, Coffeyville, Henry of Wichita; a

Charles Orien Copeland – age 77, d. Aug. 31, 1969; Harrisonville Cemetery, KS

Arlene Copeland – April 27, 1923 to June 21, 2010

Arlene Copeland, 87, of Coffeyville, passed away this morning, June 21, 2010 at Windsor Place.

She was born April 27, 1923 in Coffeyville, Kansas to Roll Elmer and Stella C. (Price) Webb. She grew up in rural Wayside, Kansas and graduated from Wayside High School. She received a Bachelor of Arts Degree from the Coffeyville Junior College in 1943.

She married Ralph Copeland on May 27, 1953 in Coffeyville, Kansas. Following their marriage they made their home in Coffeyville. She worked as an office manager for S.H Kress & Co. in Coffeyville for 27 years and for TG&Y for eight years.

She was an active member of the Westside Christian Church.

Survivors include her husband, Ralph Copeland of Coffeyville, Kansas and numerous cousins.

She was preceded in death by her parents.

Funeral Services will be held at 11:00 a.m. Friday, June 25, 2010 at the Westside Christian Church in Coffeyville, Kansas with Pastor Mike Elrod officiating. Interment will follow at the Elmwood Cemetery in Coffeyville

Friends may call on Thursday, June 24, 2010 from 9:00 a.m. to 9:00 p.m. at the David W. Barnes Funeral Home in Coffeyville. The family is receiving friends from 7:00 p.m. to 8:30 p.m. at the funeral home.

Arlene and Ralph Copeland's headstone; Elmwood Cemetery, Coffeyville, Kansas

Casket Bearers
Bob Kriebel
Heath Higbie
Gene Hamlin
Kenneth Emery
Melvin O'Connor
Dee Loyd Roberts

Musical Selections
"Precious Lord Take My Hand"

Vocalist
Emaleigh Mote

Pianist
Kevin Mote

Memorial
Westside Christian Church

We ask those driving in the procession to kindly turn on headlights for safety

306 North Cline Road
Coffeyville, Kansas
(620) 251-6008
www.dwbfh.com

In Loving Memory of

Arlene Copeland

Safely Home

I am home in Heaven, dear ones;
Oh, so happy and so bright!
There is perfect joy and beauty
In this everlasting light.

All the pain and grief is over,
Every restless tossing passed;
I am now at peace forever,
Safely home in Heaven at last.

Did you wonder I so calmly
Trod the valley, of the shade?
Oh! But Jesus' love illuminated
Every dark and fearful glade.

And He came Himself to meet me
In that way so hard to tread;
And with Jesus' arm to lean on
Could I have one doubt or dread?

Then you must not grieve so sorely,
For I love you dearly still;
Try to look beyond Earth's shadows.
Pray to trust our Father's Will.

There is work still waiting for you,
So you must not idly stand;
Do it now, while life remaineth –
You shall rest in Jesus' land.

When that work is all completed,
He will gently call you Home;
Oh, the rapture of the meeting,
Oh the joy to see you come!

In Memory of

Arlene Copeland

Date of Birth
April 27, 1923
Coffeyville, Kansas

Date of Death
June 21, 2010
Coffeyville, Kansas

Services From
Westside Christian Church
Coffeyville, Kansas
Friday, June 25, 2010
11:00 a.m.

Officiating
Pastor Mike Elrod
Westside Christian Church
Coffeyville, Kansas

Interment
Elmwood Cemetery
Coffeyville, Kansas

Ralph Owen Copeland – Nov. 5, 1923 to August 11, 2011

Ralph Copeland, 87, of Coffeyville, passed away Thursday, August 11, 2011 at Coffeyville Regional Medical Center.

He was born November 5, 1923 at Bolton, KS to Charlie and Marie (Hudson) Copeland. Ralph grew up in the Harrisonville community where he received his elementary education at Harrisonville School, and graduated from Wayside High School. In 1941 he moved to Coffeyville.

On May 24, 1953 he married Arlene Webb in Coffeyville. Following their marriage they made their home in Coffeyville. Ralph worked as a security guard for Wells Fargo, as a orderly at Coffeyville Memorial Hospital, and for many years delivered groceries, and prescriptions. Arlene preceded him in death on June 21, 2010.

Ralph was a member of Westside Christian Church.

He is survived by numerous cousins. Ralph was preceded in death by his parents, his wife, Arlene, and one brother Henry Copeland.

Services will be at 11:00 a.m. Monday, August 15, 2011 at Westside Christian Church in Coffeyville with Pastor Mike Elrod officiating. Burial will follow in Elmwod Cemetery

Friends may call on Sunday from 12:00 p.m. to 9:00 p.m. at the David W. Barnes Funeral Home in Coffeyville.

Memorials are suggested to Tyro Christian School in Tyro, or Holy Name School in Coffeyville; contributions may be left with the funeral home or mailed c/o David W. Barnes Funeral Home, 306 North Cline Road, Coffeyville, KS 67337.

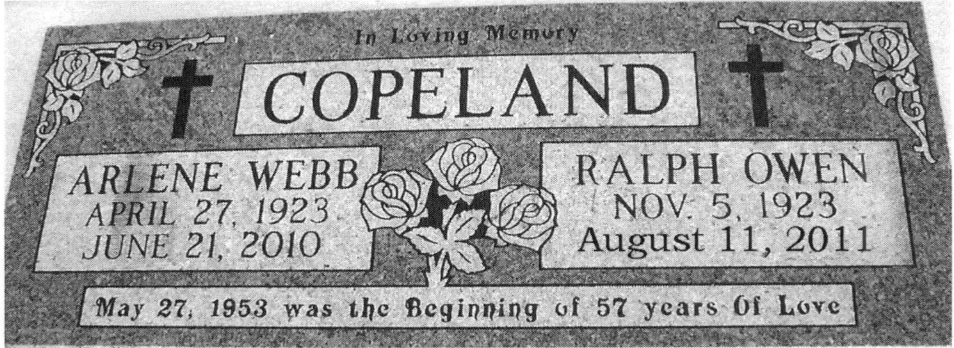

Arlene & Ralph Copeland's headstone; Elmwood Cemetery, Coffeyville, Kansas

In Memory of

Ralph Owen Copeland

Date of Birth
November 5, 1923
Bolton, Kansas

Date of Death
August 11, 2011
Coffeyville, Kansas

Services From
Westside Christian Church
Coffeyville, Kansas
Monday, August 15, 2011
11:00 a.m.

Officiating
Pastor Mike Elrod
Westside Christian Church
Coffeyville, Kansas

Interment
Elmwood Cemetery
Coffeyville, Kansas

Casket Bearers
M.R. Hershey
Lee O'Connor
Harold Finney
Kenneth Emery
Frank McCullough

Vocalist
Emaleigh Mote

Pianist
Kevin Mote

Memorial
Tyro Christian School
Holy Name Catholic School

Please turn on headlights in the procession

306 North Cline Road
Coffeyville, Kansas
(620) 251-6008
www.dwbfh.com

In Loving Memory of

Ralph Copeland

Safely Home

I am home in Heaven, dear ones;
Oh, so happy and so bright!
There is perfect joy and beauty
In this everlasting light.

All the pain and grief is over,
Every restless tossing passed;
I am now at peace forever,
Safely home in Heaven at last.

Did you wonder I so calmly
Trod the valley, of the shade?
Oh! But Jesus' love illuminated
Every dark and fearful glade.

And He came Himself to meet me
In that way so hard to tread;
And with Jesus' arm to lean on
Could I have one doubt or dread?

Then you must not grieve so sorely,
For I love you dearly still;
Try to look beyond Earth's shadows.
Pray to trust our Father's Will.

There is work still waiting for you,
So you must not idly stand;
Do it now, while life remaineth -
You shall rest in Jesus' land.

When that work is all completed,
He will gently call you Home;
Oh, the rapture of the meeting,
Oh the joy to see you come!

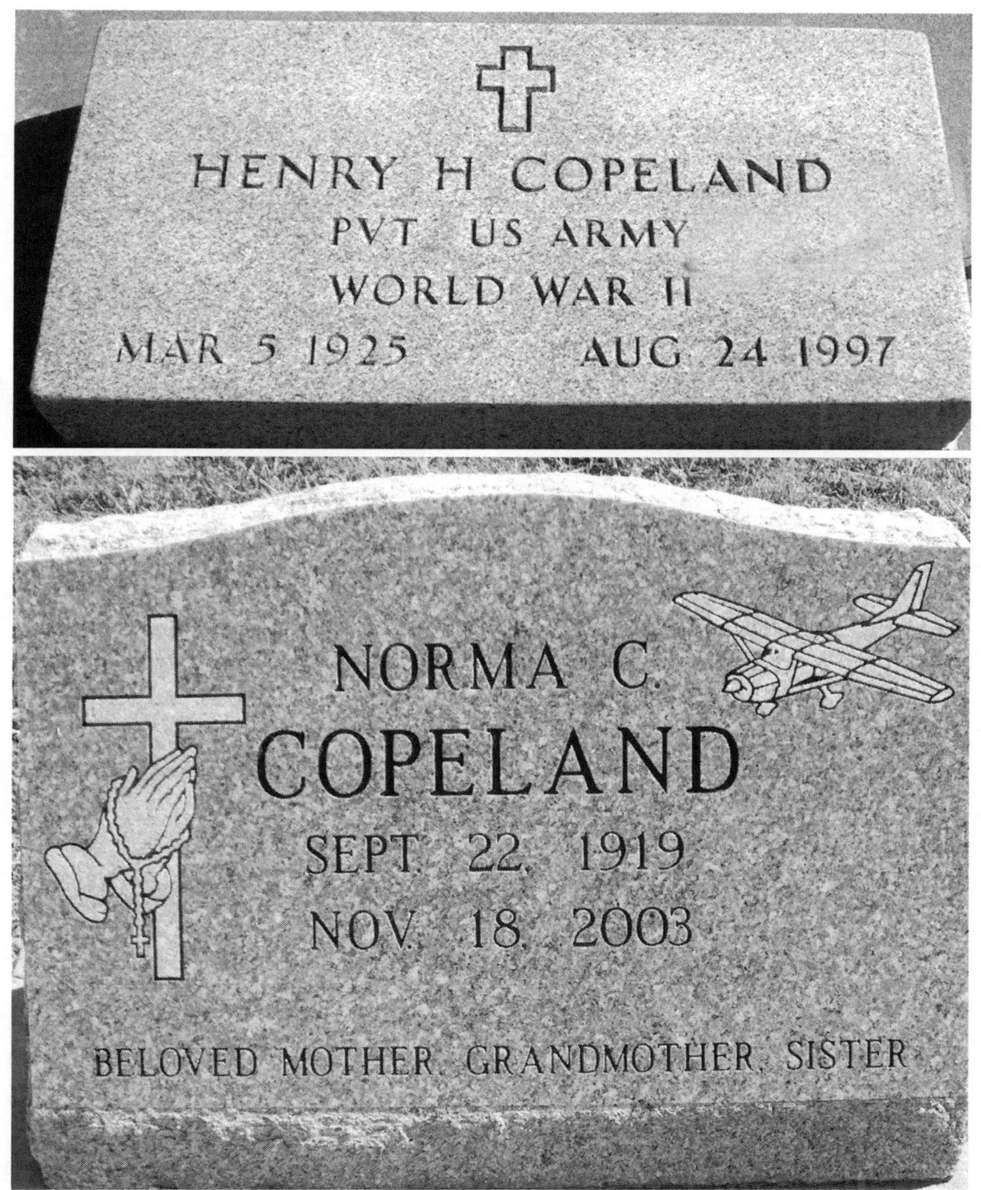

Henry Hudson Copeland – age 72, d. Aug 24, 1997; Harrisonville Cemetery, KS ; Norma Copeland – age 87 , d. Nov 18, 2003; Harrisonville Cemetery, KS

Mrs. Pearl Koons dies; services set Sunday in Wynona

Funeral services for Mrs. Pearl Koons, 69, a resident of Wynona since 1944, are tentatively scheduled for 2:30 p.m. Sunday at the First Baptist Church in Wynona. Mrs. Koons died Thursday morning in a Skiatook nursing home where she had been about one week.

Mrs. Koons was born November 9, 1895 at Bolton, Kans., and married Frank W. Koons at Independence, Kans., on December 22, 1920. They made their home in Osage County and Mr. Koons died on

(Continued on Page Two)

Pearl Koons——

(Continued From Page One)

January 7, 1959. Mrs. Koons was a member of the Baptist Church at Wynona and of the Home Demonstration Club.

Survivors include four sons, Claude, with the Air Force in Formosa; Melvin, Farmington, Minn.; Wayne, Shawnee Mission, Kans.; and Robert of Tulsa. One Sister, Miss Clarissa Copeland of Independence, Kans.; two brothers, Ezra Copeland, Independence, and Charles Copeland, Wichita. Also, four grandchildren.

Burial will be in the Hominy City Cemetery.

Copelands Attend Services For Pearl Koons, 69

Miss Clarissa Copeland, Ezra Copeland and Mrs. Mary Copeland of this city and Miss Virginia Copeland, Coffeyville, attended funeral services Sunday in Wynona, Okla. for Mrs. Pearl Koons, 69. Mrs. Koons, a resident of Wynona since 1944 was a sister of Miss Clarissa Copeland and Ezra Copeland. She died Thursday morning in a Skiatook nursing home where she had been a week.

Mrs. Koons was born on November 9, 1895 at Bolton, Kansas. Her marriage to Frank W. Koons took place in this city on December 22, 1920. The couple resided in Osage County, Mr. Koons died in January, 1959.

Survivors include four sons, Claude with the U.S. Air Force in Formosa, Melvin, Farmington, Minn., Wayne, Shawnee Mission, Kans., and Robert, Tulsa. A sister, Miss Clarissa Copeland, and two brothers, Ezra Copeland of this city, and Charles Copeland, Wichita, along with four grandchildren are other survivors.

Burial was in the Hominy City Cemetery at Wynona.

Mrs. Koons was a member of the Baptist Church at Wynona and of a home demonstration unit.

Pearl (Copeland) Koons – age 69, d. Nov. 26, 1964; Hominy City Cemetery, OK

Frank Wilburn Koons – Sept 16, 1892 to Jan. 7, 1959; Pearl (Copeland) Koons – Nov. 9, 1895 – Nov. 26, 1964

CLAUDE W. KOONS, 48, of 2322 Ida, North American Van Lines employe, services at 10 a.m. Tuesday in DeVorss Mortuary, graveside services at 2 p.m. in Hominy, Okla. He died Friday of cancer. Survivors include his widow, Velma; two daughters, Mrs. Sharon King, Phoenix, Ariz., and Miss Claudia Koons, Los Angeles, and three brothers, Myron Wayne, Overland Park, Kan., Melvin, Rosemount, Minn., and Robert, Tulsa, Okla.

Claude Wilburn Koons – obituary

Paying Respects

Harrisonville Cemetery – Kansas: The Harrisonville Kansas cemetery is lovely – up on a hill where the sun shines and the winds blow freely.

Pearl (Copeland) Koons visiting her parents grave in the 1950s

Clarissa, Pearl Copeland Koons, and Daniel Ezra Copeland visiting their parents grave in the 1950s

> ***From Ralph Copeland***
>
> Grandma bought the first grave lot on the drive she is on up there. The cemetery is up on a hill and you can go up there and see the fireworks go off on the 4th of July. You can't hear what they say but you can see them go off in Independence and Coffeyville.

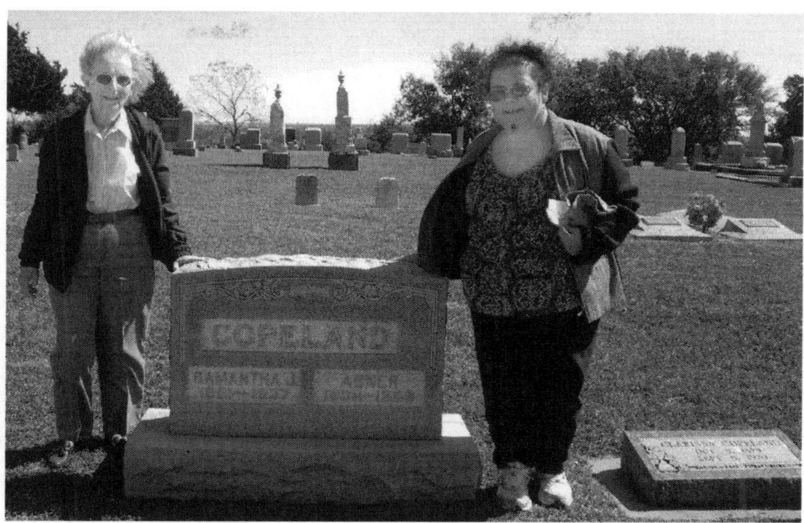

Virginia (Copeland) Noble and Cousette Copeland by Samantha and Abner Copeland's headstone; Clarissa's headstone is to the right

Mt. Hope Cemetery – Kansas: The Mt. Hope Cemetery is a large attractive cemetery in the heart of Independence Kansas.

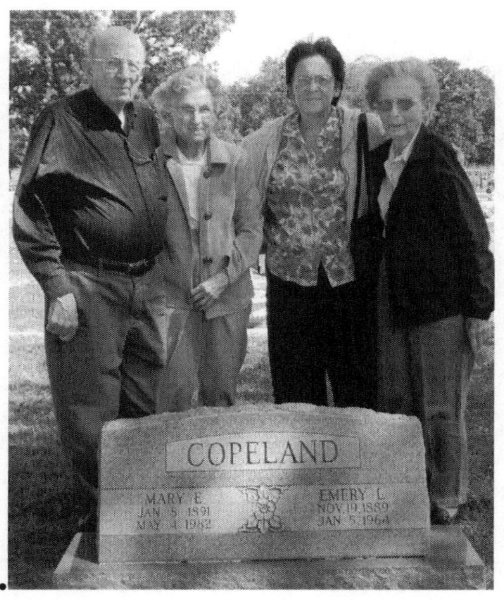

Ralph and Maxine Copeland, Fran (Copeland) Gardner, Virginia (Copeland) Noble at Mary and Emery Copeland's grave – Mt. Hope Cemetery

Jacksonville Cemetery – Oregon: The Jacksonville Oregon Cemetery is a historic cemetery on the top of hill. A great tall tree shades the Copeland family plot.

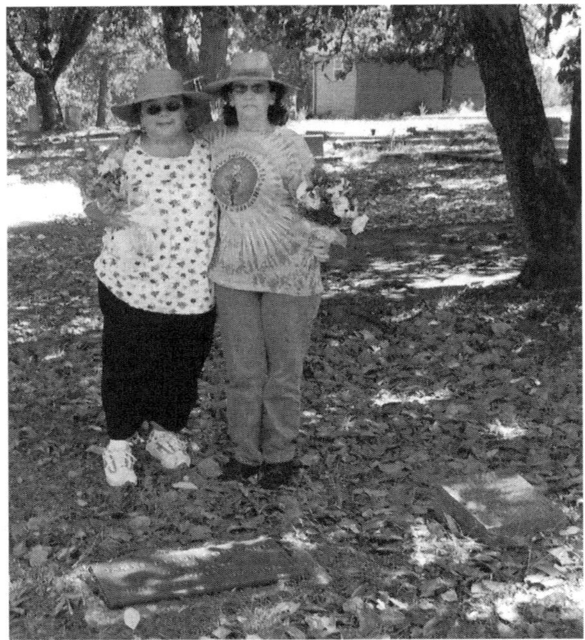

Cousette and Donna Copeland bringing flowers to Cousette's Dad and Donna's Mom – Jacksonville Cemetery, OR

Entrance to historic Jacksonville Cemetery in Jacksonville, OR

For the other Finney family and relations

Tilghman Wood, husband of Anna (Finney) Wood – suicide 1927

Anna Elizabeth (Finney) Wood – d. 1929

Perry Wood – d. 1962

A SUICIDE AT TYRO

Tilghman Wood, 75, a Retired Farmer, Slashed Throat With Razor Early Yesterday.

His throat slashed with a razor, the body of Tilghman Wood, 75, retired farmer, was found in his garage at Tyro at 4 o'clock yesterday morning. Brooding over ill health probably led Wood to take his life.

Mr. Wood arose shortly after 3 o'clock and was heard to leave the house by other members of the family. When he failed to return promptly a search was started. It was not until 4 o'clock, however, that the body was found by Perry Wood, a son, who had been summoned from his home northeast of Tyro.

An illness of several months' standing had been diagnosed as cancer of the liver. The dead man's widow has been an invalid for several years. He owned two large farms near Tyro and was well-to-do financially.

The surviving relatives are his widow, Mrs. Anna E. Wood, a daughter, Nellie Wood of the home, and a son, Perry Wood of near Tyro. Three brothers and a half-sister live in Indiana where Mr. Wood was born. The deceased had lived in and near Tyro for about thirty-five years.

The body will be taken from the Skinner funeral home to the family home at 10 o'clock tomorrow morning and the funeral services will be conducted at the home at 2 o'clock tomorrow afternoon. Burial will be in Fawn Creek cemetery, a mile east and three miles north of Tyro.

Perry Wood – son of Tilghman and Anna (Finney) Wood

Daniel Webster Finney, husband of Mary Ann Farlow – Dec. 1927

OBITUARY

Daniel Webster Finney.

Daniel Webster Finney, son of Wesley and Matilda Finney was born Nov. 7, 1868 near Anapolis, Park county, Indiana. His parents moved to Montgomery county, Kas. in 1882, locating on a farm two miles south of Bolton, Kas.

In 1896, Mr. Finney was united in marriage to Mary Farlow and to this union two children were born: Mabel Estella who passed away at the age of three years, and Carl Chester. Besides the wife and son, Carl Chester of Independence, he leaves one brother, John W. Finney of Niotaze, and three sisters: Mrs. Anna Woods of Tyro, Mrs. Samantha Copeland of Wayside, and Mrs. Ella Farlow of Wayside. Besides these there are a number of nieces and nephews, a grandson and a great number of friends.

Mr. Finney had lived in Montgomery county for years, having lived on the home place east of Wayside for twenty years and had proven himself a good neighbor and Christian gentleman.

His father was a United Brethren minister for years and Mr. Finney, due to the influence of the home, became a Christian and united with the church at an early age. He held his membership in the United Brethren church at Bolton and was a trustee of that church for some time. He showed by his life he had faith in God and a love for his fellowmen. When told that he had only a brief time to live he told those about him that he was ready to go.

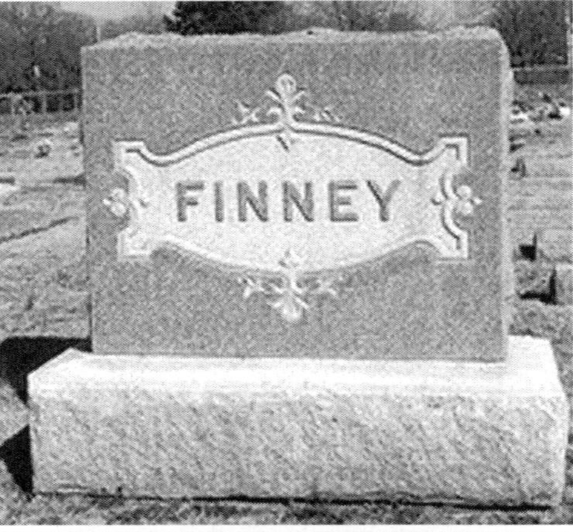

D. W. FINNEY DIED AFTER LONG ILLNESS

D. W. Finney, aged 59 years, a pioneer in Montgomery county and a successful farmer, died at 3:30 Saturday afternoon in Mercy hospital where he had been for the past three weeks. Death was due to cancer. He had been ailing since last May and it was not until an operation came that the cause of his illness was definitely established.

Funeral services were held at 2 o'clock this afternoon from the Friends church of this city, in charge of the Rev. Donovan Smith, pastor of the United Brethren church. Interment was made in Mount Hope cemetery.

The obituary containing the list of surviving relatives and other information will be published in the Reporter tomorrow.

Dannie Merle Finney, infant child of John Wesley and Nonnie Brooks – April 6, 1937

Dannie Merl Finney Dies

Dannie Merl Finney, month-old son of Mr. and Mrs. Clarence Finney, of near Niotaze, died this morning. He had never been well since birth, March 4. Funeral services will be held at the Christian church at Niotaze tomorrow afternoon at 2:30 with Rev. W. M. McKinney officiating. Burial will be in Sunnyside cemetery under the direction of Lloyd W. Graves of the Atwood-Carinder Funeral home.

Surviving are the parents, two brothers, Johnnie and Gene, three sisters, Alta, Mary and Hilda, the grandparents, Mr. and Mrs. J. W. Finney of Niotaze and Mr. and Mrs. E. H. Hann of Chautauqua, and other relatives and friends

Daniel Robert Finney (son of Carl and Vivia Finney) Oct 13 – 14, 1935

Cousette Copeland

John Wesley Finney – died Oct. 6, 1945

Nannie Finney (wife of John Wesley Finney) – died Nov. 6, 1953

DEATH TO AGED NIOTAZE MAN

JOHN W. FINNEY, 83, HAD LIVED IN THAT COMMUNITY PAST 59 YEARS

John W. Finney, 83, died at 9:30 o'clock, October 6 at his home at Niotaze. He had been a resident of that community 59 years, living on the same farm 56 years. He was a charter member of the Niotaze Methodist church.

Mr. Finney died on the 59th wedding anniversary of he and Mrs. Finney, the former Nannie Brooks, to whom he was married October 6, 1886 at Sedan. Mrs. Finney survives.

Mr. Finney was born February 14, 1862 at Indianopolis, Ind. He came with his parents, Wesley and Matilda Finney, to Bolton, Kan., in 1882. From there they moved to Niotaze.

Four daughters and four sons survive. They are: Mrs. Nora Norris, Ponca City, Mrs. Eva McCarthey, Amhurst, Va., Mrs. Stella Hilbert, Sedan,. Mrs. Emma Hatten, Tulsa; Frank Finney, Caney, Fred Finney, Wayside, Clarence Finney. and Clinton Finney, Niotaze. A sister, Ella Farlow, also survives as do 39 grandchildren and 18 great-grandchildren.

Funeral services will be held tomorrow afternoon (Tuesday) at 2:30 o'clock in the Methodist church at Niotaze, with Rev. J. B. Brown of Dearing, officiating. Burial will be in Fairview cemetery at Niotaze. The funeral will be under direction of the Graves funeral home.

Mrs. Nannie Finney Passes Away At Home In Niotaze

Mrs. Nannie Finney, a resident of the Niotaze community since 1872, passed away at her home there November 6, 1953 at the age of 86.

Funeral services were held at 2 P. M. Monday November 9 at the Methodist Church of which she was a member. The Rev J. B. Brown of Dearing, Kansas officiated with Interment in the Fairview Cemetery near Niotaze. Pall bearers were her grandsons; Warren Finney, Paul Finney, Jack Finney, Johnny Finney, Billy Hilbert and George Finney.

Mrs. Finney was the daughter of William and Elizabeth Brooks and was born near Bridgeport in Cook County Tenn. She and John W. Finney were married in 1866 at Sedan, Kansas. He passed away in 1945. Two sisters, Mrs. Cora Kocker and Mrs. Flora Wilson also preceeded her in death.

Survivors include four daughters: Mrs. Nora Norris of Ponca City, Mrs. Eva McCarthy of Houston, Mrs. Emma Hatton of Tulsa, Mrs. Stella Hilbert, Yates Center and four sons, Frank of Caney, Fred of Wayside, Clarence and Clinton, both of Niotaze; one brother, Walter Brooks of Pacoima, California; 40 grandchildren and 47 great grandchildren.

Two of Mrs. Finney's grandsons lost their lives in service, Carl Shafer in World War II and Glen Finney in Korea

Mrs. Finney came to Kansas with her parents in a covered wagon at the age of seven. She lived the greater part of her life before marriage near the Little Caney river and was there when the flood of 1885 came. She and her parents were forced to seek safety in the trees until help came the following day.

The cyclone that passed through that vicinity in 1889 took their home but they were at the home of her parents and were unharmed.

Mr. and Mrs. Finney lived on the farm south of Niotaze 57 years before moving to Niotaze in 1945 where they spent the remainder of their lives held yesterday at 2 p. m. in the Niotaze Methodist church, with Rev. J. B. Brown, her former pastor, officiating.

He used John 14: 1-3 for his text. This had been requested by Mrs. Finney.

Rev. Brown presented a comforting message. He spoke of having known Mrs. Finney for many years and said that she was a fine, Christian woman.

Mrs. Oza Wallace and Mrs. Joe Harmon sang "What a Friend We Have in Jesus" and "Goodnight Here and Good Morning Up There." Mrs. D. R. Redding accompanied them at the piano.

Casketbearers were grandsons of the deceased, and included Johnny Finney, Willie H. Hilbert, Jack Finney, Warren E. Finney, Paul J. Finney and George Finney. Interment was made in the Fairview cemetery at Niotaze under direction of the Graves Funeral Home.

Out-of-town relatives and friends attending the services were Mr. and Mrs. James Norris, Mr. and Mrs. Lyman Norris, Mr. and Mrs. Lloyd Norris, Mr. and Mrs. C. H. Clevenger and Mrs. Leo Norris, Ponca City, Okla.; Mr. and Mrs. Harold Norris, Oklahoma City; Mr. and Mrs. Ben Simms and Mary Ellen, Wichita; Mr .and Mrs. E. C. Hutton, Tulsa; Mr. and Mrs. Fred Finney and family, Mr. and Mrs. Paul Finney and family, Mr. and Mrs. Warren Finney and family, Mr. and Mrs. E. L. Copeland and Clarissa, and Austin Hamilton, Wayside; Mr. and Mrs. William Hilbert, Yates Center, Kan.; Willie Hilbert, Jr., Manhattan, Kan.; Mr. and Mrs. Harold Kirchner, Sedan; Mr. and Mrs. A. W. Hertwick, Jack Finney, Perry Wood, Mrs. Al Herrington, Mr. and Mrs. Earl Moody, Mrs. Dan E. Smith, Mr. and Mrs. Charles Wilson and Don, Coffeyville; Mrs. Floyd Bowles and Mr. and Mrs. Arthur James, Tyro; Mrs. Steve Bowman, Paducah, Ky.; Mr. and Mrs. Monroe Bailey, Cherryvale; Mrs. A. K. Druley and Mrs. Clarence Cales, Peru; Sgt. Bill R. Clevenger, Camp Polk, La.; Mr. and Mrs. D. Lennox and Mrs. Forest Williams, Wann, Okla.; Mr. and Mrs. Alvie Wilson, Mr. and Mrs. A. W. Wilke and Mrs. Harold Sullivan, Havana; Mr. and Mrs. Frank Finney, Mr. and Mrs. George Finney, Ben Shafer, Mr. and Mrs. Ralph Coltharp, Mr. and Mrs. Johnny Finney and family, Mrs. Ed Clark, Mr. and Mrs. George Reed, Mr. and Mrs. Arthur Reed, Mr. and Mrs. F. Ellingworth, Mrs. George Freidline, Mr. and Mrs. Art Denny, Mrs. Joe Harmon, Mrs. Oza Wallace and Mrs. D. R. Redding, Caney, and Rev. and Mrs. J. B. Brown, Dearing.

---o---

In Memory of

Mrs. Nannie Finney

BORN

Dec. 18, 1866
Cook County, Tennessee

ENTERED INTO REST

Nov. 6, 1953
Niotaze, Kansas

SERVICES FROM

Niotaze Methodist Church
Monday, Nov. 9, 1953—2 P. M.

OFFICIATING CLERGYMAN

Rev. J. B. Brown

FINAL RESTING PLACE

Fairview Cemetery
Niotaze, Kansas

MUSIC

Processional - Recessional
Mrs. D. R. Redding

"What a Friend We Have in Jesus"
"Goodnight Here and Good Morning Up There"

Sung by

Mrs. Oza Wallace
Mrs. Joe Harmon

CASKETBEARERS

(Grandsons)

George Finney
Warren Finney
Paul Finney
John Finney
Bill Hilbert
Harold Norris

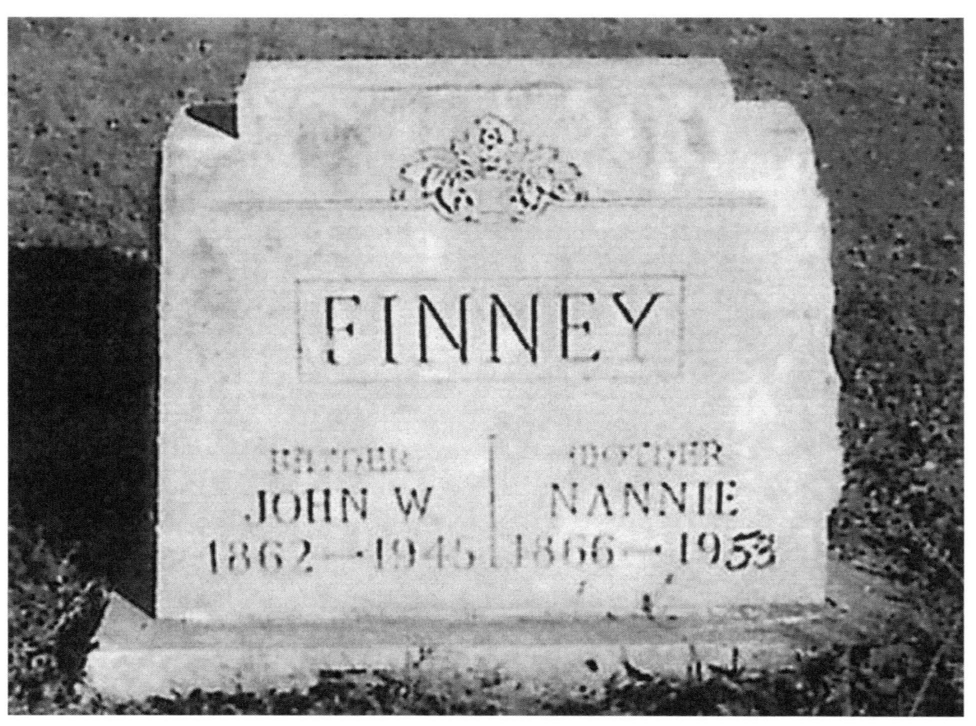

Elmer Farlow – d. 18 Sept. 1942

Clara Ellen (Finney) Farlow – died Dec. 13, 1945

MRS. ELLEN FARLOW DIES WEDNESDAY

Funeral Services to Be Held Friday

Mrs. Clara Ellen Farlow, 73 years old, died yesterday evening at 7:20 at the Mercy hospital, after being seriously ill for about a week. She had been in poor health for a number of years.

Funeral services will be held Friday at the Webb Funeral home at 2 p. m. with the Rev. Blaine Stands of the Friends church officiating and burial will be made in Mt. Hope cemetery.

Clara Ellen Finney, daughter of Mr. and Mrs. Wesley Finney, was born in Park county, Indiana, May 27, 1872. At the age of eight years she came to Kansas with her parents and settled on a farm two miles south of Bolton, Kansas. She was united in marriage to Elmer Farlow February 13, 1896, near Bolton and she resided in that vicinity until 1941, when her husband died, and she moved to Independence. She was a member of the Friends church.

She is survived by two sons, Orville W. Farlow of Tulsa, Oklahoma, and Merl N. Farlow of Independence and two grandchildren, Mary Belle and Orville, jr.

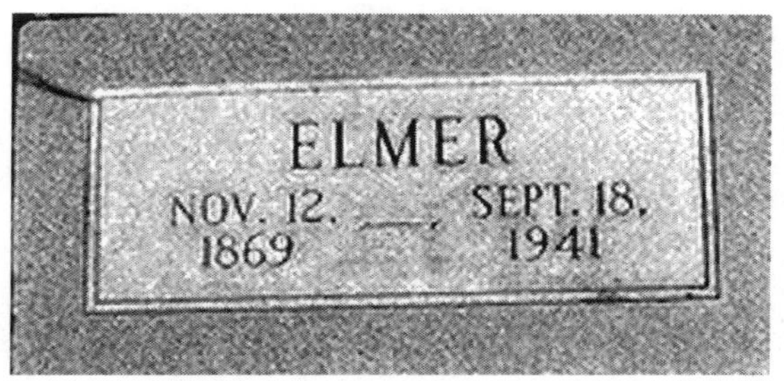

CLARA ELLEN
MAY 27, 1872 — DEC. 12, 1945

Mary Ann (Farlow) Finney (wife of Daniel Webster Finney) – died Jan. 2, 1952

Obituary

Mary Ann Farlow Finney

Mary Ann Farlow, a daughter of Nathan and Martha Farlow, was born March 12, 1873, near Paoli, in Orange County, Indiana. She passed away January 2, 1952.

In 1887, she came to Kansas with her parents and lived in the Rutland Township where she attended school at Sunnyside.

She was united in marriage to Daniel W. Finney in 1896 and lived in Harrisonville District on a farm until December 1927, when her husband passed away. She moved to 400 North 12th and shared her home with roomers.

She was the mother of two children: Mable Estella who passed away at the age of 3½ and Carl Chester who lives in South Gate, California. There are five grandchildren and one great-grandchild. She had three brothers: Harry Farlow of Coffeyville, Kansas; Will Farlow of rural Independence; and Elmer Farlow, deceased.

Since the age of 14 she has been a member of the Friends Church.

Funeral services were held Saturday morning and interment was made in Mt. Hope cemetery.

Mrs. Mary Finney Dies In Mercy Hospital Today

Mrs. Mary A. Finney, 78, died at 6 a.m., today in Mercy hospital where she had been a patient since suffering a heart attack Sunday night. She resided at 400 North Twelfth. She was the widow of Dan Finney and before his death lived in the Bolton vicinity.

She is survived by a son, Carl, who is enroute here from his home at South Gate, Calif. The Webb Funeral home will make arrangements for the services after his arrival. Additional information of her biography will be available after the son arrives.

Frank Finney, son of John Wesley and Nonnie Finney; husband of Hattie Nicholson Cole Finney – d. Dec. 13, 1954

NUMBER 86.

Injuries Fatal to Frank Finney

Frank Finney, 66, 109 West Third, died at 9:20 last night in Coffeyville Memorial Hospital as a result of injuries received a week ago yesterday in a highway accident at the east edge of Caney.

He had been in the hospital since the accident, and had undergone surgery yesterday morning.

Mr. Finney was the son of John and Nannie Finney and was born near Niotaze, Nov. 27, 1888. His parents were pioneer residents of that community.

He was married to Hattie Nichelson Cole on Nov. 23, 1916, at Sedan. They resided on farms in the Niotaze-Caney vicinity before moving to Caney about 15 years ago.

Mr. Finney was a farmer, but was employed by the Sinclair company in Coffeyville from 1944 to 1949. He had spent the past few years in retirement and in limited farming activities.

Mr. Finney was a member of the Caney Methodist church.

Survivors, in addition to his wife, are two daughters, Mrs. Arnold (Melrena) Hertweck, Coffeyville, Mrs. Virgil (Monica) Kidwell, Sterling, Colo.; and twd sons, George W. Finney, Caney, and Gordon Jack Finney, Coffeyville.

Four sisters and three brothers also survive. They are Mrs. James Norris, Ponca City, Okla.; Mrs. Edward Hatton, Tulsa; Mrs. Blair McCarty, Amherst, W. Va.; Mrs. William Hilbert, Yates Center; Clarence and Clinton Finney, Niotaze, and Fred Finney, Wayside.

Six grandchildren also survive.

Funeral services, directed by the Ford Funeral Home, Coffeyville, will be conducted at 2 p. m. Sunday in the Caney Methodist church, with Rev. Mark Smith officiating. He will be assisted by Rev. Joe Brown of Dearing. Burial will be in Sunnyside cemetery.

The body will be brought to Caney at 3 p. m. Saturday and will lie in state at the Graves Funeral Home until the funeral hour.

Frank Finney Succumbs to Crash Injuries

Frank Finney, 66-year-old Caney man, critically injured Dec. 8 near Caney when the pickup truck he was driving was struck from the rear by a car driven by Grover C. Fitzpatrick of Coffeyville, died last night in Coffeyville Memorial Hospital. Mr. Fitzpatrick also was hospitalized following the accident but released shortly afterwards.

Funeral services for Mr. Finney will be conducted at 2 Sunday afternoon in the First Methodist Church at Caney with the Rev. Mark E. Smith officiating, assisted by the Rev. Joe B. Brown of Dearing. Burial will be in Sunnyside Cemetery at Caney. The body will lie in state at the Ford Funeral Home until 3 Saturday afternoon when it will be removed to Graves Memorial Chapel in Caney to lie in state until the funeral hour.

Mr. Finney, a former Sinclair Refinery employe in Coffeyville, was born Nov. 27, 1888 near Niotaze, the son of the late John W. and Nannie Finney, pioneer residents of that vicinity. On Nov. 23, 1916, he married Hattie Nichelson Cole at Sedan. They lived on farms in the Havana; Caney and Niotaze communities before moving to Caney about 15 years ago. From 1944 until the refinery closed in 1949, he was employed by the Sinclair Oil Co., in Coffeyville. Since that time, he has farmed in the Caney vicinity. He was a member of the First Methodist Church at Caney and former member of the Woodmen of the World.

Survivors include the wife of the home; two daughters, Mrs. Arnold W. (Melrena) Hertweck, Route 1, Coffeyville; and Mrs. Virgil (Monica) Kidwell, Sterling, Colo.; two sons, George W. Finney, Caney; and Gordon Jack Finney, Route 1, Coffeyville; four sisters, Mrs. James (Nora) Norris, Ponca City, Okla.; Mrs. Edward (Emma) Hatton, Tulsa; Mrs. Blair (Eva) McCarty, Amherst, W. Va.; and Mrs. William H. (Stella) Hilbert, Yates Center; three brothers, Clarence F. and Clinton, both of Niotaze; and Fred B., Wayside; and six grandchildren.

Fred Dewey Finney (son of Nannie and John Wesley Finney; husband of Pearl Norris) – died Feb. 12, 1960

Fred Finney, 61, Dies

Fred D. Finney, 61, an oil field pumper, died at his home, 907 North State, at 9 a.m. today. He had been in failing health three years and in serious condition since October.

Mr. Finney was a lifelong resident of Chautauqua and Montgomery counties. He had resided in the Wayside and Caney communities before moving to Caney last September.

He was born Feb. 27, 1898 at Niotaze, a son of Nannie and John W. Finney. He was married to Pearl Norris at Sedan on May 2, 1917, and she survives.

He was employed by the Wiser Oil Co., which later became the Forrest Oil Co. He was a member of the Methodist church at Niotaze.

Four daughters and five sons survive. They are Mrs. Steve (Letha) Bowman, Mrs. Arthur (Nancy) James, both of Caney, Mrs. Verne (Fern) Gilliland, Sterling, Colo., Miss Twyla Finney of the home; Paul Finney, rural Havana, Warren Finney, rural Caney, Russell Finney, Navy Air Force, Oak Harbor, Wash.; Jerry Finney of the home and Gerald Finney, rural Caney.

A son, Pvt. Glen Finney, was killed in action in Suray Ni, Korea, June 11, 1953.

Fourteen grandchildren and two great grandsons survive.

Surviving sisters are Mrs. Jim Norris of Ponca City, Okla.; Mrs. Blair McCarthey of Amherst, Va.; and Mrs. William Hilbert of Yates Center. Two brothers, Clarence Finney and Clinton Finney, both of Niotaze, survive.

A sister, Emma Hatton, a brother, Frank Finney, his parents and son, Glen, preceeded him in death.

Funeral services will be held at 2:30 p.m. Sunday, February 14, in the Graves Memorial Chapel. Rev. J. B. Brown will officiate and burial will be in Fairview Cemetery, Niotaze.

Paul James Finney (son of Fred. D. and Pearl C. Finney) – died Sept. 15, 1962

In Memory of

Paul James Finney

Born

December 4, 1924
Havana, Kansas

Entered into Rest

September 15, 1962
Rural Havana, Kansas

Services From

Graves Memorial Chapel
Tuesday, September 18, 1962
2 P. M.

Officiating Minister

Rev. Joe Brown

Interment

Havana Cemetery
Havana, Kansas

Music

Processional - Recessional
Organ Selections
Mrs. D.R. Redding, Organist

"In The Garden"
"Sunrise Tomorrow"

Sung by
Harry E. Graves

Casketbearers

Hubert Horton
Elvern Bales
Glen Freidline
Jack Ward
Charles Bright
William Casement

Flag Service

By Lloyd W. Graves - Earle D. Biggerstaff
Veterans of World Wars I and II

Hiram Alexander Rayl – Feb. 1, 1856 to June 27, 1927

Cousette Copeland

Martha Myrtle (Hann) Finney (wife of Clarence Finney) – died May 8, 1965

Clarence Fay Finney (husband of Martha Myrtle Hann) – died June 21, 1972

Martha Finney Dies Suddenly

Mrs. Martha M. Finney, wife of Clarence Finney of Niotaze, died Saturday in Sedan City hospital. She became suddenly ill at her home and died one hour after admission to the hospital.

Funeral services were held Wednesday afternoon in the First Christian church at Sedan with Rev. Donald Anderson officiating. Burial was in Fairview cemetery at Niotaze under the direction of Graves-Baird funeral home.

Mrs. Finney was born June 25, 1907 at Chautauqua and had lived in this community all her life. She was married at Sedan in 1924.

Survivors include her husband and five sons, Gary, Melvin, David, Roy and Eugene, all of the home; four other sons, Johnny, and Kyle, both of Collinsville, Okla., Gene of Redmond, Wash., and Harold, with the Air Force in Germany; four daughters, Mrs. Alda Kirchner and Mrs. Wanda Riley, both of Sedan, Mrs. Mary Dufoe of Golden, Colo., and Mrs. Hilda Gorby of Nowata; her mother, Mrs. Amanda Hann of Claremore, Okla.; a sister, Mrs. Allen [illegible]ster of Claremore; two brothers, Elmer Hann of Medicine Lodge, and Aaron Hann of Colorado Springs; and 27 grandchildren.

CLARENCE F. FINNEY

SEDAN — Clarence F. Finney, a retired railroad worker and carpenter, died Wednesday in King's Nursing Home at Sedan where he had been a resident for the past three years. He was 68.

Born Jan. 18, 1904, at Niotaze, Finney spent most of his life there, and was a member of the Niotaze Methodist Church.

Survivors include four daughters, Mrs. Harold (Alta) Kirchner of Sedan, Mrs. Claude (Mary) Dufoe of Nampa, Idaho, Mrs. Kenneth (Hilda) Gorby of Nowata and Mrs. Carl (Wanda) Riley of Sedan; nine sons, Johnny E. of Collinsville, Rollie G. of Nampa, Kyle B. of Arvada, Colo., Harold E. of Tulsa, Gary L. of Fort Smith, Ark., Melvin R. of Dearing, David W. of Niotaze, Roy K. of Sycamore and Lyle E. of Dearing; two sisters, Mrs. Stella hilbert of Yates Center and Mrs. Eva McCarthy of Amhurst, Va.; a brother, Clint of Pawhuska, Okla.; 30 grandchildren and nine great-grandchildren.

Funeral services will be held at 2 p.m. Friday in the Graves-Baird Funeral Home Chapel. The Rev. Lemert Whitmer of the First Christian Church will officiate. Burial will be in Fairview Cemetery at Niotaze.

Merl Nathan Farlow (son of Elmer and Clara Ellen Finney Farlow) – died June 17, 1969

Wife, Elizabeth (Castillo) Farlow – d. June 20, 1993

Merl N. Farlow, Retired Banker, Dies on Tuesday

Merl N. Farlow, 69, of [illegible]20 W. Oak, retired veteran bank employe, died at 2:50 p.m. Tuesday in Mercy Hospital where he had been a patient since June 6. He had been in ill health for some time.

Funeral services will be held Friday at 10:30 a.m. in the Webb Funeral Home Chapel with the Rev. Donald Burt, pastor of the First United Presbyterian Church, officiating. Burial will be in Mount Hope Cemetery. There will be Masonic services.

The family will receive friends at the Webb Chapel Thursday from 7:30 to 9 p.m.

Merl N. Farlow was born June 28, 1899, in the Bolton area, the son of Elmer and Ellen (Finney) Farlow. He was a lifetime resident of Montgomery County and graduated from Montgomery County High School in 1920.

He was first employed by the Citizens First National Bank in 1920 and for several years in the 1920's worked for the Kansas Savings and Trust Co., a division of the Citizen Bank. He continued to work for the same bank for 48 years and retired as assistant cashier of the Citizens National Bank Dec. 1, 1968.

He married Elizabeth Castillo Oct. 5, 1923, at Independence and she survives at the home.

Mr. Farlow was a member of the First United Presbyterian Church and of the Kiwanis Club. He was a member and for many years served as treasurer of four Independence Masonic bodies including Fortitude Lodge No. 1[illegible] AFAM; Keystone Chapter No. 22 RAM, Independence Council No. 15 R&SM, and St. Bernard Commandery No. 10 KT.

Survivors in addition to the widow include one daughter, Mrs. Bill (Mary Belle) Butts, St. Joseph, Mo.; one brother, Orville of Tulsa, Okla.; and four grandchildren.

The family suggests contributions to the Presbyterian Church, or the American Cancer Fund.

Birth: Jun.28,1899 Bolton Montgomery County Kansas

Death: Jun.17,1969
Independence Montgomery County Kansas,

MERLE NATHAN FARLOW

INDEPENDENCE (JNS) -- Funeral services for Merl Farlow, 69, who died Tueday at Mercy Hospital will be at 10:30 a.m. Friday at Webb Funeral Home with the Rev. Donald Burt presiding.

Burial will be at Mount Hope Cemetery.

Mr. Farlow, born June 28, 1899, at Bolton, was a retired cashier of the Citizens Bank and a member of the First Presbyterian Church, Masonic Lodge, and Kiwanis Club.

Survivors include the widow, Elizabeth of the home; a daughter, Mrs. Mary Butts of St. Joseph, Mo., and a brother, Orville of Tulsa.

Stella M. Finney Hilbert (daughter of John Wesley and Nannie Finney) – died Aug. 21, 1981

Stella M. Hilbert

Mrs. Stella M. Hilbert, 79, Yates Center, died Friday, Aug. 21, 1981 at a Topeka hospital.

She was born Jan. 5, 1902. at Niotaze in Chautauqua County, the daughter of Wesley and Nannie Brooks Finney.

Mrs. Hilbert taught in Round Mound and High Rock schools and later worked at Sue's Cafe in Yates Center.

She was a member of the Yates Center United Methodist Church.

She is survived by her husband, Willie Hilbert; a son, William Hilbert, Topeka; a brother, Clinton Finney, Copan, Oklahoma; and two grandchildren.

Services were Monday, Aug. 24, 1981 at 2:00 p.m. at Graves Funeral Home, Caney. Burial was in Fairview Cemetery, Niotaze. Memorial contribution may be made to the Yates Center United Methodist Church in care of the funeral home.

Virginial Lee Finney (daughter of Carl and Vivia Finney) – died 17 Sept. 1971

Jonathan David Presley (son of David and Sandra (Finney) Presley) – died May 18, 1986

Finney grandson dies in Texas

Jonathan David Presley, 4, son of David and Sandra (Finney) Presley of Katy, Tex., died Tuesday, Dec. 22, 1987, in a Houston hospital.

The youth became ill one week ago with a virus infection which attacked his breathing system, finally closing it off completely. He had been in a coma for the past several days.

Surviving are his parents, one sister, Amber Dawn, and a brother, Matthew, all of the home. His surviving maternal grandfather is Warren Finney, Tyro, and his surviving paternal grandmother is Mrs. Virginia Presley, Katy, Tex.

Jonathan's parents are former residents of the Caney and Tyro areas.

Funeral arrangements were incomplete at press time today.

Carrol Sue (Bays) Finney (wife of Roy Finney) – died May 18, 1986

Death claims Carrol Sue Finney

Carrol Sue Finney, 33, died Sunday, May 18, 1986 in Colorado Springs, Colo., and funeral services were held at the Caney Church of Christ on Friday, May 23 with Elvis Denny officiating. Interment was in the Fairview Cemetery near Niotaze.

Carrol Sue Finney was born Nov. 30, 1952 in Independence, Kans., to her parents, Calvin Dale and Letha (Pendergraft) Bays.

On May 29, 1971 she was married at Caney to Roy Keith Finney and he survives at the home in Security, Colo. Mrs. Finney was a homemaker and a member of the Caney Church of Christ.

Surviving are two daughters, Karen Lynn Finney and Amanda Marie Finney; and a son, Shawn Keith Finney, all of the home.

Four sisters survive: Linette Hook, Berlin, Germany; Stacy Castleberry, Charolette Jones, and Delories Eckles, all of Pratt, Kans., and five brothers, Edward Bays of Independence; David Bays, Mulvane, Kans.; William Bays, Independence; U.S. Marine Corporal Douglas Bays, Okinawa, Japan; and Matthew Bays, Pratt, Kans.

Both parents also survive.

Carl Chester Finney (son of Daniel Webster and Mary Ann (Farlow) Finney) – died 15 Nov. 1987

Vivia J. (McLure) Finney (wife of Carl C. Finney) – d. 3 Sept. 2002

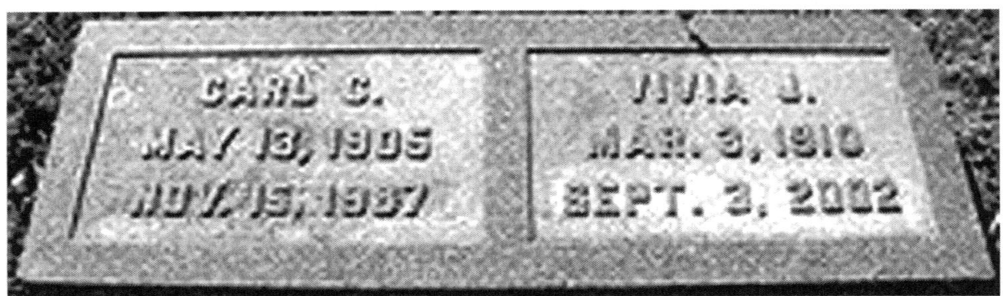

George Wesley Finney (son of Frank and Hattie Finney) – died Sept. 26, 1989

George Finney passes away

A former Caney resident, George W. "Red" Finney, 67, died Tuesday, Sept. 26, 1989, in the KU Medical Center at Kansas City, Kans. Finney had been residing at Olathe.

Funeral services have been set for Friday, Sept. 29, at 2 p.m. in the Graves Memorial Chapel with Rev. Marvin Alley, pastor of the First Baptist Church officiating. Burial will be in the Sunnyside Cemetery.

Friends may call at the Graves Funeral Home after 11 a.m. Thursday.

George Finney was born Feb. 23, 1922, in Caney, to his parents, Frank and Hattie (Cole) Finney. He attended Caney schools and graduated from Caney High School before entering the United States Army, serving during World War II.

Mr. Finney worked as a mail carrier while residing here, and served as a member of the Caney Volunteer Fire Department for 25 years. He also operated a television repair shop in Caney for 25 years.

He moved to Independence in the mid 1970s, then to the Kansas City area two years ago.

He was married in July of 1943 to Mary Swank and the couple later divorced.

Survivors include his mother, Hattie Finney of Caney; two sons, Major Jerrold M. Finney, Copperas Cove, Texas, and Van W. Finney, Olathe; a daughter, Gwendora Johnston, St. Louis, Missouri; one brother, Jack Finney of Coffeyville; and two sisters, Melrena Bishop of Coffeyville and Monica Webb of Tulsa. Three grandchildren also survive.

The Twenty-Third Psalm
The Lord is my shepherd; I shall not want.
He maketh me to lie down in green pastures:
He leadeth me beside the still waters.
He restoreth my soul: He leadeth me in the
paths of righteousness for His name's sake.
Yea, though I walk through the valley of the
shadow of death, I will fear no evil:
for Thou art with me;
thy rod and thy staff they comfort me.
Thou preparest a table before me in the
presence of mine enemies:
thou anointest my head with oil;
my cup runneth over.
Surely goodness and mercy shall follow
me all the days of my life:
and I will dwell in the house of the Lord for ever.

IN MEMORY OF
GEORGE WESLEY FINNEY

DATE OF BIRTH
February 23, 1922
Niotaze, Kansas

DATE OF DEATH
September 26, 1989
Kansas City, Kansas

SERVICES FROM
Graves Memorial Chapel
Friday, September 29, 1989
2:00 p.m.

OFFICIATING
Reverend Marvin Alley
First Baptist Church
Caney, Kansas

INTERMENT
Sunnyside Cemetery
Caney, Kansas

Hattie Nicholson Cole Finney (wife of Frank Finney) – died Jan. 1, 1990

Hattie Finney

Hattie N. Finney, 90, a lifelong resident of this area, died Monday, Jan. 1, 1990, at her home, 118 N. Spring.

Funeral services will be held Friday at 2 p.m. in the Graves Memorial Chapel with burial in the Sunnyside Cemetery. Friends may call at the Graves Funeral Home in Caney.

Hattie Finney was born March 13, 1899, to George R. and Lottie D. (Graham) Cole, in Mount Hope, Kans., and resided most of her life in the Niotaze and Caney areas.

A housewife, she also worked for the Caney Valley National Bank and the City of Caney in cleaning and janitorial work.

She was married in 1916 to Frank Finney and he preceded her in death in 1954.

She is survived by a son, Gordon Jack Finney of rural Coffeyville, and two daughters, Melrena Bishop of Coffeyville, and Monica Webb of Tulsa.

She is also survived by seven grandchildren, five great-grandchildren, and four great-great-grandchildren.

She was preceded in death by a son and two brothers. George W. F

Mrs. Finney was a member of the United Methodist Church in Niotaze.

IN MEMORY OF
HATTIE FINNEY

DATE OF BIRTH
March 13, 1899
Mount Hope, Kansas

DATE OF DEATH
January 1, 1990
Caney, Kansas

SERVICES FROM
Graves Memorial Chapel
Friday, January 5, 1990
2:00 p.m.

OFFICIATING
Reverend Dean Knewtson
United Methodist Church
Caney, Kansas

INTERMENT
Sunnyside Cemetery
Caney, Kansas

The Twenty-Third Psalm

The Lord is my shepherd: I shall not want.
He maketh me to lie down in green pastures.
He leadeth me beside the still waters.
He restoreth my soul. He leadeth me in the
paths of righteousness for His name's sake
Yea, though I walk through the valley of the
shadow of death, I will fear no evil:
for Thou art with me.
thy rod and thy staff they comfort me.
Thou preparest a table before me in the
presence of mine enemies:
thou anointest my head with oil;
my cup runneth over
Surely goodness and mercy shall follow
me all the days of my life:
and I will dwell in the house of the Lord for ever

Georgia Katherine (Lewis) Finney (wife of Clinton "Red" Finney) – Aug. 27, 1997

The County Chronicle

Georgia K. Finney

CANEY — Georgia Katherine Finney, 87, formerly of Bartlesville, Okla., died Wednesday, Aug. 27, 1997, at the Caney Nursing Center.

Graveside services were held Aug. 30 in Sunnyside Cemetery, Caney, with Rev. Mike Graham of the Caney First Christian Church officiating.

Mrs. Finney was born April 9, 1910, at Caney to John W. and Julie (Ledbedder) Lewis. She grew up and attended school in Caney, and later spent several years in Bartlesville. She was a homemaker and of the Christian faith.

She is survived by her sons, Thomas B. Finney, Caney, Timothy R. Finney, Wanette, Okla.; a daughter, Julie K. (Katie) Perry, Garfield, Ark.; nine grandchildren, several great-grandchildren and a sister, Zada King, Independence.

She was preceded in death by her parents, a daughter, Susan Grace Perry on Jan. 2, 1979, two sisters, and one brother.

Stumpff Funeral Home of Bartlesville was in charge of arrangements.

Warren Eugene Finney (son of Fred D. Finney and Pearl C. Norris) – Apr. 26, 1998

Warren E. Finney

CANEY — Warren E. Finney, 69, of rural Tyro, died Sunday evening at his home.

Services will be at 2 p.m. Thursday at the Caney United Methodist Church with the Rev. Ronald J. Williams, pastor, officiating. Burial will be in Fairview Cemetery in Nio-

WARREN FINNEY

taze. Visitation will be from 8 a.m. to 8 p.m. Wednesday and 8 a.m. to 10 a.m. Thursday at Graves Funeral Home, Caney. The family will greet friends at their home from 7 p.m. to 9 p.m. Wednesday.

Memorials are suggested to New Hope Hospice and may be left with the funeral home.

Mr. Finney was born on Nov. 1, 1928, on the family farm near Wayside to Fred D. and Pearl C. (Norris) Finney. He graduated from Wayside High School in 1946.

Upon graduation, he entered the Air Force in 1946 and was honorably discharged in 1949. He was a farmer, rancher and custom combiner.

He was a member of the Caney United Methodist Church and the American Legion post in Wellington.

On Dec. 31, 1949, he married Betty Tolbert. They were later divorced. On June 4, 1967, he married Wyden Owens in Caney, and she survives.

Other survivors include three sons, Jeffery Finney, Tyro, Brandon Owens, rural Tyro, and Ryan Finney, Northridge, Calif.; five daughters, Linda Kroesche, Rosenberg, Texas, Sandra Presley, Katy, Texas, Robin Kaminska, rural Independence, Reggin Kastler, South Coffeyville, and Meggin Hogsett, Alta Vista; four sisters, Fern Gilliland, Skiatook, Okla., Letha Bowman, rural Caney, Nancy Buster, Dewey, Okla., and Twyla Sawdy, Wichita; two brothers, Gerald Finney, rural Havana, and Russell Finney, Caney; 15 grandchildren and one great-grandchild.

Fern Gilliland (daughter of Fred D. Finney and Pearl C. Norris; wife of Verne Gilliland) – May 28, 1998

Fern Gilliland

SKIATOOK, Okla. — Fern Gilliland, 79, of Skiatook, Okla., died Thursday, May 28 in Skiatook. 1998

Services were Monday at Peters-Stumpff Funeral Home in Skiatook. Burial was in Robbins Cemetery west of Coffeyville.

Mrs. Gilliland was born on Jan. 5, 1919, in Towanda to Fred and Clarinda (Norris) Finney. She grew up in Wayside, Havana and Tyro and graduated from Wayside High School in 1936.

On Aug. 15, 1936, she married Verne E. Gilliland in Sedan. At first, they lived in Tyro, but they later moved to Independence; Cozad, Neb.; and Sterling, Colo. After living for three years in Kenya, they moved to Skiatook, where Mr. Gilliland finished his career in the oil industry and retired.

She was a member of the Tyro United Methodist Church.

Survivors include her husband; a son, Larry Dean Gilliland, Sterling, Colo.; three daughters, Shirley Smidt, Cozad, Neb., Karen Anderson, Greeley, Colo., and Sharon Kay Weber, Holyoke, Colo.; two brothers, Gerald Finney, Havana, and Russell Finney, Caney; three sisters, Letha Bowman, Caney, Nancy Buster, Dewey, Okla., and Twila Saudy, Wichita; 13 grandchildren and 17 great-grandchildren.

Verne Gilliland (husband of Fern Finney) – Jan. 26, 2000

Verne Gilliland

GREELEY, Colo. — Verne Gilliland, 83, of Greeley, Colo., formerly of Skiatook, Okla. and Tyro, Kan., died Wednesday, Jan. 26, 2000, in Greeley, Colo.

Verne Gilliland was born Nov. 24, 1916, in Tyro to Amalek and Effie (Ringeisen) Gilliland. He was raised in Tyro and graduated from Tyro High School. He also attended one year of junior college.

On August 15, 1936, he married Fern Finney in Sedan, Kan. They first lived in Tyro and later moved to Independence. They also lived in Cozad, Neb., and Sterling, Colo. After working and living in Libya for three years, they moved to Skiatook, Okla., where he completed his career in the oil industry and retired. He enjoyed fishing, golfing, bowling and playing baseball in his earlier years. He was a member of the B.P.O.E. in Sterling, Colo., and a member of the Tyro Methodist Church.

Verne Gilliland is survived by one son, Larry and his wife, Sandra, of Sterling. Colo.; three daughters, Shirley and her husband, LaDean Smidt of Cozad, Neb.; Karen Anderson of Greeley, Colo.; Sharon and her husband, Larry Weber of Holyoke, Colo.; one brother Dean and his wife, Margie of Tulsa, Okla.; 13 grandchildren and 19 great-grandchildren.

He was preceded in death by his wife Fern, on June 1, 1998, and by his parents and one brother, Lawrence.

Funeral services for Verne Gilliland were held Saturday, Jan. 29, at the Graves Memorial Chapel in Caney. Rev. John Durham of the Caney United Methodist Church officiated with burial at Robbins Cemetery, west of Coffeyville.

Arrangements were under the direction of Graves Funeral Home.

Rhonda Sue (McSpadden) Finney (wife of Van Finney) – Aug. 13, 2001

RHONDA SUE MCSPADDEN FINNEY

Rhonda Sue McSpadden Finney, Olathe, died Monday, Aug. 13, 2001, at her home after a long battle with cancer.

She was born on Oct. 17, 1957, in Amarillo, Texas, to Bert and Mary Ann McSpadden. She graduated from Shawnee Mission West High School. She worked for the Olathe Medical Center in the billing department until her illness.

She is survived by her husband, Van W. Finney, a son, Brandon, and a daughter, Kayla, all of the home; her parents, Bert and Mary Ann McSpadden, Overland Park; a sister, Felicia A. Body, and her husband, David, Olathe; two brothers, Joseph McSpadden, and wife Ramona, Aurora, Ill., and Kevin McSpadden, Overland Park; her grandparents, Mr. and Mrs. Wayne Kissinger, Granbury, Texas; her husband's parents, Edgar and Mary Ellen Youngberg, Chanute, Kan.; and numerous nieces, nephews and cousins.

Services will be at 2 p.m. Thursday at Heritage Family Worship Center, 13715 W. 151st St., Olathe. Visitation will be from 7 to 9 p.m. Wednesday at the W.L. Frye and Son Mortuary and Crematory, 105 E. Loula, Olathe. Burial in the Pleasant Valley Cemetery, located east of 159th and Switzer.

The family suggests memorial contributions be made to a memorial fund for her children at the First National Bank of Olathe, 444 E. Santa Fe, Olathe, KS 66061, in lieu of flowers.

Johnny Finney (husband of Paula Pearl Courtney) – d. 4 July 2002

Johnny E. Finney

COLLINSVILLE, Okla. — Johnny E. Finney, 76, of Collinsville, Okla., died Thursday at his home.

Graveside services are 2 p.m. Wednesday at Niotaze Fairview Cemetery in Niotaze. Services are under the direction of Nick Reynolds Funeral Service in Collinsville.

Mr. Finney was born Dec. 13, 1925 in Chautauqua to Clarence Faye and Martha Myrtle Finney.

He was a veteran of the United States Army and he was employed by American Airlines until his retirement.

He is survived by his wife, Virginia, at the home; a son, Ira Finney, Niotaze; two daughters, Debra Mason and Donna Loffer, both of Owasso, Okla.; eight brothers, Rollie Gene Finney, Idaho, Kyle B. Finney, Niotaze, Harold Edward Finney, Coffeyville, Gary Lee Finney, Ft. Smith, Ark., Melvin Ray Finney, Independence, Wesley David Finney, Niotaze, Roy Keith Finney, Manhattan, and Lyle Eugene Finney, Idaho; four sisters, Alta Fuller, Collinsville, Mary McMurray, Duncan, Okla., Wanda Riley, Sedan, and Hilta Gurby, Nowata, Okla.; seven grandchildren, and two great-grandchildren.

Johnny Finney's obituary (provides incorrect name for wife – Virginia; his wife was Pearl)

Gerald "G. W." Bowman (son of Woodson Bowman) – died Aug. 16, 2003

Gerald Woodson "G.W." Bowman

SANTA CRUZ, N.M. – Gerald Woodson "G.W." Bowman, 29, of Santa Cruz, N.M., was killed in an automobile accident near Mountain Home, Ark., on Saturday, Aug. 16, 2003.

G.W. Bowman was born in Espanola, N.M. on Sept. 4, 1973, to Woodson Bowman and Donna Armitage. He grew up and attended elementary school in Jemez Springs, N.M. The family moved to Caney in the early 1980s, and G.W. attended Caney schools.

Survivors include his father, Woodson Bowman, of Caney; his mother and stepfather, Donna and Don Armitage, of Havana; one sister, Sholene Willis of Joplin, Mo.; two brothers, Shawn Bowman of Pittsburg and Shane Bowman of Havana; grandparents, Leatha Bowman and Stephen Bowman, both of Caney; two nieces and two nephews.

G.W. was preceded in death by his maternal grandparents.

Services were held for family only.

Caney native killed, others injured in Arkansas wreck

A former Caney man was killed an two other area natives were injured in a one-vehicle accident near Baxter, Ark., on Saturday.

The Arkansas State Police says Gerald W. "G.W" Bowman, 29, of Santa Cruz, N.M., was killed as a passenger in a 2000 Chevrolet Impala that ran off the side of a county road. Bowman was ejected from the vehicle and killed.

Two other passengers, Shaun M. Dryer and Marcus Berry, both of Mountain Grove, Mo., and both of whom are Montgomery County natives, were injured and taken to regional hospitals for medical treatment. Also injured after being ejected from the vehicle was the driver: Michael Landry, 35, of Mountain Grove, Mo. Landry was charged with driving while intoxicated, the Arkansas State Police said.

Bowman was a former Caney resident and attended local schools. Berry is a native of the Havana area and also attended Caney schools.

As of presstime, the condition of the three injured persons was not known. A memorial service for Bowman was also being planned by family members.

G.W. Bowman

CANEY - Caney native Gerald W. "G.W" Bowman, 29, of Santa Cruz, New Mexico, was killed in an automobile accident near Baxter, Ark., on Saturday, Aug. 16, 2003.

Burial information will be printed at a later date.

Leatha Finney Bowman (wife of Stephen Woodson Bowman; daughter of Fred and Pearl (Norris) Finney) – died Sept. 1, 2003

2003

Leatha Bowman

CANEY — Leatha Bowman, 82, Caney, died Monday, Sept. 1, 2003, at the Jane Phillips Medical Center in Bartlesville.

Her graveside service will be held Friday, Sept. 5, at 2 p.m. at Fairview Cemetery, Niotaze, with David Bycroft officiating.

Visitation at Graves Funeral Home in Caney will be held from 8 a.m. to 8 p.m. on Thursday.

Memorial donations can be made to the donor's choice and left at the funeral home.

Leatha Bowman was born Oct. 26, 1920, at Niotaze, Kan., to Fred and Pearl (Norris) Finney. She grew up in the area and graduated from Wayside High School.

She held numerous jobs in her life. She ran a snack bar at the Tewalans Bowling Allen in New Mexico. She later moved back to the area and operated a cafe with Nancy Buster and Wydene Finney in Tyro called Lee's Cafe. Leatha also helped care for the family of Warren and Wydene Finney when they needed extra help. She also worked at the Box Factory in Caney. Her main occupation was a homemaker most of her life and she enjoyed gardening, cooking and taking care of her family.

Survivors include one son, Woodson Bowman, Caney; two brothers, Russell Finney, Havana, and Gerald Finney, Independence; two sisters, Nancy Buster, Dewey, Okla., and Twyla Sawdy, Wichita; two grandsons, Shawn Bowman of Pittsburg and Shane Bowman of Havana; one granddaughter, Sholene Willis of Joplin, Mo.; four great-grandchildren and numerous nieces and nephews.

She was preceded in death by her parents; one sister; four brothers; and one grandson, G.W. Bowman.

Graves Funeral Home of Caney is in charge of arrangements.

Cousette Copeland

Nancy Aileen Buster – died Oct. 24, 2003

IN LOVING MEMORY OF
NANCY AILEEN BUSTER

DATE OF BIRTH	**DATE OF DEATH**
May 5, 1922	October 24, 2003
Niotaze, Kansas	Bartlesville, Oklahoma

FUNERAL SERVICES
Graves Memorial Chapel
2:00 p.m., Wednesday
October 29, 2003

OFFICIATING
Reverend David Brown

MUSIC SELECTIONS
"What A Friend We Have In Jesus"
"How Great Thou Art"
"Amazing Grace"

SOLOIST
Lana Grayum

INTERMENT
Fairview Cemetery
Niotaze, Kansas

THE TWENTY-THIRD PSALM

The Lord is my Shepherd; I shall not want.
He maketh me to lie down in green pastures;
He leadeth me beside the still waters.
He restoreth my soul; He leadeth me in the
paths of righteousness for his name's sake,
Yea, though I walk through the valley of the
shadow of death, I will fear no evil;
for thou art with me;
thy rod and thy staff they comfort me.
Thou preparest a table before me in the
presence of mine enemies;
thou annointest my head with oil;
my cup runneth over.
Surely goodness and mercy shall follow
me all the days of my life:
and I will dwell in the house of the Lord forever.

George H. Hendrickson – Nov. 10, 1882 – Nov. 20, 1954

IN MEMORY OF
GEORGE H. HENDRICKSON
Omak, Washington

BORN
November 10th, 1882
Wayside, Kansas

DATE OF DEATH
November 20th, 1954

SERVICES FROM
Wayside Church
Wayside, Kansas
November 29th, 1954

CLERGYMAN OFFICIATING
Reverend W. D. McKinney
Caney, Kansas

Final Resting Place
HARRISONVILLE CEMETERY
BOLTON, KANSAS

The Lord is my shepherd; I shall not want. He maketh me to lie down in green pastures: he leadeth me beside the still waters. He restoreth my soul: he leadeth me in the paths of righteousness for his name's sake. Yea, though I walk through the valley of the shadow of death, I will fear no evil: for thou art with me; thy rod and thy staff they comfort me. Thou preparest a table before me in the presence of mine enemies: thou anointest my head with oil; my cup runneth over. Surely goodness and mercy shall follow me all the days of my life: and I will dwell in the house of the Lord for ever.

Funeral Conducted by
Potts Funeral Home
Independence, Kansas

Jackie Lee "Jack" Perry (son of Ray and Pearl (Scott) Perry) – died Aug. 23, 2004

Jackie Lee "Jack" Perry

GARFIELD, Ark. – Jackie Lee "Jack" Perry, 60, retired fireman, and former resident of Bartlesville, Okla., died on Monday, Aug. 23, 2004, in the Washington Regional Medical Center at Fayetteville, Ark.

His funeral service was held at 2 p.m. on Friday in the Stumpff Funeral Home Chapel with Dr. Michael G. McBride, pastor of the Highland Park Baptist Church, officiating.

Interment was in the Sunnyside Cemetery, Caney. Funeral services and interment were under the direction of Stumpff Funeral Home, Bartlesville.

Jack Perry was born Nov. 27, 1943, at Caney, Kan., to Ray and Pearl (Scott) Perry. He was raised and attended schools in Caney.

Mr. Perry was employed as a mechanic for the City of Bartlesville from 1963 to 1966. In 1966 he joined the Bartlesville Fire Department and worked there until his retirement in 1986. Mr. Perry was a member of the Oklahoma Firefighters Association.

He moved to Garfield, Ark., in 1991.

Survivors include his wife, Gwynda S. Perry, of the home in Bella Vista, Ark.; his former wife, Katie (Finney) Perry, Rogers, Ark.; his mother, Pearl Perry, Bartlesville; one son, Jackie Ray Perry, Bartlesville; three stepdaughters, Julie Koonce, Whitehall, Ark., Ashley and Jessica Berry, of the home; three brothers, Danny Perry of Maryland, Johnny Perry, Copan, Okla., and Carl Perry, Chelsea, Okla.; four sisters, Emma Jean Shaw, Tulsa, Okla., Alice Bennett, Oklahoma City, Okla., Kathryn Doggett, Bartlesville, and Carol Bradford, Caney; and two grandchildren, Mitchell Perry, Bethany, Okla. and Dakota Lee Perry, Bartlesville.

Mr. Perry was preceded in death by his father, Ray Perry; one son, Kevin Lee Perry; and a brother, Eugene Perry.

Melrena J. Bishop (daughter of Frank and Hattie Finney) – died Apr. 26, 2006

Melrena J. Finney-Bishop 1917-2006

Melrena J. Finney-Bishop, 88, Coffeyville, Kansas resident, entered into rest on April 26, 2006 at the Medical Lodge of Coffeyville, Kansas.

She was born to Frank and Hattie (Cole) Finney, June 6, 1917, at Niotaze, Kansas.

She attended grade school at Havana and Wayside, Ks. Graduated from Caney High and attended Coffeyville Community College.

She taught school for twelve years at Dearing, Fredonia, Sedan and Robbins School. Mrs. Bishop received her Master's Degree from Emporia State University.

She married A.W. "Buck" Hertweck in December 1943. They owned and operated Hertweck Electric for thirty-five years. They later divorced.

She married Clyde Bishop on June 17, 1973. He preceded her in death.

She was a long time member of the First Baptist Church.

She is survived by one Sister, Monica Webb of Broken Arrow, Oklahoma, and several nieces and nephews.

She was preceded in death by her parents, and two brothers, George and Jack Finney.

Mrs. Bishop will lie in state at Penwell-Gabel Ford-Wulf-Bruns Chapel, 2405 Woodland Ave., in Coffeyville, Kansas on Friday, April 28, 2006 from 1:00 p.m. until 9:00 p.m.

Funeral Services will be held 1:00 p.m., Saturday, April 29, 2006 at the Penwell-Gabel Ford-Wulf-Bruns Chapel, 2405 Woodland Ave., in Coffeyville, KS. The Reverend Dr. Wayne Norton will be presiding. Burial will follow in the Sunnyside Cemetery in Caney, Kansas.

THE TWENTY-THIRD PSALM
The Lord is my shepherd; I shall not want.
He maketh me to lie down in green pastures:
He leadeth me beside the still waters.
He restoreth my soul: He leadeth me in the
paths of righteousness for His name's sake.
Yea, though I walk through the valley of the
shadow of death, I will fear no evil:
for Thou art with me;
thy rod and thy staff they comfort me.
Thou preparest a table before me in the
presence of mine enemies:
thou anointest my head with oil;
my cup runneth over.
Surely goodness and mercy shall follow
me all the days of my life:
and I will dwell in the house of the Lord for ever.

IN LOVING MEMORY OF
Melrena J. Bishop
June 6, 1917 - April 26, 2006

Funeral Service
1:00 p.m. Saturday April 29, 2006
Penwell-Gabel Ford-Wulf-Bruns Chapel
The Reverend Dr. Wayne Norton

Special Music
"How Great Thou Art"
"In The Garden"
"Precious Memories"

Casket Bearers
Dale George Tim Burdick Clarence Green
Don Crawford Gordon Finney Vannie Finney

Entombment
Sunnyside Cemetery
Caney, Kansas

Memorials
First Baptist Church
c/o Penwell-Gabel Funeral Home

Timothy Finney (son of Clinton (Red) Finney and Georgia Kathryn Irene LEWIS; grandson of John Wesley Finney) – died June 7, 2006

In Loving Memory

Timothy Finney

In Loving Memory

Timothy Finney

Born
February 27, 1947

Passed Away
June 7, 2006

Services Held
2:00 p.m. Monday
June 12, 2006
Graveside

Conducted By
Stuart Rising
Worldwide Church of God

Interment
Wanette Cemetery
Wanette, Oklahoma

Arrangements By
Cooper Funeral Home
Tecumseh, Oklahoma

Stephen W. Bowman (son of Stephen and Sarah Bowman) – died July 16, 2008

Stephen W. Bowman

CANEY — Stephen W. "Steve" Bowman, 88, of Caney died Wednesday, July 16, 2008, in the Coffeyville Regional Medical Center.

He was born on October 11, 1919 in Aline, Okla., to Stephen H. and Sarah (Perkins) Bowman. He graduated high school at Kaw City, Okla. He served during World War II in the Air Force for a short time before receiving injuries and an honorable discharge.

He was a pipefitter, employed by Local 412 of Albuquerque, N.M., until his retirement in 1985. Stephen also worked at Boeing and because of the experience he had working on aircraft, was hired to work on planes during WWII.

Stephen is survived by one son, Woody Bowman of Caney; two grandsons, Shawn Bowman of Kauai, Hawaii, and Shane (Kasey) Bowman of Caney; one granddaughter, Sholene (Kevin) Willis of Joplin, Mo.; and four great-grandchildren.

Mr. Bowman is preceded in death by his parents and grandson, G.W. Bowman who passed away in 2003.

Following Mr. Bowman's wishes, cremation has taken place under the direction of David W. Barnes Funeral Home.

The family suggests donations in Stephen's memory be given to the Caney Valley High School Athletic Department. Memorials may be left at the funeral home or mailed c/o David W. Barnes Funeral Home, 306 N. Cline Rd., Coffeyville, KS, 67337.

View the obit online and leave a comment for the family at www.dwbfh.com

Nickie G. "Nikki" Simpson (daughter of Gordon Jack Sr and Ellene (Johnson) Finney) – died Jan. 18, 2009

NICKIE G. "NIKKI" SIMPSON

ikki Simpson was born Nickie Geneva Finney on October 31, 1949. She received her education at Wann High School, and went on to become the first college graduate in her family by earning her Associate Degree in Nursing from Independence Community College and Parsons College in 1984.

After exploring different facets of nursing, Nikki found her calling in the field of psychiatric nursing, where she worked as a registered nurse in Independence, KS, Wichita, KS, St. Louis, MO, and Bartlesville, OK. She was a gifted nurse and counselor, and was beloved by many in the medical community.

Nikki considered her greatest accomplishment to be raising her three children into loving adults who respect and serve God. Nikki was blessed with: two daughters and one son, Lee Ann Pierce and her husband, Chris, of Bartlesville, OK, Billy Clayton and wife, Candace, of Clarksville, TN; Birgindi Clayton of Wichita, KS; five grandchildren, Brett Pierce and wife, Erin, Corleigh Cranor, Autumn Cranor, Adrienne Clayton, and Kenan Clayton; her mother and stepfather, Ellene and Boyd Peery, of McPherson, KS; two brothers and two sisters, Nancy Belknap and husband, Claude, of McPherson, KS, Gordon Finney and wife, Evelyn, of Lake Pomme De Terre, MO, Marguerite Crockett and husband, Butch, of McPherson, KS, and Kevin McKean and wife, Chris, of McPherson, KS; and several nieces and nephews.

Nikki was preceded in death by her father, Gordon Jack Finney, Sr., and a brother, Tom McKean.

Nikki entered peacefully into eternal rest on Sunday, January 18, 2009, at her home in McPherson. She was fifty-nine.

In addition to her incredible love for her family, Nikki will be remembered for her multiple talents in the arts, most notable of which was her beautifully distinctive singing voice.

Nikki placed great value on her relationship with God, and drew her strength from the Lord throughout her life. Her family and friends will miss her greatly.

Forrest Dale Williams (great great grandson of Mary Catherine Finney and William Henry Allen) – died Nov. 8, 2009

FOREST DALE WILLIAMS
1934 - 2009

Mr. Forest Dale Williams, 75, of Bartlesville, died at 10:56 a.m. Sunday at the Jane Phillips Medical Center.
Funeral services will held at 10 a.m. on Thursday in the Stumpff Funeral Home Chapel with Shane Keeter of Oktaha, Oklahoma officiating. Interment will be in the Sunnyside Cemetery in Caney, Kansas under the direction of the Stumpff Funeral Home & Crematory.
Charitable contributions may be made to the charity of the donor's choice.
Forest Dale Williams was born August 14, 1934 at Wann, Oklahoma to Forest E. and Mary Inez (Hendrickson) Williams. He was raised and received his education in Pleasant View and Copan, Oklahoma, graduating from Copan High School in 1952. Dale was employed with REDA Pump Company for five years before moving to Arizona in 1957. He was married to Barbara Plumb on June 3, 1959 at Tolleson, Arizona. Dale began his career with the U.S. Postal Service in 1962 at Show Low, Arizona. They moved to Goodyear, Arizona in 1969 and retired in 1992. Mr. and Mrs. Williams moved to Bartlesville in December 1995 to enjoy their retirement. Dale was a VERY LOVING Father, Husband, Grandfather and friend. "A job well done".
Survivors include; his wife Barbara Williams of the family home; two sons Charlie Williams and his wife Connie of Bartlesville and Larry Williams of Bartlesville; one daughter Kristen Slocum of Phoenix, Arizona; fifteen grandchildren and seventeen great-grandchildren. Mr. Williams was preceded in death by his parents, two brothers George Marion Williams and Nelson Williams and a sister Wanda Morgan.

Shawn Lee Bowman (son of Woodson and Pali Montoya Bowman) – died Jan. 21, 2010

Shawn Lee Bowman

CANEY – Shawn Lee Bowman, age 43, of Caney, Kan., died Thursday, Jan. 21, 2010, at his home in Caney.

His funeral service was held at 2 p.m., Monday, Jan. 25, 2010, at the First Christian Church in Caney with Brad Sanders officiating. Burial followed at the Fairview Cemetery in Niotaze, Kan., under the direction of Potts Chapel, Caney.

Shawn was born June 25, 1966, in Espanola, New Mexico, to Woodson and Pali Montoya Bowman. Shawn grew up in Albuquerque, N.M. At 12 years of age he moved to Caney. Shawn graduated from Caney Valley High School in 1984. He received vocational training through Coffeyville Community College, graduating in 1986, and then graduated from Pittsburg State University with a bachelor of arts degree in communication.

In 1994 Shawn joined the Army Reserves Supply and Services in Independence, Kan. He served during Desert Storm. Shawn worked in the Bacon Factory in Pittsburg, Kan., as a maintenance engineer for 10 years. Shawn moved to Hawaii in 2004 and worked in maintenance at a resort. In 2009, Shawn moved back to Caney.

Survivors include his father, Woodson Bowman, of Caney, Kan.; his mother, Pali Montoya-Bowman of Hawaii; two brothers, Chris Montoya of Hawaii and Shane Bowman of Caney; two sisters, Shelly Campbell of Santa Fe, N.M., and Sholene Willis of Joplin, Mo.; and his Grandmother Nanny of Phoenix, Ariz.

He was preceded in death by one brother, Gerald Bowman, and his grandparents, Steve and Leatha Bowman.

Nancy Lee Belknap (daughter of Gordon Jack Sr and Ellene (Johnson) Finney) – died Apr. 24, 2010

In Loving Memory
Nancy L. Belknap

Nancy L. Belknap, 63, of McPherson, passed away on Saturday, April 24, 2010, at Memorial Hospital, McPherson. She was a former Executive Director of Mount Hope Sanctuary. She also was an interior decorator and operated the Inside-Out Shop in McPherson.

Nancy was born on January 24, 1947, in Coffeyville, KS, the daughter of Gordon Jack, Sr. and Ellene Josephine (Johnson) Finney. She graduated from McPherson High School and the LaSalle School of Interior Design. On August 31, 1991, she was united in marriage to Claude A. Belknap in Bartlesville, OK.

Nancy served on the board of directors for Mount Hope Sanctuary, was a member of New Hope Evangelical Church and Beta Sigma Phi Sorority, all of McPherson.

The funeral service will be at 10:30 AM, Wednesday, April 28, 2010, at the New Hope Evangelical Church with Pastor Jim Keil officiating. Burial will be in the Crestwood Memorial Park, McPherson. Visitation is from 3:00 to 8:00 PM, Tuesday, at Stockham Family Funeral Home, with the family receiving friends from 6:00 to 8:00 PM.

Survivors include: husband, Claude of the home; son, Zachary of the home; mother, Ellene Peery and husband, Boyd, of McPherson; brothers, Gordon Finney and wife, Evelyn, of Lake Pomme de Terre, MO and Kevin McKean and wife, Chris, of McPherson; sister, Marguerite Crockett and husband, Butch, of McPherson; and several nieces & nephews. She was preceded in death by her father, brother, Tom McKean, and sister, Nikki G. Simpson.

Memorial donations may be given to Mount Hope Sanctuary, McPherson in loving memory of Nancy.

Stockham Family Funeral Home

Joseph H. Finney (IL) – attended by his brother Robert Finney from KS, notice Sept. 9, 1857 (not in Wesley's family)

Robert Finney and wife attended the funeral of their brother, Joseph H. Finney, at Newman, Ill. Joseph was born and raised on the farm now owned by T. D. Byers. He had been in the dry goods business for 25 years. He was laid to rest last Saturday in the family lot in the cemetery at Tuscola, Ill., aged 48 years.

Edgar, son of Daniel and Gilla Finney – 15 Dec. 1861 – 21 Feb. 1866 (this was printed March 25, 1865) he died in Parke County, IN (Edgar's great grandparents were Joseph and Mary Polly Finney)

FINNEY—On Wednesday morning, Feb. 21st, of spotted fever, little Edgar, only son of Daniel and Gilla Finney, in the 5th year of his age, after an illness of only thirteen hours.

I know your hearts are lonely and sad,
And filled with deepest gloom—
For one you dearly love is dead,
And sleeping in the tomb.

To you the days are dreary now,
And lonely every hour.
Since death crept in your cheerful home
And nipped your tender flower.

You little dreamed that he would go
And leave you all so soon.
But death had marked him for his own,
And stole him for the tomb.

No more you'll hear his gentle voice;
You say, Oh! can it be
That Eddie has left us all in tears
And crossed death's stormy sea.

Yes, he is gone, forever gone;
You cannot call him back:
But soon you'll go to meet your child
And leave life's beaten track.

For oh! I trust the boatman's pole
Hath rowed him safely o'er;
For all that's bright and fair is found
Upon that dazzling shore

His little sisters they will miss him
When they run about and play,
For Eddie now is no more with them,
But lives in endless day.

His fairy form no more will flit
Around about the door,
For, smiling now, he waits for all
Upon the other shore.

Then let such hopeful thoughts as these
Your drooping spirits cheer,
And from the mount delectable
Oh! view the country near.

We soon shall reach it as we tread,
Oftimes by sorrow driven;
May Jesus guide our wandering steps,
And save us all in Heaven. M. E. F.

Cousette Copeland

Jerry Raymond Reding, 55 of Nampa, went home to his Lord and Savior on Monday September 12, 2011 due to an airplane accident near Stanley Idaho. A Memorial Service will be held at 1:00 P.M., Tuesday, September 20, 2011 at Crossroads Community Church, 4152 E. Amity, Nampa. Private family burial will precede the services at the Hillcrest Memorial Gardens, Caldwell. Services are under the direction of the Nampa Funeral Home, Yraguen Chapel.

He was born in Nampa Idaho on April 30, 1956 the son of Raymond and Arlene (Flowers) Reding. He was raised on the family farm and was educated in Nampa, graduating from Nampa High in 1975. Jerry enjoyed life to the fullest and was a friend to more people than can be numbered. Family was his #1 priority and farming was his livelihood. He had a passion for flying and obtained his pilot's license in 1997. He also enjoyed spending time with his loving wife and wonderful children and grandchildren. Jerry was the rock of the family and was willing to go above and beyond for anyone in any situation. His smile and laughter will be greatly missed by all who knew him. Jerry's love for Jesus was evidenced by his dedication to church and his everyday way of life. Many described Jerry as always there to help without expecting anything in return.

He met and married his sweetheart Jane Dufoe on June 22, 1978. They began their life together on the farm where they raised their 4 children with hard work and lots of love. Jerry instilled the value of hard work, commitment, faithfulness and generosity along with selflessness to and through his family.

Jerry leaves behind his wife Jane and 4 children: daughter Michelle and husband Augustine Pereira, daughter Brenda, son Andrew and his wife Brittany Kingrey, and son Lucas along with 3 grandchildren: Jennifer, Irene "Fred", and Bentley "My Little Flying Buddy". He was expected to be a grandfather 4 times over in December to Addison. He was also a great grandfather to Lexani. He is also survived by his parents, Raymond and Arlene Reding; and his siblings, Darlene (Leonard) Cross, Mary Caywood, John (Brenda) Reding, Sue Sexton, Angie (Lamond) Thueson and Jeff (Misty) Reding. He was a beloved Husband, Father, Grandfather, Brother, Son, Uncle, and Friend who will be greatly missed leaving a void that can't be filled. Jerry was so very proud of the accomplishments of his children and wife; he was continually encouraging them to do their absolute best in all they do.

He was preceded in death by his brothers in law, Bruce Caywood and Jamie Sexton, brother Lynn Reding and his grandparents.

Part Six - INDEX

NOTE: The Index page numbers are from Rosamary High Finney's original text. This Index does not contain entries from updates to the original text.

Made in the USA
Charleston, SC
05 November 2011